High Impact Data Visualization with Power View, Power Map, and Power BI

Adam Aspin

Apress·

High Impact Data Visualization with Power View, Power Map, and Power BI

ISBN-13 (pbk): 978-1-4302-6616-7

ISBN-13 (electronic): 978-1-4302-6617-4

President and Publisher: Paul Manning
Lead Editor: Jonathan Gennick
Technical Reviewer: Rodney Landrum
Editorial Board: Steve Anglin, Mark Beckner, Ewan Buckingham, Gary Cornell, Louise Corrigan, Jim DeWolf, Jonathan Gennick, Jonathan Hassell, Robert Hutchinson, Michelle Lowman, James Markham, Matthew Moodie, Jeff Olson, Jeffrey Pepper, Douglas Pundick, Ben Renow-Clarke, Dominic Shakeshaft, Gwenan Spearing, Matt Wade, Steve Weiss
Coordinating Editor: Jill Balzano
Copy Editor: Rebecca Rider
Compositor: SPi Global
Indexer: SPi Global
Artist: SPi Global
Cover Designer: Anna Ishchenko

Distributed to the book trade worldwide by Springer Science+Business Media New York, 233 Spring Street, 6th Floor, New York, NY 10013. Phone 1-800-SPRINGER, fax (201) 348-4505, e-mail orders-ny@springer-sbm.com, or visit www.springeronline.com. Apress Media, LLC is a California LLC and the sole member (owner) is Springer Science + Business Media Finance Inc (SSBM Finance Inc). SSBM Finance Inc is a Delaware corporation.

For information on translations, please e-mail rights@apress.com, or visit www.apress.com.

Apress and friends of ED books may be purchased in bulk for academic, corporate, or promotional use. eBook versions and licenses are also available for most titles. For more information, reference our Special Bulk Sales–eBook Licensing web page at www.apress.com/bulk-sales.

Any source code or other supplementary material referenced by the author in this text is available to readers at www.apress.com. For detailed information about how to locate your book's source code, go to www.apress.com/source-code/.

To Timothy.

Contents at a Glance

Contents

About the Author

Adam Aspin is an independent business intelligence (BI) consultant based in the United Kingdom. He has worked with a range of Microsoft products for 25 years. During this time, he has developed several dozen reporting and analysis systems based on SQL Server, Access, Excel and SharePoint.

A graduate of Oxford University, Adam began his career in publishing before moving into IT. Databases soon became a passion, and his experience in this arena ranges from dBase to Oracle, and Access to MySQL, with occasional sorties into the world of DB2. He is, however, most at home in the Microsoft universe when using SQL Server Analysis Services, SQL Server Reporting Services, SQL Server Integration Services, and more recently, the Microsoft self-service business intelligence suite and Power BI.

Business intelligence has been his principal focus for the last 15 years. He has applied his skills for a range of clients, including J.P. Morgan, The Organisation for Economic Co-operation and Development (OECD), Tesco, Centrica, Harrods, Vodafone, Crédit Agricole, Cartier, the RAC and EMC Conchango.

Adam has been a frequent contributor to SQLServerCentral.com for several years; he has written numerous articles for various French IT publications; he has spoken at various SQL Server events including SQLBits; and he is the author of *SQL Server 2012 Data Integration Recipes* (Apress 2012).

A fluent French speaker, Adam has worked in France and Switzerland for many years.

Contact him at adam@calidra.co.uk.

About the Technical Reviewer

Rodney Landrum went to school to be a poet and a writer. And then he graduated, so that dream was crushed. He followed another path, which was to become a professional in the fun filled world of Information Technology. He has worked as a systems engineer, UNIX and network admin, data analyst, client services director, and finally as a database administrator. The old hankering to put words on paper, while paper still existed, got the best of him, and in 2000, he began writing technical articles, some creative and humorous, some quite the opposite. In 2010 he wrote *The SQL Server Tacklebox*, a title his editor disdained, but a book closest to the true creative potential he sought; he wanted to do a full book without a single screen shot. He promises his next book will be fiction or a collection of poetry, but that has yet to transpire.

Acknowledgments

Writing a technical book can be a lonely occupation. So I am all the more grateful for the help and encouragement that I have received from so many fabulous friends and colleagues.

First, my considerable thanks go to Jonathan Gennick, the commissioning editor of this book. Throughout the publication process, Jonathan has been both a tower of strength and an exemplary mentor. He has always been available to share his vast experience selflessly and courteously. It is thanks to him that this book has seen the light of day.

Heartfelt thanks go to Jill Balzano, the Apress coordinating editor, for managing this book through the publication process. She succeeded in the impossible task of making a potentially stress-filled trek into a pleasant journey filled with light and humor. Her team also deserves much praise for their calm under pressure. So thanks to Rebecca Rider for her tireless and subtle work editing and polishing the prose, and also to Dhaneesh Kumar for the hours spent formatting—and reformatting—the text.

When lost in the depths of technical questions, it is easy to lose sight of what should be one's main objectives. Fortunately, the technical reviewer, Rodney Landrum, has worked unstintingly to remind me of where the focus should be. He has placed his considerable experience at my disposal and has enriched the subject matter enormously with his suggestions and comments.

However, my deepest gratitude must be reserved for the two people who have given the most to this book. They are my wife and son. Timothy has put up with a mentally absent father for months, while providing continual encouragement to persevere. Karine has given me not only the support and encouragement to continue, but also the love without which nothing would be worth it. I am a very lucky man to have both of them.

Introduction

Business intelligence (BI) is a concept that has been around for many years. Until recently, it has too often been a domain reserved for large corporations with teams of dedicated IT specialists. All too frequently, this has meant developing complex solutions using expensive products on timescales that did not meet business needs.

All this has changed with the advent of self-service business intelligence. Now a user with a reasonable knowledge of Microsoft Excel can leverage their skills to produce their own analyses with minimal support from central IT. Then they can deliver their insights to colleagues safely and securely via the cloud.

This democratization has been made possible by four Excel add-ins that combine to revolutionize the way in which data is discovered, captured, structured, and shaped so that it can be sliced, diced, chopped, queried, and presented in an interactive and intensely visual way.

The four Excel add-ins that together make up the Excel BI toolkit are these:

- **Power Query**—to find and load external data

- **PowerPivot**—to design a coherent data model for analysis

- **Power View**—to present your findings visually and interactively

- **Power Map**—to display insights with a geographical slant

They are completed by Power BI—a simple way of sharing your analyses and insights on PCs and mobile devices from the Microsoft cloud.

Some of these tools (Power Query and Power Map, for instance) are relatively new. Others, such as Power View, have been around as part of SharePoint for a short while. PowerPivot, indeed, has been a dependable Excel add-in for four years or so. Yet it is when these elements are integrated that their combined strengths take business intelligence to a whole new level. When used together, these tools empower the user as never before. They provide you with the capability to analyze and present your data and to shape and deliver your results easily and impressively. All this can be achieved in a fraction of the time that it would take to specify, develop, and test a corporate solution. To cap it all off, self-service BI produces reports at a fraction of the cost of more traditional solutions, with far less rigidity and overhead.

The aim of this short book is to introduce the reader to the brave new world of self-service business intelligence. This will involve a complete tour of the Excel BI toolkit and Power BI. Although it assumes a basic knowledge of Excel, this book presumes that you have little or no knowledge of the Microsoft self-service business intelligence suite of products. These tools are therefore explained from the ground up. The aim is, nonetheless, to provide the most complete coverage possible of each facet of the entire Microsoft self-service BI toolkit, and the way in which its components work together to deliver user-driven business intelligence. Hopefully if you read the book and follow the examples given, you will arrive at a level of practical knowledge and confidence that you can subsequently apply to your own BI requirements.

This book should prove invaluable to business intelligence developers, Excel power users, IT managers, and finance experts—indeed anyone who wants to deliver efficient and practical business intelligence to their colleagues. Whether your aim is to develop a proof of concept or to deliver a fully-fledged BI system, this book can, hopefully, be your guide and mentor.

Although you can read this book from start to finish, it is not designed to be a progressive self-tutorial. The Microsoft self-service BI suite consists of multiple tools that can be used completely independently, and so the same applies to this book. Consequently, you are free to dip only into the chapters that cover the aspect of the self-service BI suite that interests you. You can consider this book as consisting of five independent parts, each of which you can read without needing any of the others. Each part covers one aspect of the self-service BI product suite. These five parts map to the following chapters:

- **Power View**—Chapters 2 through 8

- **PowerPivot**—Chapters 9 through 11

- **Power Query**—Chapters 12 and 13

- **Power Map**—Chapter 14

- **Power BI**—Chapter 15

This book comes with a small sample data set that you can use to follow the examples that are provided. It may seem paradoxical to use a tiny data sample when explaining a product suite that is capable of analyzing medium and large data sets. However, I prefer to use an extremely simplistic data structure so that the reader is free to focus on the essence of what is being explained, and not the data itself.

Inevitably, not every question can be answered and not every issue can be resolved in one book. I truly hope that I have answered many of the essential self-service BI questions that you will face and have provided ways of solving a reasonable number of the challenges that you may encounter.

I wish you good luck in using the Microsoft self-service business intelligence suite to prepare and deliver your insights. And I sincerely hope that you have as much fun with it as I had writing this book.

—Adam Aspin

CHAPTER 1

■ ■ ■

Self-Service Business Intelligence

If you are reading this book, it is most likely because you need to use data. More specifically, it may be that you need to take a journey from data to insight in which you have to take quantities of facts and figures, shape them into comprehensible information, and give them clear and visual meaning.

This book is all about that journey. It covers the many ways that you, an Excel user, can transform raw data into high-impact analyses delivered by Microsoft's new self-service business intelligence (BI) paradigm. This fresh approach presumes presumes that you are not dependent on central IT nor do you need their help on a regular basis It is based on enabling the user to handle industrial-strength quantities of data using familiar tools and to share stunning output in the shortest possible timeframe.

The keywords in this universe are

- Fast

- Decentralized

- Intuitive

- Interactive

- Delivery

Using the tools and techniques described in this book, you can discover and load your data, create all the calculations you need, and then develop and share stylish interactive presentations.

It follows that this book is written from the perspective of the user. Essentially it is all about empowerment—letting users define their own requirements and satisfy their own needs simply and efficiently by building on their existing skills.

The Microsoft Self-Service Business Intelligence Solution

It is important to understand from the start that Microsoft's self-service business intelligence solution is a constantly evolving process. It has been assembled from a series of parallel technologies and is in a continuous state of flux. Fortunately this perpetual motion is now at a peak of readiness, and although it is still undergoing some enhancements and revisions, it is already in a state in which you can use it with confidence.

The Microsoft self-service business intelligence solution has two parts

- **The Excel BI Toolkit**—Allows users to import and model data then create jaw-dropping visualizations.

- **Power BI**—Lets the creators share their insights and data with colleagues on a variety of devices.

By combining these technologies, Microsoft has made an amazingly powerful set of tools available that you can use to find and mash up data that you can then display in crisply interactive reports. Let's take a more in-depth look at this solution.

The Excel BI Toolkit

At the core of Microsoft's self-service BI is the Excel BI Toolkit. This consists of Excel (inevitably) and four add-ins that allow you to import, model, prepare, and display your analyses. These elements are

- **Power Query**—To import and transform data

- **PowerPivot**—To model data and carry out all necessary calculations

- **Power View**—To display your results interactively

- **Power Map**—To show your data from a geographical perspective

You may find that you do not need all these products all the time. Indeed, you may find that you use them independently or in certain combinations. This is because self-service business intelligence is designed to be flexible and respond to a variety of needs. Nonetheless, we will be exploring all of these tools in the course of this book so that you can handle most, if not all, of the challenges that you may meet.

Power BI

Once you have developed reports (or presentations, if you prefer to call them that) using PowerPivot and Power View, you will probably want to share your insights with your colleagues. This is where Power BI enters the equation. Power BI, which technically is an aspect of SharePoint online, lets you load Excel workbooks into the cloud and share them with a chosen group of co-workers. Not only that, but your colleagues can interact with your reports to apply filters and slicers and to highlight data. Power BI also lets information workers share the queries and, possibly complex, data ingestion routines that they have created using Power Query. This way your organization can avoid the duplication of effort that can arise when staff work in "data silos." In addition, you can validate certain data sources as being the key route to an approved data set. Power BI can also ensure that the Excel workbooks that have been shared are updated automatically and regularly so that users are always looking at the most recent data.

■ **Note**   There is no Power BI for on-premises SharePoint sites at the time of writing.

Taken together, this combination of tools and technologies creates a unique solution to the challenges of creating and sharing analytical insights. However, let me say again that you may not need *all* that the solution can offer. If all you need to do is share workbooks, then you do not need to share queries. The advantage of self-service BI is that it is a smorgasbord of potential solutions, where each department or enterprise can choose to implement the tools and technologies that suit its specific requirements.

The Excel BI Toolkit and Power BI

To understand how all these elements fit together, it will probably help if I begin with a more detailed overview of the various technologies that are employed. This should help you see how they can let you discover and load your data and then calculate and shape your data model so that you can create and share presentations and insights.

Power Query

Power Query is one of the most recent additions to the self-service BI toolkit. It allows you to discover, access, and consolidate information from varied sources. Once your data is selected, cleansed, and transformed into a coherent table, you can then place it in an Excel worksheet, or better still, load it directly into PowerPivot, which is a natural source for data when you are using Power View and Power Map.

Power Query allows you to do many things with source data, but the four main steps are likely to be

- *Import* data from a wide variety of sources. This covers corporate databases to files, and social media to big data.

- *Merge* data from multiple sources into a coherent structure.

- *Shape* data into the columns and records that suit your uses.

- *Cleanse* your data to make it reliable and easy to use.

There was a time when these processes required dedicated teams of IT specialists. Well, not any more. With Power Query, you can mash up your own data so that it is the way you want it and is ready to use as part of your self-service BI solution.

Power Query is discussed in more depth Chapters 12 and 13.

PowerPivot

PowerPivot is essentially the data store for your information. Indeed, many people refer to the Excel Data Model when they talk about data in PowerPivot. Power Query lets you import data and make it useable; PowerPivot then takes over and lets you extend and formalize the cleansed data. More specifically, it allows you to

- Create a data model by joining tables to develop a coherent data structure from multiple separate sources of data. This data model will then be used by Power View, Power Map, and the Power BI natural language querying engine.

- Enrich the data model by applying coherent names and data types.

- Create calculations and prepare the core metrics that you want to use in your analyses and presentations.

- Add hierarchies to enhance the user experience and guide your users through complex data sets.

- Create KPIs (Key Performance Indicators) to allow benchmarking.

It is worth noting that you can load data into PowerPivot directly without using Power Query. As you will see in this book, you have the choice. Whether you want or need to use Power Query at all will depend on the complexity of the source data and whether or not you need to cleanse and shape the data first.

PowerPivot is discussed in Chapters 9 through 11.

Power View

I think of Power View as the "jewel in the crown" of self-service business intelligence. It is a dynamic analysis and presentation tool that lets you create professional-grade

- Tables
- Matrixes
- Charts
- Maps

Not only that, but it is incredibly fast and highly intuitive. It provides advanced interactivity through the use of

- Slicers
- Filters
- Highlighting

A Power View report is only a special type of Excel worksheet, and you can have many reports in an Excel file. In most cases, users tend to create Power View reports using a PowerPivot data model, but you can also create Power View reports using data tables in an Excel worksheet if you prefer. However (at the risk of laboring the point), a PowerPivot data set can be tweaked to make Power View reports much easier to create and modify than can a table in Excel.

Power View is discussed in Chapters 2 through 8.

Power Map

Power Map is, as its name implies, a mapping tool. As long as your data contains some form of geographical data, and you can connect to Bing Maps, you can use Power Map to create geographical representations of the data.

The types of presentation that you can create with Power Map include

- Maps
- Automatic presentations of geographical data
- Time-based representations of geographical data

As is the case with Power View, Power Map is at its best when you use the data in a PowerPivot data set. However, you can use data in Excel if you prefer.

Power Map is discussed in Chapter 14.

Power BI

Power BI is a cloud-based data sharing environment. Power BI leverages existing Excel 2013 PowerPivot, Power Query, and Power View functionality and adds new features that allow you to

- Share presentations and queries with your colleagues.
- Update your Excel file from data sources that can be on-site or in the cloud.
- Display the output on multiple devices. This includes PCs, tablets, and HTML 5-enabled mobile devices as well as Windows tablets that use the Power BI app.
- Query your data using natural language processing (or Q&A, as it is known).

Power BI is discussed in Chapter 15.

Preparing the Self-Service BI Environment

Before you can begin to use the Excel BI Toolkit you need to make sure that your PC is set up correctly and that everything is in place. This is not difficult, but it is probably less frustrating if you get everything set up correctly before you leap into the fray rather than get annoyed if things do not work flawlessly first time. If you are working in a corporate environment where these add-ins are the norm, then all your problems are probably solved already. If not, you might have a few tweaks to perform. So let's see how to ensure that your version of Excel is ready to fly with self-service BI.

PowerPivot

To begin with, PowerPivot is only available in Microsoft Office Professional Plus, Office 365 Professional Plus, and in a standalone edition of Excel 2013. It is not available in Office on a Windows RT PC. PowerPivot does exist in Excel 2010, but it uses a different version of the Excel Data Model (which can be converted to the 2013 data model). So if you open an Excel 2013 workbook containing a data model created with Excel 2010, you will get a warning that you will have to convert the data model and that this step is irreversible. Note also that a data model created with the 2013 version of Excel is not backward compatible with the previous version

You will know if PowerPivot is enabled if you can see a PowerPivot menu and ribbon in Excel. If this ribbon is not available, you will have to enable it like this:

1. In the File menu click Options.

2. Click Add-Ins on the bottom of the menu on the left. The Excel Options dialog will look like Figure 1-1.

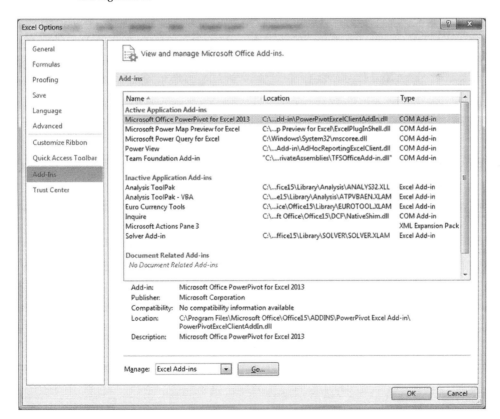

Figure 1-1. *The Excel Options dialog*

3. In the Manage popup list, and select COM Add-ins.

4. Click Go. The COM Add-ins dialog will appear as shown in Figure 1-2.

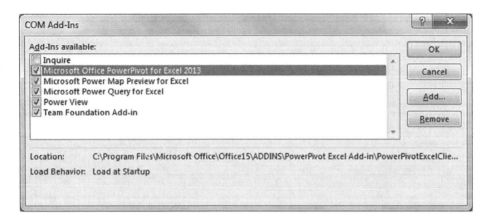

Figure 1-2. *The COM Add-ins dialog*

5. Check the Microsoft Office PowerPivot For Excel 2013 check box.

6. Click OK.

The PowerPivot menu and ribbon should now be available in Excel.

■ **Note** Depending on your exact configuration of Excel, you may see more or fewer add-ins displayed in the COM Add-ins dialog on your PC.

Power View

Power View is also currently only available in Office Professional Plus 2013 and Office 365 Professional Plus, as well as in the standalone edition of Excel 2013. Power View is not available in Office on a Windows RT PC. Not only that, but you will have to install Microsoft Silverlight 5 for Power View to work. Fortunately, however, Power View will detect if you have Silverlight installed and if it is not present, Power View will install it the first time that it is run.

Normally Power View is an integral part of Excel. Indeed, if you open Excel and activate the Insert ribbon, you will see the Power View button, as shown in Figure 1-3.

Power
View
Reports

Figure 1-3. *The Power View button in the Excel Insert ribbon*

There may be times when the Power View button is grayed out. If this is the case, you will need to enable the Power View add-in. You can do this almost exactly as I described in the previous section for PowerPivot, except that at step 5, you need to check the Power View box, which you can see in Figure 1-2.

You should then see that the Power View button in the Insert ribbon is no longer grayed out.

▦ **Note** Power View is also available in SharePoint and is virtually identical to the Excel version. If you need an introduction to this version of Power View, refer to Chapters 2–8, which will cover most of your requirements. I will not, however, be discussing SharePoint BI in this book.

Power Query

Power Query is currently an optional add-in for Excel—providing that you are using one of the following versions:

- Microsoft Office 2010 Professional Plus with Software Assurance

- Microsoft Office 2013 Professional Plus

- Office 365 Pro Plus

- Excel 2013 Standalone

Since it is optional, you may have to download and install the add-in. If it is already installed, you will see a Power Query ribbon available in Excel. If you do not, here is how you can install it:

1. Close Microsoft Excel.

2. Download the Power Query install file. At the time of writing this is available at the following URL: http://www.microsoft.com/en-gb/download/details.aspx?id=39379.

3. On the download page click Download. You will see the Choose The Download That You Want page.

4. On this page, ensure that you select the correct version for your version of Excel (32-bit or 64-bit).

5. Click Next and select a directory to which you want to download the .msi file. The March 2014 file is named PowerQuery_2.10.3598.81 (64-bit) [en-US].msi.

6. Go to the directory where you downloaded the .msi file in the previous step, and double-click the file. The security warning dialog will appear as in Figure 1-4.

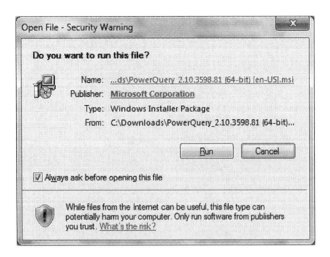

Figure 1-4. *The security warning dialog*

7. Click Run. The Power Query Setup dialog will appear as in Figure 1-5.

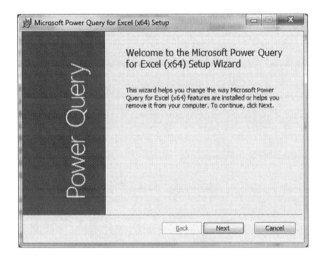

Figure 1-5. *The Power Query Setup dialog*

8. Click Next. The License Terms dialog will be displayed. You can see this in Figure 1-6.

Figure 1-6. *The License Terms dialog for Power Query*

9. Check the I Accept The Terms In The License Agreement box.

10. Click Next. The Destination Folder dialog will appear as in Figure 1-7.

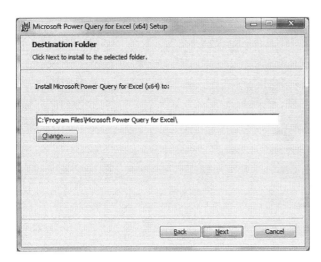

Figure 1-7. *The Destination Folder dialog*

11. Leave the suggested destination folder unless you have a specific reason to select another and click Next. The final installation dialog will be displayed, as shown in Figure 1-8.

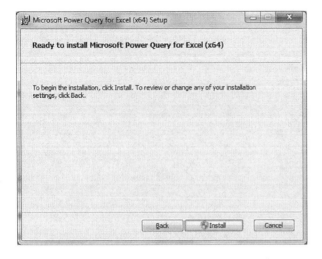

Figure 1-8. The final installation dialog for Power Query

12. Click Install. The install process will run. You may see a User Account Control dialog requesting permission to run the install program. If you do, click Yes. Once the process has finished you will see the completion dialog, as in Figure 1-9.

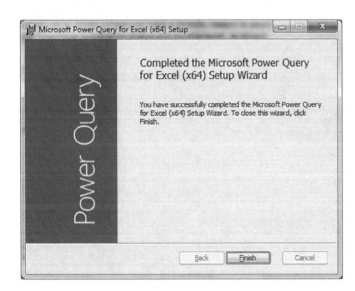

Figure 1-9. The completion dialog once Power Query is installed

13. Click Finish.

Power Query is now installed, and the Power Query menu and ribbon will be available in Excel.

Power Map

As of Microsoft Office 2013 Service Pack 1, Power Map is now an integral part of Excel. If you are running an older version of Excel, then you may have to download the add-in and install it separately. Since this process is virtually identical to the process I just described for Power Query, I will not reiterate all the details here. Suffice it to say that you follow all the steps you followed for Power Query, except that at step 2, you use the following URL instead (as at April 2014): `http://www.microsoft.com/en-gb/download/details.aspx?id=38395`. If you have Power Map already installed, you will have an active Map button in the Excel Insert ribbon, as shown in Figure 1-10.

Power Map

Figure 1-10. *The Power Map button in the Excel Insert ribbon*

Power BI

Power BI is the online solution that enables you to share the presentations and queries that you have created using the Excel BI Toolkit. It is an enhancement to SharePoint online and requires a subscription to use. As things stand, Power BI does not include Excel (unless you have a Power BI with Office 365 subscription), and at the time of writing there are three different pricing plans. As this state of affairs could evolve over time, I will not go into the details here, but I suggest that you see what is available on the Microsoft web site if you are considering a Power BI subscription.

One you have taken out a subscription to Power BI—and you have a valid Excel license—you can use the SharePoint online Power BI site application to add a robust, dynamic location where you can share Excel workbooks in the Microsoft cloud.

▓ **Note**   At the time of writing there is a free trial offer for Power BI. I can only recommend that you take advantage of this if you want to test out all that it can deliver.

Adding a Power BI Site

To take full advantage of the enhanced functionality that Power BI can bring to SharePoint online, you will need to add a Power BI site to your cloud-based portal. This only takes a few clicks, but it will enable you to

- View workbooks up to 250 MB in a browser on Office 365 if you save and enable them on the Power BI site.

- Highlight certain spreadsheets as "Featured Reports."

- Display thumbnail images of Power View reports in a spreadsheet in the Power BI site.

Assuming that you have a working subscription to Office 365 with Power BI and you also have a starter site, you now need to create the Power BI site To do this,

1. In the navigation bar on the left of the portal window, click Site Contents. The Site Contents page will be displayed, as in Figure 1-11.

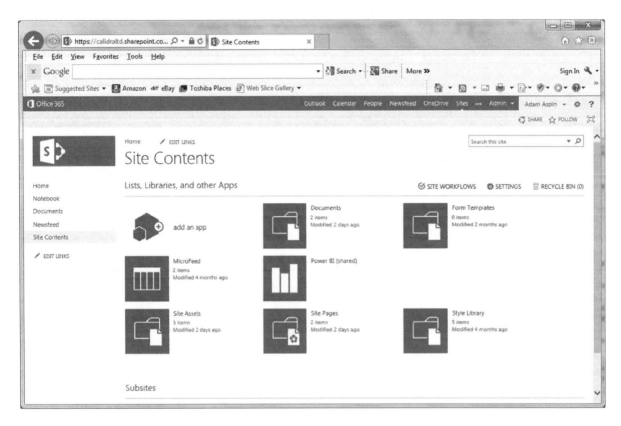

Figure 1-11. *Adding the Power BI app*

2. Click the Power BI icon—or possibly click Add An App first to display all the available apps, including the Power BI app, and then click it—and it will be installed after a few seconds. You will then be taken into the Power BI app, which looks like Figure 1-12.

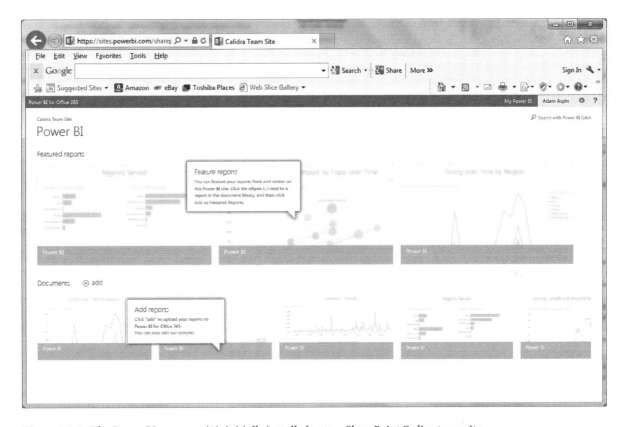

Figure 1-12. *The Power BI app once it is initially installed onto a SharePoint Online team site*

It really is that simple to enable the Power BI site on your portal. Once this is done, you should see Power BI listed in the navigation bar on the left of the portal window when you use your site.

The Windows Power BI App

If you are using a Windows 8.1 tablet, then you may well want to download and install the Power BI app for Windows. This app is available for free in the Windows App store; the current URL is `http://apps.microsoft.com/windows/en-gb/app/b7e7c94d-2ea3-4fa6-a277-9d19a1f697ba`.

This app will allow you to view and interact with Power View reports from multiple Power BI sites.

A version of this app for the iPad has been promised for mid 2014, and could be available by the time that you are reading this book. An Android version is rumoured to be in the works.

Corporate BI or Self-Service BI?

This book is all about self-service business intelligence. Although this concept stands in opposition to corporate business intelligence, the two interact and relate. However, the distinctions are not only blurred, they are evolving along continually changing lines.

In any case, I do not want to describe these two approaches as if they are mutually antagonistic. They are both in the service of the enterprise, and both exist to provide timely analysis. The two can, and should, work together as much as possible. After all, much self-service business intelligence needs corporate data, which is often the result of many months (or years) of careful thought and intricate data processing and cleansing. So it is really not worth rejecting all that a corporate IT department can provide for avid users of self-service BI. At the same time, the speed at which a purely self-service approach can deliver rapid discovery, analysis, and presentation can relieve hard-pressed IT departments from the kind of ad-hoc jobs that distract from larger projects. So it pays for central IT to see self-service BI as a friend, and for users to appreciate all the support and assistance that an IT department can provide.

Self-service business intelligence, then, is part of an equation. It is not a total solution—and neither is it a panacea. Anarchic implementation of self-service BI can lead to massive data duplication and so many versions of "the truth" that all facts become mere opinions. Consequently, I advise a measured response. When managers, users, or, heaven forbid, external consultants announce in tones of hyperactive excitement that Microsoft have produced a new miracle-working solution to replace all your existing BI solutions, I suggest you take a step backward and a deep calming breath. I would never imply that you use Power BI to replace "canned" corporate reports, for instance (to solve this requirement see *Pro SQL Server 2012 Reporting Services* [Apress 2012] by Rodney Landrum, Brian McDonald, and Shawn McGehee). Yet if you need interactive reports based on volatile and varied data sources, then the Excel BI Toolkit and Power BI could be a perfect solution.

The Excel Data Model

When introducing PowerPivot toward the start of this chapter I made a passing reference to the Excel Data Model. As this is fundamental to the practice of self-service BI using Excel and Power BI, you really need to understand what this data model is, and how it helps you to create valid analyses.

The data model is a collection of one or more tables of data that are loaded into PowerPivot and then joined together in a coherent fashion. The data can come via Power Query, be obtained from existing Excel tables or worksheets, or be imported from a variety of sources. There can only be a single data model for an Excel file.

Admittedly, you can place all your data in a single "flat" table in Excel and use that as the basis for Power View reports and Power Map output. However, it is highly likely that you will want to develop a data model using PowerPivot if you intend to use data sets of any complexity. There are occasions when building a good data model can take awhile to get right, but there are many valid justifications for spending the time required to build a coherent data model using PowerPivot. The reasons for this investment include

- You can go way beyond the million-row limit of an Excel worksheet if you are using the Excel Data Model in PowerPivot. Indeed, in PowerPivot tables of tens of millions of rows are not unknown.

- A coherent data model makes understanding and visualizing your data easier.

- A well thought out data model means less redundant information stored in a single table when it can be referenced from another table rather than repeated endlessly.

- PowerPivot saves space on disk and in memory because it uses a highly efficient data compression algorithm to store the data set. This means that a workbook using a data set will take up considerably less space than storing data in Excel worksheets.

- Since a data set is loaded entirely into the PC's memory, calculations are faster.

- A data model can be prepared for data output. More specifically, you can apply formatting and define data types (such as geographical types, for instance) for specific columns so that Power View and Power Map will recognize them instantly and make the correct deductions as to the best ways to use them.

- A data model can contain certain calculations (some of which can get fairly complex) that are designed to ensure that the correct results are returned when slicing and filtering data in Power View and Power Map.

- A data model can contain hierarchies and KPIs.

- A data model can be used to create complex pivot tables in Excel if you not want to use Power View or Power Map.

- A data model can be the basis, or the proof of concept, for a fully-fledged SSAS (SQL Server Analysis Services) tabular data warehouse.

As an example of a data set, this book will use a simple model that uses the sales data for an imaginary company that sells classic and modern British sports cars throughout Europe and that is starting to expand into the United States. This fictitious corporation is called Brilliant British Cars, and it has been going for a couple of years. Their data is relatively simple, and the data model for the company can be seen in Figure 1-13.

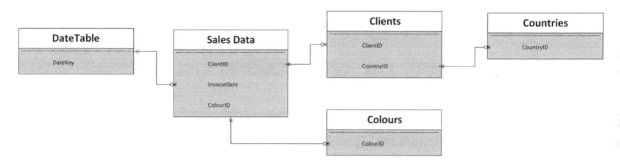

Figure 1-13. *The Excel Data Model used by Brilliant British Cars*

The art and science of developing data models could easily be the subject of a separate tome. It is, in fact, not unrelated to basic relational database design, which has been described exhaustively in dozens (or hundreds) of books over the last couple of decades. As a reader, you can breathe a sigh of relief as I have no intention of attempting to cover this subject in this book. As far as our sample data model is concerned, I will just take it as is and suggest that you consult one of the many excellent resources already available should you need further guidance when developing your own specific data model.

Throughout this book I will be using the established best practice, which is to use the Excel Data Model as the basis for self-service BI. However, as I remarked earlier, you can use plain old Excel tables as a source of data for both Power View reports and Power Map deliverables if you wish.

How This Book Is Designed to Be Read

The suite of technologies that makes up the Microsoft self-service business intelligence offering are essentially independent products. It follows that you may need only to focus on one or two of them to solve a particular problem. Or it may be that you already know how to use part of the toolset but need to learn, or revise, other elements.

Because we are looking at a set of tools, each of which can be learned individually, this book is not designed to be read *only* in a linear fashion. Given that the primary focus of this text is on delivering output that has the "wow" factor, it begins with Power View to show what can be done with the new presentation tool that is now integrated into Excel.

The chapters on Power View, however, do not presume any knowledge of how to assemble or develop an underlying data set. Their aim is to get you up and running with interactive presentations as fast as possible. Nevertheless, it is likely that you will one day need a data model to use as the basis for your reports. So after the chapters on Power View, you learn how to use PowerPivot to create data sets and get them ready to be the bedrock of your Power View deliverables.

Frequently PowerPivot is all you need to connect to source data. Yet sometimes you need something more advanced to load and prepare data from multiple varied sources. If this is the case, you can learn how to perform these tasks using Power Query in the couple of chapters that follow the three on PowerPivot.

You can then see all that Power Map can do for you in the penultimate chapter and learn, in the final chapter, how to pull it all together by sharing your data and insights with Power BI.

There are, however, other possible reading paths, if you prefer. So, depending on your requirements, you may wish to try one of the following approaches.

Discovering Data

If your primary focus is on discovering data and then preparing it for later use—that is, you need to load, mash up, rationalize, and cleanse data from multiple diverse sources—then Chapters 13 and 14, which introduce Power Query, should be your first port of call. Chapter 13 explains how to connect to many of the data sources that Power Query can read, and Chapter 14 gives the reader a thorough grounding in how to process and transform source data to make it coherent and usable by PowerPivot as part of a logical data set.

Creating a Data Model

Conversely, if the source data that you are using is already clean and accessible, then you may be more interested in learning how to create a valid and efficient data model that is clean and comprehensible and contains all the calculations that you need for your presentations. In this case, you should start by reading Chapters 9 through 11.

Taking Data and Preparing It for Output

If you are faced with the task of finding, cleansing, and modeling data that is ready to be used for reporting, then you will probably need to use both Power Query and PowerPivot. If this is the case, you may be best served by reading Chapters 13 and 14 on Power Query (to import and shape the source data) and then Chapters 9, 10, and 11 on PowerPivot (to model the data).

Taking Existing Excel BI and Sharing It

You may well be a PowerPivot expert already and have possibly learned to use Power View in its initial incarnation as part of SharePoint. If this describes your situation, you may want to move straight to the part where you learn to share your reports in the cloud. This means that Chapter 15 on Power BI is for you. Here you will learn how best to load and share Excel BI workbooks and Power Query queries as well as how to update workbooks in the cloud with the latest data from on-premises data sources.

Delivering Geodata

It is not just tables and charts that create the "Eureka!" moment. Sometimes an insight can come from seeing how data is dispersed geographically, or how geographic data evolves over time. If this is what you are looking for, then you need to look at Chapter 8 (which covers maps in Power View) and Chapter 14 (which covers Power Map) to learn how these two tools can create and deliver new insights into your data.

Delivering Excel BI to Mobile Devices

If you need to ensure that you and your colleagues can access their data on mobile devices, then Chapter 15 on Power BI is the one for you. Here you will see how to use the Power BI app on a Windows tablet, as well as how to use Power View on many other mobile devices.

To Learn the Product Suite Following a Real-World Path

If you are coming to self-service BI as a complete novice, then one way to learn it is by taking the path that you could need to follow in a real-world situation. If this suits you, then you could try reading the entire book, but in this order:

- **Discover and prepare data**—Start with Chapters 13 and 14 on Power Query.

- **Create and enhance a data model**—Next, read Chapters 9, 10, and 11 on PowerPivot.

- **Create visualizations**—Continue with Chapters 2–7 on Power View.

- **Add geodata outputs**—Move on to Chapter 8 and Chapter 12, which cover maps in Power View and Power Map.

- **Share your insights**—Finish with Chapter 15 on Power BI.

Anyway, these proposed reading paths are only suggestions. Each chapter is designed to cover a complete aspect of self-service BI in as thorough a fashion as is possible. Feel free to jump in and pick and choose the path that best suits you.

The Self-Service Business Intelligence Universe

The amalgam of products and technologies that make up the world of Microsoft self-service business intelligence can seem complex and even confusing at first glance. This is, to some extent, because some Excel add-ins seem to have overlapping aims, or that the interface between creating reports and sharing them is not always immediately clear.

Figure 1-14 attempts to provide a more comprehensible vision of the total toolset so that you can better see how all the pieces work together.

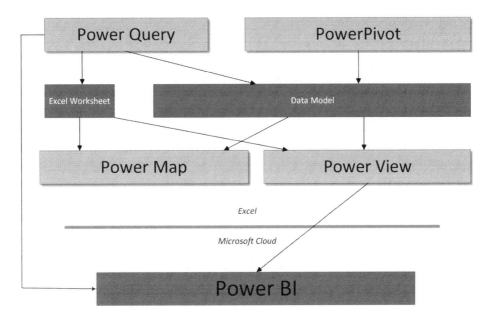

Figure 1-14. *The self-service business intelligence universe*

Conclusion

Microsoft self-service business intelligence, then, is not an application, but a suite of tools and technologies that allow you to find, import, join, and structure data that you then extend with any necessary calculations; you then use this data as the basis for interactive presentations that you can subsequently share in the cloud and access using a variety of devices.

More precisely, you will be using a set of Excel add-ins and a cloud-based subscription service to create and share data and high-impact analyses with your colleagues. The output can be viewed using a PC or a mobile device and can allow your public to select and filter the reports to discover their own insights.

In any case, that is enough of a preamble. The best way to learn any instrument is to practice using it. So it is time for you to move on to the chapters that interest you and start your journey into the wonderful world of self-service business intelligence.

CHAPTER 2

■ ■ ■

Power View and Tables

Welcome to Power View! This chapter, along with the next six, aims to give you a comprehensive introduction to Microsoft's new presentation and analysis add-in for Excel. You will learn how to use this incredible tool to

- Delve deep into data and produce valuable information from the mass of facts and figures available.

- Create interactive views of your insights, where you can test your analyses quickly and easily.

- Enhance the presentation of your results to grab your audience's attention.

Power View may be easy to use, but it can present your insights in many and varied ways. So, to provide some structure, I have decided on an approach that mimics the analysis and presentation process (for many of us, at least). As data analysis often begins with a look at the data itself, presenting the facts will be the immediate focus. More precisely, what you will be seeing in this chapter is

- How to use the Power View interface.

- How to create and enhance tabular visualizations of your data. This covers simple lists and more advanced matrix-style tables.

- How to drill down into your tables to dig into the meaning of the numbers.

- How to use cards as a new and innovative way to display facts and figures.

- How to display tabular KPIs (Key Performance Indicators).

I realize that it may seem contradictory to spend time on things that are generally described as intuitive. I can only say to this that while getting up and running is easy, attaining an in-depth understanding of all of the potential of this powerful tool does require some explanation. The approach in this book is to go through all the possibilities of each aspect being handled as thoroughly as possible. So feel free to jump ahead (and back) if you don't need all the detail just yet.

In the chapters on Power View I will be using a set of data from an Excel data model. This data is in the sample Excel worksheet CarSales.xlsx in the directory C:\HighImpactDataVisualizationWithPowerBI (assuming that you have followed the instructions in Appendix A). As I explained in Chapter 1, accessing the right source data, and ensuring that this data is coherent and in a valid data model, is vital for successful self-service business intelligence. However, I feel that preparing the data is a separate (although clearly related) subject, and so I will be treating it separately in Chapters 9, 10, and 11. For the moment I want to concentrate on all that Power View has to offer, and so I will use this sample data set as a basis for all the data visualizations that you will learn to produce in the next few chapters.

As Power View is now a core part of Excel, I will assume you have some basic Excel knowledge. You do not need to be an Excel maestro by any stretch of the imagination, however. Indeed one of the major aspects of Power View is that it really is highly intuitive and requires only basic familiarity with its host application.

Anyway, that is enough said to set out the ground rules. It is time to get started. So, on to Power View.

The Power View Experience

I realize that you probably just want to start creating punchy presentations straight away. Well, that is fair enough. So feel free to jump ahead to the next section if you can't wait. However, if you are the sort of person who prefers to have concepts and terms explained first, then this section will describe the Power View interface so you know what is available, what it does, and possibly most important of all, what everything is called. Of course, you can always refer back to this section at a later time, whatever your approach to learning Power View.

Adding a Power View Sheet to an Excel Workbook

Assuming that you have launched Excel and that Power View is enabled (as described in Chapter 1), then this is how you start using Power View:

1. Open the CarSales.xlsx sample workbook (or any workbook where you have prepared a data model).

2. Click Insert to activate the Insert ribbon.

3. Click Power View.

You will find yourself face to face with an empty Power View report.

The Power View Interface

The Power View interface—as with everything about it—is designed for simplicity so that you can use it almost instantaneously rather than learn how to use it. However, as you can see, being simple does not make it austere. Essentially you are looking at four main elements, as illustrated in Figure 2-1:

- The *Power View report* (where most things happen) in the center of the screen.

- The *Filters Area*, to the right of the Power View report. This lets you select the data that will appear in the report and even in specific parts of the report.

- The *Field List*, at the right of the screen. Here you will see all the available data for your report abd any data that you re using for a selected visualization.

- Finally—not to say inevitably—the *Power View Ribbon*, at the top of the screen.

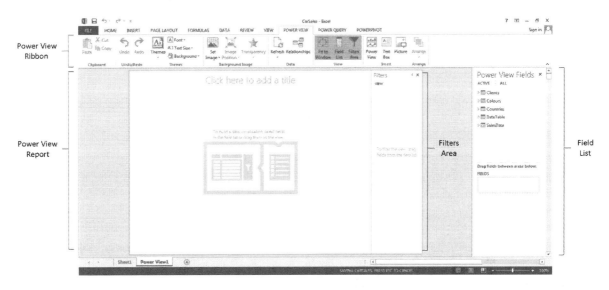

Figure 2-1. *The Power View interface*

Now that you have an overall feeling for the Power View interface, two initial aspects need some further explanation: the Ribbon and the Field List.

The Power View Ribbon

The Power View ribbon is something that you will be seeing a lot of, so it is probably worth getting to know it sooner rather than later. Table 2-1 describes the buttons in the Power View ribbon. Don't worry, I will not be explaining what each one can do in detail straight away, as I prefer to let you see how they can be used in the context of certain operations; you will see what each one can do over the course of the next few chapters.

Table 2-1. *Buttons Available in the Power View Ribbon*

Button	Description
Paste	Pastes a copied element from the clipboard
Cut	Removes the selected element and places it in the clipboard
Copy	Copies the selected element and places it in the clipboard
Undo	Undoes the last action
Redo	Undoes the last undo action
Themes	Lets you select a theme (color palette and font) for your report
Font	Lets you choose a font from the popup menu of those available
Text Size	Allows you to set a text size percentage
Background	Displays a selection of backgrounds to add to the report
Set Image	Lets you insert a background image into your report

(continued)

Table 2-1. (*continued*)

Button	Description
Image Position	Lets you alter the dimensions of the background image in the report
Transparency	Sets the transparency of an image
Refresh	Refreshes the source data for a Power View report
Relationships	Enables you to add, modify, or delete joins between source data tables
Fit To Window	Fits the report to the screen window
Field List	Displays or hides the list of data fields
Filters Area	Displays or hides the Filter Area
Power View	Inserts a new, blank, Power View report
Text Box	Adds a freeform text box to the report
Picture	Lets you add a freeform image into the report
Arrange	Allows you to alter the way in which objects are placed on top of each other in the report

Figure 2-2 shows you how the buttons are grouped in the Power View ribbon:

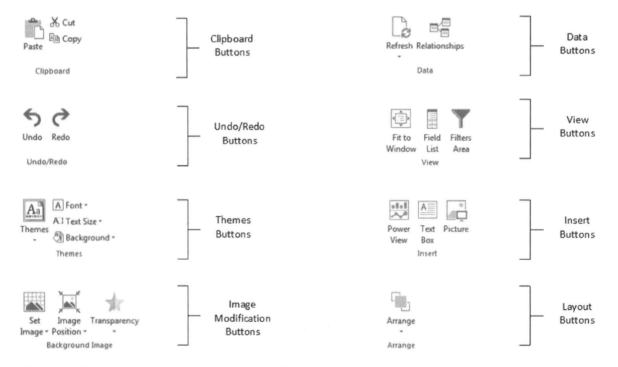

Figure 2-2. *The buttons available in the Power View ribbon*

The Power View ribbon can be minimized just like any other MS Office ribbon to increase the screen space available for report creation. To hide the ribbon.

1. Click on the Minimize icon (the small upward facing caret at the bottom right of the ribbon).

Once the Power View ribbon has been minimized, all Excel ribbons are minimized. You can, however, make a ribbon reappear temporarily by clicking on the ribbon name in the Menu bar at the top of the Excel application. Once you have finished with a Ribbon option, the ribbon will be minimized once more.

To make the ribbon reappear permanently, just click on the small pin icon which has replaced the initial caret at the bottom right of any ribbon.

The Field List

The Field List, as I mentioned earlier, is where you can see and select all the fields that contain the data in the underlying data model.

To display the Field List

1. In the Power View ribbon, click the Field List icon.

The field list will (re)appear to the right of the Power View canvas.

The Field List icon will also hide the field list—it is a simple on/off switch. The Field List also has a Close icon, just like a normal window. So you can hide the Field List by clicking the Close button (the small X at the top right corner of the Field List) if you wish.

You can also adjust the width of the Field List. While the default width is probably suitable in most circumstances, you may wish to

-   Widen the Field List to display particularly long field names.

-   Narrow the Field List to increase the size of the Power View canvas.

To resize the Field List

1. Place the mouse pointer over the left-hand border of the Field List. The cursor will become a two-headed lateral arrow.

2. Drag the mouse pointer left or right until the Field List is the width you want.

Once you have resized the Field List, it will remember the size that you set, even if you hide and redisplay it.

Remember that to create any visualization, or to modify the data behind an existing visualization, you will need to have the Field List visible. My advice is to leave it visible, at least in the initial stages of developing Power View reports.

Using the Field List

The Field List is quite probably one of the most fundamental parts of Power View. Consequently, it is well worth making its acquaintance earlier rather than later.

Figure 2-3 shows you part of a Power View Field List, using the data model from the CarSales.xlsx workbook. Only some of the available data tables are visible, and the Layout section may look very different from what you see on screen. Moreover, the popup menus can vary depending on the context of the current operation. However this image enables you to get an idea of what the Field List has to offer.

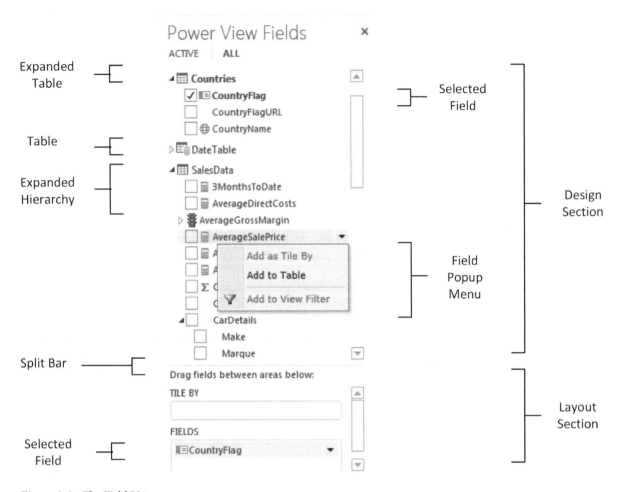

Figure 2-3. The Field List

The Field List is divided into two parts. The upper part (known as the Design section) is the available data, seen as tables that you can expand in order to view the fields, and possibly any hierarchies that they contain. The lower part is the Layout section, which contains any selected fields. The Layout section will change considerably depending on which visualization is being used. You can alter the relative sizes of the upper and lower parts of the Field List by dragging the Split Bar up and down.

■ **Note**   You can see if you are using data from a data table in the current report, as the name of the table will be in bold in the Field List.

Renaming or Deleting a Power View Report

So you have created a Power View report. This new report has been added as a new Excel sheet, as you can guess from looking at the tabs at the bottom of the screen. This report is now part and parcel of the Excel workbook in which it was created. You can save it with the Excel .xlsx file extension (indeed it cannot be saved independently). A Power View report is an Excel sheet like any other (worksheet, chart, etc...) and can be manipulated like any other sheet. This means that it can be hidden, deleted, or renamed using standard Excel techniques. Just in case, here is a quick refresher on deleting or renaming an Excel tab:

1. Right-click on the tab at the bottom of the screen.

2. Select Rename (for instance).

3. Enter the new Power View Sheet name.

4. Press Enter to confirm.

If you chose to delete the Power View report, then you will see a dialog asking for confirmation that you really want to delete the report.

Tables in Power View

Now that you understand the Power View interface, let's look at getting some data from the data model into a report. I suggest a progression that begins with the simplest type of list first—a standard table. From there we will move on to matrix tables and, finally, cards and Key Performance Indicators (KPIs). Tables are an essential starting point for any PowerPivot visualization. Indeed, everything that is based on data (which is to say virtually everything) in Power View starts out as a table. So it is worth getting to know how tables work—and how to get them into action the fastest possible way.

Let's start with the simplest possible type of table: a list. This is what you could well find yourself using much of the time to create visualizations in your Power View reports.

Adding a Table

Adding a basic table is probably the simplest thing that you can do in Power View. After all, a table is the default visualization that Power View will create. So, here is how you can create a table that shows total sales to date by make of car from the sample dataset:

1. Display the Field List, unless it is already visible.

2. Expand the table containing the field that you wish to display (SalesData to begin with). You do this by clicking on the hollow triangle to the left of the table name. The triangle becomes a black triangle, and the field names are displayed, slightly indented, underneath the table name.

3. Find the hierarchy named CarDetails and expand this, too, by clicking the triangle to its left. The fields that make up the hierarchy will be displayed.

4. Select the check box to the left of the field name for the first field that you wish to display in a table. In our example this is Make. When you do this, a table containing a list of all the makes of car in the dataset appears in the Power View canvas. The field that you selected will also appear in the FIELDS box in the Layout section (the lower part) of the Field List.

5. Repeat steps 2 through 4 for all the fields that you wish to display. In this simple example, the SalePrice field will suffice. You will see that any field that you add appears in the existing table.

The table immediately displays the data that is available from the source, and all new fields appear to the right of any existing fields. If there is a lot of data to display, then a vertical scroll bar appears at the right of the table, allowing you to scroll up and down to view the data. Totals will be added automatically to the bottom of the table—though you may have to scroll down to see them. The basic list-type table that you created is shown in Figure 2-4.

Make	SalePrice
Aston Martin	£3,507,660.00
Bentley	£1,622,000.00
Jaguar	£1,997,750.00
MG8	£315,000.00
Rolls Royce	£2,413,800.00
Triumph	£286,500.00
TVR	£201,500.00
Total	**£10,344,210.00**

Figure 2-4. *A first table*

This is, self-evidently, a very tiny table. In the real world you could be looking at tables that contain thousands, or tens of thousands, of records. Power View accelerates the display of large data sets by only loading the data that is required as you scroll down through a list. So you might see the scroll bar advance somewhat slowly as you progress downward through a large table.

___

■ **Note**   In this example, we leapt straight into a concept that might be new to you—that of hierarchies. These are essentially an organizational technique you can use to help you manage access to data. You will learn how to create them in Chapter 11.

___

You can always see which fields have been selected for a table either by selecting the table or by clicking inside it. The fields used will be instantly displayed in both the Field List (as checked fields) and in the FIELDS box in the Layout section of the Field List. To get you used to this idea, see Figure 2-5, which shows the Field List for the table you just created.

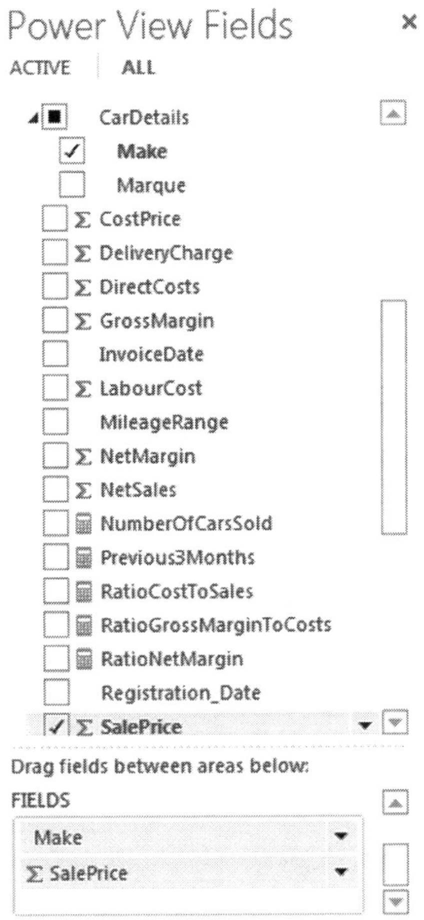

Power View Fields ✕

ACTIVE | ALL

- ▲ ■   CarDetails
  - ✓   **Make**
  - ☐   Marque
- ☐ Σ CostPrice
- ☐ Σ DeliveryCharge
- ☐ Σ DirectCosts
- ☐ Σ GrossMargin
- ☐   InvoiceDate
- ☐ Σ LabourCost
- ☐   MileageRange
- ☐ Σ NetMargin
- ☐ Σ NetSales
- ☐ ▦ NumberOfCarsSold
- ☐ ▦ Previous3Months
- ☐ ▦ RatioCostToSales
- ☐ ▦ RatioGrossMarginToCosts
- ☐ ▦ RatioNetMargin
- ☐   Registration_Date
- ✓ Σ **SalePrice** ▼

Drag fields between areas below:

FIELDS

| Make | ▼ |
| Σ SalePrice | ▼ |

Figure 2-5. *The Field List for the table of Sales By Make*

As befits such a polished product, Power View does not limit you to just one way of adding fields to a table. Other ways in which you can add fields to a table are

- By dragging the field name into the Fields section at the bottom of the Field List.

- By hovering the mouse pointer over a field in the Fields section (the upper part) of the Field List. When you do this, the field is highlighted and a down-facing triangle appears on the right of the field name. You can then click on the down-facing triangle and select Add To Table from the popup menu.

You can add further fields to an existing table at any time. The key thing to remember (if you are using the two techniques just described) is that you must select the table that you want to modify first. This is as simple as clicking inside it. After you click, you instantly see that the table is active because tiny handles appear at the corners of the table as well as in the middle of each side of the table.

■ **Note** If you do not select an existing table before adding a field, Power View will create a new table using the field that you are attempting to add to a table.

To create another table, all you have to do is click outside any existing visualizations in the Power View report and begin selecting fields as described earlier. A new table will be created as a result. Power View will always try to create new tables in an empty part of the canvas. You will see how to rearrange this default presentation shortly.

Deleting a Table

Suppose that you no longer need a table in a Power View report. Well, that is simple, just

1. Select the table. You can do this by hovering the pointer over any of the table borders (in practice the left, right, and bottom borders are easiest).

2. Click to select; the table will briefly flash another color, and the borders will remain visible, even if you move the mouse pointer away from the table.

3. Press Delete.

Another way to select a table is to click inside it. This is a bit like selecting a cell in Excel. You will even see the "cell" that you selected appear highlighted.

If you are used to controlling your software through avid use of the right mouse button, then you can also remove a table by right-clicking on it. You will not get a Delete menu choice, but you can use the Cut option. This will store the table in the clipboard for later use, leaving it deleted if you choose not to reuse it.

Deleting a table is so easy that you can do it by mistake, so remember that you can restore an accidentally deleted table by pressing Ctrl-Z, or clicking the Undo icon (the very large left-turning arrow) in the Power View ribbon. And, yes, you guessed it, you can undo an Undo action by clicking the Redo icon (the very large right-turning arrow) in the Power View ribbon.

■ **Note** You will have to return to the Power View ribbon to use the Power View Undo and Redo buttons. Interestingly, the Excel Undo and Redo buttons in the Quick Access toolbar do not work with Power View.

Changing the Table Size and Position

A table can be resized just like any other visualization in a Power View report. All you have to do is to click on any of the table handles and drag the mouse.

Moving a table is as easy as placing the pointer over the table so that the edges appear and, once the cursor changes to the hand shape, dragging the table to its new position. You will know that the table is correctly selected as it will be highlighted in its entirety as long as the mouse button is depressed.

Changing Column Order

If you have built a Power View table, you are eventually going to want to modify the order in which the columns appear from left to right. To do this

1. Activate the Field List—unless it is already displayed.

2. In the FIELDS box in the Layout section (the lower part) of the Field List, click on the name of the field (which, after all, is a column in a table) that you wish to move.

3. Drag the field vertically to its new position. This can be between existing fields, at the top or at the bottom of the Field List. A thick gray line indicates where the field will be positioned. A small right-facing blue arrow icon under the field name tells you that the field can be moved there.

Figure 2-6 shows how to drag a field from one position to another.

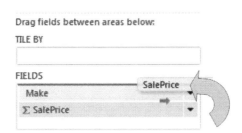

Figure 2-6. *Changing column order by moving fields*

■ **Note**   You cannot change the position of a column in a table by dragging it sideways inside the table itself.

Removing Columns from a Table

Another everyday task in Power View is removing columns from a table when necessary. As is the case when rearranging the order of columns, this is not done directly in the table but is carried out using the Field List. There are, in fact, at least four ways of removing columns from a table, so I will begin with the way that I think is the fastest and then describe the others.

1. Activate the Field List—unless it is already displayed.

2. Uncheck the field name in the Design section of the Field List.

The other three ways to remove a field are

- Hover the mouse pointer over the field you want to remove. Click on the popup menu icon (the downward-facing triangle at the right of the field name) and select Remove Field.

- Drag the field from the FIELDS box back up into the upper area (the Design section) of the Field List. You will see that the field name is dragged with the mouse pointer and that the pointer becomes a cross (·) when you are over the Field List. Just release the mouse button to remove the field.

- Click, in the FIELDS box in the lower area (the Layout section) of the Field List on the name of the field (or column) that you wish to remove; then press the Delete key.

Figure 2-7 shows how to remove a field (or column if you prefer) by dragging it out of the Layout section of the Field List.

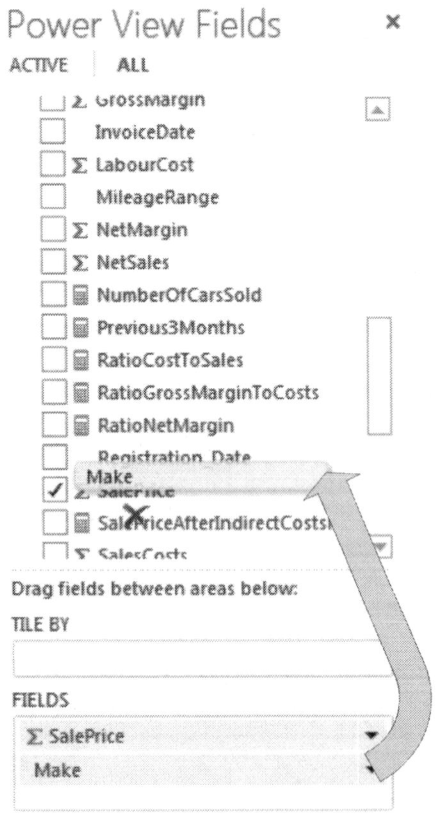

Power View Fields   ✕

ACTIVE   ALL

☐ Σ GrossMargin

☐   InvoiceDate

☐ Σ LabourCost

☐   MileageRange

☐ Σ NetMargin

☐ Σ NetSales

☐   NumberOfCarsSold

☐   Previous3Months

☐   RatioCostToSales

☐   RatioGrossMarginToCosts

☐   RatioNetMargin

☐   Registration Date

Make

☑ Σ SalePrice

☐   SalePriceAfterIndirectCosts

☐ Σ SalesCosts

Drag fields between areas below:

TILE BY

FIELDS

Σ SalePrice

Make

Figure 2-7.   *Removing a field from a table*

Types of Data

Not all data is created equal, and the data model that underlies Power View will provide you with different types of data. The initial two data types are

- Descriptive (non-numeric) attributes

- Values (or numeric measures)

Power View indicates the data type by using a descriptive icon beside many of the fields that you can see when you expand a data table in the Field List. These data types are described in Table 2-2.

Table 2-2. *Data Types*

Data Type	Icon	Comments
Attribute	None	This is a descriptive element and is non-numeric. It can be counted but not summed or averaged.
Aggregates	Σ	This is a numeric field whose aggregation type can be changed.
Calculation	▦	This is a numeric field whose aggregation type cannot be changed as it is the result of a specific calculation.
Geography	⊕	This field can potentially be used in a map to provide geographical references.
Binary Data	▣	This field contains data such as images.
Hierarchy	▷	This indicates that a hierarchy needs to be expanded to see any fields that it contains.
KPI	▹▓	This indicates a Key Performance Indicator (KPI) has been defined as the source data.

▓ **Note** Numeric fields are not the only ones that can be added as aggregates. If you add an attribute field by clicking on its popup triangle in the Field List and then selecting Add To Table As Count, you will get the number of elements for this attribute.

Data and Aggregations

When you create a table, Power View will always aggregate the data to the highest possible level. Not only will it do this, but it will add up (sum) the data, if it can, by default. This is not, however, the only possible way to aggregate data in Power View.

Selecting the type of aggregation required is a useful way to fine-tune the final output. As this is done on a column by column basis, you will need to

1. Click inside the column whose aggregation you wish to change.

2. Display the popup menu for the relevant field name in the Fields section at the bottom of the Field List by clicking on the small black triangle at the right of the field.

3. Select the type of aggregation you want.

There are seven available aggregation types. These are explained in Table 2-3.

Table 2-3. *Data Aggregation Options*

Aggregation Type	Description
Do not Summarize	No aggregation is applied and every record is displayed.
Sum	The total of the values is displayed.
Average	The average of the values is displayed.
Minimum	The smallest value is shown.
Maximum	The largest value is shown.
Count (Not Blank)	The number of all records/rows/elements is displayed, providing that there is data available.
Count (Distinct)	The number of all unique data elements in the column is returned.

Enhancing Tables

So you have a basic table set up and it has the columns you want in the correct order. Quite naturally, the next step is to want to spice up the presentation of the table a little. So let's see what Power View has to offer here. Specifically, we will look at

- Adding and removing totals
- Formatting columns of numbers
- Changing columns widths
- Sorting rows by the data in a specific column
- A few other aspects of table formatting

The Design Ribbon

The starting point for modifying the appearance of a table is the Design ribbon. You will be using this much of the time to tweak the presentation of your tables, so it is well worth getting to know. This ribbon will appear whenever a visualization is selected. It is likely to become your first port of call when you are enhancing the look and feel of Power View reports.

Figure 2-8 shows you the buttons in the Design ribbon.

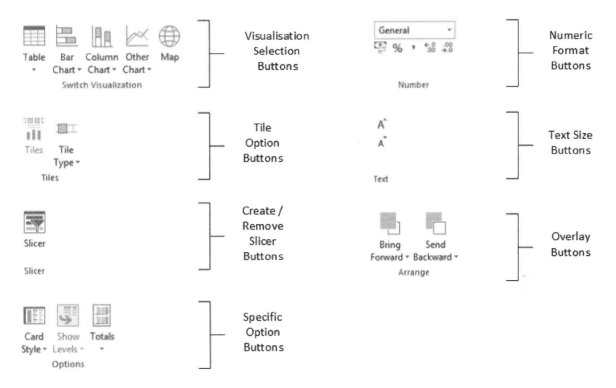

Figure 2-8. *The Design ribbon*

It is not my intention to go through all the options that the Design ribbon offers in detail straight away. I prefer to explain things as required over the course of the next few chapters. Nonetheless, as a succinct overview (and as a reference, should you require it), the options available in all the Design ribbon buttons are explained in Table 2-4.

Table 2-4. *Buttons Available in the Design Ribbon*

Button	Description
Table	Lets you select the table type, including the card type of visualization.
Bar Chart	Converts the visualization to one of the available Bar Chart types.
Column Chart	Converts the visualization to one of the available Column Chart types.
Other Chart	Displays the other available chart types.
Map	Converts the visualization to a map.
Tiles	Adds tiles to a visualization. This is explained in Chapter 6.
Tile Type	Lets you choose the tile type. This is explained in Chapter 6.
Slicer	Adds a slicer to a report. This explained in Chapter 6.
Card Style	Lets you choose the card style. This is explained in Chapter 6.
Show Levels	Lets you switch between grouping and drill-down in a matrix table.
Totals	Shows or hides the totals.

(*continued*)

Table 2-4. (*continued*)

Button	Description
Number Format Selector	Lets you select a number format for a column from the popup list of those available.
Currency	Applies the Currency format.
Percentage	Applies the Percentage format.
Thousands Separator	Adds a thousands separator.
Increase Number of Decimal places	Increases the number of decimal places displayed.
Decrease Number of Decimal places	Decreases the number of decimal places displayed.
Increase Text Size	Increases the text size in the selected visualization.
Decrease Text Size	Decreases the text size in the selected visualization
Bring Forward	Brings a visualization, text, image or other object to the top/front.
Send Backward	Sends a visualization, text, image or other object to the bottom/back.

Row Totals

Row totals are added automatically to all numeric fields. You may, however, wish to remove the totals. Conversely, you could want to add totals that were removed previously. In any case, to remove all the totals from a table.

1. Select the table, or click anywhere inside it. In this example I will use the table you saw earlier in Figure 2-4.

2. Click Totals - None in the ribbon.

To add totals where there are none, merely click Totals - Rows in the Design ribbon (with the table selected). You can see the table you created previously—without totals—in Figure 2-9.

Make	SalePrice
Aston Martin	£3,507,660.00
Bentley	£1,622,000.00
Jaguar	£1,997,750.00
MGB	£315,000.00
Rolls Royce	£2,413,800.00
Triumph	£286,500.00
TVR	£201,500.00

Figure 2-9. *The initial table without totals*

▓ **Note** You can only add or remove totals if a table displays multiple records. If a table is displaying the highest level of aggregation for a value, then no totals can be displayed, as you are looking at the grand total already. In this case, the Totals button will be grayed out.

Formatting Columns of Numbers

Power View will make an educated guess as to the correct type of numeric formatting to apply to a column of numbers in a table based on the source data type. More specifically, if you have applied a format in an Excel table that has been added to the data model, or if you have formatted a column in the data model using PowerPivot, then these formats will be carried into Power View. However, there could well be times when you wish to override the formatting that Power View has chosen and apply your own. Once again, this is an extremely intuitive process, which consists of doing the following:

1. Click anywhere in the column you wish to reformat—except on the title.

2. Switch to the Design ribbon (unless it is already active).

3. Click on one of the available formatting icons (or click the popup menu in the Number section of the Design ribbon and select the type of formatting you require).

Power View will apply the formatting to the entire column, including totals if there are any. You can then increase or decrease the number of decimal places displayed by clicking on the Increase Decimal places and Decrease Decimal places icons.

▓ **Tip** Clicking the Increase Decimal places or Decrease Decimal places icons will apply the Number style if the current style is General. Any other style will remain in force if these icons are clicked—but the number of decimal places will be changed, of course.

You may well be familiar with the available number formatting options, as they are essentially a subset of the Excel formatting options, and you may be extremely well acquainted with this tool already. Alternatively, if you have used PowerPivot, then you could have a strong sense of déjà vu. In the interest of completeness the available options are described in Table 2-5.

Table 2-5. *Number Formatting Options*

Format Type	Icon	Description	Example
General		Does not apply any uniform formatting and leaves the current number of decimal places in place.	100000.011
Number		Adds a thousands separator and two decimal places. This is also called Comma style.	100,000.01
Currency		Adds a thousands separator and two decimal places as well as the current monetary symbol.	£100,000.01
Accounting		Adds a thousands separator and two decimal places as well as the current monetary symbol at the left of the column.	£100,000.01

(*continued*)

Table 2-5. (*continued*)

Format Type	Icon	Description	Example
Percentage		Multiplies by 100, adds two decimal places and prefixes with the percentage symbol.	28.78%
Scientific		Displays the numbers in Scientific format.	1.00E+05
Long Date		Displays a date column as a long date, that is, with the month name in full.	25 July 2014
Short Date		Displays a date column as short date, that is, in figures.	25/07/14
Time		Displays the time part of a date or date/time field.	16:55:01
Increase Decimal places		Adds another decimal place to the display of the figure.	
Decrease Decimal places		Removes a decimal place from the figure's display.	

Default Formatting

Power View will apply the Date, Time, and Currency formats that are set for your PC. For an Excel-based Power View worksheet, you can use Control Panel to set the regional defaults and select the appropriate settings for the Long Date, Short Date, and Time (Short Time) format. Remember that

- Altering the Date, Time, and Number formats using Control Panel will only take effect once you close and reopen any open Power View reports.

- Modifying the default Date, Time, and Number formats using Control Panel will affect all applications that use these formats—that is, not just all past and future Power View reports, but many other applications as well.

Changing Column Widths

Power View will automatically set the width of a column so that all the data is visible. Here also, at times you may wish to narrow or widen columns to suit the aesthetics of a particular table or report.

To alter the column widths, which is shown in Figure 2-10.

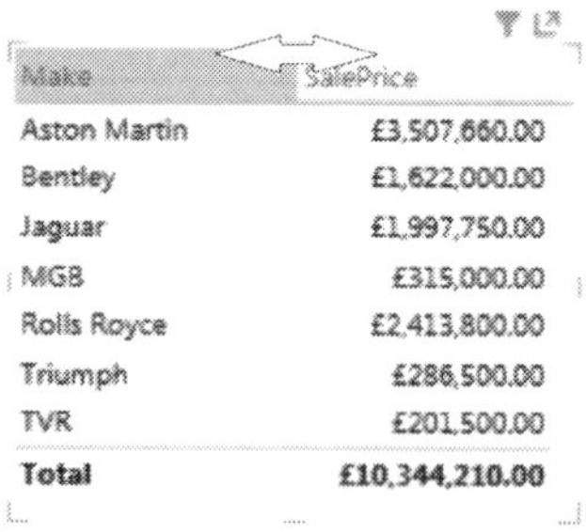

Figure 2-10. Altering column width

1. Hover the mouse pointer over the column title. The column title will be highlighted.

2. Place the mouse pointer on the right edge of the column. The pointer will become a two-headed sideways arrow.

3. Drag left or right to increase or decrease the column width.

There are, inevitably, a few points to take on board once you start overriding Power View's default column sizing:

- If you widen one or more columns to the point that all the columns of data are not visible in the table, then the horizontal scroll bar will appear at the bottom of the table. Power View will *not* resize the table as you resize a column.

- If you reduce a column's width so that text or numbers will no longer fit, then Power View will add ellipses (...) to indicate that data has been truncated.

- You cannot reduce a column's width to zero and hide the column, as Power View will always leave a narrow sliver of a column (and its contents) visible.

- Double-clicking the right edge of the column will set the column width automatically to the width of the widest element that is currently visible. If there is a wider element further up or down in the data set, then you might have to re-widen the column again.

- You can, of course, adjust the width of your table to take the new column widths into account by making the table larger; this is done by dragging the left or right lateral handles or the corner handles.

- If you subsequently change the size of the text in a table, then the column widths will not change. You may have to resize certain columns, however, if you feel that this is required for the general appearance of the report.

- Applying a different theme from the Power View ribbon can apply different fonts to the table, and thus cause the column widths to change, as Power View will continue to display the same number of characters per column as were visible using the previous theme. For more information on themes, please see Chapter 7.

Font Sizes in Tables

You may prefer to alter the default font size that Power View applies when a table is first created. This is easy:

1. Click anywhere inside the table (or select the table).

2. Switch to the Design ribbon if it is not active already.

3. Click on the Increase Font Size and Decrease Font Size icons until the table text size suits your requirements.

I really should add a couple of points to conclude on font sizes in tables:

- You cannot select a font size; you can only use the Increase Font Size and Decrease Font Size icons until you have found a size that suits you. My impression is that the available range is from 6 to 36 point.

- Altering the font size can cause the table to grow or shrink, as Power View will continue to display the same number of characters per column as were visible using the previous font size. So you may end up having to alter the column widths or the table size (as described previously) to make your table look exactly the way you want it.

Copying a Table

You will need to copy tables on many occasions. There could be several reasons for this:

- You are creating a new visualization on the Power View report and need the table as a basis for the new element, such as a chart, for instance.

- You are copying visualizations between reports.

- You want to keep an example of a table and try some fancy tricks on the copy, but you want to keep the old version as a failsafe option.

In any case, all you have to do is

1. Select the table (as described previously).

2. Right-click and select Copy (or press Ctrl-C).

To paste a copy, click outside any visualization in a current or new Power View report, right-click, and select Paste (or press Ctrl-V).

Sorting by Column

Any column can be used as the sort criterion for a table, whatever the type of table. To sort the table, merely click on the column header. Once the rows in the table have been sorted according to the elements in the selected column, a small triangle will appear to the right of the column header to indicate that this column has been used to sort the data, as you can see in Figure 2-11. A downward-facing triangle tells you that the sort order is A to Z (or lowest to highest for numeric values). An upward-facing triangle tells you that the sort order is Z to A (or highest to lowest for numeric values).

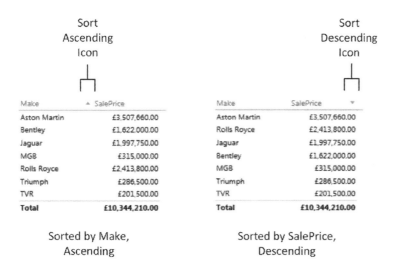

Figure 2-11. *Sorting a table by column*

Once a table has been sorted, you cannot unsort it. You can, however, use another column to resort the data. As an example of sorting a column, look at Figure 2-11 (once again I will use the table we created at the very beginning of this chapter):

Sometimes you are sorting a column on one field (as was the case in all the examples so far), but the actual sort uses another column as the basis for the sort operation. For example, you could sort by month name but see the result by the month number (so that you are not sorting months alphabetically, but numerically). You can see how this is set up in Chapter 11.

Table Granularity

A Power View table will automatically aggregate data to the lowest available level of grain. Put simply, this means that it is important to select data at the lowest useful level of detail but not to add pointlessly detailed elements.

This is probably easier to understand if I use an example. Suppose you start with a high level of aggregation—the country for instance. If you create a table with CountryName and Sales columns, it will give you the total sales by country. If you use the sample data given in the examples for this book (the file CarSales.xlsx on the Apress web site), this table will only contain half a dozen or so lines.

Then add the ClientName after the country. When you do this, you will then obtain a more finely-grained set of results, with the aggregate sales for each client in each country. If you (finally) add the InvoiceNumber, you will get an extremely detailed level of data. Indeed, adding such a fine level of grain to your table could produce an extremely large number of records. This example is shown in Figure 2-12.

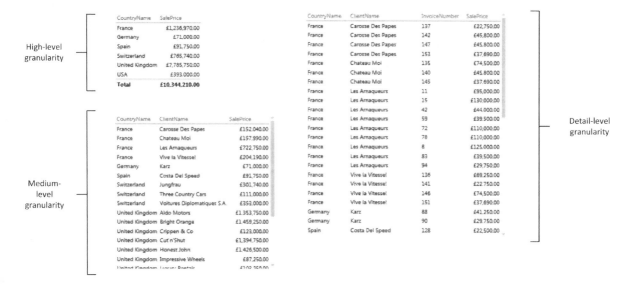

CountryName	SalePrice
France	£1,236,970.00
Germany	£71,000.00
Spain	£91,750.00
Switzerland	£765,740.00
United Kingdom	£7,785,750.00
USA	£393,000.00
Total	**£10,344,210.00**

High-level granularity

CountryName	ClientName	SalePrice
France	Carosse Des Papes	£152,040.00
France	Chateau Moi	£157,990.00
France	Les Arnaqueurs	£722,750.00
France	Vive la Vitesse!	£204,190.00
Germany	Karz	£71,000.00
Spain	Costa Del Speed	£91,750.00
Switzerland	Jungfrau	£301,740.00
Switzerland	Three Country Cars	£111,000.00
Switzerland	Voitures Diplomatiques S.A.	£353,000.00
United Kingdom	Aldo Motors	£1,353,750.00
United Kingdom	Bright Orange	£1,459,250.00
United Kingdom	Crippen & Co	£123,000.00
United Kingdom	Cut n'Shut	£1,394,750.00
United Kingdom	Honest John	£1,426,500.00
United Kingdom	Impressive Wheels	£87,250.00
United Kingdom	Luxury Rentals	£202,250.00

Medium-level granularity

CountryName	ClientName	InvoiceNumber	SalePrice
France	Carosse Des Papes	137	£22,750.00
France	Carosse Des Papes	142	£45,800.00
France	Carosse Des Papes	147	£45,800.00
France	Carosse Des Papes	153	£37,690.00
France	Chateau Moi	135	£74,500.00
France	Chateau Moi	140	£45,800.00
France	Chateau Moi	145	£37,690.00
France	Les Arnaqueurs	11	£95,000.00
France	Les Arnaqueurs	15	£130,000.00
France	Les Arnaqueurs	42	£44,000.00
France	Les Arnaqueurs	59	£39,500.00
France	Les Arnaqueurs	72	£110,000.00
France	Les Arnaqueurs	78	£110,000.00
France	Les Arnaqueurs	8	£125,000.00
France	Les Arnaqueurs	83	£39,500.00
France	Les Arnaqueurs	94	£29,750.00
France	Vive la Vitesse!	136	£69,250.00
France	Vive la Vitesse!	141	£22,750.00
France	Vive la Vitesse!	146	£74,500.00
France	Vive la Vitesse!	151	£37,690.00
Germany	Karz	88	£41,250.00
Germany	Karz	90	£29,750.00
Spain	Costa Del Speed	128	£22,500.00

Detail-level granularity

Figure 2-12. *Progressive table granularity*

Power View will always attempt to display the data using the information available to it in the underlying data model. Exactly how this can be optimized for the best possible results is described in Chapter 11.

Matrix Tables

So far in this chapter we have limited ourselves to tables that display the information as full columns of lists, just like the source data in an Excel spreadsheet or database, for instance. Lists, however, do not always give an intuitive feeling for how data should be grouped at various levels. Presenting information in a neat hierarchy with multiple grouped levels is the task of a matrix-type table.

Row Matrix

When creating a matrix table, I find that it helps to think in terms of a hierarchy of information and to try and visualize this information as flowing from left to right. For instance, suppose that we want to create a matrix with the country name as the highest level in the hierarchy (and consequently the leftmost item). Then we want the make of car to be the second level, and the next element in from the left. (In Figure 2-13, I've labeled this Make.) Finally we want the color of car sold, followed by all the numeric fields that interest us.

So our Hierarchy is shown in Figure 2-13.

Country Name ⟹ Make ⟹ Colour

Figure 2-13. *An information hierarchy*

When creating a matrix, it is important to have the Field List reflect the hierarchy. Put another way, you must ensure that the order of the fields that you select for the table follows the display hierarchy that you want for the matrix. Consequently, to create a matrix table like the one just described, you will need to

1. Click outside any existing visualizations (or start with a new Power View report).

2. Add the fields CountryName, Make (from the CarDetails hierarchy), and Colour (in this order) to the field selection (remember that you can drag them onto the Power View canvas, drag them into the FIELDS box in the Layout section at the bottom of the Field List, or select them using the popup menu for each field). Then add the fields SalePrice and GrossMargin. The table will be very long, but we will not worry about that at this point. The table should look something like Figure 2-14.

CountryName	Make	Colour	SalePrice	GrossMargin
France	Aston Martin	Blue	£69,250.00	49,525.00
France	Aston Martin	Canary Yellow	£207,190.00	40,740.00
France	Aston Martin	Green	£60,440.00	3,365.00
France	Aston Martin	Night Blue	£45,800.00	26,325.00
France	Aston Martin	Red	£245,300.00	166,600.00
France	Aston Martin	Silver	£37,690.00	13,215.00
France	Bentley	British Racing Green	£39,500.00	-24,200.00
France	Bentley	Canary Yellow	£110,000.00	47,000.00
France	Bentley	Red	£110,000.00	83,025.00
France	Jaguar	Canary Yellow	£44,000.00	5,500.00
France	Jaguar	Night Blue	£39,500.00	13,500.00
France	Rolls Royce	Black	£22,750.00	-2,600.00
France	Rolls Royce	Canary Yellow	£130,000.00	66,250.00
France	Rolls Royce	Night Blue	£45,800.00	26,075.00
France	TVR	Silver	£29,750.00	-7,950.00
Germany	TVR	Blue	£43,250.00	3,550.00

FIELDS
- ⊕ CountryName
- Make
- Colour
- Σ SalePrice
- Σ GrossMargin

Figure 2-14. *A table before conversion to a matrix*

3. In the ribbon, select Table ⇨ Matrix. The Layout section of the Field List changes to add two new boxes: COLUMNS and Σ VALUES. The table and the Layout section of the Field List will now look like those shown in Figure 2-15.

CountryName	Make	Colour	SalePrice	GrossMargin
France	Aston Martin	Blue	£69,250.00	49,525.00
		Canary Yellow	£207,190.00	40,740.00
		Green	£60,440.00	3,365.00
		Night Blue	£45,800.00	26,325.00
		Red	£245,300.00	166,600.00
		Silver	£37,690.00	13,215.00
		Total	**£665,670.00**	**299,770.00**
	Bentley	British Racing Green	£39,500.00	-24,200.00
		Canary Yellow	£110,000.00	47,000.00
		Red	£110,000.00	83,025.00
		Total	**£259,500.00**	**105,825.00**
	Jaguar	Canary Yellow	£44,000.00	5,500.00
		Night Blue	£39,500.00	13,500.00
		Total	**£83,500.00**	**19,000.00**

Figure 2-15. *A matrix table*

As you can see, a matrix display not only makes data easier to digest, but it automatically groups records by each element in the hierarchy and also adds totals. What is more, each level in the hierarchy is sorted in ascending order.

You can also add fields directly to a table by dragging them onto the table. However, you need to remember that Power View will always add a field to the right of existing fields. In a matrix, this means that any aggregate/numeric field will be added to the right of existing aggregate fields (and appear in the ∑ VALUES box), whereas any text or date/time fields will be added to the right of any existing hierarchy fields (and appear in the ROWS box). However, it is always a simple matter to reorganize them by dragging the required fields up and down in the ROWS and ∑ VALUES boxes.

When creating matrix tables, my personal preference is to drag the fields that constitute the hierarchy of non-numeric values into the ROWS box, which means I am placing them accurately above, below, or between any existing elements. This ensures that your matrix looks right the first time, which can help you avoid some very disconcerting double takes!

Column Matrix

Power View does not limit you to adding row-level hierarchies; you can also create column-level hierarchies, or mix the two. Suppose that we want to get a clear idea of sales and gross margin by country, make, and vehicle type and how they impact one another. To achieve this, I suggest extending the matrix that you created previously in the following ways:

- Remove the Colour level from the row hierarchy.

- Add a VehicleType level as a column hierarchy.

Here is how you can do this:

1. Click inside the table that you created previously to select it. The Field List will update to display the fields that are used for this table.

2. Drag the Colour field from the FIELDS box in the Layout section (the lower part of the Field List) back up into the upper part of the Field List. This will remove it from the table.

3. Drag the VehicleType field down into the COLUMNS box in the Layout section of the Field List. This will add a hierarchy to the columns in the table. The Field List will look like it does in Figure 2-16.

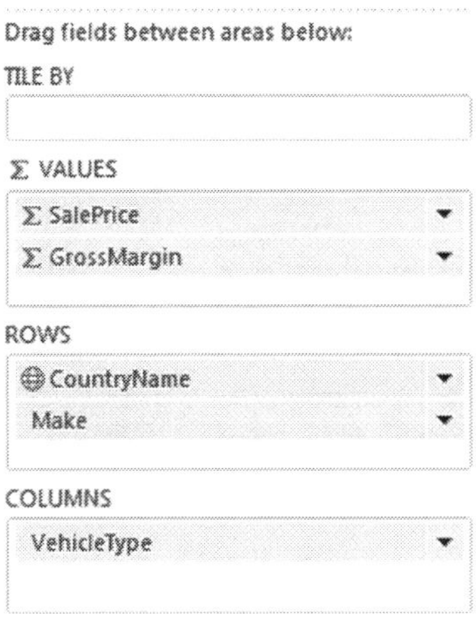

Drag fields between areas below:

TILE BY

Σ VALUES

Σ SalePrice ▼
Σ GrossMargin ▼

ROWS

⊕ CountryName ▼
Make ▼

COLUMNS

VehicleType ▼

Figure 2-16. *The Field List for a row and column matrix table*

The table will now look like the one in Figure 2-17. As you can see, you now have the sales and gross margin by country name, make, and vehicle type, but it is in a cross-matrix, where the data is broken down by both rows and columns.

CountryName	Make	Convertible SalePrice	GrossMargin	Coupe SalePrice	GrossMargin	Saloon SalePrice	GrossMargin	Total SalePrice	GrossMargin
France	Aston Martin	£149,880.00	73,830.00	£515,790.00	225,940.00			£665,670.00	299,770.00
	Bentley					£259,500.00	105,825.00	£259,500.00	105,825.00
	Jaguar			£44,000.00	5,500.00	£39,500.00	13,500.00	£83,500.00	19,000.00
	Rolls Royce					£198,550.00	89,725.00	£198,550.00	89,725.00
	TVR			£29,750.00	-7,950.00			£29,750.00	-7,950.00
	Total	£149,880.00	73,830.00	£589,540.00	223,490.00	£497,550.00	209,050.00	£1,236,970.00	506,370.00
Germany	TVR			£71,000.00	-4,400.00			£71,000.00	-4,400.00
	Total			£71,000.00	-4,400.00			£71,000.00	-4,400.00
Spain	Jaguar			£29,750.00	-7,950.00	£39,500.00	1,800.00	£69,250.00	-6,150.00
	Triumph			£22,500.00	5,300.00			£22,500.00	5,300.00
	Total			£52,250.00	-2,650.00	£39,500.00	1,800.00	£91,750.00	-850.00
Switzerland	Aston Martin	£74,000.00	35,675.00	£194,990.00	113,990.00			£268,990.00	149,665.00
	Bentley					£110,000.00	83,025.00	£110,000.00	83,025.00
	Jaguar	£120,000.00	82,300.00	£39,500.00	1,050.00	£83,500.00	18,000.00	£243,000.00	101,350.00
	Rolls Royce			£74,500.00	41,650.00	£69,250.00	50,975.00	£143,750.00	92,625.00
	Total	£194,000.00	117,975.00	£308,990.00	156,690.00	£262,750.00	152,000.00	£765,740.00	426,665.00
United Kingdom	Aston Martin			£2,573,000.00	881,609.99			£2,573,000.00	881,609.99
	Bentley	£193,500.00	76,375.00	£305,250.00	88,800.00	£670,250.00	264,750.00	£1,169,000.00	429,925.00
	Jaguar			£452,500.00	56,000.00	£911,000.00	222,400.00	£1,363,500.00	278,400.00
	MGB	£87,250.00	69,150.00	£227,750.00	169,450.00			£315,000.00	238,600.00
	Rolls Royce					£2,071,500.00	896,160.00	£2,071,500.00	896,160.00
	Triumph			£264,000.00	100,300.00			£264,000.00	100,300.00
	TVR			£29,750.00	-7,950.00			£29,750.00	-7,950.00

Figure 2-17. *A row and column matrix table*

To conclude the section on creating matrix tables, there are a few things that you might like to note:

- If you add totals, then every level of the hierarchy will have totals.

- Adding non-numeric data to the aggregated data will make Power View display the Count aggregation.

- Matrix tables can get very wide, especially if you have a multilevel hierarchy. Power View matrix tables reflect this in the way in which horizontal scrolling works. A matrix table will freeze the non-aggregated data columns on the left and will allow you to scroll to the right to display aggregated (numeric) data.

- Moving the fields in the VALUES box of the Field List (using drag and drop as described previously) will reorder the aggregated data columns in the table.

Sorting Data in Matrix Tables

When you sort data in a matrix table, the sort order will respect the matrix hierarchy. This means that if you sort on the second element in a hierarchy (Make, in the example table we just created) then the primary element in the hierarchy (CountryName, the leftmost column) will not be altered, but all the subgroupings by Make for each country will be sorted. This means, in effect, that you can carry out multiple sort operations, by sorting on several columns, and in any order. The net result will be independent sorts on multiple elements.

As an example of this, look at Figure 2-18, which is based on the matrix table displayed in Figure 2-15. Here I sorted on make, country name, and color. Power View even indicates that there was a multiple sort operation by displaying the sort triangles to the right of all the fields. CountryName and Make are sorted in ascending order and Colour in descending order.

CountryName ▲	Make ▲	Colour ▼	SalePrice	GrossMargin
France	Rolls Royce	Night Blue	£45,800.00	26,075.00
		Canary Yellow	£130,000.00	66,250.00
		Black	£22,750.00	-2,600.00
	TVR	Silver	£29,750.00	-7,950.00
Germany	TVR	Silver	£29,750.00	-7,950.00
		Blue	£41,250.00	3,550.00
Spain	Jaguar	Red	£29,750.00	-7,950.00
		Green	£39,500.00	1,800.00
	Triumph	Canary Yellow	£22,500.00	5,300.00
Switzerland	Aston Martin	Silver	£111,500.00	72,800.00
		Red	£37,690.00	18,665.00
		Green	£45,800.00	26,825.00
		Blue	£37,000.00	18,150.00
		Black	£37,000.00	13,225.00
	Bentley	Black	£110,000.00	83,025.00
	Jaguar	Dark Purple	£39,500.00	1,050.00

Figure 2-18. Sorted matrix table

If you sort by an aggregate figure, then the total for the highest level of the hierarchy will be used to reorder the whole table. You can see this in Figure 2-19, where the matrix from the previous figure has been sorted on gross margin in descending order. This has made the best-selling country move to the top of the table. As well, if you have a column matrix (as in this example), then you must sort on the grand total of the columns (the two rightmost columns in this example) to make the matrix sort by numeric values.

CountryName	Make	Colour	SalePrice	GrossMargin ▼
United Kingdom	Rolls Royce	Red	£692,000.00	342,380.00
		British Racing Green	£411,000.00	158,250.00
		Silver	£178,500.00	114,750.00
		Dark Purple	£178,500.00	102,160.00
		Blue	£219,000.00	67,500.00
		Green	£198,000.00	44,370.00
		Black	£102,500.00	38,250.00
		Canary Yellow	£92,000.00	28,500.00
	Aston Martin	Blue	£490,000.00	271,300.00
		Dark Purple	£288,500.00	154,860.00
		Silver	£253,500.00	113,410.00
		Red	£418,500.00	102,550.00
		British Racing Green	£288,500.00	85,610.00
		Green	£124,500.00	61,050.00
		Black	£273,500.00	35,610.00
		Night Blue	£222,500.00	21,110.00

Figure 2-19. Matrix table sorted by value

Drilling Through with Matrix Tables

By default a matrix table will show all the levels in the hierarchy of information that you have selected. With smaller data sets there is not usually a problem in displaying and finding the records that interest you. However, with larger data sets (or if you want to isolate a subset of data to drive a point home), you may prefer not to display all the levels at once, but to drill down, level by level, until you reach the figures that interest you.

A drill-down approach can be particularly useful with large and complex data sets. As an extension to matrix tables, it can avoid having to display too many columns at once, which makes the table easier to view (and consequently easier to scroll through). Using drill-down matrix tables, you can display only one key column at a time with all the correctly aggregated data visible for each level of information.

Drilling Down

To switch from the default overall view of the grouping hierarchy and then drill down through the data, all you need to do is

1. Click on Show Levels in the Design ribbon and select Rows - Enable Drill-Down One Level At A Time. The matrix will hide all but the first grouping level (the leftmost column, CountryName) in the hierarchy. If we take the matrix table you saw in Figure 2-15 as a basis for this, you will now see a drill-down table as shown in Figure 2-20.

CountryName	SalePrice	GrossMargin ▼
United Kingdom ⬇	£7,785,750.00	2,817,044.99
France	£1,236,970.00	506,370.00
Switzerland	£765,740.00	426,665.00
USA	£393,000.00	109,775.00
Spain	£91,750.00	-850.00
Germany	£71,000.00	-4,400.00

Figure 2-20. *The topmost level of a drill-down matrix table*

2. Double-click an element (the United Kingdom in this example) and the next level down in the hierarchy (Make) will be displayed as in Figure 2-21. This was, if you remember, the second column in the matrix.

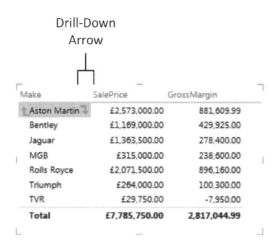

Drill-Down
Arrow

Make	SalePrice	GrossMargin
Aston Martin	£2,573,000.00	881,609.99
Bentley	£1,169,000.00	429,925.00
Jaguar	£1,363,500.00	278,400.00
MGB	£315,000.00	238,600.00
Rolls Royce	£2,071,500.00	896,160.00
Triumph	£264,000.00	100,300.00
TVR	£29,750.00	-7,950.00
Total	£7,785,750.00	2,817,044.99

Figure 2-21. *The second level of a drill-down table*

3. To drill down to the next level (if there is one), double-click on an element of the current grouping level, and so on, until the lowest level is reached. Figure 2-22 shows the lowest level for Aston Martin—the color of the cars sold. This was the third column from the left in the matrix.

Drill-Up
Arrow

Colour	SalePrice	GrossMargin
Black	£273,500.00	35,610.00
Blue	£490,000.00	271,300.00
British Racing Green	£288,500.00	85,610.00
Canary Yellow	£102,500.00	26,109.99
Dark Purple	£288,500.00	154,860.00
Green	£124,500.00	61,050.00
Night Blue	£333,500.00	31,110.00
Red	£418,500.00	102,550.00
Silver	£253,500.00	113,410.00
Total	£2,573,000.00	881,609.99

Figure 2-22. *The final level of drill-down in a matrix table*

▪ **Tip** The easy way to see if there are further drill-down levels available is to click on any descriptive element in the leftmost column of the table. If Power View displays a downward-facing arrow to the right of the selected element, then you can continue drilling down into the data. Power View will indicate when no further drill-down is possible by *not* displaying the downward-facing arrow when you click on an element at the lowest available level.

You can continue drilling down through a grouping hierarchy until you have reached the lowest available level. You can drill down in a hierarchy without double-clicking if you prefer. The alternative solution is as follows (assuming that you have already enabled drill-down):

1. Click on any non-numeric element in the drill-down table. A small right hand downward-facing arrow appears at the right of the selected element.

2. Click on the downward-facing arrow.

An example of an element in a table, just before clicking on the downward-facing arrow is given in the previous figure, Figure 2-21.

Drilling Up

Drilling back up through a hierarchy is as easy as clicking on the upward-facing arrow that appears at the top of the column of data on the left of the table. Power View will move up to the previous level of data in the hierarchy.

You can see the drill-up arrow earlier in Figure 2-22.

Reapplying Matrix Visualization

To switch back to the default view of all the hierarchy of grouping levels

1. Click on Show Levels in the ribbon and select Rows - Show All Grouping Levels At Once.

2. The drill-down table will revert to a matrix table. All the columns in the table will be visible once more.

Drilling Through with Column Hierarchies

Drill-through is not limited to rows. It can also be applied to columns either together with row-based drill-through, or on its own.

I prefer to use different data to show you a table that will use row-based drill-through and column-based drill-through together. This will also serve as a revision of the matrix and drill-through possibilities that Power View offers. So, here we go:

1. Add a new Power View report by clicking on the Power View button in the Power View ribbon.

2. Create a table based on the following fields, and in this order:

    a. CountryName

    b. Colour

    c. VehicleType

    d. CarAgeBucket

    e. SpareParts

3. Convert the table to a matrix by selecting Matrix from the Table button in the Design ribbon.

4. Drag the fields VehicleType and CarAgeBucket from the ROWS box to the COLUMNS box in the Layout section of the Field List. You now have a column-based matrix to extend the row matrix.

5. Select Both Groups from the Totals button in the Design ribbon. The table should look like Figure 2-23, after a little bit of resizing and aesthetic adjustment.

	VehicleType	Convertible					Coupe							Saloon	
CountryName	Colour	1 - 5	6 - 10	11 - 15	Over 30	Total	6 - 10	11 - 15	16 - 20	21 - 25	26 - 30	Over 30	Total	1 - 5	6 - 10
France	Black														895.00
	Blue						750.00						750.00		
	British Racing Green														2,570.00
	Canary Yellow			895.00		895.00	500.00	1,950.00			750.00		3,200.00		2,550.00
	Green						1,790.00						1,790.00		
	Night Blue						500.00						500.00	895.00	1,950.00
	Red		895.00			895.00	500.00			900.00			1,400.00		1,950.00
	Silver	895.00				895.00	400.00						400.00		
	Total	895.00	895.00	895.00		2,685.00	4,440.00	1,950.00		900.00	750.00		8,040.00	895.00	9,915.00
Germany	Blue						400.00						400.00		
	Silver						400.00						400.00		
	Total						800.00						800.00		
Spain	Canary Yellow											250.00	250.00		
	Green														400.00
	Red						400.00						400.00		

Figure 2-23. *A column and row matrix table*

6. Click Show Levels in the Design ribbon and select Rows - Enable Drill-Down One Level At A Time.

7. Click Show Levels in the Design ribbon and select Columns - Enable Drill-Down One Level At A Time.

You now have a table where you can drill down both by column and by row. It should look like the one in Figure 2-24.

CountryName	Convertible	Coupe	Saloon	Total
France	2,685.00	8,040.00	10,810.00	21,535.00
Germany		800.00		800.00
Spain		650.00	400.00	1,050.00
Switzerland	2,190.00	5,345.00	7,365.00	14,900.00
United Kingdom	7,840.00	50,465.00	56,865.00	115,170.00
USA	1,950.00	4,700.00	6,470.00	13,120.00
Total	14,665.00	70,000.00	81,910.00	166,575.00

Figure 2-24. *A matrix table ready for row and column drill-down*

Now if you double-click on any row or column header, you will drill down to the next level in the corresponding hierarchy. Figure 2-25 shows you the same table after drilling down by country (United Kingdom) and vehicle type (convertible).

Colour	↑ 6 - 10	Over 30	Total
↑ Canary Yellow	2,570.00		2,570.00
Dark Purple	4,520.00		4,520.00
Green		250.00	250.00
Red		250.00	250.00
Silver		250.00	250.00
Total	**7,090.00**	**750.00**	**7,840.00**

Figure 2-25. *A matrix table after drill-down by row and column*

As you can see, the principles for drilling up and down through a column hierarchy are the same as those that you used with a row hierarchy.

Card Visualizations

Tabular data can also be displayed in an extremely innovative way using the Power View card style of output. As is the case with matrix tables, you begin by choosing the fields that you want to display as a basic table and then you convert this to another type of visualization. Here is an example of how this can be done:

1. Create a new Power View report or select a report with some available space.

2. Add the following fields, in this order (as before, this can be done by selecting the relevant check boxes in the upper part of the Field List, dragging fields into the FIELDS box in the Layout section of the Field List, or by dragging the fields onto the Power View report and into an existing table if you are adding fields):

   a. CountryName

   b. CostPrice

   c. TotalDiscount

   d. LabourCost

   e. SpareParts

3. Set all the numeric fields to be the average of the value by clicking on the popup menu for each field (the small black triangle to the right of the field name in the FIELDS Box in the Layout section of the Field List) and selecting Average.

4. Select Table ➪ Card in the ribbon; you now have a card-type table, as shown in Figure 2-26.

Figure 2-26. *A card visualisation*

Card-type tables will display the selected fields in the order in which they appear in the Fields section at the bottom of the Field List, and it is here that they can be reordered, as with any table. This makes each card into a data record. The fields will flow left to right and then on to the following line in each card. What is interesting here is that adjusting the size of the table can change the appearance of the table quite radically. A very narrow table will list the fields vertically, one above the other. If you can fit all the fields onto a single row, then you will get a highly original multiple record display.

In the initial example of a card visualization, we only added one attribute (or non-numeric) field. Power View correspondingly took this to be the title of each card and made its text larger than that of the other elements. However, try adding a second descriptive element to the FIELDS box in the Layout section of the Field List (I used vehicle type); as you can see from Figure 2-27, this resets all the fonts in each card to the same size.

United Kingdom	Convertible	£21,816.67
CountryName	VehicleType	Average of CostPrice
408.33	532.83	1,306.67
Average of TotalDiscount	Average of LabourCost	Average of SpareParts

France	Convertible	£23,708.33
CountryName	VehicleType	Average of CostPrice
666.67	1,150.00	895.00
Average of TotalDiscount	Average of LabourCost	Average of SpareParts

Switzerland	Coupe	£23,937.50
CountryName	VehicleType	Average of CostPrice
791.67	1,206.17	890.83
Average of TotalDiscount	Average of LabourCost	Average of SpareParts

Switzerland	Convertible	£24,166.67
CountryName	VehicleType	Average of CostPrice
716.67	941.67	730.00
Average of TotalDiscount	Average of LabourCost	Average of SpareParts

Switzerland	Saloon	£26,425.00
CountryName	VehicleType	Average of CostPrice
562.50	918.25	1,841.25
Average of TotalDiscount	Average of LabourCost	Average of SpareParts

Spain	Coupe	£27,250.00
CountryName	VehicleType	Average of CostPrice
150.00	405.50	325.00
Average of TotalDiscount	Average of LabourCost	Average of SpareParts

Figure 2-27. *A card visualization with multiple non-numeric fields*

In any case, card-style tables will only scroll vertically, unlike basic tables and matrix tables. If you add multiple fields to a table, you will note that Power View will always attempt, initially, to keep the data for a record on one line, shrinking the text as more fields are added. Once there is simply too much data to fit on a single row, Power View will flow the data onto the next line in a card, and possibly alter the font size.

A card-style table will always display the column headers for each field in the record. Cards are also a perfect vehicle for images. This is described in Chapter 7. Also, there is a technique to set a field as the title field; however, many non-numeric fields are added. This is part of the way that the underlying data set is prepared for Power View, and it is described in Chapter 11.

Card Visualization Styles

Just to make things even more interesting—and diversified—Power View lets you switch card styles if you want. The style of cards that we have seen up until now is called simply Card. However, there is another card style that is completely different, called Callout. To switch the existing card visualization to the Callout style

1. Click inside, or select, the card visualization.

2. Select Callout from the Card Style button in the Design ribbon. Your card visualization should look like Figure 2-28.

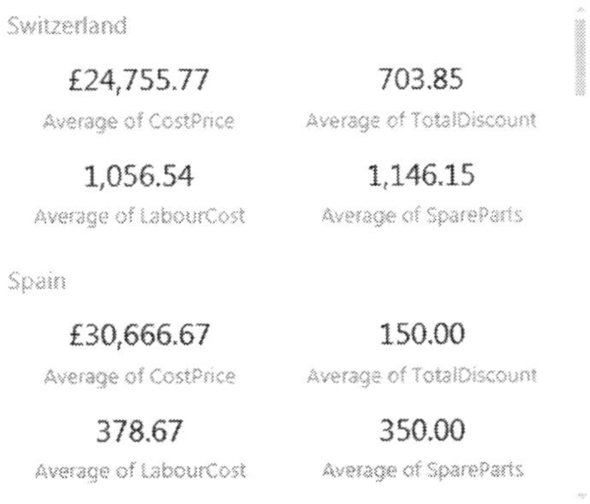

Switzerland
£24,755.77
703.85
Average of CostPrice
Average of TotalDiscount
1,056.54
1,146.15
Average of LabourCost
Average of SpareParts
Spain
£30,666.67
150.00
Average of CostPrice
Average of TotalDiscount
378.67
350.00
Average of LabourCost
Average of SpareParts

Figure 2-28. *Card Callout style*

Callout cards do take up a lot of space, which makes them ideal candidates for Pop-out display should you want a detailed look at the figures that they contain. This is explained in Chapter 4.

Sorting Data in Card-View Tables

You sort data in card-type tables slightly differently than the way we saw previously for basic and matrix tables. As you can see in Figure 2-29, when you hover the mouse pointer over a card-type table Sort By, a field name will appear above the top left of the table. If the table is not yet ordered, then Power View will display the first field in the table. If the table is already ordered, then the column used to sort the data will be displayed.

sort by Average of CostPrice asc
CountryName
Average of CostPrice
Average of TotalDiscount
Average of LabourCost
Average of SpareParts
703.85
1,146.15

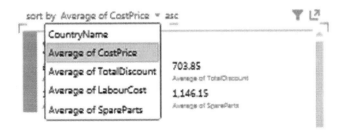

Figure 2-29. *Sorting cards in a card visualization*

To sort the records, you have two choices:

- Click on the downward-facing triangle to the right of the sort field, and select the field that you wish to order the data by from the popup list that will appear. This is shown in Figure 2-29.
  If you prefer, you can simply click on the sort field, which will then display the next field in the table, and order the data by this field.

To change the sort order—that is, to switch between ascending and descending order—simply click on the Asc (or Desc) that appears to the right of the sort field when you hover the mouse pointer over a card-type table. As you can see, this is very similar to the way in which you sorted data in table columns.

Switching Between Table Types

One of the fabulous things about Power View is that it is designed from the ground up to let you test ideas and experiment with ways of displaying your data quickly and easily. So, quite naturally, you can switch table types easily to see which style of presentation is best suited to your ideas and the message that you want to convey. To switch table types, all you have to do is click on Table in the ribbon, and select one of these options:

- Table

- Matrix

- Card

What is even more reassuring is that Power View will remember the attributes of the previous table type you used. So, for instance, if you set up a matrix with a carefully crafted hierarchy and then switch to a card-type table, Power View will remember how you set up the matrix should you want to switch back to it.

Key Performance Indicators (KPIs)

There is a tabular presentation that can be considered a little special, and consequently, it is worthy of being looked at separately. This kind of table is a Key Performance Indicator table, and it contains a visual indication of how an objective is being met (if at all). A KPI does require that the underlying data has been prepared to display the data as a KPI, so this is explained in Chapter 11. Fortunately we have KPI data in the sample file, so here is how to display it.

1. Drag the Make field to the FIELDS box in the Field List.

2. Expand the KPI field (AverageGrossMargin) and drag the field's Value and Status to the FIELDS box in the Field List.

A table will be created, but the columns will be named AverageGrossMargin and AverageGrossMarginStatus. The AverageGrossMarginStatus field will contain the KPI indicators (Xs and check marks or exclamations in this case) to indicate if the metric is on track or not. This can be seen in Figure 2-30.

Make	AverageGrossMargin	AverageGrossMargin Status
Aston Martin	37,528.92	✓
Bentley	26,758.33	✓
Jaguar	12,984.52	!
MGB	20,083.33	✓
Rolls Royce	52,939.29	✓
Triumph	9,000.00	✗
TVR	-3,916.67	✗
Total	**26,060.68**	✓

Figure 2-30. *A Key Performance Indicator*

Conclusion

I hope that you are now comfortable with the Power View interface and are relaxed about using it to present your data, whether you are using standard tables, matrix tables, KPIs, or the new and innovative card visualizations that Power View offers. Equally, I hope that you are at ease sorting your tables using the various techniques that are available. Finally, never forget that you can, if you prefer, set up tables so that you can drill down into the data—and back up, of course.

This chapter is just a taster of the many ways in which Power View can help you analyze and display the information that you want your audience to appreciate. Yet, as tables are the basis for just about every other form of visualization, it is well worth mastering the techniques and tricks of table creation. This way you will be well on the way to a fluent mastery of Power View, which will lay the foundations for some truly impressive presentations.

CHAPTER 3

Filtering Data in Power View

Power View is built from the ground up to enable you, the user, to sift through mounds of facts and figures so that you can deliver meaningful insights. Consequently, what matters is being able to delve into data and display the information it contains quickly and accurately. This way, you can always follow up on a new idea or simply follow your intuitions without needing either to apply complex processes or to struggle with an impenetrable interface. After all, Power View is there to help you come up with new analyses that could give your business an edge on the competition.

Filtering the potentially vast amounts of data that stand between you and the insights that could make all the difference to your business is profoundly important. The people who developed Power View recognized this, which is why you can filter on any field or set of fields in the underlying data model. This is not only intuitive and easy, it is also extremely fast, which ensures that you almost never have to wait for results to be returned.

You can add filters before, after, or during the creation of a Power View report. If you add filters before creating a table, say, then your table will only display the data that the filter allows through. If you add a filter to an existing report, then the data visualization will alter before your eyes to reflect the new filter. If you modify a filter when you have visualizations on a Power View report, then (as you probably guessed by now), all the visualizations will also be updated to reflect the new filter criteria—instantaneously.

You can filter any type of data:

- Text

- Numeric values

- Dates

Each data type has its own ways of selecting elements and setting (where possible) ranges of values that can be included—or excluded. This chapter will explain the various techniques for isolating only the data that you want to display. You will then be able to create Power View reports based only on the data that you want them to show.

This chapter, like the previous one, will presume that you have downloaded the file CarSales.xlsx into the folder C:\HighImpactDataVisualizationWithPowerBI, assuming you want to try out the filtering techniques for yourself.

Filters

Subsetting data in Power View is based on the correct application of filters. Consequently, the first thing that you need to know about filters is that they work at two levels. You have

- View-level filters

- Visualization-level filters

The characteristics of these two kinds of filter are described in Table 3-1.

Table 3-1. *Power View Filters*

Filter Type	Application	Comments
View-level	Applies to every visualization in the current report	This kind of filter will filter data for every visualization in the current view.
Visualization-level	Only applies to the selected visualization	This kind of filter will apply only to the selected visualization (table, chart, etc.).

Hiding and Displaying the Filters Area

When you first open Power View you will probably see the Filters Area displayed to the immediate right of the Power View report; it looks like a narrow empty sheet of paper. There could be times when you will not be filtering data, and so you may prefer to hide the Filters Area to increase the available screen space you need to hone your report. So, if you wish to remove the Filters Area from view

1. Activate the Power View ribbon (if it is not already active).

2. Click the Filters Area button and the Filters Area will slide out of view.

To Display the Filters Area

1. Activate the Power View ribbon (if it is not already active).

2. Click the Filters Area button and the Filters Area will reappear.

Alternatively, to hide the Filters Area, you can click on the Close Filters Area button (the small X in the top right-hand corner of the Filters Area) and it will obligingly remove itself from view.

If you prefer to collapse the Filters Area while leaving a thin strip visible to the immediate right of the Power View report, you can click the Minimize icon (a lesser-than symbol in the top right-hand corner of the Filters Area) and the Filters Area will collapse nearly completely out of sight. You can make it reappear at any time by clicking the Expand icon (a greater-than symbol) in the top right-hand corner of the slimmed-down Filters Area. The elements of a typical Filters Area are set out in Figure 3-1.

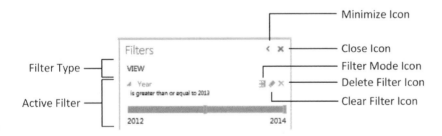

Figure 3-1. *The essential parts of the Filters Area*

View Filters

Saying that there are two types of filter available in Power View is a purely descriptive distinction. For Power View, any filter is a filter, and all filters work in the same way. However, as there is a clear hierarchy in their application, I will begin with view filters and then move on to their descendants—the visualization filters. Given the general similarity between the two, it is probably worth noting that it is important that you check that you are creating or modifying the appropriate filter. As this is not always obvious, at least when you are starting out with Power View, you need to look out for the word View, which is at the top of the view area. If it is not grayed out, this will tell you that you are working on a view filter. To be really sure that you are creating or modifying a view filter, a good trick is to ensure that no visualizations are selected in the Power View report—or even to click on a blank part of the report canvas to be extra sure that you are dealing with a view filter. In this case, only the word View will be displayed at the top of the view area.

Adding Filters

The Filters Area helpfully advises you To Filter The View, Drag Fields From The Fields List. And yes, it really is that simple. Here is how to add a filter to select only a couple of countries from those available in the source data. In this case, we will add the filter before creating a Power View table:

1. In the Power View Field List, expand the table containing the field that will be a filter criterion (Countries in this example).

2. Drag the CountryName field into the Filters Area. The Filters Area will display all the unique elements in the source table; in this case it will be a list of countries.

3. Select two or three elements by clicking on the appropriate check boxes (France, Germany, and Spain, in this example). The Filters Area will look like Figure 3-2.

Figure 3-2. *A simple filter to select specific countries*

■ **Note**   The filter will include the number of elements in the data table for each filter element. For a reference-style table such as this one for countries, this will probably always be "1." For a table containing metrics, the figures will be much larger.

To see the filter working, I suggest creating a table using the following fields:

- CountryName (from the Country table)
- Colour (from the Colours table)
- SalePrice (from the SalesData table)

You will see that data is only displayed for the countries that were selected in the filter. Of course, you do not need to display the CountryName field in the table just because it is used to filter the data. In a real-world Power View report, you will probably not display a field in a table or chart if it is being used to filter data. However, if you want to confirm to yourself that filters work, then you can always display them in a table or chart, and once you are happy that the results are what you expect, you can remove the filtering field from the table. The resulting table should look like Figure 3-3.

CountryName	Colour	SalePrice
France	Black	£22,750.00
France	Blue	£69,250.00
France	British Racing Green	£39,500.00
France	Canary Yellow	£491,190.00
France	Green	£60,440.00
France	Night Blue	£131,100.00
France	Red	£355,300.00
France	Silver	£67,440.00
Germany	Blue	£41,250.00
Germany	Silver	£29,750.00
Spain	Canary Yellow	£22,500.00
Spain	Green	£39,500.00
Spain	Red	£29,750.00
Total		£1,399,720.00

Figure 3-3. A simple filtered table

You will have noticed that when the filter was first applied, every check box was empty, including the (All) check box. The default is (fairly logically) to set up a filter ready for tweaking, but not actually to filter any data until the user has decided what filters to apply. Once you start adding filter elements, they will be displayed in the Filters Area just above the name of the field that is being used to filter data. Well, as many filters as will fit on one line will be displayed to indicate that filters are active.

■ **Tip**   There is a subtle difference that you need to watch out for when selecting filter elements. If you click on the check box, then an element is added to filter (or removed if the check box was already checked). If, however, you click on the name of an element, then all currently selected elements are deselected, and only the element that you clicked on is active in filtering the data.

You modify filters the same way you apply them. All you have to do to remove a selected filter element is to click on the check box with a check mark to clear it. Conversely, to add a supplementary filter element, just click on a blank check box.

The (All) Filter

The only subtlety concerning simple filters is that you also have the (All) check box. This acts as a global on/off switch to select, or deselect, all the available filter elements for a given filter field. The (All) filter field has three states:

- Blank—No filters are selected for this field.

- Checked—All filters are selected for this field.

- Filled-in—Some (but not all) filters are selected for this field.

Clicking a filled-in (All) filter field will deselect all filter elements for this field, in effect rendering the filter inactive. Checking the (All) filter field will select all filter elements for this field, also rendering the filter inactive. Removing the check mark from the (All) filter field will deselect all filter elements for this field, also rendering the filter inactive. Clicking multiple times on the (All) filter field will cycle through the available options.

The (All) filter field is particularly useful when you want not only to remove multiple filter selections in order to start over but also want to select all elements in order to deselect certain elements individually (and avoid manually selecting reams of elements).

■ **Note** When selecting multiple elements in lists, you may be tempted to apply the classic Windows keyboard shortcuts that you may be in the habit of using in, for instance, Excel or other Windows applications. Unfortunately Control- or Shift-clicking to select a subset of elements will simply not work. In addition, although you can select and deselect a check box using the spacebar, it is not possible to use the cursor keys to pass from one element to another in a filter list.

Clearing Filters

Setting up a finely honed filter so that you are drilling through the noise in your data to the core information can take some practice. Fortunately, the virtually instantaneous application of filters means that you can see almost immediately if you are heading down the right path in your analysis. However, there are frequent occasions when you want to start over and remove any settings for a particular filter. This can be done as follows:

1. Click the Clear Filter icon to the right of the selected filter. This icon is shown in Figure 3-4.

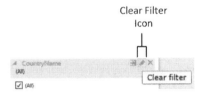

Figure 3-4. *Clearing a filter*

Once a filter has been cleared the only way to get it back to its previous state is to click Undo (or press Ctrl-Z) immediately. Otherwise you will have to rebuild it from the ground up.

■ **Tip** An interesting trick to note is that if you click on the filter field in the Filters Area, you can expand and collapse the filter.

Deleting Filters

When working with filters, at times you may want to clear the decks and start over. The fastest way to do this is to delete a filter; once a filter is deleted, it produces no effect on the data in the Power View report. This can be done as follows:

1. Click the Delete Filter icon to the right of the selected filter. This icon is shown in Figure 3-5.

Delete Filter
Icon

Figure 3-5. *Deleting a filter*

Once a filter has been deleted the only way to get it back is to click Undo (or press Ctrl-Z) immediately. Otherwise you will have to rebuild it from scratch. Interestingly, although you can add filters by dragging elements into the Filters Area, you cannot drag them out of the Filters Area to remove them.

Expanding and Collapsing Filters

When you only have a few filters active in a Power View report, and when those filters only contain a few elements, then having all the filter elements visible at the same time is no real problem. However, when you are using multiple filters and/or are employing filters that contain dozens, or hundreds, of elements, then managing filters may require a little attention.

To give a more uncluttered aspect to the Filters Area, the simplest thing to do is to collapse any filters once you have defined them. To do this

1. Click the Collapse icon (a filled triangle facing down and to the right situated to the left of the filter title). The filter elements will disappear, leaving only the filter title and the list of selected elements.

Note that if no elements are selected for a filter, then (All) will be displayed under the filter title. A collapsed filter is shown (with some selected elements) in Figure 3-6.

Expand/Collapse
Filter Icon
(Collapsed)

Figure 3-6. *Collapsing a filter*

To expand a filter and continue refining the selection

1. Click the Expand icon (an empty triangle facing right, situated to the left of the filter title). The filter elements will reappear, as you saw previously in Figure 3-2.

Subsetting Large Filter Lists

Depending on the source data that you are using, you could have only a few elements making up each filter. If so, then you should probably consider yourself lucky, because many data sets can contain dozens, or hundreds of filter elements. If this is the case, then you will probably need to know a few simple techniques for handling long lists of filter elements.

First, we need to specify what exactly a "large" filter list is. Fortunately Power View helps us here, as it will start helping to manage lists once there are more than 10 (or so) elements in the list. If more than 20 elements are in a filter (this will depend on several factors including your screen resolution and how many filters you have placed in the Filters Area), then Power View will limit the number of elements displayed and will display a vertical scroll bar. This way you can scroll through the available filter elements.

Searching for Specific Elements in a Filter

So, assuming you have a large list of filter elements, just how can Power View help you?

Very simply, you can search for any text inside a list of elements. For instance, assuming you have added a filter on ClientName (by dragging the ClientName field from the Clients table into the Filters Area), you will see immediately that for Power View, this is a large set of filter elements, because it adds a Search box between the filter name and the filter detail (this is the box with a magnifying glass to the right). To search for a specific element

1. Click inside the Search box.

2. Enter the (hopefully few) characters that are enough to isolate the element that you are looking for. I suggest entering the word **England**.

3. Click the magnifying glass to the right of the Search box (or press Enter).

Power View will return only a subset of the filter elements that contain the characters that you have searched on. The characters that you entered will be highlighted inside each of the filter elements that is returned. It is worth noting that the character string you entered will be found anywhere inside the filter elements. An example of this search facility is shown in Figure 3-7.

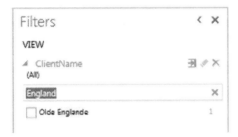

Figure 3-7. *Searching inside a filter*

Once you have returned the subset of filter elements, you can select the ones you want as described earlier. Do remember that when searching in a filter, you can only find elements that are available. So, if there are other active filters, you might not get all the results you were expecting.

Clearing a Filter Subset

To clear the filter on a filter that you created using the Search box, all you have to do is

1. Click the small X to the right of the Search box. This X replaced the magnifying glass once you activated the filter search.

The search string will be removed, as will the filter on the filter elements. All the filter elements (or at least, as many as can be displayed) will reappear in the filter. Be aware that just deleting the contents of the Search box might not produce the result you were expecting!

Filtering with Wildcards

When searching through a large and varied set of filter elements, you might want to bring back elements based not on a specific search string, but on a string containing certain letters or combinations of letters. This is called a *wildcard search*. For instance, when searching car colors, you could indicate to Power View that you want all filter elements that contain the letter "a" followed anywhere further in the element by the letter "e." So, if you take this as an example of a subset of filter elements that you want to isolate, this is what you have to do:

1. Add the Colours field to the Filters Area (unless you have already done so).

2. Enter the search string **a*e** in the search box, as show in Figure 3-8.

Figure 3-8. *Wildcard filter search*

3. Click the magnifying glass to the right of the Search box (or press Enter).

4. Select the elements from the filter subset to which you want to apply the filter. Only cars of the selected colors will appear in any visualization.

As you can see, the wildcard search returned only the following colors in the filter:

*   British Racing Green

*   Canary Yellow

*   Dark Purple

All of these colors contain the letter "a" followed further in the element by the letter "e." Of course, this example is not necessarily very practical, but it shows how you can extend the search facility for filter elements to widen a search by using the asterisk wildcard. This will return any number of characters in the place of the asterisk.

Finally, if you want a slightly narrower search—for just one character—you can use the question mark (?) character. Entering the search string **g?e** in the search box will return

*   British Racing Green

*   Green

Using the question mark wildcard character will force Power View to find a character; for instance, entering **?r** will find several colors, but not Red, because the search string states "any r preceded by a single character." As the initial R in Red is not preceded by any character, it is consequently not found. However, searching for ***r** will find Red, as the asterisk implies zero or more characters.

▓ **Note** This search facility is not case sensitive.

Clearing a Filter Element Search

To cancel a filter element search (and remove the search string from the Search box), click the X (which replaces the magnifying glass when a Filter element search is active). The search string will be removed and the subset of filter elements will be replaced with the available filter elements—or at least by as many elements as Power View can display.

Filtering Different Data Types

So far we have only seen how Power View can filter text elements in a view. Although text-based elements are a major part of many data filters, they are far from the only available type. There are also

- Numeric Data
- Date and Time Data

Numeric Data

You can filter on numeric elements just as you can filter on text-based elements in Power View. However, although the core principles are the same, there are some interface differences and tricks that you probably need to know.

Range Filter Mode

The first trick worth knowing is that, when filtering on numeric data, you do not *only* have the choice of selecting elements from a list. You *also* have a *range selector,* which is the default filter for numeric filters. The range selector is a slider, which allows you to set the lower and upper limits of the range of numbers that you want to display in a Power View report.

To set the range of figures for which data will be displayed

1. Drag a numeric field into the Filters Area (CostPrice in this example). The field title and a blue range slider bar appear in the Filters Area. The initial range filter is given in Figure 3-9. You can see that the range filter starts with the lowest available value and ends with the highest available value.

Figure 3-9. *A range filter for numeric values*

2. Place the mouse pointer over the left-hand (lower) extremity of the blue range slider bar for the selected filter. The mouse pointer becomes a two-headed arrow.

3. Slide the left-hand range limiter to the right. You will see the constituent elements of the field appear above the slider and below the field title, preceded by Is Greater Than Or Equal To *X,* where *X* is the figure from the source data. The figures will increase from smaller to larger the further to the right you slide the range boundary. Stop when you have reached a suitable lower bound for the data. This is shown in Figure 3-10.

Figure 3-10. *Setting a range filter*

4. Place the mouse pointer over the right-hand (upper) extremity of the blue range slider bar for the selected filter. The mouse pointer becomes a two-headed arrow.

5. Slide the upper range limiter to the left. You will see the constituent elements of the field appear above the slider and below the field title, preceded by Is Between *lower range boundary* And *X*, where *X* is the figure from the source data. Stop when you have reached a suitable upper bound for the data.

That is it; you have set a range for all data in the Power View report corresponding to the selected field. It should look like Figure 3-11.

Figure 3-11. *A filter range*

When selecting a range of numeric data you do not, of course, have to set both upper and lower bounds. You may set one, the other, or both. Also you will have noticed that the figures that are displayed as you alter the boundaries are not in any regular progression. This is because they are extrapolated from the actual data, as it is in the data source.

■ **Note**   Numeric filters seem to support 400-plus increments—less if the data has a smaller range.

List Filter Mode

In some cases you may prefer to select real values to filter numeric data. This is, in my experience, more rarely required, but it can be useful when you wish to exclude outliers at either end of the data spectrum.

To switch a numeric list to List Filter Mode (I will use the CostPrice filter, which we just set up)

1. Hover the mouse pointer over the filter title (the field name you selected when you created the filter). The filter title will turn blue.

2. Click on the Filter Mode icon to the right of the filter title. This is the first of the three icons at the top right of the filter. You should see something like Figure 3-12.

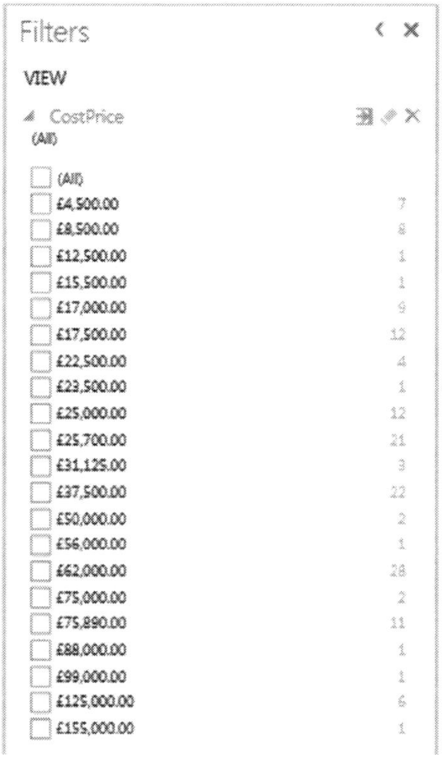

Filters	‹ ✕
VIEW	
◢ CostPrice	⬚ ✎ ✕
(All)	
☐ (All)	
☐ £4,500.00	7
☐ £8,500.00	8
☐ £12,500.00	1
☐ £15,500.00	1
☐ £17,000.00	9
☐ £17,500.00	12
☐ £22,500.00	4
☐ £23,500.00	1
☐ £25,000.00	12
☐ £25,700.00	21
☐ £31,125.00	3
☐ £37,500.00	22
☐ £50,000.00	2
☐ £56,000.00	1
☐ £62,000.00	28
☐ £75,000.00	2
☐ £75,890.00	11
☐ £88,000.00	1
☐ £99,000.00	1
☐ £125,000.00	6
☐ £155,000.00	1

Figure 3-12. *A list filter*

That is it; you will now see the numeric data in list mode, and you can select specific values.

■ **Tip**   Be warned, however, that it is not because no values are selected that the filter is inactive. You need to be careful and check the filter title, which could still say Is Between *value* And *value*. This indicates that a filter is active. To reset the filter so that the range filter is deactivated, you need to click the (All) filter field, twice, preferably. This will select, then clear, all the check boxes for all the elements in the list.

You can then select, or exclude, any specific elements, as you did earlier in the chapter for colors. In practice, you may want to exclude any values that are suspiciously high or low and presume that they are outliers that need to be filtered out of the dataset. Alternatively, you may want to select any suspicious-looking values in order to take a closer look at them.

To flip back to Range Filter mode

1.   Hover the mouse pointer over the filter title (the field name you selected when you created the filter). The filter title will turn blue.

2.   Click twice on the Filter Mode icon to the right of the filter title. This is the first of the three icons at the top right of the filter.

You will see that the list filter disappears, and in its place the range filter reappears.

When cycling through the filter modes (by clicking on the Filter Mode icon to the right of the filter title) you will see that there is also an Advanced Filter mode. As this will be described very shortly, I will not describe it here. Power View is also very helpful in providing a tooltip when you hover the mouse pointer over the Filter Mode icon that tells you what the next filter mode will be if you click on the icon.

Quickly Excluding Outliers

A few paragraphs ago I mentioned the possibility of excluding outliers. There is a quick trick to getting this done efficiently that you may find useful:

1.   Drag the filter for the field containing the outlier value to the Filters Area.

2.   Click on the Filter Mode button to switch to List Filter mode.

3.   Click (All) to select all the values in the list filter.

4.   Uncheck the values that are at the upper and lower limits of the filter elements and that you consider to be outliers.

By definition, there should only be a few outliers, so this process should only take a few seconds.

Date and Time Data

At its simplest, date and time data is merely list data, like the List Filter mode for numeric data. Consequently, dragging a Date, Time, or DateTime field into the Filters Area will add a list of discrete elements from the data source. You can then select all, none, or a chosen subset of elements from the list as was described for text-based data. If your data has a Date table (or as datawarehousing people would call it, a Date Dimension), then you could well be using this to select date filter criteria. What you need to know here is that dragging a date hierarchy (or any other hierarchy for that matter) to the Filters Area will add every element in the hierarchy as a separate filter. Let's see this in action.

1.   Expand the Date table in the Field List.

2.   Drag the Year hierarchy to the Filters Area. Figure 3-13 demonstrates this.

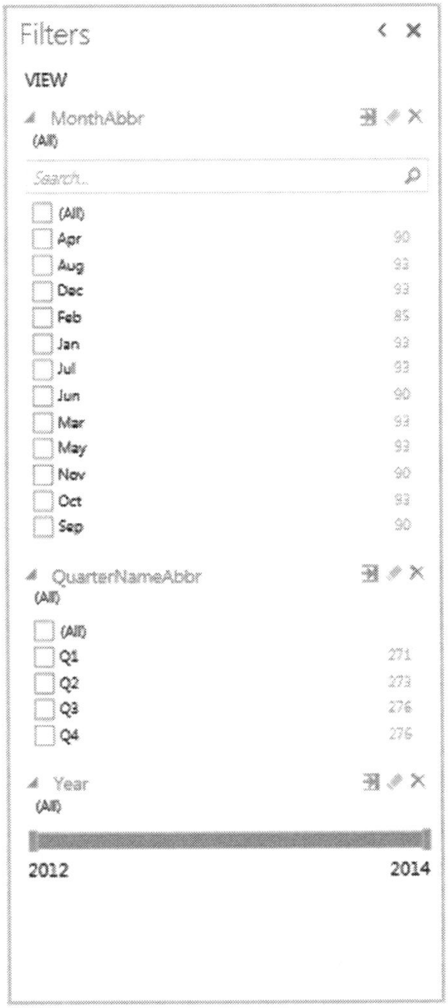

Filters	‹ ✕
VIEW	

▲ MonthAbbr   ⊞ ✎ ✕
(All)

| Search... | 🔍 |

☐ (All)
☐ Apr   90
☐ Aug   93
☐ Dec   93
☐ Feb   85
☐ Jan   93
☐ Jul   93
☐ Jun   90
☐ Mar   93
☐ May   93
☐ Nov   90
☐ Oct   93
☐ Sep   90

▲ QuarterNameAbbr   ⊞ ✎ ✕
(All)

☐ (All)
☐ Q1   271
☐ Q2   273
☐ Q3   276
☐ Q4   276

▲ Year   ⊞ ✎ ✕
(All)

```
▐▬▬▬▬▬▬▬▬▬▬▬▬▬▬▬▬▬▬▬▬▬▬▬▬▬▬▐
2012                        2014
```

Figure 3-13. *A date filter based on a hierarchy*

What you are looking at is, in essence, multiple filters, where you can select elements from each of the different filters: Year, Quarter, and/or Month. Alternatively, if you will be filtering on successive elements in a date hierarchy (Year, followed by Month, for instance) you may find it more intuitive to drag the filter elements from the date hierarchy to the Filters Area in the temporal order in which you will be using them (that is, Year followed by Month, and probably not even Quarter). This way, you can proceed in a logical manner, from top to bottom in the Filters Area, to apply the date criteria that interest you.

▓ **Note** If, or when, you want to delete filters that were added as a hierarchy, you will have to delete them individually, as you cannot remove all the fields that make up the hierarchy together. Fortunately this only takes a few seconds.

However, if you are faced with multiple dates that are taken directly from source data, and you do not have a time table in your PowerPivot data, it is frequently easier to set ranges for dates. This is best dealt with by using the advanced filters for all the available data types. These kinds of filters are explained in a following section.

Other Data Types

There are, of course, other data types in the source data that you are likely to be handling. You might have boolean (True or False) data, for instance. However, for Power View, this is considered, for all intents and purposes, to be a text-based filter. So if you filter on boolean data, Power View will display True and False in the expanded filter for this data type. You can see this if you expand the Client table and drag IsCreditWorthy to the Filters Area. On the other hand, there are some data types that you cannot use to filter on, and that will not even appear in the Filters Area. Binary data (such as images) is a case in point.

Multiple Filters

So far we have treated filters as if only one was ever going to be applied at a time. Believe me, when dealing with large and intricate data sets, it is unlikely that this will be the case. As a matter of course, Power View will let you add multiple filters to a report. This entails some careful consideration of the following possible repercussions:

- All filters will be active at once (unless you have cleared a filter), and their effect is cumulative. That is, data will only be returned if the data matches *all* the criteria set by all the active filters. So, for example, if you have requested data between a specified date range and above a certain sales figure, you will not get any data back where the sale figure is lower than the figure that you specified or the sales date is before or after the dates that you set.

- It is easy to forget that filters can be active. Remember that all active filters in the Filters Area will remain operational whether the Filters Area itself is expanded or collapsed. If you are going to collapse filters to make better use of the available space on the screen, then it is worth getting into the habit of looking at the second line below any filter title that will give you a description of the current filter state. It will display something like Contains Rolls. Of course, the exact text will vary according to the filter that you have applied.

- Filters can interact in the Filters Area. The time hierarchy is a case in point. If you select Quarter 3, for instance, you will only see the months for that quarter in the Months filter.

Advanced Filters

In many cases, when you are delving into your data, merely selecting a "simple" filter will be enough to highlight the information that interests both you and your audience. There will, however, inevitably be cases when you will need to filter your data more finely in order to return the kinds of results that sort the wheat from the chaff. This is where Power View's advanced filters come to the fore. Advanced filtering lets you search inside field data with much greater precision, and it is of particular use when you need to include, or exclude, data based on parts of a field (if it is text) or a precise range (if it is a number or a date).

Advanced filters, just like standard filters, are adapted to the three main data types that Power View handles, namely

- Text
- Numbers
- Dates

so it is best to look at each of these separately. However, before going through all the details, you first need to know how to switch to Advanced Filter mode in Power View.

Applying an Advanced Filter

Let's begin with a simple example of how to apply an advanced filter to a text field. You have to

1. Add a field on which you want to filter to the Filters Area (unless, of course, the filter is already in place). In this example, it will be the ClientName field.

2. Expand the filter field (you can see a list of individual data elements from the field) unless it has already been done.

3. Click on the Advanced Filter Mode icon to the right of the filter header. The body of the filter switches to show the Advanced Filter boxes, and the text under the filter title now reads Show Items For Which The Value. This is shown in Figure 3-14.

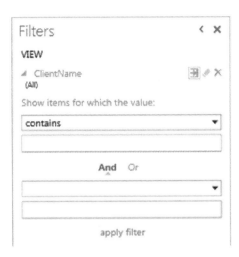

Figure 3-14. *Advanced filters*

4. Click inside the filter text box (under the box displaying Contains) and enter the text to filter on (**Aldo** in this example).

5. Click Apply Filter, or press the Enter key, and all objects in the Power View report will only display data where the client contains the text Aldo. The result (a sample table) is shown in Figure 3-15; the advanced filter used to produce it is also shown.

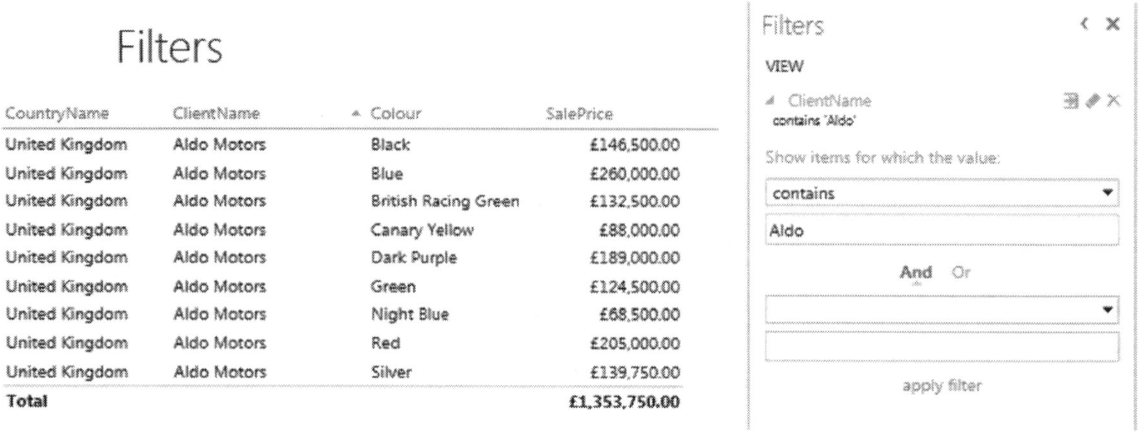

Filters

CountryName	ClientName	▲ Colour	SalePrice
United Kingdom	Aldo Motors	Black	£146,500.00
United Kingdom	Aldo Motors	Blue	£260,000.00
United Kingdom	Aldo Motors	British Racing Green	£132,500.00
United Kingdom	Aldo Motors	Canary Yellow	£88,000.00
United Kingdom	Aldo Motors	Dark Purple	£189,000.00
United Kingdom	Aldo Motors	Green	£124,500.00
United Kingdom	Aldo Motors	Night Blue	£68,500.00
United Kingdom	Aldo Motors	Red	£205,000.00
United Kingdom	Aldo Motors	Silver	£139,750.00
Total			**£1,353,750.00**

Filters ‹ ✕

VIEW

◢ ClientName 🗐 ✏ ✕
  contains 'Aldo'

Show items for which the value:

| contains ▼ |

| Aldo |

And   Or

| ▼ |

| |

apply filter

Figure 3-15. *The results of applying an advanced filter*

Here are several comments that it is important to make at this stage:

- Advanced filtering is *not* case sensitive. You can enter uppercase or lowercase characters in the filter box; the result will be the same.

- Spaces and punctuation are important, as they are taken literally. If you enter, for instance "**A** " (without the quotes, but note the space after the A), then you will only find elements containing an A (uppercase or lowercase) followed by a space.

- Advanced filters, just like standard filters, are cumulative in their effect. So, if you have applied a filter and do not get the results you were expecting, be sure to check that no other filter is active that might be narrowing the data returned beyond what you want.

- If your filter excludes all data from the result set, then any tables in the Power View report will display This Table Contains No Rows.

- Similarly, if your filter excludes all data, charts will be empty, and multiple charts will display Contains No Small Multiples To Display.

In any case, if you end up displaying no data, or data that does not correspond to what you wanted to show, just clear the filter and start over!

Clearing an Advanced Filter

Inevitably you will also need to know how to remove an advanced filter. The process is the same as for a standard filter; all you have to do is

1. Click the Clear Filter icon (the middle icon of the three to the right of the filter field name). The filter elements are removed for this filter.

You can, of course, if you have no further need for the entire filter, delete the filter by clicking the Delete Filter icon (the right-hand one of the three to the right of the filter field name). This will not only clear the filter settings, but it will delete the entire filter.

Advanced Wildcard Filters

A few pages previously we saw how to use wildcards to create a subset of filter elements that would then be used to select specific values. Well, you can also use wildcards directly to filter data using the Advanced Filter mode. To apply a wildcard filter to your data

1. Add a field on which you want to apply a wildcard filter to the Filters Area (unless, of course, the filter is already in place). I suggest using the ClientName field.

2. Expand the filter field (you can see a list of individual data elements from the field) unless this has already been done.

3. Click on the Advanced Filter Mode icon to the right of the filter header. The body of the filter switches to show the Advanced Filter boxes, and the text under the filter title now reads Show Items For Which The Value.

4. Click inside the filter text box (under the box displaying Contains) and enter the filter text containing one or more wildcards. In this example it will be **u*e**.

5. Click Apply Filter, or press the Enter (Return) key, and all visualizations in the Power View report will only display data where the Client contains the character "u" followed anywhere by the character "e."

As you can see in Figure 3-16, the result is that the Power View report only displays clients containing a "u" followed by an "e."

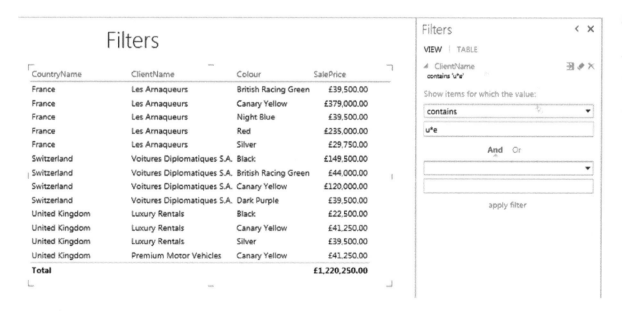

Figure 3-16. *Applying an advanced wildcard filter*

The wildcard variations that you can apply are described in Table 3-2.

Table 3-2. *Wildcard Filter Options*

Wildcard Character	Description	Comments
*	Asterisk	Searches for zero or more characters in the data
?	Question mark	Searches for a single character in the data

Note that using the question mark wildcard character will force Power View to find at least one character. Also, using wildcards in advanced filtering is not case sensitive.

Numeric Filters

Setting an advanced filter for a numeric value is, if anything, easier than when instantiating a filter for a text-based value—and it is very similar. Here is the process to filter Gross Margin so that only sales for makes of car with a gross margin value above £50,000 are displayed in the report.

1. Create a new Power View report (this way we know that no other filters are active).

2. Create a table based on the ClientName and SalePrice fields.

3. Drag the field GrossMargin to the Filters Area.

4. Click on the Advanced Filter Mode icon to the right of the filter header. The body of the filter switches to show the Advanced Filter boxes, and the text under the filter title now reads: Show Items For Which The Value. The filter option is Greater Than Or Equal To. Do not change this as it suits our requirements as is.

5. Click inside the box under the filter option text and enter the figure **50000**. Do not add formatting elements to this figure.

6. Click Apply Filter (or press the Enter [Return] key).

The report, including the Filters Area, looks like the one in Figure 3-17. The filter title now says Gross Margin Is Greater Than Or Equal To 50,000.00. As you can see, the filter title adopts the formatting used in the source data.

Figure 3-17. *Using numeric filters*

When you have added a numeric filter, you can increase and decrease the value by clicking on the tiny up and down triangles that appear to the right of the value box. This saves you from having to reenter figures. It will, however, only change by single increments.

Date and Time Filters

If you are filtering on a Date or DateTime field, then you will quickly notice that Power View adds a couple of popup elements to the advanced filter to help you select dates and times more easily. These additions are

- A calendar popup, which lets you click on a day of the month (and scroll through the months of the year, forward and backward)

- A time series popup, which lets you select times preset to every five minutes throughout the day

The calendar popup is shown in Figure 3-18.

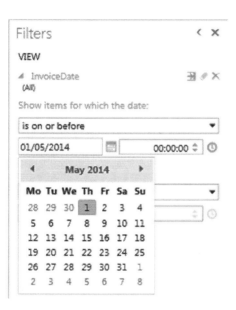

Figure 3-18. *The calendar popup*

There are a couple of tricks that may save you time when you are selecting dates from the calendar popup (you may be used to these techniques already in other desktop packages, so forgive me if I add them anyway in the interests of completeness):

- When using the calendar popup, clicking on the right-facing triangle to the right of the month and year will display the following month.

- When using the calendar popup, clicking on the left-facing triangle to the left of the month and year will display the previous month.

- When using the calendar popup, clicking on the month and year will display a Year popup, in which you can click on the right-facing triangle to the right of the year to display the following year, and then you can select the month from those displayed.

- When using the calendar popup, clicking on the month and year will display a Year popup, in which you can click on the left-facing triangle to the left of the year to display the previous year, and then you can select the month from those displayed.

- When using the time popup, clicking inside any constituent part of the time (hour, minute, or second) and then clicking on the up and down scroll triangles to the right of the time field allows you to scroll rapidly through the available options.

- Clicking on the clock icon to the right of the time box lets you scroll through the time of the day in five-minute intervals.

If you do not want to select a date using the calendar popup, then you can enter a date directly in the date box of the advanced filter for a Date (or DateTime) field. Just remember that you must enter the date in the date format corresponding to the environment that you are using. That is to say, it must be formatted exactly as a Date field appears in a Date column in any Power View table.

■ **Note** If you enter a date where the format does not correspond to the system format, or if the date is purely and simply invalid (the 30th of February, for instance), then Power View will not let you apply the filter. In this case the Apply Filter link will remain grayed out, and pressing the Enter (Return) key will not apply the filter. To correct this, merely select a correct date using the calendar popup. Similarly, if you enter a nonexistent time, the Power View will refuse to accept it and will revert to the previous (acceptable) time that was chosen.

Complex Filters

All the examples I've given so far in this chapter have used a single filter criterion for each filter that was applied, even if multiple filters were used. You can, however, add a second criterion to a single filter (using the Advanced Filter mode) if you want to extend or limit the effect of the filter. Each filter that you apply can contain two possible criteria at most. This is how it can be done:

1. Add an advanced filter as described in steps 1–4 of the "Applying an Advanced Filter" section earlier. Enter only an **A** in the upper filter text box. Do not apply the filter.

2. Click And under the filter text box.

3. Select Does Not Contain from the lower filter type popup.

4. Enter **O** in the lower filter text box.

5. Click Apply Filter, or press the Enter (Return) key, and all objects in the Power View report will display data only where the Client's name contains an "A" but not an "O."

This filter should look like the one given in Figure 3-19.

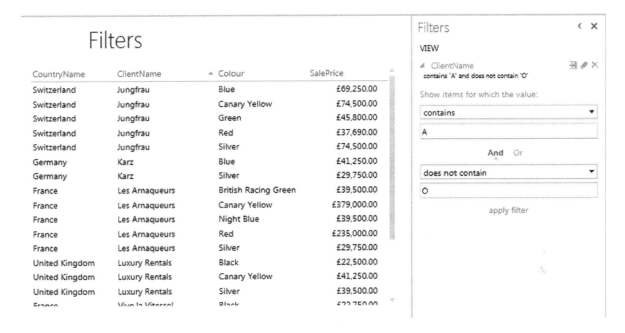

Figure 3-19. *A complex filter*

In this past example, you selected an *And* filter. In fact, as you can see from the Power View screen, you have two choices of complex filter. They are explained in Table 3-3.

Table 3-3. *Complex Filter Options*

Filter Type	Comments
And	Applies both filter elements to *reduce* the amount of data allowed through the filter
Or	Applies either of the filter elements separately to *increase* the amount of data allowed through the filter

Advanced Text Filter Options

When filtering on the text contained in a data field, you can applied the string you are filtering on to the underlying data in several ways. These are the same for both the upper and lower of the two advanced filter options for a text field. They are described in Table 3-4.

Table 3-4. *Advanced Text Filter Options*

Filter Option	Description
Contains	The selected field contains the search text anywhere in the field data.
Does Not Contain	The selected field does not contain the search text anywhere in the field data.
Starts With	The selected field begins with the search text, followed by any data.
Does Not Start With	The selected field does not begin with the search text, followed by any data.
Is	The selected field matches the search text exactly.
Is Not	The selected field does not match the search text exactly.
Is Blank	The selected field is blank.
Is Not Blank	The selected field is not blank.

Advanced Numeric Filter Options

Numbers cannot be filtered in exactly the same ways as text. Consequently, the advanced filtering options are slightly different from those you use when filtering text. They are described in Table 3-5.

Table 3-5. *Advanced Numeric Filter Options*

Filter Option	Description
Is Less Than	The selected field is less than the number you are searching for.
Is Less Than Or Equal To	The selected field is less than or equal to the number you are searching for.
Is Greater Than	The selected field is greater than the number you are searching for.
Is Greater Than Or Equal To	The selected field is greater than or equal to the number you are searching for.
Is	The selected field matches exactly the number you are searching for.
Is Not	The selected field does not exactly match the number you are searching for.
Is Blank	The selected field is blank.
Is Not Blank	The selected field is not blank.

When applying a numeric filter you must—not altogether surprisingly—enter a numeric value. If you enter text by mistake, you will get the following message:

The value is not valid. Enter a valid number between -Infinity and Infinity.

In this case you will have to delete the characters that you entered and enter a numeric value in the place of the erroneous text. You can, if you really want, format numbers (by adding a thousands separator, for instance), but Power View will remove all number formatting.

Advanced Date Filter Options

Dates also cannot be filtered in exactly the same ways as text or numbers. Consequently, the advanced filtering options for date filters are slightly different from those used when filtering other data types. They are described in Table 3-6.

Table 3-6. *Advanced Date Filter Options*

Filter Option	Description
Is	The selected field contains the date that you are searching for.
Is Not	The selected field does not contain the date that you are searching for.
Is After	The selected field contains dates after the date that you entered, that is, later dates that do not include the date you entered.
Is On Or After	The selected field contains dates beginning with the date that you entered or later.
Is Before	The selected field contains dates before the date that you entered, that is, earlier dates, not including the date you entered.
Is On Or Before	The selected field contains dates on or before the date that you entered, that is, earlier dates, up to and including the date you entered.
Is Blank	The selected field is blank.
Is Not Blank	The selected field is not blank.

Visualization-Level Filters

So far in this chapter we have looked at View filters, that is, filters that will be applied to the entire view and every visualization it contains. Although filtering the source data at a global level will certainly ensure coherence among the tables, charts, and other visualizations that you are using, there will inevitably be times when you want to filter a specific visualization at a finer level. This is where visualization-level filters come in.

Fortunately, visualization-level filters are virtually identical to view filters. The essential thing to remember is that you must select (or click inside) a visualization to apply a visualization-level filter. You will see when this option is available, as the word Table or Chart will appear at the top right of the Filters Area to the immediate right of the word View.

As with nearly everything in Power View, this is probably best experienced in practice, so, to apply a visualization-level filter

1.   Return to an existing Power View report.

2.   Display the Filters Area (unless it is already visible).

3.   Click on an existing visualization. In this example, I will be using the initial table created in this chapter, which you can see in Figure 3-3.

4.   Click on the word Table, which has appeared at the top right of the Filters Area to the immediate right of the word View in the View area. You will see that all the fields that are used by the selected table appear in the View area.

5.   Expand any filter fields that you wish to use, or add any further fields from the Power View Field List, and apply any filters that you require, as described previously in this chapter. I suggest selecting a couple of the colors for this example. This is shown in Figure 3-20.

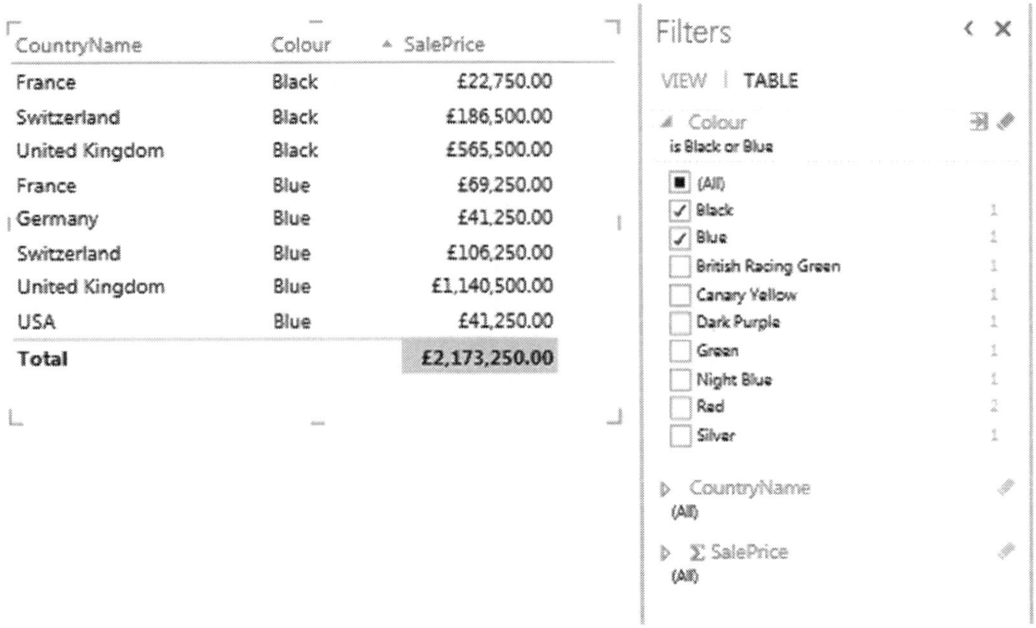

CountryName	Colour	▲ SalePrice
France	Black	£22,750.00
Switzerland	Black	£186,500.00
United Kingdom	Black	£565,500.00
France	Blue	£69,250.00
Germany	Blue	£41,250.00
Switzerland	Blue	£106,250.00
United Kingdom	Blue	£1,140,500.00
USA	Blue	£41,250.00
Total		**£2,173,250.00**

Filters   ‹ ✕

VIEW | TABLE

⊿ Colour
is Black or Blue

- ■ (All)
- ✓ Black   1
- ✓ Blue   1
- ☐ British Racing Green 1
- ☐ Canary Yellow   1
- ☐ Dark Purple   1
- ☐ Green   1
- ☐ Night Blue   1
- ☐ Red   2
- ☐ Silver   1

▷ CountryName
(All)

▷ ∑ SalePrice
(All)

Figure 3-20. *A visualisation-level filter*

You will notice right away that the filter(s) that you have applied only affect the selected visualization (the table in this example). When you create more complex reports that contain several visualizations, you will see that no other visualizations in the report have their underlying data modified in any way.

You can clear any filter at the visualization level just as you can at the view level—by clicking the Clear icon at the top right of the filter name. You can also delete any filter that you have added to the Filters Area for a visualization (but not those that are based on the fields used by the visualization) by clicking the Delete icon at the top right of the filter name. Adding and removing fields from a visualization will automatically add and remove the corresponding filters from the Filters Area for the visualization. This will include any filters that you added manually before you add them to the list of fields used by the visualization.

Filter Hierarchy

As I mentioned previously, a hierarchy of filters is applied in Power View:

- **First**, at the data level, any selections or choices you apply to the underlying data will restrict the data set that Power View can use to visualize your information.

- **Second**, at the report or view level, any view-level filters that you apply will affect all visualizations in the view, using the (possibly limited) available source data.

- **Finally**, for each visualization, any visualization-level filters that you apply will further limit the data that is allowed through the view-level filter—but only for the specific visualization.

As a quick example of this you could

1. Apply a country filter to the view (which means you would either deselect any selected visualization, or, alternatively, click on the word View at the top of the view area).

2. Drag the CountryName field into the Filters Area and select all countries except the UK. You will see that all current visualizations are updated to reflect the new filter.

3. Click on the table for which you added a table filter earlier. Click on the Table indicator at the top of the Filters Area.

4. Now expand the CountryName filter in the Filters Area. You will see that the UK is not available to filter on, as shown in Figure 3-21.

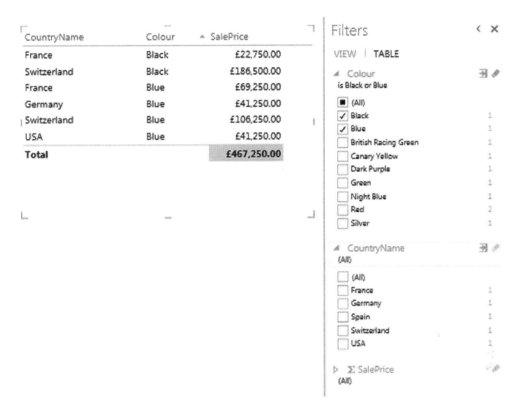

Figure 3-21. *The filter hierarchy*

It is worth noting the following points:

- You have no way to apply a selection to a visualization filter if it has been filtered out at view level. Clicking (All) will only select from the subset of previously filtered elements.

- If you apply a filter at visualization level and then reapply the same filter at view level, but with different elements selected, you will still be excluding all non-selected elements from the filter at visualization level. I stress this because Power View will remember the previously selected elements at visualization level, and leave them visible even if they cannot be used in a filter, because they have already been excluded from the visualization-level filter by being ruled out at view level. This, in my opinion, adds a certain visual confusion, even if the hierarchical selection logic is applied.

Hopefully this shows you that Power View is rigorous in applying its hierarchy of filters. Should you need to apply a filter at visualization level when the filter choice is excluded at view level, you have no choice but to remove the filter at view level and then reapply visualization-level filters to all necessary visualizations to apply the view filter individually to each visualization.

Filtering Tips

Power View makes it incredibly easy to filter data, and to exclude any and all data that you feel is not helpful in your data analysis. However, like many powerful tools, this ability to apply filters so quickly and easily can be something of a double-edged sword. So here are a few words of advice and caution when applying filters to your data.

Don't Filter Too Soon

As an initial point, I would say that a key ground rule is "Don't filter too soon." By this, I mean that if you are examining data for trends, anomalies, and insights, you have to be careful not to exclude data that could contain the very insights that can be game-changing.

The problem is, of course, that when you first delve into a haystack of data in search of needles of informational value, you have no idea what you could be looking for. So I can only suggest the following approaches:

- Begin with no filters at all, and see what the data has to say in its most elemental form.

- Apply filters one at a time, and remember to delete a filter before trying out another one.

- Try to think in terms of "layers" of filters. So, once you have defined an initial set of filters, add further filters sequentially.

- Go slowly. The temptation is to reach a discovery in order to shout about it from the rooftops. This can lead to inaccurate analysis.

- Always remove any filters that are not absolutely necessary.

- Be careful when hiding the Filters Area. It is too easy to forget that there are active filters.

- Remember that you can have filters specific to a visualization that cannot be visible in the Filters Area. So always check if any visualization filters are active for each table and chart in a report.

Drill-Down and Filters

In Chapter 2 we saw how to drill down in a matrix table. In the following chapter, you will see how to drill down into charts. In either case, you need to know that performing a drill-down operation (or indeed a drill-up) will have a subtle effect on the Filters Area.

What happens is that the Filters Area for the visualization will reflect the selected drill-down element. As an example, you could try out the following (I will not give all the details for all the steps as a bit of revision for you):

1. Create a matrix based on the following fields, in the following order:

   a. Colour

   b. ClientType

   c. CountryName

   d. CostPrice

2. Remove the totals.

3. Set the matrix to be a drill-down table (by rows).

4. Drill down to the second level by double-clicking Night Blue and then Dealer.

5. Expand the Filters Area (if necessary) and click on Matrix to see the visualization-level filters.

6. Expand the Colour and ClientType filters.

The table, and the Filters Area, will look like Figure 3-22.

CountryName	CostPrice
⬆France	42,500.00
United Kingdom	418,290.00
USA	37,500.00

Figure 3-22. *Drill-down and filters*

As you can see, the filters indicate the drill-down elements, both by indicating the selected elements and selecting the appropriate check boxes. So drilling down is essentially a filter operation.

Annotate, Annotate, Annotate

If you are presenting a key finding based on a data set, then it can save a lot of embarrassment if you make it clear in every case what the data does, and does not, contain. You could, for instance, be so pleased with the revelatory sales trend that you have discovered that you forget to note an important exclusion in the underlying data. Now, no one is suggesting that you are doing anything other than making a point, but your audience needs to know what has been excluded, and possibly why—just in case it makes a difference. After all, you don't want a rival using this point to try and invalidate your findings in the middle of a vital meeting, do you?

Annotation techniques are described in Chapter 7 if you need to jump ahead to check this out now.

Conclusion

This chapter has shown you how to apply and fine tune a series of techniques to enable you to select the data that will appear in your Power View reports. The main thing to take away is that you can filter data at two levels: the overall report and each individual visualization.

You have also seen a variety of selection techniques that allow you to subset data. These range from the avowedly simple selection of a few elements to the specification of a more complex spread of dates or values. Finally it is worth remembering that you can filter data using any fields in the underlying dataset, whether the field is displayed in a report or not.

CHAPTER 4

■ ■ ■

Charts in Power View

It is one thing to have a game-changing insight that can fundamentally alter the way your business works. It is quite another to be able to convince your colleagues of your vision. So what better way to show them—intuitively and instantaneously—that you are right than with a chart that makes your point irrefutably?

Power View is predicated on the concept that a picture is worth many thousands of words. Its charting tools let you create clear and convincing visualizations that tell your audience far more than a profusion of figures ever could. This chapter, therefore, will show you how simple it can be not just to make your data explain your analysis, but to make it seem to leap off the screen. You will see over the next few pages how a powerful chart can persuade your peers and bosses that your ideas and insights are the ones to follow.

A little more prosaically, Power View lets you make a suitable data set into

- Pie charts

- Bar charts

- Column charts

- Line charts

- Scatter charts

- Bubble charts

- Multiple charts

In this chapter we will get up and running by looking at creating pie, bar, column, and line charts. The other chart types will be discussed in the next chapter. Once you have decided upon the most appropriate chart type, you can then enhance your visualization with titles, data labels, and legends, where appropriate. We will also see how to apply drill-down techniques to charts and how to filter the data that underlies them.

The sample file for this chapter is CarSales.xlsx, which you should find in the directory C:\HighImpactDataVisual izationWithPowerBI—assuming you have installed the samples as described in Appendix A.

A First Chart

As with so much in Power View, it is easier to appreciate its simplicity and power by doing rather than talking. So I suggest leaping straight into creating a first chart straightaway. In this section we will look only at "starter" charts that all share a common thread—they are based on a single column of data values and a single column of descriptive elements. This data will be

- A list of clients

- Car sales for a given year

So, let's get charting!

Creating a First Chart

Any Power View chart begins as a data set. So, let me introduce you to the world of charts; this is how to begin:

1. Create a new Power View report by clicking Power View in the Insert ribbon.

2. Display the Field List by clicking the Field List button in the Power View ribbon (unless the Field List is already visible).

3. Drag the field ClientName from the Clients table onto the Power View report canvas.

4. Drag the field SalePrice from the SalesData table onto the table that was created in the report canvas during the previous step.

5. Expand the YearHierarchy in the Date table and add the Year field to the Filters Area. Select the year 2013 (I'll let you refer back to Chapter 3 if you need reminding how this is done). The data table should look something like Figure 4-1.

ClientName	SalePrice
Aldo Motors	£637,750.00
Bright Orange	£1,034,250.00
Carosse Des Papes	£152,040.00
Chateau Moi	£157,990.00
Costa Del Speed	£91,750.00
Crippen & Co	£123,000.00
Cut'n'Shut	£964,250.00
Honest John	£914,000.00
Impressive Wheels	£87,250.00
Jungfrau	£301,740.00
Karz	£71,000.00
Les Arnaqueurs	£348,750.00
Luxury Rentals	£103,250.00
Olde Englande	£143,750.00
Premium Motor Vehicles	£41,250.00
Rocky Riding	£150,000.00
Smooth Riders	£64,750.00
Three Country Cars	£111,000.00
Vive la Vitesse!	£204,190.00
Voitures...	£159,500.00
Wheels'R'Us	£1,297,250.00

Figure 4-1. *A source data table for charting*

6. Leaving the table selected, click Bar Chart, then Clustered Bar in the Design ribbon. Your chart should look like Figure 4-2.

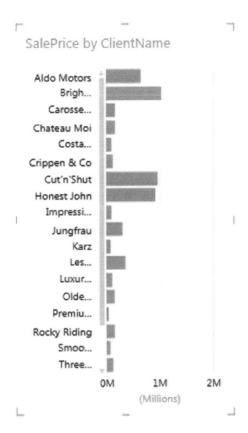

Figure 4-2. *Your first chart*

7. Resize the chart—I suggest widening it—by dragging the handle in the middle of the right edge to the right until the axis labels are clearly visible, as shown in Figure 4-3.

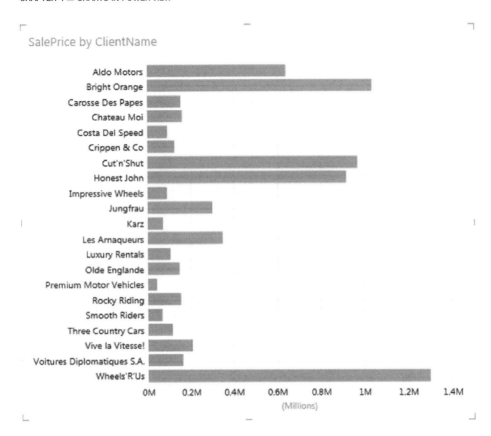

Figure 4-3. *A basic chart after resizing*

And that is all that there is to creating a simple starter chart. This process might only take a few seconds, and once it is complete, it is ready to show to your audience, or be remodeled to suit your requirements.

Nonetheless, a few comments are necessary to clarify the basics of chart creation in Power View:

- *First*, when creating the table on which a chart is based, you can use any of the techniques described in Chapter 2 to create a table. You can drag fields into the FIELDS box of the Design section of the Field List rather than onto the Power View canvas if you prefer.

- *Second*, when you transform a table into a chart, the Layout section of the Field List changes to reflect the options available when creating or modifying a chart. If you select the chart that you just created, you will see that the ClientName field has been placed in the AXIS box, and the SalePrice field has been placed in the VALUES box. Neither of these boxes existed when the visualization was a table. This can be seen in Figure 4-4.

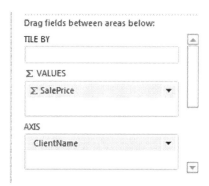

Figure 4-4. *The layout section of the fields list for a clustered bar chart*

- *Third,* when using *only a single data set,* you can choose either clustered or stacked as the chart type for a bar or column chart; the result will be the same in either case. As you will see as we progress, this will not be the case for multiple data sets.

- *Fourth,* Power View will add a title at the top left of the chart explaining what data the chart is based on. You can see an example of this in Figure 4-3.

- *Fifth,* you can disregard the totals in the initial table. These are not used in a chart.

- *Finally,* creating a chart is very much a first step. You can do so much to enhance a chart and accentuate the insights that it can bring. However, all of this will follow further on in this chapter and in the next one.

Deleting a Chart

Deleting a chart is as simple as deleting a table. All you have to do is

1. Click inside the chart.

2. Press the Delete key.

If you remove all the fields from the Layout section of the Field List (with the chart selected), then you will also delete the chart.

Basic Chart Modification

So you have an initial chart. Suppose, however, that you want to change the actual data on which the chart is based. Well, all you have to do to change both the axis elements, the client names, and the values represented, is

1. Click on, or inside, the chart that you created previously. Avoid clicking on any of the bars in the chart for the moment.

2. In the Field List, click on the popup menu for SalePrice in the VALUES box, and select Remove Field. The bars will disappear from the chart.

3. Drag the field GrossMargin from the SalesData table into the VALUES box.

4. In the Field List, click on the popup menu for ClientName in the AXIS box, and select Remove Field. The client names will disappear from the chart and a single bar will appear.

5. Click on the popup menu for the Colour field in the Colours table and select Add As Axis (or drag the Coluor field from the Colours table into the AXIS box). The list of colors will replace the list of clients on the axis, and a series of bars will replace the single bar. Look at Figure 4-5 to see the difference.

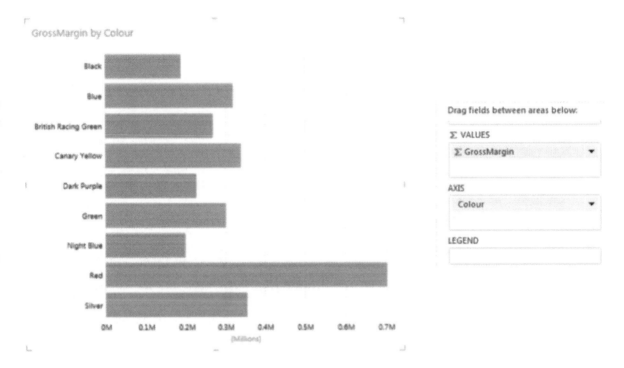

Figure 4-5. *A simple bar chart with the corresponding layout section*

That is it. You have changed the chart completely without rebuilding it. Power View has updated the data in the chart and the chart title to reflect your changes.

Basic Chart Types

When dealing with a single set of values, you will probably be using the following four core chart types:

- Bar chart
- Column chart
- Line chart
- Pie chart

Let's see how we can try out these types of chart using the current data set—the colors and Gross Margin that you applied previously.

Column Charts

A column chart is, to all intents and purposes, a bar chart where the bars are vertical rather than horizontal. So, to switch your bar chart to a column chart

1. Click on, or inside, the bar chart that you created previously. Avoid clicking on any of the bars in the chart for the moment.

2. Click Column Chart, then Clustered Column, in the Design ribbon. Your chart should look like Figure 4-6.

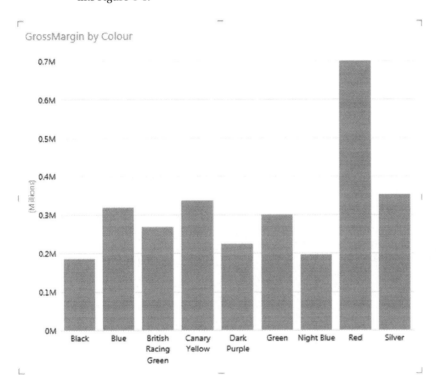

Figure 4-6. *An elementary column chart*

Line Charts

A line chart displays the data as a set of points joined by a line. To switch your column chart to a line chart

1. Click on, or inside, the bar chart that you created previously. Avoid clicking on any of the bars in the chart for the moment.

2. Click Other Charts, then Line, in the Design ribbon. Your chart should look like Figure 4-7.

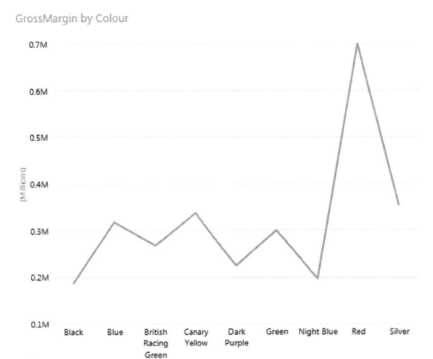

Figure 4-7. *A simple line chart*

Pie Charts

Pie charts can be superb at displaying a limited set of data for a single series—like we have in this example. To switch the visualization to a pie chart

1. Click on, or inside, the line chart that you created previously. Avoid clicking on the line in the chart for the moment.

2. Click Other Charts, then Pie, in the Design ribbon. Your chart should look like Figure 4-8. You will notice that the Layout section has changed slightly for a pie chart, and the AXIS box has been replaced by a COLOR box.

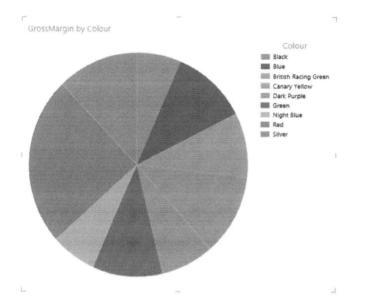

Figure 4-8. *A basic pie chart*

A pie chart will be distorted if it includes negative values at the same time as it contains positive values. What Power View will do is display the negative values as if they were positive, because otherwise the values cannot be displayed. This is probably not the effect that you were hoping for. If your data set contains a mix of positive and negative data, then Power View will display an alert above the chart warning you that the Pie Chart Contains Positive And Negative Values. You can see which pie slices contain negative values by hovering the mouse pointer over each slice and reading the values in the popup that appears.

In practice, you may prefer not to use pie charts when your data contains negative values, or you may want to separate out the positive and negative values into two data sets and display two charts, as explained in the "Chart Filters" section later in this chapter.

■ **Note**   Juggling chart size and font size to fit in all the elements and axis and/or legend labels can be tricky. One useful trick is to prepare "abbreviated" data fields in the source data, as has been done in the case of the QuarterAbbr field in the Date table that contains Q1, Q2, and so on, rather than Quarter 1, Quarter 2, and so on to save space in the chart. Techniques for this sort of data preparation are given in Chapter 10.

Essential Chart Adjustments

Creating a chart in Power View is, I hope you will agree, extremely simple. Yet the process of producing a telling visualization does not stop when you take a table of data and switch it into a chart. At the very least, you will want to make the following tweaks to your new chart:

- Resize the chart.

- Reposition the chart.

- Sort the elements in the chart.

- Alter the size of the fonts in the chart.

None of these tasks is at all difficult. Indeed it can take only a few seconds to transform your initial chart into a compelling visual argument—when you know the techniques to apply.

Resizing Charts

A chart is like any other visualization on the Power View report and can be resized to suit your requirements. To resize a chart

1. Place the mouse pointer over any of the eight handles that appear at the corners and in the middle of the edges of the chart that you wish to adjust. The pointer becomes a two-headed arrow.

2. Drag the mouse pointer. As you are resizing the chart, its background changes color to indicate that it is selected.

■ **Note**   You do not have to select or click inside a chart before you resize it. Remember that the lateral handles will let you resize the chart only horizontally or vertically, and that the corner handles allow you to resize both horizontally and vertically.

When resizing a chart, you will see that this can have a dramatic effect on the text that appears on an axis. Power View will always try and keep the space available for the text on an axis proportionate to the size of the whole chart.

For bar charts, this can mean that the text can be

- Adjusted to spread over two or more lines

- Cut, with words split over two rows

- Truncated, with an ellipsis (three dots) indicating that not all the text is visible.

For column and line charts, this can mean that the text can be

- Adjusted to spread over two or more lines

- Angled at 30, 60, or 90 degrees

- Truncated, with an ellipsis (three dots) indicating that not all the text is visible

If you reduce the height (for a bar chart) or the width (for a column or a line chart) below a certain threshold, Power View will stop trying to show all the elements on the non-numeric axis. Instead it will only show a few elements and will add a scroll bar to allow you to scroll through the remaining data. You can see an example of this for a bar chart in Figure 4-9.

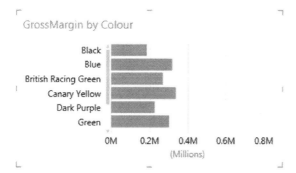

Figure 4-9. *A chart with a scroll bar visible*

All this means is that you might have to tweak the size and height to width ratio of your chart until you get the best result. If you are in a hurry to get this right, I advise using the handle in the bottom right corner to resize a chart, as dragging this up, down, left, and right this will quickly show you the available display options.

Repositioning Charts

You can move a chart anywhere inside the Power View report:

1. Place the mouse pointer over the border of the chart. The pointer changes into a hand. As you are repositioning the chart, its background changes color to indicate that it is selected.

2. Drag the mouse pointer.

Sorting Chart Elements

Sometimes you can really make a point about data by changing the order in which you have it appear in a chart. Up until this point you have probably noticed that when you create a chart, the elements on the axis (and this is true for a bar chart, column chart, line chart, or pie chart) are in alphabetical order by default. If you want to confirm this, then just take a look at Figures 4-5 to 4-8 on the preceding pages.

Suppose now, for instance, you want to show the way that sales are affected by the color of the vehicle. In this case, you want to sort the data in a chart from highest to lowest so that you can see the way in which the figures fall, or rise, in a clear order. Here is how to do this:

1. Select the Clustered Bar chart type, as described earlier (and shown in Figure 4-5).

2. Place the mouse pointer over the chart. You will see that Sort By Color Asc appears over the chart on the top left. This is shown in Figure 4-10.

95

Figure 4-10. *The sort area in a chart*

3. Click on the word Colour. This will change to GrossMargin, and the sort order of the elements in the chart will change.

4. Let's suppose now that you want to see the sales by color in descending order. Place the mouse pointer over the chart. You will see that Sort By GrossMargin Asc appears over the chart on the top left.

5. Click Asc. This becomes Desc, and the chart changes to become like it is in Figure 4-11.

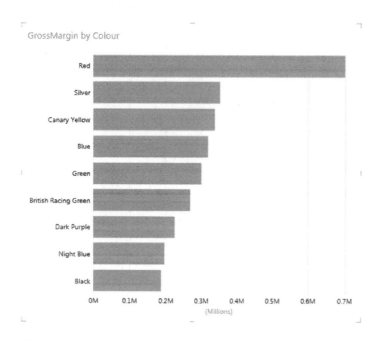

Figure 4-11. *Sorting data in a bar chart*

If a chart has multiple values, as will be the case for some of the charts that you will see further on in this chapter, then you have two options when selecting the field on which the chart will be ordered:

- Click on the field name that appears above the top left of the chart when the mouse pointer is placed over the chart (as we did a moment ago). Each click will change the sort to the next available field used by the chart and then continue to cycle through the fields.

- Click on the downward-facing triangle to the right of the currently selected sort field to get a popup list of available fields to sort on. Then click on the field you want to use as a basis for the sort. This is shown in Figure 4-12.

Figure 4-12. *Selecting the sort element in a chart*

I should add just a short remark about sorting pie charts. When you sort a pie chart, the pie chart will be sorted clockwise, starting at the top of the chart. So if you are sorting colors by GrossMargin in descending order, the top selling color will be at the top of the pie chart (at 12 o'clock), with the second bestselling color to its immediate right (2 o'clock, for example) and so on. An example of this is shown in Figure 4-13.

GrossMargin by Colour

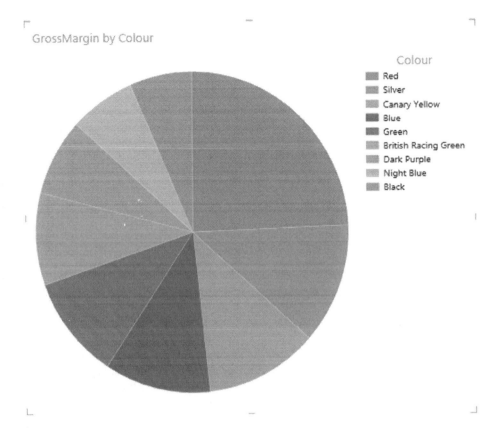

Colour
Red
Silver
Canary Yellow
Blue
Green
British Racing Green
Dark Purple
Night Blue
Black

Figure 4-13. *Sorting data in a pie chart*

Font Size

When a chart is initially created, Power View will apply a default font size. This font size will not change proportionally if you resize the chart. This does not, however, mean that Power View fixes font sizes definitively. You can influence matters by choosing proportionally to reduce, or increase, the size of the fonts used on both axes of the chart. You can do this in the following way:

1. Select the chart (but do not click on any of the bars, columns, or lines).

2. In the Design ribbon, click on the Increase Font Size button to make the fonts in the chart larger, or on the Decrease Font Size button to make the fonts in the chart smaller.

Adjusting the font size will produce many of the same effects that you saw when you were resizing a chart; namely, text on the axes will be

- Adjusted to spread over two or more lines

- Truncated, with an ellipsis (three dots) indicating that not all the text is visible

- Angled at 30, 60, or 90 degrees

If Power View considers the text too large to display all the elements in the chart, then it will only show a few elements and will add a scroll bar to allow you to scroll through the remaining data.

Applying Color to Bar and Column Charts

The bar and column charts that we have created so far are a little lacking in color, as every bar or column is the same shade. If you want to add a splash of color, then you can override the default and make Power View apply a palette of colors to the bars and columns for a chart based on a single data element.

For example, take the column chart shown in Figure 4-5; all you have to do is

1. Drag the Colour field from the AXIS box into the LEGEND box in the Layout section of the Field List.

You can see the result in Figure 4-14. The axis titles are now the legend elements, and the bars are in different colors. Admittedly, on the printed page you cannot see the colors, but the shading indicates that your changes have worked! You can get a similar result for a bar chart.

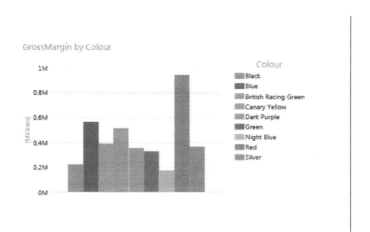

Figure 4-14. *Applying a color palette to individual columns*

___

■ **Note**   You cannot sort a chart like this one—one that does not have any axis values.

___

Multiple Data Values in Charts

So far in this chapter we have seen simple charts that display a single value. Life is, unfortunately, rarely that simple, and so it is time to move on to slightly more complex, but possibly more realistic, scenarios where you need to compare and contrast multiple data elements.

For this set of examples, I will presume that we need to take an in-depth look at the indirect cost elements of our car sales to date. These are

- Delivery

- Parts

- Labor

All of these can be found in the CarSalesData table.

Consequently, in order to begin with a fairly simple comparison of these indirect costs, let's start with a clustered column chart:

1. Starting with a clean Power View report, create a table that displays the following fields:

    a. ClientName (from the Clients table)

    b. SpareParts (from the SalesData table)

    c. DeliveryCharge (from the SalesData table)

    d. LabourCost (from the SalesData table)

2. Filter to include only data for the year 2013 as described for the initial chart that you created at the start of this chapter.

3. Leaving the table selected, click Bar Chart, then Clustered Bar, in the Design ribbon.

4. Resize the chart to make it clear and comprehensible, as shown in Figure 4-15 (I have included the Fields List so that you can see this too).

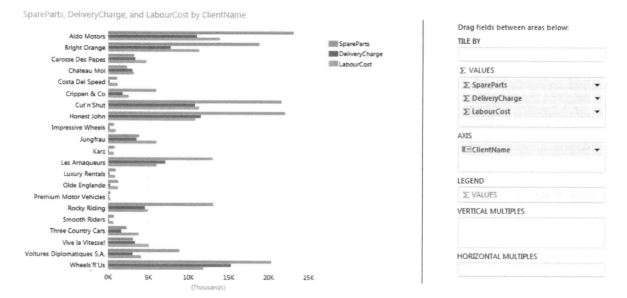

Figure 4-15. *Multiple data values in charts—a clustered bar chart with the layout section shown*

You will notice that a chart with multiple data sets has a legend by default, and that the automatic chart title now says SpareParts, DeliveryCharge, And LaborCost By ClientName.

The same data set can be used as a basis for other charts that can effectively display multiple data values. These are

- Stacked bar

- Clustered column and stacked column

- Line charts

As column charts are essentially bar charts pivoted through 90 degrees, I will not show examples of these here. However, in Figures 4-16 and 4-17, you will see examples of a stacked bar chart and a line chart. You will also see that when creating these types of visualization, the Layout section of the Field List remains the same for all of these charts.

SpareParts, DeliveryCharge, and LabourCost by ClientName

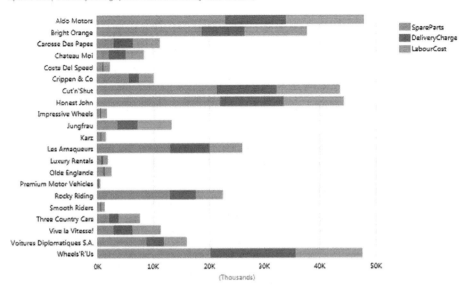

Figure 4-16. *A simple stacked bar chart*

SpareParts, DeliveryCharge, and LabourCost by ClientName

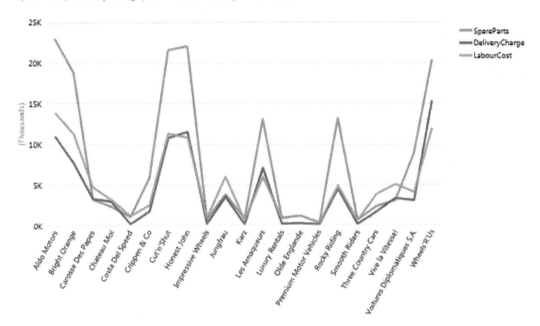

Figure 4-17. *An introductory line chart*

■ **Note** You cannot create a stacked bar or stacked column chart directly from a table that has multiple numeric data values; so you have two choices: *either* you start with a table containing only one numeric data value and then drag the other numeric fields that you wish to use onto the stacked chart (or into the Σ VALUES box), *or* you start with a clustered chart that you then convert into a stacked chart.

Data Details

To conclude our tour of basic charts, I just want to make a couple of comments.

First, you can always see exactly what the figures behind a bar, column, line, point, or pie segment are just by hovering the mouse pointer over the bar (or column, or line, or pie segment). This will work whether the chart is its normal size, or whether it has been popped out to cover the Power View report area. An example of this is given in Figure 4-18.

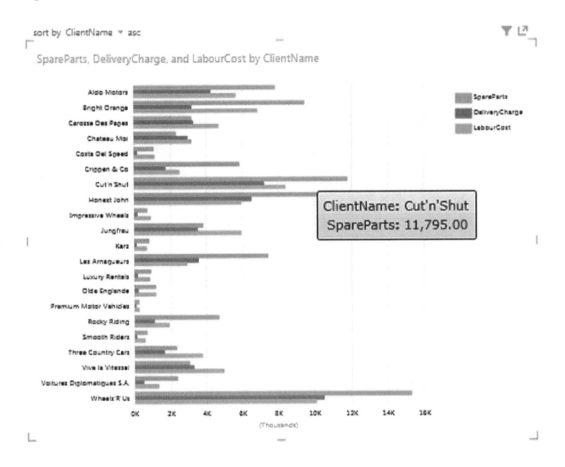

Figure 4-18. *A clustered bar chart with the popup displayed*

Second, however much work you have done to a chart, you can always switch it back to a table if you want. Simply select the chart, and select the required table type from the Table button in the Design ribbon. If you do this, you will see that the table attempts to mimic the design tweaks that you applied to the chart, keeping the font sizes the same as in the chart, and the size of the table identical to that of the chart. Should you subsequently switch back to the chart, then you should find virtually all of the design choices that you applied are still present—unless, of course, you made any changes to the table before switching back to the chart visualization.

The Layout Ribbon

You have already seen most of the basic charting techniques. I hope that you found them as simple as I promised they would be. So, before we move on to the next level, I really should explain a new Power View ribbon that appears every time you click on a chart. It is the Layout ribbon.

The Layout ribbon is largely devoted to enhancing charts in Power View. The buttons it contains are outlined in Figure 4-19.

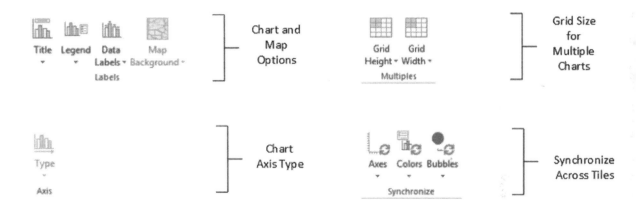

Figure 4-19. The Layout ribbon

There are only a few buttons in the Layout ribbon, and they are, fortunately, largely intuitive. Should you need a reference, then a detailed explanation of their use is given in Table 4-1.

Table 4-1. The Layout Ribbon Buttons

Button	Description
Title	Adds or removes a title from the chart.
Legend	Lets you choose where (if at all) the legend is placed on a chart.
Data Labels	Lets you decide to add or hide data labels and choose where they are placed.
Map Background	Adds a thematic background to a map. This is explained in Chapter 7.
Axis Type	Lets charts have continuous or interrupted axes.

(*continued*)

Table 4-1. (*continued*)

Button	Description
Grid Height	Allows you to choose the number of vertical charts that can be displayed if multiples are selected.
Grid Width	Allows you to choose the number of horizontal charts that can be displayed if multiples are selected.
Axes	Synchronizes chart axes when tiles are added to a chart.
Colors	Synchronizes chart colours across the tiles when tiles are added to a chart.
Bubbles	Synchronizes chart bubble sizing when tiles are added to a chart.

Enhancing Charts

Now that you have been introduced to the Layout ribbon and have mastered basic charts, it is time to move on to the next step and learn how to tweak your charts to the greatest effect. The next few sections are, consequently, devoted to the various techniques available in Power View to give your charts real clarity and power.

Chart Legends

If you have a chart with more than one field that provides the values on which the chart is based, then you will see a legend appear automatically. The default for the legend is for it to be placed on the right of the chart. However you can choose where to place the legend, or even whether to display it at all, by choosing from one of the options that appear when you click on the Legend button in the Layout ribbon.

The available options are given in Table 4-2.

Table 4-2. *Legend Position Options*

Legend Option	Comments
None	No legend is displayed for this chart.
Show Legend At Right	The legend is displayed at the right of the chart.
Show Legend At Top	The legend is displayed above the chart.
Show Legend At Left	The legend is displayed at the left of the chart.
Show Legend At Bottom	The legend is displayed below the chart.

If one of the legend options is grayed out, it is because this is the option that is currently active.

Legends can require a little juggling until they display their contents in a readable way. This is because the text of the legend is often truncated when it is initially displayed. If this is the case, you have two options:

- Decrease the font size for the chart (as described earlier).

- Modify the chart size.

Do not hesitate to try both these methods, and to switch between the two, as Power View will often end up by displaying the legend in a way that suits your requirements as you adjust these two aspects of the chart display.

▓ **Note**   A legend can contain a scroll bar (vertical for legends to the left or right or horizontal in the case of legends above or below the chart). This can be both extremely useful if you are dealing with many elements in a legend and extremely disconcerting if you are not expecting it!

Chart Title

Each chart is created with a title explaining what the chart is displaying, that is, the fields on which it is based. Here, the available options are fairly simple, as you can only choose between displaying the title or not.

1. To hide the chart title, all you have to do is click on the Title button in the Layout ribbon and select None.

2. To make a title reappear, click on the Title button in the Layout ribbon, and select Above Chart.

You can always add further annotations to a chart using free-form text boxes. This is described in Chapter 7.

Chart Data Labels

As we have seen already, you can display the exact data behind a column, bar, or point in a line chart simply by hovering the mouse pointer over the data that interests you. Yet there could be times when you want to display the values behind the chart permanently on the visualization. This is where data labels come into play.

To add data labels to a chart (in this example I will use the chart shown in Figure 4-11, which we created previously), all you have to do is

1. Click inside the chart to which you wish to add data labels.

2. Go to the Layout ribbon.

3. Select Outside End from the Data Labels button.

Power View will add data labels to the chart as shown in Figure 4-20.

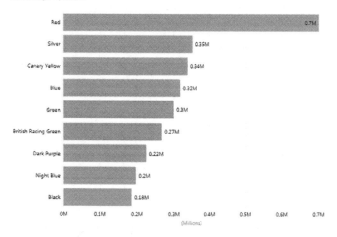

GrossMargin by Colour

Figure 4-20. *A bar chart with data labels applied*

As you will have seen when you were clicking on the Data Labels button, Power View gives you several options concerning the placement of data labels in a chart. These options are explained in Table 4-3.

Table 4-3. *Data Labels for Column and Bar Charts*

Data Label Option	Comments
None	No data labels will be superimposed on the chart.
Center	The data label will be displayed (if possible) inside the data area.
Inside End	The data label will be displayed (if possible) inside the data area, at the top end of the bar or column.
Inside Base	The data label will be displayed (if possible) inside the data area, at the top end of the bar or column.
Outside End	The data label will be displayed (if possible) outside the data area, at the top end of the bar or column.

When applying data labels to line charts, the possible options are somewhat different than those offered for bar and column charts. Options for line charts are given in Table 4-4.

Table 4-4. *Data Labels for Line Charts*

Data Label Option	Comments
None	No data labels will be superimposed on the chart.
Auto	Power View will place the data labels as it sees best.
Center	Data labels will be placed across each point on the chart.
Left	Data labels will be placed to the left of each point on the chart.
Right	Data labels will be placed to the right of each point on the chart.
Above	Data labels will be placed above each point on the chart.
Below	Data labels will be placed below each point on the chart.

■ **Note**   When applying data labels to column, bar, and line charts, you will notice that sometimes Power View cannot, physically, place all the data labels exactly where the option that you have selected implies that they should appear. This is because on some occasions there is simply not enough space inside a bar or column at the upper or lower end of a chart, to fit the figures as, the bar or column is too small. In these cases, Power View will place the data outside the bar or column. On other occasions, the data cannot fit outside a line, column, or bar without being placed above the upper end of the axis. Here again, Power View will tweak the presentation to get as close as possible to the effect that you asked for.

There are a few final points to note on the subject of data labels:

- If one of the data label options is grayed out when you click the Data Labels button on the Layout ribbon, it is because this is the option that is currently active.

- Pie charts cannot display data labels, so the Data Labels button is grayed out on the Layout ribbon.

- Scatter charts and balloon charts can also display data labels. However, they will not display figures; instead, they will display the labels (the descriptive text) for the point or balloon in a chart.

Drilling Down

In Chapter 2, we saw that Power View lets you drill down into tables, level by level, to pursue your analyses of the underlying data. Well, it probably comes as no surprise to discover that you can also drill down into the data that is displayed as charts, as well as drill back up again. As an example of this, let's imagine that you want to take a look at average direct costs and average sale costs. Yet you want to see these

- At the top level, by country

- Then, for a given country, by car age bucket (this is explained in Chapter 10, and is a way of grouping car ages into a set of thresholds)

Let's see how this can be done.

1. Start with a new Power View report, where the report filter is set to allow data only for the year 2013.

2. Add the following fields to the FIELDS box in the Field List:

   a. CountryName (from the Countries table)

   b. CarAgeBucket (from the SalesData table)

   c. DirectCosts (from the SalesData table)

   d. SalesCosts (from the SalesData table)

3. Click on the popup triangle at the right of the DirectCosts and SalesCosts fields, and set the aggregation to Average for each of these fields.

4. Switch the visualization from Table to Matrix, using the Table button in the Design ribbon.

5. Also in the Design Ribbon, click Show Levels, and select Rows, Enable Drill Down One Level At A Time.

6. Switch the visualization to clustered column (using the Column button in the Design ribbon). You will see a column chart with only the top level of axes (CountryName) visible. It should look like Figure 4-21. Note that the title is "Average Of DirectCosts, Average Of SalesCosts By CountryName".

Average of DirectCosts, and Average of SalesCosts by CountryName

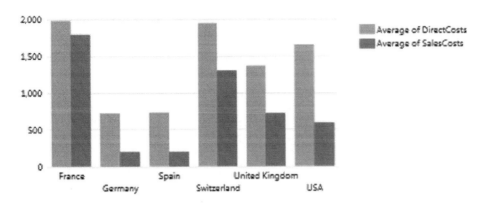

Figure 4-21. The top level in a drill-down chart

7.   Double-click on either of the columns for the UK. You will drill down to the next axis level, CarAgeBucket. The chart should look like Figure 4-22. Note that the title is now Average Of DirectCosts, Average Of SalesCosts By CarAgeBucket:

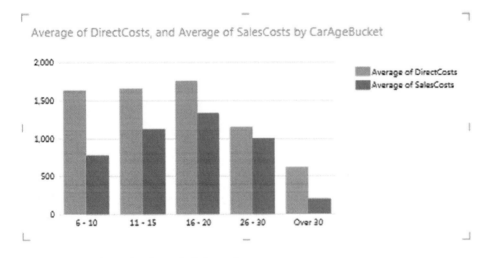

Figure 4-22. A lower level in a drill-down chart

8.   To drill back up to the preceding level, click on the Drill-Up , which appears at the top right of the chart (this is shown in Figure 4-23).

Figure 4-23. *The Drill-Up icon in a chart visualization*

Drilling up will return you to the initial chart, as seen in Figure 4-20.

Now, the technique that I just explained is not the only way to create a drill-down chart. I would argue that it is probably the easiest to do when you are new to Power View, or if you are testing things out as you try and find a suitable visualization to express your findings in visual form. However, and in the interests of completeness, there is another way that I tend to use in practice. It consists of

- Creating a single-level chart
- Adding a second level (or indeed, several more levels) to this chart

To create a drill-down chart using this alternative approach

1. Add the following fields to the FIELDS box in the Field List in a Power View report:

   a. CountryName (from the Countries table)

   b. DirectCosts (from the SalesData table)

   c. SalesCosts (from the SalesData table)

■ **Note** AS you can see, you did not add CarAgeBucket (from the SalesData table) yet. Also you need to make sure that the values are set to use the Average aggregation type.

---

2. Switch the visualization to a clustered bar chart (to ring the changes a little). You should see a chart like Figure 4-24.

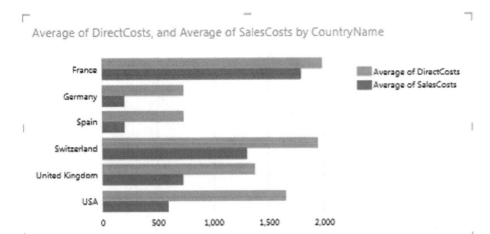

Figure 4-24. *A clustered bar chart using average aggregations*

3. Leaving the chart selected, add the CarAgeBucket (from the SalesData table) to the AXIS box in the Field List Design area, under the CountryName field. The Field List Design area should look like Figure 4-25.

Figure 4-25. *The Fields List Layout section for a clustered bar chart and average aggregations*

Nothing in the chart has changed; yet, if you double-click on any bar, you drill down to the next level. If you were to try this with Switzerland, for instance, you would see what appears in Figure 4-26.

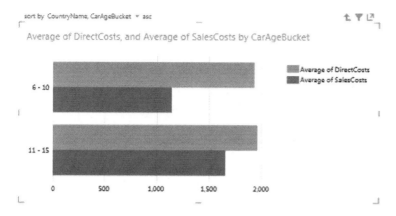

Figure 4-26. *Drilling down inside a chart*

You can add multiple levels to the axis of a chart into which you wish to drill down. If you want to change the order of the elements used to provide the levels you use to drill down, then all you have to do is alter the arrangement of the field names in the AXIS box of the field names Design area by dragging them up or down.

You can remove a level in this hierarchy in one of two ways:

- Clicking on the popup icon for the level at the right of the field name and selecting Remove Field

- Dragging the field out of the AXIS box of the field names Design area and up into the Field List area.

As it is all too easy to get lost when using charts with multiple hierarchical levels, I advise you to take a look at the chart title before drilling up or down. This way you can always see which level in the data hierarchy is currently displayed. Also, you can always see if you are at the top of a hierarchy—the drill up icon will never appear at the top right of a chart.

Popping Charts Out and In

Once you have perfected the appearance of a chart, you could decide to zoom in to the chart for a detailed look. This is incredibly easy:

1. Move the mouse pointer over the chart (I will use the one you saw in Figure 4-15). You will see two tiny icons appear over the top right of the chart. You can see these icons in Figure 4-27.

Figure 4-27. *The Pop Out icon*

2.   Click on the rightmost of these icons—the Pop Out icon.

The chart will expand to cover the entire area of the Power View report. Not only that, but the following changes will be visible:

- The axis text will be adjusted and should not contain ellipses (unless the text is extraordinarily long).

- The number of elements displayed will be adjusted to attempt to show as much data as clearly as possible. This can mean that any scroll bars that are visible in the chart before you clicked Pop Out could disappear.

- The major gridline on the values axis could change to allow finer increments.

Take a look at the chart you created previously in Figure 4-15; once it has been popped out, you can see that a much clearer representation of the underlying data is available. Indeed, to get the full effect of a pop out, it is probably better to see the entire Power View report, as is shown in Figure 4-28.

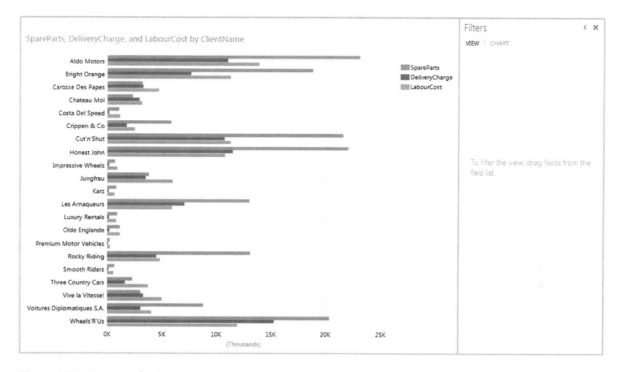

Figure 4-28. *A popout chart*

■ **Note** A popout visualization cannot be saved in its expanded version. A Power View report will always open with all visualizations in their normal state. Interestngly, you cannot delete a chart which is expanded, either.

Chart Filters

Any chart can be filtered to show a subset of the data that you want to display. Fortunately applying filters is easy, as all the filtering techniques are identical to those that I described in the previous chapter. So I will assume that you have already taken a look at Chapter 3, and here I will try and build on the knowledge you have already acquired and explain how it can be used effectively when creating chart visualizations with Power View.

To give a practical example of this, let's take up a point that I made earlier about negative values in pie charts. To avoid giving the idea that negative gross margin is somehow positive, it would be a good idea to display two pie charts that show, respectively, clients where we made money and clients where we lost money in 2013. This is how you can do it:

1. Create a new Power View report and set the report filter to include data for the year 2013 only.

2. Drag the field ClientName from the Clients table onto the report area.

3. Drag the field GrossMargin from the SalesData table onto the table containing the client names.

4. Make this table into a pie chart. You will see the warning that the chart contains negative data, as shown in Figure 4-29.

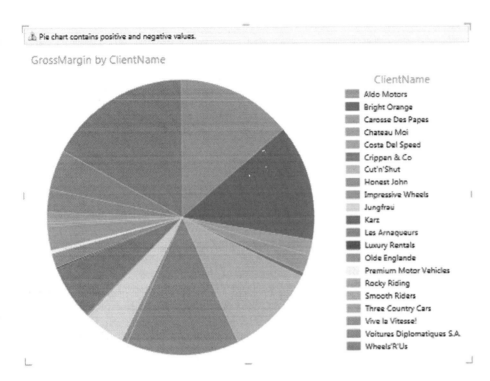

Figure 4-29. A pie chart containing negative values

5. Sort the chart by GrossMargin, in descending order (hover the mouse pointer over the chart and when Sort By ClientName, Asc appears at the top of the chart, click ClientName and Asc to switch them to GrossMargin and Desc).

6. Click inside this chart (but not on any pie segment) and display the Filter pane (unless it is already visible).

7. Click on Chart in the Filters Area, expand GrossMargin, and click on the Advanced Filter Mode icon.

8. From the popup Show Items For Which The Value, select Is Greater Than Or Equal To.

9. From the box under this selection, enter **0** (zero), and press Enter. This will prevent negative numbers from being displayed.

10. Tweak the font size, and resize the chart if you want to, to give it the allure that you prefer.

11. Copy the pie chart and ensure that the copy is selected.

12. Click on Chart in the Filters Area; GrossMargin should be expanded and in Advanced Filter mode.

13. In the popup Show Items For Which The Value in the Filter pane, select Is Less Than 0, and press Enter.

14. Sort the values in the second stacked bar chart by GrossMargin, Ascending (as these are negative values, we want to see the biggest loss-maker first).

15. Tweak the font sizes and adjust the legend position for the second chart.

16. Position the two pie charts on the Power View report.

The report should look like Figure 4-30. I have left a popup visible to remind you that when you have extended data sets, you can always see the exact figures by floating the mouse pointer over a pie segment.

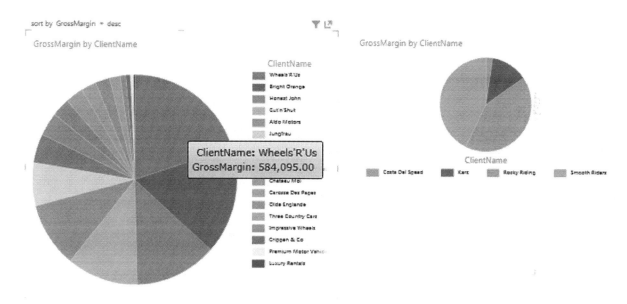

Figure 4-30. *Pie charts with separate filters for each chart*

Data visualization purists are, I imagine, looking at the pie chart of positive sales and muttering that there are too many elements for a single pie chart and that there are too many clients for whom the sales figures are too small to be read easily. I agree, and the solution is to split the pie chart of positive values into two charts: one for major clients, and one for the smaller clients. I will also set the chart of all middle-sized clients to be a bar chart, as there are (in my opinion) too many elements for a pie chart. So, to separate out the clients with sales under 200,000.00 (I came up with this figure by looking at the sales figures in the popup for the pie slices; I chose what seemed to be a good break point between major sales and lower sales figures), we will extend the chart filter used previously to set a filter of upper and lower boundaries for the data in the chart:

1. Click on the initial pie chart for positive sales.

2. Click on Chart in the Filter pane.

3. Change the value for Is Greater Than Or Equal To to **200000**, and press Enter.

4. Copy the initial pie chart for positive sales and ensure that the copy is selected.

5. Convert this chart to a clustered bar chart by selecting Clustered Bar from the Bar Chart button in the Design ribbon. This is to show you that filters are applied independently of the chart type.

6. In the Filter pane for the third (clustered bar) chart, change the value for Is Greater Than Or Equal To to **0**, and press Enter.

7. Click And under the box where you entered the value 0.

8. Select Is Less Than Or Equal To from the second popup.

9. From the box under this selection, enter **200000**, and press Enter.

10. Set the Chart Type to Clustered Column.

11. Tweak the layout of all three charts until you have a telling presentation.

An example of how the data can be filtered to create three separate charts is given in Figure 4-31.

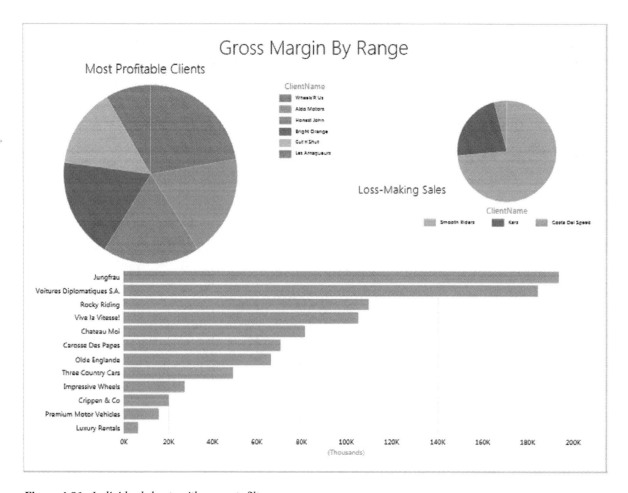

Figure 4-31. *Individual charts with separate filters*

I have jumped ahead slightly here by adding some explanatory text boxes so that the reader can see what each chart is showing. These are explained in Chapter 7 if you want to flip a few pages and find out. However what matters here is that you have seen how to fine-tune individual visualizations so that they display only the data that you want them to show.

Conclusion

The techniques described in this chapter should help you produce a real "wow" effect on your audience. You can now deliver punchy presentations where crisp clear charts help you make your point with definite panache.

We have seen how to create a set of basic chart types (pie charts, bar charts, column charts, and line charts) using one or more data values. We have also seen how to filter charts using the same filtering techniques that you learned previously.

However, charts do not end at this in Power View. There is a further range of more advanced charting possibilities that you can learn to exploit; they are the subject of the next chapter.

CHAPTER 5

■ ■ ■

Advanced Charting with Power View

Now that you have mastered the core skills required to create simple but powerful charts with Power View, the time has come to extend your knowledge and discover some of the more advanced charting possibilities that are open to you. The techniques that we will look at in this chapter are

- Multiple charts

- Scatter charts

- Bubble charts

- Using a play axis to animate charts

These more advanced charting techniques are well worth learning, in my opinion, as they allow you to make your point with greater subtlety and originality. Used effectively, they can enhance considerably the clarity of a presentation and can make your analysis stand out in the crowd.

In this chapter, too, we will be using the sample file CarSales.xlsx from the folder C:\HighImpactDataVisualizationWithPowerBI. How to download the contents of this folder is explained in Appendix A.

Multiple Charts

Teasing out real meaning from a mass of data occasionally requires an approach that goes beyond the traditional charts that you may be used to using. Power View comes to your aid in this area by giving you the possibility of creating multiple charts simultaneously, which can allow you to see individual details and trends as well as comparative distinctions. These types of visualization are also known as trellis or lattice charts.

Multiple chart visualizations, as is the case with single chart visualizations, display and enhance data differently according to the chart type. So, to give you a flavor of what you can achieve using Power View, here are a few examples of multiple chart visualizations using different chart types. This way, you can decide on the type that best suits your data.

Multiple Bar or Column Charts

Let us assume that you want to see a comparative breakdown of dealer sales compared to wholesaler sales, but you want them split into multiple bar charts (which could just as easily be column charts), one for each car age range. This is how you can do it:

1. Insert a new Power View report, or open an uncluttered report, as you will need a certain amount of space for a multiple chart visualization.

2. Create a table using the following fields:

   a. Make (from the CarDetails hierarchy in the SalesData table)

   b. GrossMargin (from the SalesData table)

3. Convert the table to a bar chart (in the Design ribbon, select Bar Chart, then Clustered Bar).

4. Drag the Colour field from the Colours table into the VERTICAL MULTIPLES box in the Design area of the Field List.

5. Apply a filter to include only data for the year 2013 (as described for the initial chart that you can see in Figure 4-1 in the previous chapter).

6. Resize your multiple bar chart visualization, which, as it stands, is probably too small to be really effective.

7. Tweak the font sizes if you want to.

Your Power View report should look something like Figure 5-1. This figure includes the Layout section of the Field List so that you can see what it looks like for a multiple chart visualization.

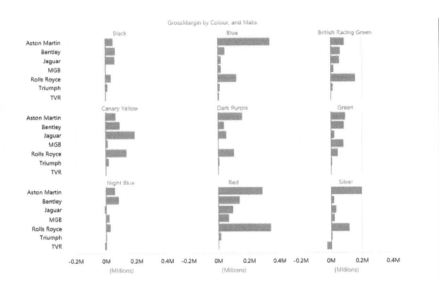
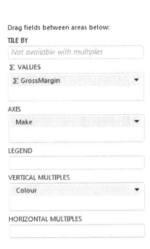

Figure 5-1. *Multiple bar charts*

You will notice that the title of the visualization is now GrossMargin By Color And Make, which draws the viewer's attention to the fact that they are looking at the multiple bar charts as a whole, not as a separate set of unconnected analyses. Also, if you chose to resize the visualization, you will have seen that Power View will not only alter the size of the overall chart "container," but it will also resize the individual charts inside it. However, all the charts inside the outer container will stay the same size.

■ **Tip** There is just one point to add specifically about multiple pie charts. Multiple pie charts can contain slices, just as single pie charts can. So if you place the mouse pointer over a bar chart segment (color) or slice, you will get a popup that gives you the exact details of the data you are examining.

Specifying Vertical and Horizontal Selections

In the previous section you saw how to visualize multiple charts to see how the color and make of a car affected the Gross Margin. Now let's take this one step further, by adding another element of comparison. Suppose that now you want to extend the analysis by adding the car age range to the mix, in order to see if this can tell you anything about your margins and how to improve them.

To do this

1. Click inside the visualization that you made previously (GrossMargin By Color And Make).

2. Drag the field CarAgeBucket into the HORIZONTAL MULTIPLES box of the Design area of the Field List.

And that is it! Your visualization now has colors on the vertical axis on the left-hand side and the age range groups on the horizontal axis across the top. Yet each individual bar chart shows you the gross margin by make for each combination of color and car age group. It should look something like Figure 5-2.

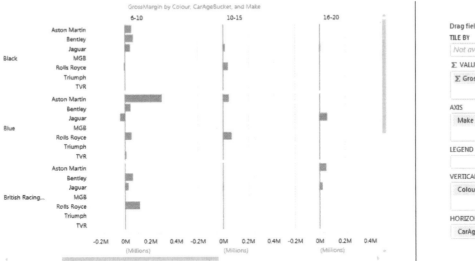

Figure 5-2. *Horizontal and vertical multiple charts*

Power View has added vertical and horizontal scroll bars to the visualization, so you can scroll through the available charts. You can also define the number of charts that are visible, and this is described in the next section.

Specifying the Layout of Multiple Chart Visualizations

In the first multiple pie chart visualization we created, it was Power View that decided how the charts would be set out together—in two rows of three charts. This layout will change depending on the number of charts that are created, which will depend on the source data—specifically the number of elements in the field that you use to define the vertical multiples. However, you can override the default chart layout so you have the final word as to how your multiple charts are displayed.

Creating Horizontal Multiples

First, be aware that if you choose to place the field where the charts will be expanded into multiple charts into the VERTICAL MULTIPLES box, Power View will distribute the charts as best it can. If you add this field to the HORIZONTAL MULTIPLES box instead, then Power View will place all the separate charts in a single row and add a scroll bar to allow you to scroll through the set of "sub" charts that make up the complete visualization. An example of this layout (with the chart type set to column) is given in Figure 5-3.

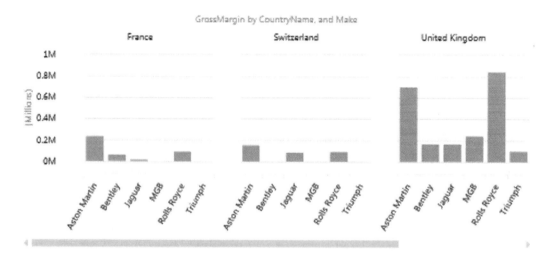

Figure 5-3. *Default use of horizontal multiples*

Defining the Multiples Grid

Depending on the complexity of your individual charts and the density of the information they contain, you may prefer to specify the dimensions of the grid that contains the individual charts in a multiple chart visualization. Put simply, you can set the number of rows and columns that make up the matrix that holds the individual charts. If there are too many charts to be displayed at once, then scroll bars will be displayed to let you navigate, vertically and horizontally, through the set of available charts.

To show you how to define the number of charts that will be displayed at once in each row or column, let us assume that you have created a multiple column chart based on the following data:

- $\sum$ SIZE: GrossMargin

- LEGEND: ClientType

- VERTICAL MULTIPLES: Colour

This chart should look like that shown in Figure 5-4.

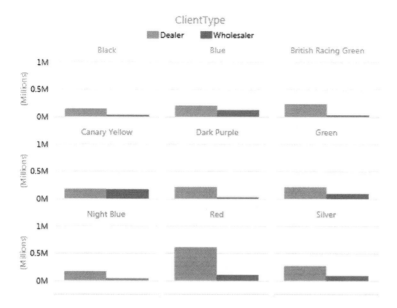

Figure 5-4. *Default use of vertical multiples*

Now, let's alter the layout and tell Power View to show the individual column charts in a 2×2 matrix. To do this

1. Click inside the multiple chart visualization or select it. Remember not to click on an individual column.

2. Switch to the Layout ribbon.

3. Click the Grid Height button and choose 2 from the popup.

4. Click the Grid Width button and choose 2 from the popup.

The visualization will change, and should look like Figure 5-5. As you can see, a vertical scroll bar has appeared to let you scroll down through the set of charts.

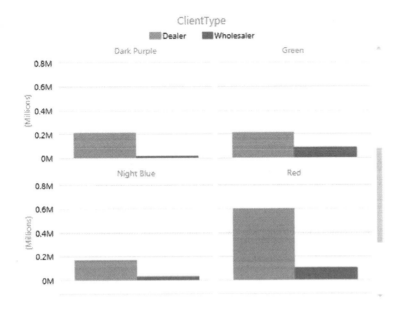

Figure 5-5. *Multiple charts with horizontal and vertical multiples grids set*

If you resize this visualization it will never display more than a 2×2 matrix of charts. You can, of course, alter the number of charts per row or column at any time by selecting a different grid height or grid width.

■ **Tip** An interesting aspect of playing with the grid size for multiple charts is that once you have overridden the default grid and specified the required number of rows and columns, you cannot revert to it later unless you undo the operation immediately. From then on Power View will not automatically try and fit all the charts as best it can in a grid that it decides is best for the number of charts. So once you have "switched to manual," you will have to make all the decisions yourself.

Multiple Line Charts

Adding a visualization that displays multiple line charts is virtually identical to displaying multiple bar or column charts. They too can show several data series. However they are particularly suited to showing how data evolves over time, and so that is what I propose to look at in this example. Anyway, now that you have seen how it is done, it might be worth clarifying the principles before creating the visualization. The process follows these steps:

1. Create the core chart that displays the data that you want repeated across multiple charts.

2. Add the elements that will separate out the charts into multiples—either horizontally, vertically, or both.

3. Set the number of charts in the grid, horizontally and vertically.

4. Resize the chart, adjust any legend, and tweak the font sizes.

To see this, let's create a multiple line chart, showing the average SalesCost and average DirectCosts for all the months in the year. To allow us some insights, we will also compare these figures by client type—dealer and wholesaler.

1. Delete the existing multiple chart visualization, leaving an empty Power View report, filtered to display only data for the year 2013. Alternatively, create a new report.

2. Create a line chart with the following fields:

   a. ∑ VALUES: AverageSalesCosts and AverageDirectCosts

   b. AXIS: CarAgeBucket

   I won't repeat all the instructions again, as it is definitely time for you to try on your own. At this point, you should see a chart like Figure 5-6.

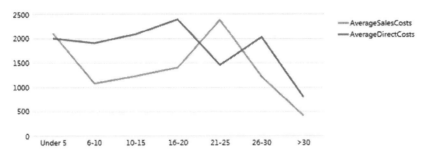

Figure 5-6. *A simple line chart ready for multiples*

3. Drag the MonthFull field from the YearHierarchy in the Date table into the VERTICAL MULTIPLES box.

4. Set the Grid Height to 4 and the Grid Width to 3 in the Layout ribbon.

5. Resize the visualization, and adjust the font sizes for the best effect.

Your visualization should now look like Figure 5-7.

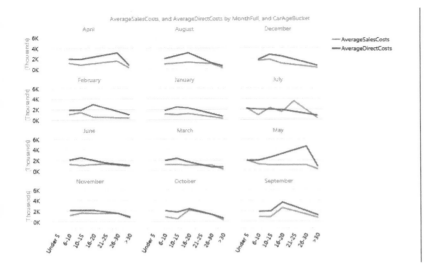

Figure 5-7. *Multiple line charts*

You can switch between all the available bar and column types (clustered, stacked, 100% stacked) and see which type of visualization best gets your insights across to your audience.

Multiple Pie Charts

Multiple pie charts are, in their turn, very similar to multiple bar, line, or column charts.

So let's imagine that you want to look at the cost of spare parts and see if this varies significantly depending on the age of the car; you also want to see these costs in multiple charts by car age group. Here is how it can be done:

1. Delete the existing multiple line visualization leaving an empty Power View report.

2. Create a pie chart with the following fields:

    a. ∑ SIZE: AverageSpareParts

    b. COLOR: QuarterNameAbbr (from the DateHierarchy)

3. Set the legend under the chart (select Show Legend At Bottom from the Layout button in the Design ribbon). You should see a chart like Figure 5-8.

Figure 5-8. *A simple pie chart before setting the vertical multiples*

4.   Drag the CarAgeBucket field from the SalesData table into the VERTICAL MULTIPLES box.

5.   As there are virtually no spare parts sold in the 21-25 bracket, display the Filter pane, and click Chart. Expand CarAgeBucket, check (All), then uncheck 26-30. (This is to remind you about filters; you might not exclude data in such a cavalier fashion in reality).

6.   Resize the visualization, and adjust the font sizes for the best effect.

Your visualization should look like Figure 5-9.

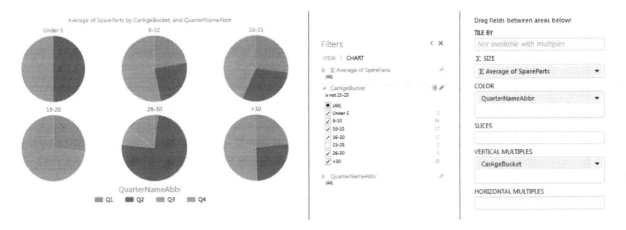

Figure 5-9. *Multiple pie charts with a filter*

Hopefully these examples will give you ideas of how you can use the power of comparative charts—first to analyze and discover the information hidden in your data, and then to present it clearly to your audience. The type of chart that you use will depend on your data, of course, and some data sets are better suited to certain types of presentation. One thing to remember is that multiple charts are inevitably small, and so I really advise you not to overload them with data or you could end up by hiding rather than clarifying your analysis.

Drilling Down with Multiple Charts

One solution to the problem of data overload is to use drill-down with multiple charts just as you did with single charts in Chapter 4. All you have to do to add a drill-down hierarchy to a multiple chart is to add another descriptive element to fields used. Here is a short example:

1.   Create the multiple pie chart example given previously.

2.   Add a VehicleType field to the COLOR box in the Design area of the Field List under the existing QuarterNameAbbr field. The charts in the multiple chart will not change.

3.   Double-click on any pie slice for (say) the age range 6-10 in one of the charts. You will drill down to the vehicle types for that CarAgeBucket.

Your visualization should look like Figure 5-10.

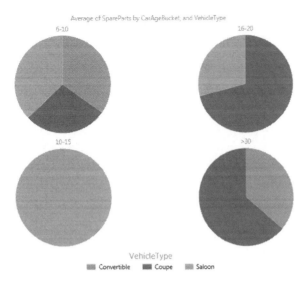

Figure 5-10. *Drill down with chart multiples*

To return to the previous level of the data (the previous set of multiple charts), just click on the Drill Up icon at the top right of the set of multiple charts. The legend (assuming that you have kept one) will indicate the drill-down level that is currently displayed.

■ **Note**   A final thing to note with multiple charts is that the Tile By option is not available. This really interesting feature will be covered in Chapter 6.

Scatter Charts

We are very near the end of our tour of Power View chart types and charting possibilities. What I want to look at now is the penultimate chart type Power View offers—the scatter chart. A *scatter chart* is a plot of data values against two numeric axes, and so by definition, you will need two sets of numeric data to create a scatter chart. To appreciate the use of these charts, let's imagine that you want to see the sales and margin for all the makes and models of car you sold in 2013. Hopefully this will allow you to see where you really made money. Here is how you can do this:

1. Create a new Power View report or go to an existing report with plenty of available space.

2. Set the report filter to include data only for the year 2013, as described previously.

3. Create a table with the following fields from the SalesData table in this order:

    a. Vehicle

    b. GrossMargin

    c. NetSales

4. Convert the table to a scatter chart by clicking Other Chart, then Scatter, from the Design ribbon.

5. Power View will display a scatter chart that looks like the one shown in Figure 5-11. Resize the chart to suit your taste.

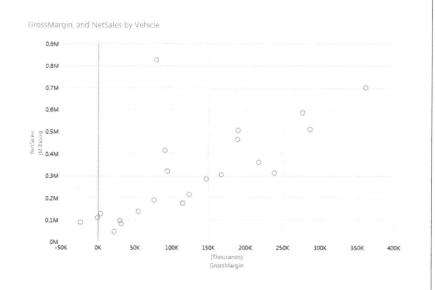

Figure 5-11. *A scatter chart*

If you look at the Design area of the Fields List (which is also shown in Figure 5-11), you will see that Power View has used the fields that you selected like this:

- Vehicle: Placed in the DETAILS box.

- GrossMargin: Placed in the Σ X VALUE box. This is the vertical axis.

- NetSales: Placed in the Σ Y VALUE box. This is the horizontal axis.

If you hover the mouse pointer over one of the points in the scatter chart, you will see, as you are probably expecting by now with Power View, the data for the specific car model.

■ **Note**   By definition, a scatter chart requires numeric values for both the X and Y axes. So if you add a non-numeric value to either the Σ X VALUE or Σ Y VALUE boxes, then Power View will convert the data to a Count aggregation.

We made this chart by adding all the required fields to the initial table first, and we also made sure that we added them in the right order so the scatter chart would display correctly the first time. In the real world of interactive data visualization, things may not be quite this coherent, so it is good to know that Power View is very forgiving, and it lets you build a scatter chart (just like any other chart) step by step if you prefer. In practice this means that you can start with a table containing just two of the three fields that are required at a minimum for a scatter chart, convert the table to a scatter chart, and then add the remaining data field. Power View will always attribute numeric or time fields to the X and Y axes (in the order in which they appear in the FIELDS box) and place the first descriptive field into the DETAILS box.

Once a scatter chart has been created, you can swap the fields around and replace existing fields with other fields from the tables in the data to your heart's content.

You can also add data labels to a scatter chart, just as you did for column charts earlier. However, unless you have very few data points (which rather goes against the raison d'être of a scatter chart in the first place), you may find that data labels just clutter up the visualization.

Drilling Down with Scatter Charts

Scatter charts also let you drill down into the data. For example, to add a second level of analysis to the existing chart, and to see sales and margin by color,

1. Add the Colour field (from the Colours table) to the DETAILS box, under Vehicle. The scatter chart will not alter.

2. Double-click on the data point for Jaguar XK (currently the car achieving the highest sales, and the data point that is near the top of the X axis, above all the others).

The scatter chart will drill down to show the sales and gross margin for this type of vehicle, but by color. This is shown in Figure 5-12.

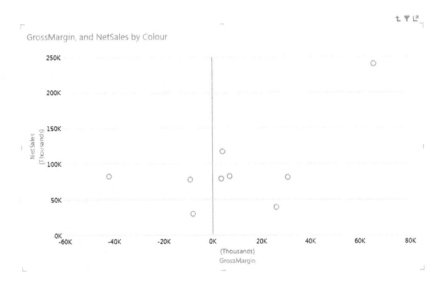

Figure 5-12. *A drill-down scatter chart*

To return to the root level of the data (the initial chart), all you have to do is to click on the Drill Up icon at the top right of the chart.

Scatter Charts to Display Flattened Hierarchies

Scatter charts generically are designed to show many, many data points. This makes them useful in, paradoxically, avoiding the need to drill down through a predefined hierarchy of data. Let's see how to display multiple data sets on one level, rather than drilling down for them. For this to happen, of course, the source data must lend itself to the type of analysis that is required. Fortunately the source data has a field named Vehicle that combines the make and model of each car and that suits this kind of analysis. What you have to do is

1. Create a new Power Pivot report.

2. Add the following fields (in this order) to the Fields List VALUES box:

    a. Vehicle

    b. Colour

    c. GrossMargin

    d. RatioCostToSales

3. Convert the resulting table to a scatter chart (click Other Chart, then Scatter from the Design ribbon, with the table selected).

As you can see in Figure 5-13, every data point appears multiple times, once for every time there is a sale for a different color. Placing the mouse pointer over a data point will let you see exactly which model of vehicle and color is being represented. I have, as you have probably guessed, tweaked the size and display of the chart to show the data in its best light.

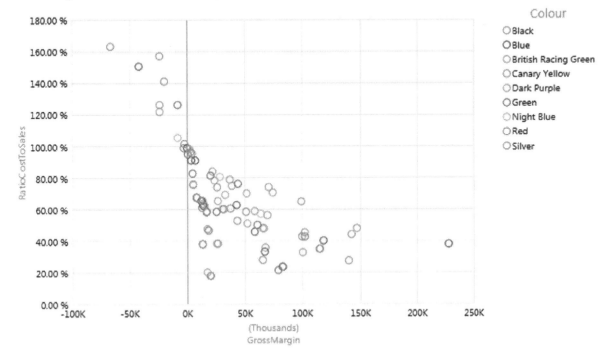

Figure 5-13. *Flattened hierarchies in a scatter chart*

In the case of some scatter charts this technique can make the chart hard to decipher. However, if your scatter chart contains relatively few data points, this technique can be useful. What is more, Power View has the ability to highlight data by the elements that compose the legend; this is explained in Chapter 6.

Scatter Chart Multiples

Scatter charts, just like bar, column, and pie charts, allow you to display the data as multiple charts. Personally, I do not always find them easy to read, but in the interests of completeness (and because all forms of visualization do, after all, depend on the data as well as each user's preferences and taste), here is how to display the sales and gross margin by color.

1. Select the chart that you made previously.

2. In the Design area of the Field List, drag the Colour field from the COLOR box to the VERTICAL MULTIPLES box.

The scatter chart will divide into a series of smaller charts, rather like the example shown in Figure 5-14.

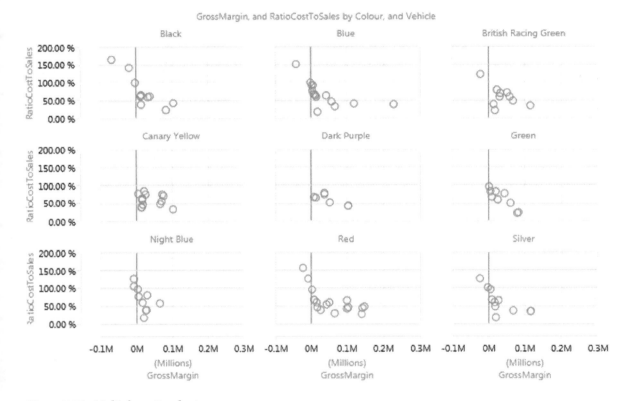

Figure 5-14. *Multiple scatter charts*

You can tailor the display of the grid—the number of charts shown horizontally and laterally—by selecting the required value from the Grid Height and Grid Width buttons in the Layout toolbar, as was described earlier for pie, column, and bar charts.

Bubble Charts

The final chart type available to you in Power View is the bubble chart. This is one of my favorite chart types, though of course you cannot over-use it without losing some of its power. A bubble chart is, essentially, a scatter chart with a third piece of data included. So whereas a scatter chart shows you two pieces of data (one on the X axis, one on the Y axis) a bubble chart lets you add a third piece of information, which becomes the size of the point. Consequently, each point becomes a bubble.

The best way to appreciate a bubble chart is to create one. So here we will assume that you want to look at the following for all makes of car sold in a single chart:

- The Net Sales

- The Net Margin Ratio

- The Gross Margin

Here is how a bubble chart can do this for you:

1. Create a new Power View report or go to an existing report with plenty of available space.

2. Set the report filter to include data only for the year 2013, as described previously.

3. Create a table with the following fields from the SalesData table, in this order:

   a. Make (from the CarDetails hierarchy)

   b. NetSales

   c. RatioNetMargin

   d. GrossMargin

4. Convert the table to a bubble chart by clicking Other Chart, then Scatter from the Design ribbon. Yes, a bubble chart is a scatter chart, with a fresh tweak added.

5. Power View will display a bubble chart that looks like that shown in Figure 5-15. Resize the chart if you need to.

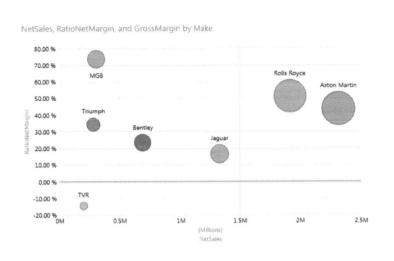

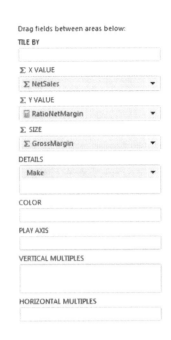

Figure 5-15. *An initial bubble chart*

If you look at the Design area of the Fields List (also shown in Figure 5-15), you will see that Power View has used the fields that you selected like this:

- Make: Placed in the DETAILS box.

- NetSales: Placed in the ∑ X VALUE box. This is the vertical axis.

- RatioNetMargin: Placed in the ∑ Y VALUE box. This is the horizontal axis.

- GrossMargin: Placed in the SIZE box. This defines the size of the points, which have consequently become bubbles.

If you hover the mouse pointer over one of the points in the bubble chart, you will see all the data that you placed in the Fields List Layout section for each make, including the GrossMargin.

Bubble Chart Data Labels and Legend

Apart from the points becoming bubbles, you will notice that a bubble chart automatically displays the data labels. If this is something you wish to remove, than all you have to do is

1. Click in the bubble chart.

2. Select None from the options available when you click on the Data Labels button in the Layout ribbon.

If you want to keep the data labels but alter their position relative to each bubble, then instead of None, you can choose one of the other data label options when you click on the Data Labels button in the Layout ribbon.

If you have chosen not to display the data labels but still need an indication of what element each bubble represents, then add a legend to a bubble chart. This is how:

1. Select the bubble chart.

2. Drag the field used for the DETAILS of the bubble chart to the COLOR box (Make, in this example).

3. Power View will add a legend to your visualization. It should look something like Figure 5-16.

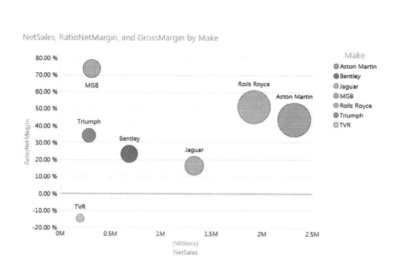

Figure 5-16. *A bubble chart with legend added*

▓ **Note** Be careful not to add the field twice to the Fields List in two different boxes. The trap that awaits the unwary here is that the chart will remain apparently the same. Yet, if you hover the mouse pointer over a bubble, you will see the field that appears in both the DETAILS and COLOR boxes **twice** in the popup.

If you were to add further fields to the DETAILS box (except if it is a field, which is in another box in the Field List as mentioned earlier), then your bubble chart will become a drill-down chart, like any other chart type that we have seen in this chapter. You can double-click on any bubble to drill down and click the Drill Up arrow to return to a previous level, exactly as you have done for other chart types.

Multiple Bubble Elements

Provided that your bubble chart is not already swamped with data points, you may be able to display multiple data elements simultaneously. Imagine that you want to see not only bubbles for each make but also by age range (or age bucket if you prefer) in the same visualization without needing to drill down to a second level in the chart.

This can be done by using a combination of the DETAILS and COLOR boxes in the Layout section of the Fields List. Here is how you can split the existing bubbles into multiple bubbles, while still identifying the make of each car.

1. Click inside the bubble chart that you created previously (or create it exactly as described earlier with the Make field placed in the COLOR box).

2. Add the CarAgeBucket field to the DETAILS box.

3. Click the DataLabels button in the Layout ribbon and select Center.

Your visualization will look like Figure 5-17. As you can see, each bubble has become multiple bubbles, one for each set of cars in each age range. You will see that each car make is always represented in the same color. In this case, a good way to see which age range a bubble represents is to add data labels.

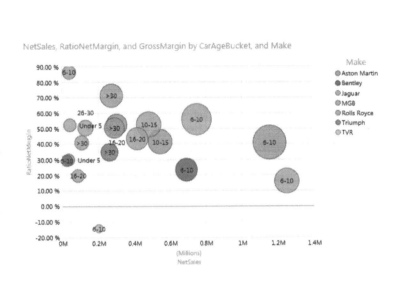
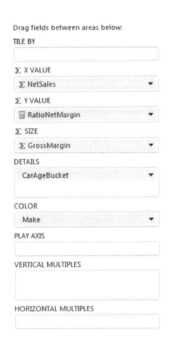

Figure 5-17. *Multiple bubble elements in a bubble chart*

If all this information clutters up your visualization, you can remove the data labels and the legend and only display the Make and CarAgeBucket when you hover the mouse pointer over a bubble.

To remove all the labels and legend

1. Click inside the chart.

2. Click on Layout to activate the Layout ribbon (unless this has already been done).

3. Select DataLabels, None.

4. Select Legend, None.

The bubble chart will look like Figure 5-18 (with a popup visible to show you how to see the details of the data).

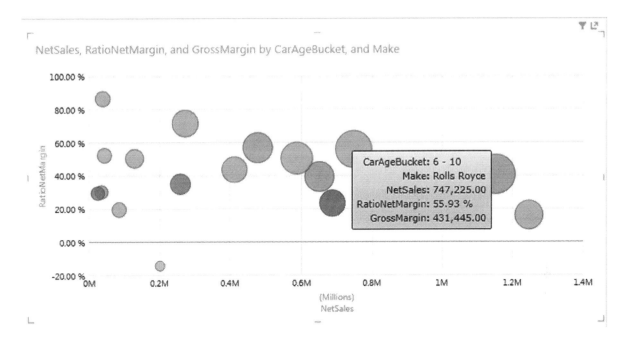

Figure 5-18. *A bubble chart without a legend or data labels*

Bubble Chart Multiples

Bubble charts can adapt well to multiple chart visualizations. I realize that this has been described earlier in this chapter, but I think that it is worthwhile to look at multiples of bubble charts as a separate topic. This will only take a few seconds, in any case. So, to display multiple bubble charts

1. Create (or revert to) the bubble chart as shown in Figure 5-15. This shows

    a. ∑ X VALUE: NetSales

    b. ∑ Y VALUE: RatioNetMargin

    c. SIZE: GrossMargin

    d. COLOR: Make

2. Add CarAgeBucket (also from the SalesData table) to the VERTICAL MULTIPLES box.

3. Select None from the Data Labels button in the Layout ribbon.

4. Adjust the grid height and the grid width if you want or need to, and possibly alter the placement of the legend. The visualization will look something like Figure 5-19.

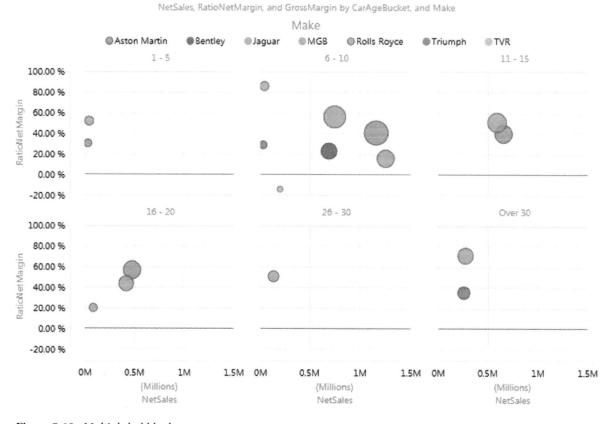

Figure 5-19. *Multiple bubble charts*

Play Axis

So far in this chapter you have seen various ways of presenting data as charts, and how to select, compare, and drill into the data using a variety of techniques. A final trick with Power View, but one that can be extremely effective at riveting your audience, is to apply a play axis to the visualization. This will animate the chart, and ideally, is suited to showing how data evolves over time. It is, unfortunately, harder to get the "wow" effect using these printed pages, so this really is a technique that you will have to try out for yourself.

You need to know that a play axis can only be applied to scatter or bubble charts. Similarly, adding a play axis will not suit or enhance all types of data. However, if you have a time-dependent element that can be added to your chart as the Y axis (such as sales to date, for instance), then you can produce some powerful and revelatory effects.

To close this chapter, then, here is how to create a bubble chart that shows the net margin ratio for colors of car sold against the sales for the year to date:

1. Create a new Power View report, with no report filter this time, so that we can see the years 2012 and 2013.

2. Create a table with the following fields from the SalesData table, in this order:

   a. Colour

   b. SalesYTD

   c. RatioNetMargin

   d. RatioGrossMarginToCost

3. Convert the table to a bubble chart by clicking Other Chart, then Scatter from the Design ribbon. You will not see any bubbles yet, as there is no date element—this element is required for the SalesYTD calculation to return a result.

4. The data fields will be placed in boxes for a bubble chart, but the default is to place the initial field (Colour) in the DETAILS box. As a legend would be useful, drag the Colour field from the DETAILS box to the COLOR box.

5. Adjust the presentation (size, legend placement, data labels, etc.) to obtain the best effect.

6. Drag the QuarterAndYear field from the DateTable (after expanding the YearHierarchy) into the PLAY AXIS box.

The visualization will look like that shown in Figure 5-20.

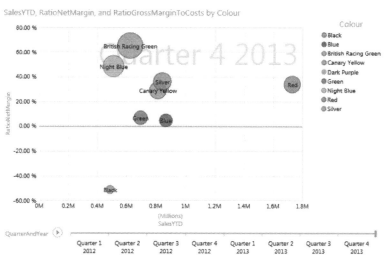

Figure 5-20. *The play axis*

Click on the Play icon to the left of the play axis, and you will see the bubbles reveal how sales progress throughout the year.

There are a few points worth noting about the play axis while we are discussing it:

- You can pause the automated display by clicking on the Pause icon, which the Play icon has become, while the animation is progressing. You can stop and start as often as you like.

- You can click on any month (or any element) in the play axis to display the data just for that element, without playing the data before that point. This essentially means that you can use the play axis as a filter for your data.

- A play axis need not be time-based. However it can be harder to see any coherence or progression in the data if time is not used as a basis for a play axis. As an example, try using NetSales (instead of NetSalesYTD) and CarAgeBucket as the play axis in the visualization that we just created for a play axis example. The data is still visible, but it is probably less indicative of underlying trends.

- You can use a play axis as another interactive filter for your data, but doing this makes you miss out on a fabulous animation technique!

- You cannot add tiles to a visualization that has a play axis.

Tiles with Charts

You can also apply tiles to any chart type (unless there is a play axis). However, this is described alongside the general use of tiles in Chapter 6.

Conclusion

If you apply the techniques that you saw in this chapter, you should be able to create bubble charts, scatter charts, and also multiple chart visualizations using any of the available chart types. You can even animate certain types of chart using a play axis to show how data evolves over time. With this gamut of possibilities at your fingertips, you can, hopefully, take your analysis and presentation skills to a higher level.

CHAPTER 6

■ ■ ■

Interactive Data Selection

In Chapter 3 we saw how to define filters both for Power View reports and for specific visualizations in a report. Filtering data in this way is extremely powerful and is perfectly suited to tweaking your analysis and trying out differing scenarios. However, altering filter elements is not really suitable for the interactive presentations to which Power View lends itself so ideally. When facing your audience you need to be able to deliver your insights in a single click. It probably comes as no surprise to discover that making dynamic selections in a report is part of the DNA of Power View. Learning these approaches is the subject of this chapter.

The other techniques that you can apply above and beyond filters in Power View reports to subset or isolate data have the following characteristics. They are

- Always visible in the Power View report

- Instantly accessible

- Interactive

- Clearly indicate which selections are being applied

So what are the effects that you can add to a Power View report to select and project your data? Essentially they boil down to three main approaches

- Slicers

- Tiles

- Highlighting

These interactive elements can be considered to function as a supplementary level of filtering. That is, they take the current filters that are set in the Filter pane (both at report-level and those tailored to a specific visualization) and then provide further fine-grained selection on top of the data set that has been allowed through the existing filters. Each approach has its advantages and limitations, but used appropriately, each gives you the ability not only to discover the essence of your data, but also to make your point clearly and effectively.

We will see how these three approaches work in detail in the rest of this chapter. In any case—and as is so often the case with Power View—it is easier to grasp these ideas by seeing them in practice than by talking about them, so let's see how tiles, slicers, and highlighting work. This chapter will follow the trend of all the Power View chapters in this book and use the sample file CarSales.xlsx from the folder C:\HighImpactDataVisualizationWithPowerBI.

Tiles

So far we have seen how one or more filters will let you exclude data from an entire Power View report as you make your point about the insights that you have unearthed. Sometimes, however, you may need to provide interactive filtering on the data in a specific visualization (whether it is a table or a chart) without affecting all the other visualizations in a report. This is where tiles come in.

A *tile* is a filter that applies only to a selected visualization. In fact, tiles are "containers" for the visualization. Not only that, but tiles look really cool and can help you review a set of data, item by item, which can make anomalies and essentials stand out in a clear and telling fashion. There are four main ways to add tiles to a visualization, so I will explain all four; then you can decide which you prefer.

Creating a Tiled Visualization from Scratch

When you want to create a visualization, which exists, so far, only in your mind's eye, I suggest that you first try and imagine all aspects of the visualization except the tile elements, and build the "core" visualization. Then all you have to do is add the tiles to enable interactive data visualization. As a starting point you could try the following:

1. Create a table or chart that displays all the fields that you want to display in your Power View report. In this example, I suggest adding Year and MonthFull from the YearHierarchy in the Date Table, and the fields SalePrice and CostPrice from the SalesData table.

2. Drag the ClientName field from the Clients table into the TILE BY box in the Layout section of the Fields List.

That is it; you have a tiled visualization as shown in Figure 6-1.

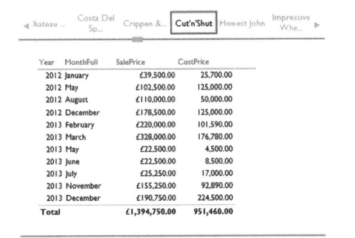

Figure 6-1. *Tiles applied to a table*

Clicking on any tile will filter the visualization to display only data for the selected tile. I suggest that you try clicking on a few of the client names in the tiles to appreciate just how fast Power View displays only the figures for the selected client. For the moment, admittedly, the tiled visualization may look a little cramped, but you will see how to adjust that in the next section.

■ **Tip** When you hover the mouse pointer over the scroll triangle at the left or right of the tile display, it will indicate exactly how many tiles there are and how many are displayed. You may see (2 – 6 / 6) for instance; this tells you that there are six tiles in all, and that you can currently see the second to the sixth.

Adjusting Tile Display

When you add tiles to a visualization, you may not always achieve a perfect display of the data instantly. So be prepared to

- Adjust the dimensions and proportion of the "outer" tile container.

- Adjust the dimensions and proportion of the "inner" visualization.

This is as simple as dragging the handles at the corners or in the middle of the sides of, respectively,

- The outer tile container

- The inner visualization

These elements are outlined in Figure 6-2. As you can see, each has corner and lateral handles and can be resized, and moved, independently.

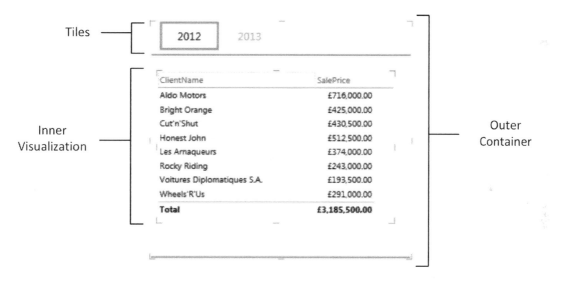

Figure 6-2. *A tiled visualization—container and inner visualization*

When resizing these visualizations, you will soon notice that it is impossible to make the inner visualization larger than the tile container, so you will always have to resize the tile container first. Then you can adjust the inner visualization as a function of its container. Just to make the point, the inner visualization is a standard Power View visualization, and can be fine-tuned using all the techniques that you would use to modify a table or chart that was not part of a tile view.

Some Variations on Ways of Creating Tiled Visualizations

You just saw one way of creating tiled visualizations. There are, however, several other ways of achieving this objective. Indeed, you have quite a variety of choices. In any case, here are some of the other techniques that you could use, if you so choose.

Creating a Tiled Visualization from Scratch—Another Variant

An alternative to the technique we just discussed is to create a visualization, probably as a simple table, that also contains the field that will be used for the tiles. Providing that the field destined to become the tiles is the *first* field in the Field List, you can create a tiled visualization with a single click. Assuming, then, that you have created a table with the following fields in this order

- The ClientName field from the Clients table

- The YearHierarchy from the Date Table

- The SalePrice field from the SalesData table

all you have to do is

1. Click on the Tile button in the Power View Design ribbon.

This approach will take the first field in the visualization as the tile element and give you a "tiled" visualization using the ClientName field as the basis for the tiles. However, unfortunately, Power View will leave this field in the visualization as well, which makes it redundant in most cases. So, presuming that you do not want to display this information twice,

1. Click on the popup menu for the first field in the FIELDS box in the Fields List Layout section (ClientName in this example).

2. Select Remove Field.

The field will be removed from the visualization but remain in the tiles above the visualization.

Adding Tiles to an Existing Visualization

If you have created a visualization already, and all that you want to do is add a layer of interactive filtering specific to this visualization, all you have to do is drag the field that will be used for the tiles into the TILE BY box in the Layout (upper) section of the Field List. To see this, let's extend the use of tiles to charts. Here, we will revise the process of creating a chart and then extend it by adding tiles.

1. Create a table using the fields Colour (from the Colours table) and GrossMargin (from the SalesData table).

2. Convert this table to a Clustered Bar chart.

3. Add the CarAgeBucket field to the TILE BY box in the Design (lower) area of the Field List.

4. Resize the chart. This could involve adjusting the size of both the inner chart itself and the outer container that displays the tiles as was explained previously.

The chart will look something like the one in Figure 6-3. If you prefer, an alternative to dragging a field to the TILE BY box is to select the chart, then click on the popup menu for the field that you want to tile by in the Field List, and select Add As Tile By.

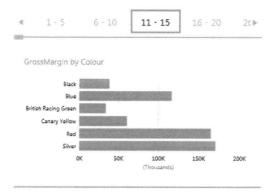

Figure 6-3. Adding tiles to a bar chart

Adding Tiles to an Existing Visualization—Another Variant

If you have created a visualization already that contains the fields that you wish to use for the tiles, then you can

1. Drag the field that will be used for the tiles from the ROWS (or possibly COLUMNS) box into the TILE BY box in the Layout section of the Field List.

Once again you have created a tiled visualization, but without the duplicate data this time.

Modifying an Existing Visualization Inside a Tile Container

Once you have added tiles to a visualization, you can alter the inner visualization in any of the ways that you learned in previous chapters. Put simply, you can

- Add and remove data fields

- Switch from table to chart and vice versa

- Change table types from table to matrix to card

- Alter the chart types

- Switch between card styles

All this only goes to show that a tiled visualization is only a standard visualization wrapped inside a selection container.

Re-creating a Visualization Using Existing Tiles

Once you have built a tile-based visualization, you may decide that the tiles are perfect but that the "inner" visualization needs a total revamp. After reaching this conclusion, you may even decide that a complete rebuild of the "inner" visualization is necessary because simply adding or removing a field and altering the visualization type is harder than starting over.

So, to delete and re-create the visualization inside a tile container, simply

1. Click on or inside the inner visualization (the chart or table).

2. Press the Delete key. You will be left with a disconcertingly empty outer tile container, as seen in Figure 6-4.

Figure 6-4. The outer tile container

3. Drag the fields that you want to use as the basis for the new tiled visualization inside the existing tile container.

4. Modify the style of visualization as described in previous chapters.

This way you can fill the container with a new visualization.

■ **Tip** What is important to remember is that the outer container remains completely independent of the inner visualization. Consequently, you can tweak, or change completely, the inner visualization without altering the outer container.

Re-creating a Visualization Using Existing Tiles—A Simple Variant

Another way to re-create a visualization inside an existing tile container is as follows:

1. Ensure that the Tile visualization remains selected.

2. Drag the fields on which you want to base your visualization into the FIELDS box in the Design area of the Field List on the right.

3. Modify the style of visualization as described in previous chapters.

You will notice that, in the Design area of the Field List on the right, the TILE BY box has remained populated with the choice of tile field. Consequently you do not need to modify this—unless, of course, you decide to alter the field that supplies the data to the tiles themselves.

Removing Tiles from a Visualization

Tiles do not always suit every type for visualization, or indeed every data set. So you may well end up deciding that the tiles that you have applied to a table or chart are just not appropriate and need to be removed, but you want to leave the rest of the visualization in place. To do this

1. Select the tile-based visualization from which you want to remove the tiles.

2. Display the Field List, unless it is already visible.

3. Drag the field currently in the TILE BY box of the Field List Design area out of the Design area and back into the Field List. A cross on the field that you are dragging away will indicate that this tile field is the one that will be deleted.

Once the field used to add the tiles has been removed from the TILE BY box in the Design area, then the tiles will also be removed from the visualization. Remember that if you have made a mistake, a quick Ctrl-Z will restore the tiles to their former glory.

If you attempt to delete tiles by dragging the Tile By field anywhere other than back into the Field area (the upper part of the Field List), then a warning icon, as shown in Figure 6-5, will appear to alert you to the fact that the field cannot be dragged anywhere but to specific areas.

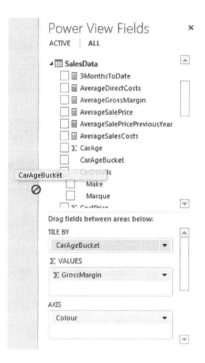

Figure 6-5. *The warning icon that appears when you attempt to remove a Tile By field*

As an alternative solution, you can click on the popup triangle to the right of the field in the Field List that is used to tile by and select Delete Field. This, too, will remove the tiles from the visualization.

Deleting a Tile Visualization

Despite your efforts, it may simply turn out that tiles are not suited to the kind of data, analysis, or presentation that you are making. So you may need to remove a tiled visualization completely (that is both the container and its content):

1. Click inside the tiled visualization but outside the inner table or chart (or whatever the visualization is).

2. Press the Delete key.

The tile-based visualization will disappear in its entirety—though, of course, a rapid click on Undo in the Power View ribbon (or Control-Z) will restore it instantly.

Tile Types

When you first add tiles to a visualization, the default is to apply a set of tiles above the inner visualization. Power View calls this the Tab Strip tile type. However, there is a second tile type available—Tile Flow. To switch between the two types of tile

1. Ensure that a tiled visualization is selected.

2. In the Design ribbon, click the Tile Type button and select Tile Flow.

To switch back to the Tab Strip tile type

1. Ensure that a tiled visualization is selected.

2. In the Design ribbon, click the Tile Type button and select Tab Strip.

The differences between the two types of tile are purely visual, and are described in Table 6-1. An example of a Tile Flow is given in Figure 6-6.

Table 6-1. *Tile Types*

Tile Type	Position	Comments
Tab Strip	Top of visualization	Displays a set of identically sized tiles above the visualization
Tile Flow	Bottom of visualization	Displays a carousel of tiles beneath the visualization

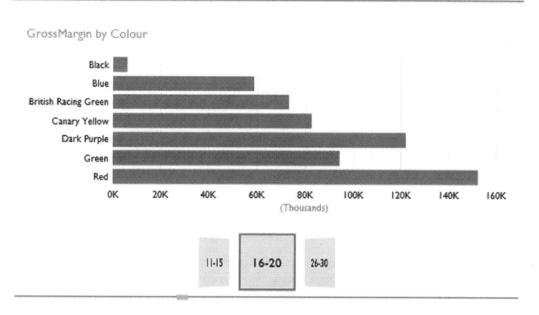

Figure 6-6. *Tiles once a filter has been applied*

Using Tiles

Given that tiles are a selection tool, all you have to do to apply filtering based on a tile is to click on the relevant tile. This tile will then be displayed in boldface, and the data visible in the inner visualization will be filtered so that only data for the selected tile will be displayed.

Unless all the elements in a set of tiles can be displayed at once, you will have to scroll through the tile set. Whatever the tile type (Tab Strip or Tile Flow), you will see a scroll bar at the bottom of the tile set. Sliding this left or right will scroll through the tile set.

A Tab Strip tile set also has scroll icons at the right and left of the tiles. Clicking on these will cause the tile set to scroll in the direction of the scroll icon. You will notice that Power View does not jump from tile to tile, but moves fluidly through the tile set. A Tile Flow tile set, however, does not have scroll icons at the right and left of the tiles. Clicking on any tile will cause that tile to move to the center of the tile set.

■ **Note**   You cannot select multiple tiles simultaneously, no matter what type of tile you are using.

Filtering Tiles

A tiled visualization is essentially just another visualization. Consequently, it too can have a visualization-level filter applied. For instance, suppose that you want to reuse the initial tiled chart from Figure 6-3, earlier in this chapter, but you only want to display some of the car age ranges. Here is how this can be done.

1.   Click inside the inner (chart) visualization—anywhere except on a bar in the chart.

2.   Click Chart in the Filters pane.

3. In the Design ribbon, click the Tile Type button and select Tile Flow (unless you have already done this).

4. Expand the filter CarAgeBucket.

5. Select the following elements:

   a. 11-15

   b. 16-20

   c. 26-30

You will see that the tiles also only display the elements that you selected. In most cases this means a reduced number of tiles in the tile set. For this to work, by the way, the option Show Items With No Data described in the following section must not be activated. The result of this process is shown in Figure 6-6.

Tiles with No Data

One point of note is that a tile set will, by default, not contain any elements for which there is no data available. At times you may want tiles to be displayed, even if they have no relevant data, possibly to make the point that nothing was sold. If this is your wish, then you can try out the following example:

1. Create a new Power View report.

2. Add the following fields:

   a. ClientName from the Clients table

   b. SalePrice from the SalesData table

   c. The Year field from the Date Table

3. Drag the Year field from the FIELDS box to the TILE BY box.

4. In the Layout section of the Field List, click on the popup option for the Year field in the TILE BY box.

5. Select Show Items With No Data.

This will cause the tiles to contain every element to be displayed from the field that you are using to tile by—even if there is no data for this selection. Initially, when you created this visualization, you did not see a tile for 2014. Once Show Items With No Data was selected, the year 2014 appeared in the tiles. The before and after effects of this choice are shown in Figure 6-7.

Default Tiles

Tiles With The Option "Show
items with no data" selected

Figure 6-7. *The effects of selecting Show items with No Data*

■ **Note**   Remember that the items in the tiles are filtered by any view filters, Table, Matrix, or Chart filters, and Slicers, which are active in the report. So if you modify any of these, you could see the items making up the tiles change dramatically. Indeed, you could remove all the existing tile elements and replace them with a completely different set, if the filters and slicer(s) that you have applied exclude the existing tile items. If this happens (and there are no common tile items shared between the filters that you switch from and the new filters that you apply), then Power View will default to selecting the first tile in the set.

Changing the Inner Visualization

You can change the visualization that is inside a tile container at any time, just as you would change it if it were a stand-alone visualization. For instance, to switch the chart from a bar chart to a pie chart (using the example that you saw earlier in Figure 6-5), all you have to do is

1. Click on the inner chart visualization.

2. Click Other Chart, then Pie in the Design ribbon.

As you can see from Figure 6-8, only the chart type has altered and the tiles have remained unchanged. So you can flip between chart and table visualizations and switch chart types independently of the tiles in place.

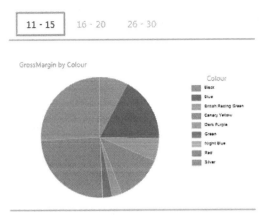

Figure 6-8. *Pie chart using tiles*

Tiles and Multiple Charts

Tiles can be added to any chart as they can to any table. The only restriction is that tiles cannot be added to charts if the chart has horizontal or vertical multiples. You will have to decide which of the two approaches you prefer to use.

Tiles can be a perfect use for images. This, along with other uses for images, is described in Chapter 7.

■ **Tip**   As a final comment on tiles in Power View, it is interesting to remark that tiled visualizations cannot be *popped out*, that is, expanded to allow for a more detailed view.

Slicers

Another form of interactive filter is the slicer. This is, to all intents and purposes, a standard multiselect filter, where you can choose one or more elements to filter data in a report. The essential difference is that a slicer remains visible on the Power View report, whereas a filter is normally hidden. So this is an overt rather than a hidden approach to data selection. Moreover, you can add multiple different slicers to a Power View report and consequently slice and dice the data instantaneously and interactively using multiple criteria. Slicers can be text-based, or indeed, they can be simple charts, as you will soon see.

Adding a Slicer

To appreciate all that slicers can do, we need to see one in action. To add a slicer

1. From the Power View Fields pane (which you need to display if it is hidden), drag the field name that you want to use as a slicer to an empty part of the report. In this example I am using the CarAgeBucket field from the SalesData table. Power View creates a single column table.

2. Click the Slicer button in the Design ribbon. The table becomes a slicer.

3. Adjust the size of the slicer to suit your requirements using the corner or lateral handles. Power View will add a vertical scroll bar to indicate that there are further elements available, or a horizontal scroll bar if the text is truncated.

You can recognize a slicer by the small squares to the left of each element in the list. This way you know that it is not just a single-column table. Figure 6-9 shows a slicer using the CarAgeBucket field from the SalesData table.

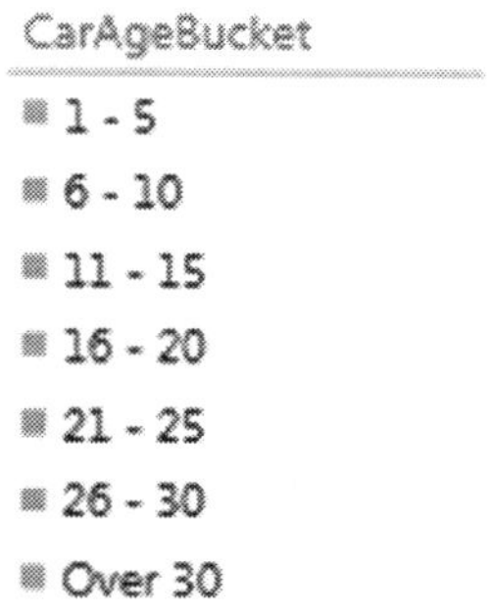

CarAgeBucket

▪ 1 - 5

▪ 6 - 10

▪ 11 - 15

▪ 16 - 20

▪ 21 - 25

▪ 26 - 30

▪ Over 30

Figure 6-9. *A slicer*

■ Note   If the Slicer icon is greyed out, then check that the table that you are trying to convert to a slicer only has one column (that is, one field in the FIELDS box of the Layout area of the Field List).

You can create multiple slicers for each view. All you have to do is repeat steps 1 through 3 for adding a slicer using a different field as the data for the new slicer.

When you start applying slicers to your Power View reports you will rapidly notice one important aspect of the Power View filter hierarchy. A slicer can only display data that is not specifically excluded by a view-level filter. For instance, if you add a Color filter at view level, and select only certain colors in this filter, you will only be able to create a slicer that also displays this subset of colors. The slicer is, in fact, dynamic, and will reflect the elements selected in a view-level filter. Consequently adding or removing elements in a filter will cause these elements to appear (or disappear) in a slicer that is based on the same field.

■ Note   You cannot, however, apply a filter specifically to a slicer. You can see this if you click on a slicer and then look at the Filters Area. There is no visualization-level filter available (you cannot see Table, Chart, Matrix, or Slicer to the right of the word Filter at the top of the Filter pane). In addition, if you applied a table-level filter to a single column table before you converted it to a slicer, the filter would be removed, and all the field elements would be displayed in the slicer, including those previously removed by the table-level filter.

Applying a Slicer

To apply a slicer and use it to filter data in a view

1.   Click on a single element in the slicer, or Shift-click (or Ctrl-click) on multiple elements.

All the objects in a Power View report will be filtered to reflect the currently selected slicer list. In addition, each element in the slicer list that is active (and consequently used to filter data by that element) now has a small rectangle to its left, indicating that this element is selected. The color of this rectangle is dictated by the Power View theme that is applied, but this is described in more detail in Chapter 7.

Figure 6-10 shows what happens when the slicer defined for Figure 6-8 is applied to the tiled visualization shown in Figure 6-7.

Figure 6-10. Applying a slicer

When you apply a slicer, think filter. That is, if you select a couple of elements from a slicer based on the CountryName field, as well as three elements based on the Color fields, you are forcing the two slicers (filters) to limit all the data displayed in the view to two countries that have any of the three colors that you selected. The core difference between a slicer and a filter is that a slicer is always visible—and that you have to select or unselect elements, not ranges of values.

If you experiment, you will also see that you cannot create a slicer from numeric fields in the source data. A slicer has to be based on a text field. If you need slicers based on ranges of data, then you will need to prepare these ranges in the data model. The CarAgeBucket field is an example of this, and Chapter 7 explains how to add these sorts of fields to a data model.

▓ **Tip**   You can (if you Shift-click or Ctrl-click on all the elements in a slicer) unselect all the data it represents. This will not, however, clear the Power View report. Unselecting everything is the same as selecting everything—despite the fact that the selection squares are no longer visible to the left of each element in the slicer.

Clearing a Slicer

To clear a slicer and stop filtering on the selected data elements in a view

1.   Click the Clear Filter icon at the top right of the slicer. This icon is pointed out earlier in Figure 6-10.

Any filters applied by the slicer to the view are now removed. You will see that each element in the slicer list now has a small rectangle to its left, indicating that this element is not selected. As this is the same thing as saying that all of the elements are selected, no data is filtered out of the report.

▧ **Tip**   Another technique to clear a slicer completely is to Shift-click (or Ctrl-click) the last remaining active element in a slicer. This will leave all elements active. So, in effect, removing all slicer elements is the same as activating them all.

Deleting a Slicer

To delete a slicer and remove all filters thatwhich it applies for a view

1.   Select the slicer and press the Delete key.

Any filters applied by the slicer to the view as well as the slicer itself are now removed. Another technique to delete a slicer is to select the slicer and then, in the Power View Fields pane, click on the popup triangle to the right of the field name toward the bottom of the pane. Then select Remove Field, and the slicer will disappear.

You can even copy and paste slicers if you wish. Although, since modifying a slicer is virtually impossible, this is largely only useful when you are copying slicers across different Power View reports.

Note that if you intend to use the field that was the basis for a slicer in a table or chart you do not need to delete the slicer and re-create a table based on the same underlying field. You can merely

1.   Select the slicer.

2.   Click on the Table button in the Design ribbon, and select the type of table (table, matrix, or card) to which you want to convert the slicer.

The instant that a slicer becomes a table, it also ceases to subset the data in the Power View report.

Modifying a Slicer

If all you want to do is replace the field that is used in a slicer with another field, then it is probably simplest to delete the slicer and re-create it.

▧ **Note**   When you save an Excel workbook containing Power View reports with active slicers, the slicer is reopened in the state in which it was saved.

Using Charts as Slicers

We have seen previously how a table can become a Slicer, which is, after all, a kind of filter. Well, charts can also be used as slicers. Knowing how charts can affect the data in a Power View report can even influence the type of chart that you create, or your decision to use a chart to filter data, rather than a standard slicer. Charts can be wonderful tools to grab and hold your audience's attention—as I am sure you will agree once you have seen the effects that they can produce.

Charts as Slicers

To begin with, let's see how a chart can be used to act as a slicer for all the visualizations in a Power View report. Initially, let's assume that we are aiming to produce a report using two objects:

- A table of Net Margin by Color
- A column chart of Net Sales by Make

I will start with the table of Net Margin by Color. This will principally be used to show the effect using a chart as a slicer in a Power View report has on other objects.

1. Create a new Power View report. You will need a whole uncluttered report for this example.

2. Filter the report to display only data for 2013, as described in the previous chapter.

3. Add a table based on the following fields:

   a. Colour (from the Colors table)

   b. NetMargin (from the SalesData table)

4. Add a bar chart based on the following fields:

   a. Make (from the SalesData table)

   b. NetSales (from the SalesData table)

5. Adjust the layout of the two visualizations so that it looks something like Figure 6-11. This includes sorting the bar chart by NetSales, in descending order.

Figure 6-11. *Preparing a chart for use as a slicer*

Now let's see how to use a chart as a slicer.

1. Click on any column in the chart of NetSales by Make. I will choose Jaguar in this example.

The Power View report will look something like Figure 6-12.

Colour	NetMargin
Black	36,450.00
Blue	-40,375.00
British Racing Green	38,263.00
Canary Yellow	75,700.00
Dark Purple	14,276.00
Green	-920.00
Night Blue	-12,550.00
Red	84,603.00
Silver	26,150.00
Total	**221,597.00**

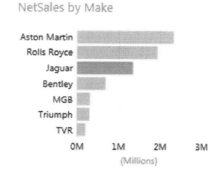

Figure 6-12. *Slicing data using a chart*

You will see that not only is the make that you selected highlighted in the chart (and the bars for other makes are dimmed), but that the figures in the table also change. They, too, only display the net margin (for each color) for the selected make.

To slice on another make, merely click on the corresponding column in the column chart. To cancel the effect of the chart acting as a slicer, all you have to do is click for a second time on the highlighted column.

Any bar chart, pie chart, or column chart can act like a slicer in this way. The core factor is that for a simple slice effect, you need to use a chart that contains only one axis; that is, there will only be a single axis in the source data and no color or legend. What happens when you use more evolved charts to slice, filter, and highlight data is explained next.

■ **Tip**   It is perfectly possible to select multiple bars in a chart to highlight data in the same way that you can select multiple elements in a slicer.

Highlighting Chart Data

So far we have seen how a chart can become a slicer for all the visualizations in a report. However, you can also use another aspect of Power View interactivity to make data series in charts stand out from the crowd when you are presenting your findings. This particular aspect of data presentation is called *highlighting*.

Once again, highlighting is probably best appreciated with a practical example. So, first we will create a stacked bar chart of costs by CountryName; then we will use it to highlight the various costs inside the chart.

1. In a new Power View report (so you do not get distracted), create a clustered column chart based on the following fields:

    a. CountryName

    b. DeliveryCharge

    c. SpareParts

    d. SalesCosts

    e. LabourCost

2. Click on SalesCosts in the legend. All the sales costs will be highlighted (that is, remain the original color) in the column for each country, whereas the other three costs will be grayed out.

The chart, after highlighting has been applied, will look like Figure 6-13.

DeliveryCharge, SpareParts, SalesCosts, and LabourCost by CountryName

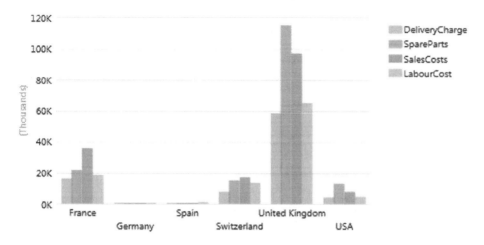

Figure 6-13. *Highlighting data inside a chart*

To remove the highlighting, all you have to do is click a second time on the same element in the legend. Or, if you prefer, you can click on another legend element to highlight this aspect of the visualization instead. Yet another way to remove highlighting is to click inside the chart, but not on any data element.

Highlighting data in this way should suit any type of bar or column chart as well as line charts. It can also be useful in pie charts where you have added data to both the COLOR and SLICES boxes, which, after all, means you have multiple elements in the chart just as you can have with bar, column and line charts. You might find it less useful with scatter charts.

Cross-Chart Highlighting

Cross-chart filtering adds an interesting extra aspect to chart highlighting and filtering. If you use one chart as a filter, the other chart will be updated to reflect the effect of selecting this new filter not only by excluding any elements (slices, bars, or columns) that are filtered out, but also by showing the proportion of data excluded by the filter.

As an example of this, create a pie chart of net sales by color and a column chart of sales costs by vehicle type. We will then cross-filter the two charts and see the results. The steps to follow are

1. Create a pie chart using the following fields:

    a. Colour

    b. NetSales

2. Create a (clustered) column chart using the following fields:

    a. VehicleType

    b. SalesCost

For charts that are this simple Power View will automatically attribute the fields to the correct boxes in the Field List once the source tables are converted into charts. The result is shown in Figure 6-14.

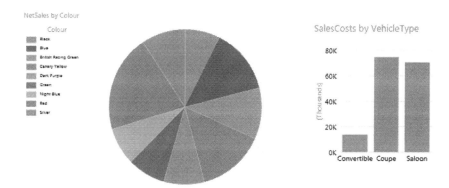

Figure 6-14. *Preparing charts for cross-chart highlighting*

Now click on the largest slice in the pie chart (or the legend element: Blue). You should see the result given in Figure 6-15.

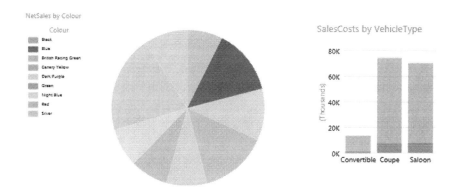

Figure 6-15. *Cross-chart highlighting*

Not only has the pie chart been updated to show the filter effect that it produces, but the bars in the bar chart have been highlighted to show the proportion of the selected color of the total sales cost per vehicle cost.

Now click on the bar in the bar chart corresponding to the vehicle type Convertible. You are now using the bar chart as a slicer. As you can see (the output is given in Figure 6-16) the pie chart displays the proportion of convertible sales for each color.

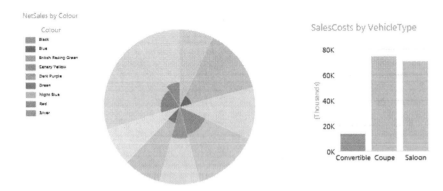

Figure 6-16. *Cross-chart highlighting applied to a pie chart*

■ **Note**   When you use a filter you will not highlight a chart but will actually filter the data that feeds into it—and consequently, you will remove elements from the chart.

Highlighting Data in Bubble Charts

Often when developing a visualization whose main objective, after all, is to help you to see through the fog of data into the sunlit highlands of comprehension, profit, or indeed, whatever is the focus of your analysis, you may feel that you cannot see the forest for the trees. This is where Power View's ability to highlight data in a chart visualization can be so effective.

Let's take a visualization that contains a lot of information; in this example, it will be a bubble chart of vehicle types. Indeed, in this example, an audience might think that there is so much data that it is difficult to see the bubbles for specific makes of car, and so analyze the uniqueness for sales data by make. Power View has a solution to isolate a data series in such a chart. To see this in action, and to make the details clearer

1.   Create a bubble chart using the following elements:

   a.   ∑ X VALUE: RatioNetMargin

   b.   ∑ Y VALUE: SalePrice

   c.   ∑ Y SIZE: NetSales

   d.   DETAILS: Colour

   e.   COLOR: VehicleType

2.   In the legend for the chart where you wish to highlight the data for one element (the make of car in our example) click on a vehicle type. I will use saloon in this example.

The data for this vehicle type is highlighted in the chart, and the data for all the other vehicle types are dimmed, making one set of information stand out. This is shown in Figure 6-17.

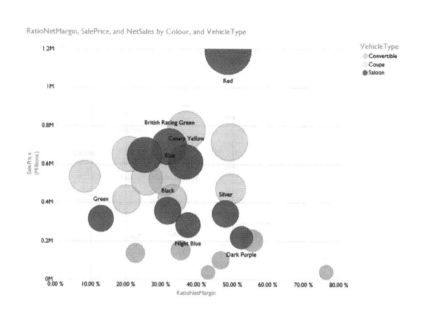
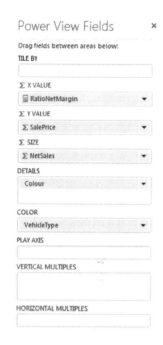

Figure 6-17. *Highlighting data in bubble charts*

This technique needs a few comments:

- To highlight another data set, merely click on another element in the legend.

- To revert to displaying all the data, click again on the selected element in the legend.

- Highlighting data in this way will also filter data in the entire report. The filter effect is described in detail in Chapter 5.

■ **Tip**   You can add drill-down to charts and still use chart highlighting in exactly the same way as you would use it normally. The chart will highlight an element at a drill-down sublevel normally as well as apply filtering to the Power View report.

Charts as Filters

Now that you have seen how charts can be used as slicers, let's take things one step further and see them used as more complex filters. To show this, I will build on the principles shown in the previous example, but add a bubble chart that will filter on two elements at once.

To make this second chart, I

1.   Build a Power View report which has

a.   A matrix of net margin by CountryName and Color

b.   A chart of net sales by Make

2. Create a bubble chart using the following data:

    a. ∑ X VALUE: NetMargin (from the SalesData table)

    b. ∑ Y VALUE: NetSales (from the SalesData table)

    c. SIZE: SalePrice (from the SalesData table)

    d. DETAILS: CountryName (from the Countries table)

    e. COLOR: Colour (from the Colors table).

3. Resize and tweak the bubble chart so that it is displayed under the existing column chart and table.

4. Click on one of the bubbles in the bubble chart (Blue in this example). The Power View report should look like Figure 6-18.

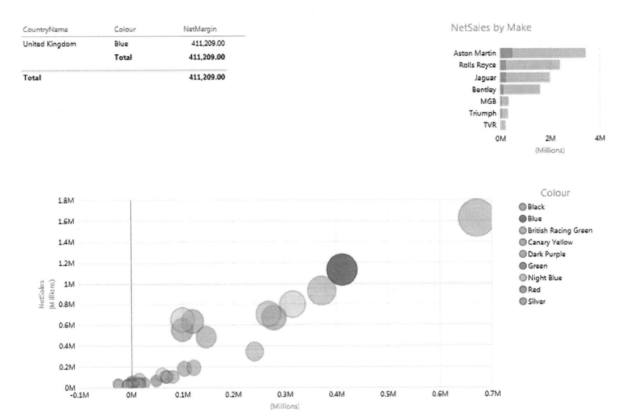

Figure 6-18. *Highlighting and filtering using a chart*

You can see that the other visualizations are filtered so that both the elements that make up the individual bubble (CountryName and Colour) are used as filters (or double-slicers if you prefer to think of them like that). This means that

- The table only shows colors where there are sales for this country and this color.

- The chart highlights data for this country and this color as a percentage of the total for each make.

As was the case with simple chart slicers, you can cancel the filter effect merely by clicking for a second time on the selected bubble. Or you can switch filters by clicking on another bubble in the bubble chart. You will also see the chart itself has data highlighted, but this is explained a little further on.

Clearly, you do not have to display the fields on which you are filtering and highlighting in all the visualizations in a report. I chose to do it in this example to make the outcome clearer. In the real world, all other visualizations in a report will be filtered on the elements in the DETAILS and COLOR boxes of the bubble chart.

Bubble charts are not, however, the only chart type that lets you apply two simultaneous filters. All chart types will allow this. However, I am of the opinion that some charts are better suited than others to this particular technique. Specifically, I am not convinced that line charts are always suited to being used as filters for a Power View report, and that scatter charts may work—visually, that is—but it is just as likely that they will not.

To show this in action, the following sections give examples of how to use the following as chart filters:

- Scatter charts

- Clustered column charts

- Clustered bar charts

Scatter Chart Filtering

As a scatter chart is virtually identical to a bubble chart (except for the third data value used to add the size of the bubbles), it follows that a scatter chart can also be used as a filter.

To see this in action, it is probably easiest to create the Power View report described earlier with the following three elements:

1. A matrix of net margin by Color.

2. A bar chart of net sales by Make.

3. A scatter chart using the following data:

   a. ∑ X VALUE: NetMargin (from the SalesData table)

   b. ∑ Y VALUE: NetSales (from the SalesData table)

   c. DETAILS: CountryName (from the Countries table)

   d. COLOR: Colour (from the Colours table)

The net result should look virtually identical to the bubble chart, except that the bubbles are now small points. If you now click on a point in the scatter chart, you will see something like Figure 6-19.

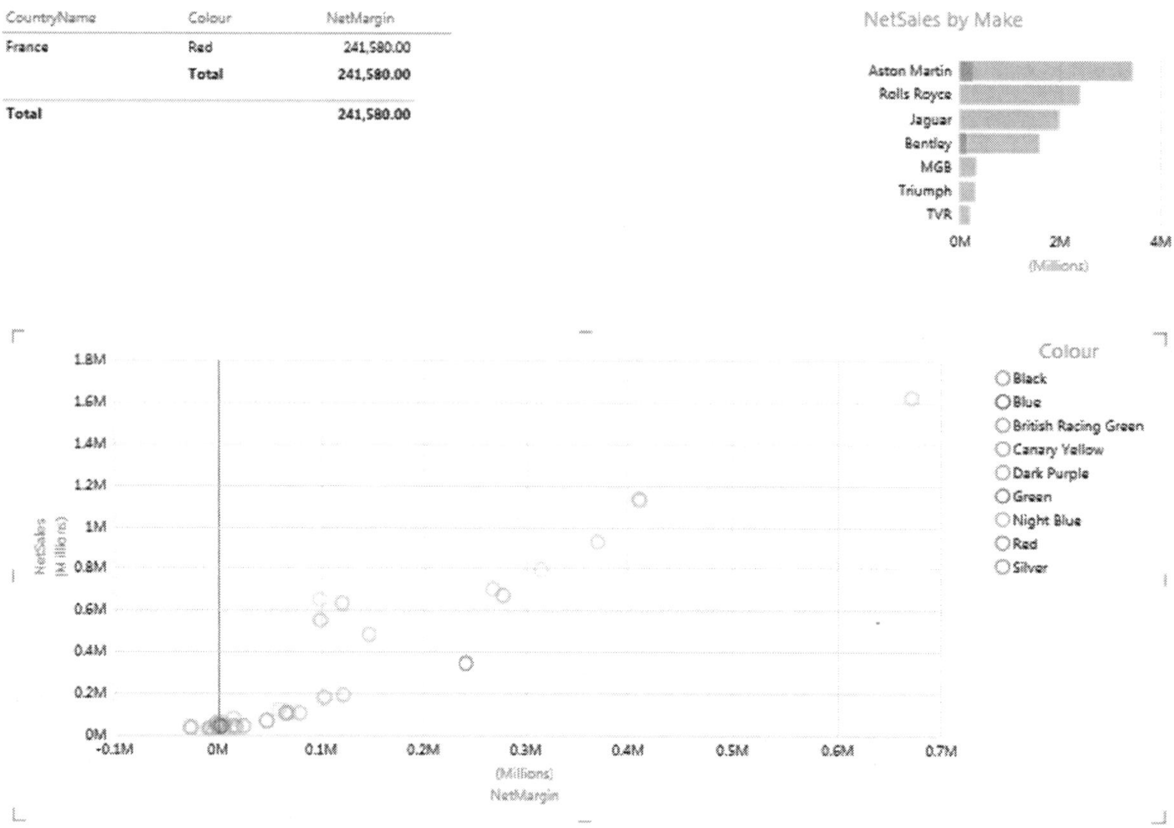

CountryName	Colour	NetMargin
France	Red	241,580.00
	Total	241,580.00
Total		241,580.00

Figure 6-19. *Scatter chart filtering*

I would suggest that using scatter charts to filter the rest of the report is slightly less intuitive, as it is harder to see exactly what you are filtering on, given that the points are so small that they make the colors hard to distinguish. Nonetheless, it certainly works! Of course, you can always hover the mouse pointer over a data point to see from the popup which elements you will be filtering on.

Column and Bar Charts as Filters

Column charts and bar charts can also be used to filter a Power View report on two elements simultaneously. The only limitation is that you can only have one set of numeric data as the $\sum$ values for the chart. If the bar or column chart is a stacked bar, then you can click on any of the sections in the stacked bar. In addition, if the chart is a clustered bar or column, you can click on any of the columns in a group to slice by the elements represented in that section.

If this limitation is not a problem, then here is how you can use bar or column charts (whether they are clustered, stacked, or 100% stacked) to apply double filters to a report.

1. Create a Power View report with the following two elements:

    a. A table based on color, country name, net sales, net margin, and cost price.

    b. A bar chart of net sales by CountryName.

2. Then create a stacked column chart using the following data:

    a. Σ VALUES: NetMargin (from the SalesData table)

    b. AXIS: CountryName (from the Countries table)

    c. LEGEND: CarAgeBucket (from the SalesData table)

Once tweaked to clarify the appearance of the chart, the net result should look like Figure 6-20.

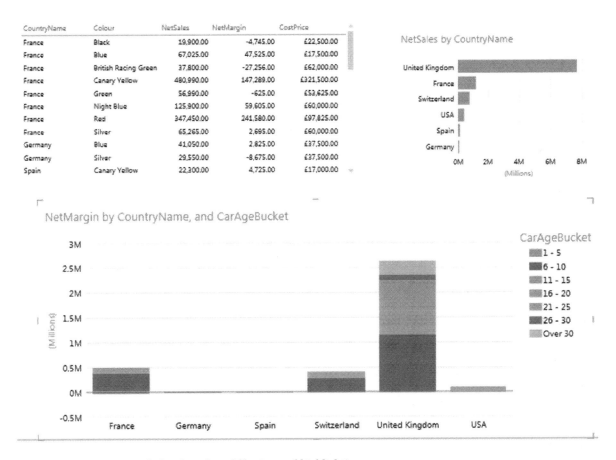

Figure 6-20. *A Report ready for chart-based filtering and highlighting*

Clicking on any segment of a bar will filter and highlight other visualizations on the same report for that country and car age range. An example of this is given in Figure 6-21, where the car age range of 6-10 has been selected for the United Kingdom bar.

CountryName	Colour	NetSales	NetMargin	CostPrice
United Kingdom	Black	386,900.00	47,032.00	£331,090.00
United Kingdom	Blue	619,925.00	211,815.00	£391,100.00
United Kingdom	British Racing Green	324,775.00	206,364.00	£113,400.00
United Kingdom	Canary Yellow	457,474.99	53,407.99	£388,290.00
United Kingdom	Dark Purple	404,550.00	142,594.00	£251,290.00
United Kingdom	Green	312,100.00	122,630.00	£180,200.00
United Kingdom	Night Blue	343,950.00	82,270.00	£251,290.00
United Kingdom	Red	683,250.00	259,583.00	£401,790.00
United Kingdom	Silver	250,050.00	24,925.00	£218,600.00
Total		3,782,974.99	1,150,620.99	£2,527,050.00

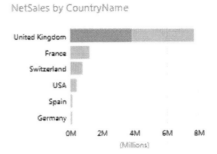

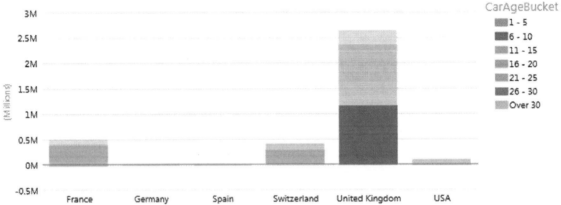

Figure 6-21. Applying filters and highlights

Clicking on any car age range in the legend will filter by car age range only. You can see this in Figure 6-22.

CountryName	Colour	NetSales	NetMargin	CostPrice
France	Night Blue	82,325.00	35,675.00	£42,500.00
France	Red	225,950.00	145,030.00	£74,325.00
France	Silver	29,550.00	-8,675.00	£37,500.00
Germany	Blue	41,090.00	2,825.00	£37,500.00
Germany	Silver	29,550.00	-8,675.00	£37,500.00
Spain	Green	39,300.00	1,075.00	£37,500.00
Spain	Red	29,550.00	-8,836.00	£37,500.00
Switzerland	Black	144,450.00	91,300.00	£48,200.00
Switzerland	Blue	104,125.00	65,125.00	£35,000.00
Switzerland	Canary Yellow	119,800.00	81,575.00	£37,500.00
Switzerland	Dark Purple	38,550.00	-1,887.00	£37,500.00

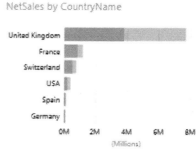

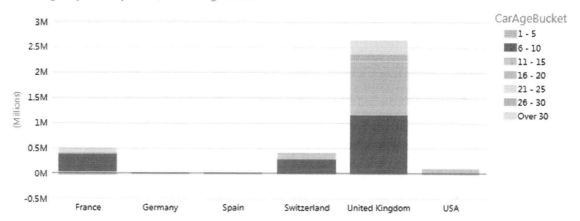

Figure 6-22. *Filtering using a legend element*

So in fact, you can choose to filter on a single element or multiple elements, depending on whether you use the chart or the legend as the filter source. It is interesting to note, finally, that if you have added tiles to a chart, then the tiles will only filter the chart itself and reduce the available possibilities for further slicing and highlighting. The choice of tile will not affect other visualizations on the same report directly.

■ **Note** A line chart will not produce the same effect, however. If you click on a series in a line chart, you are highlighting that series, which is numeric data, and so it cannot be used as a slicer. Similarly if you click on an element in the legend of a column or bar chart, you are selecting data series, and this, too, cannot serve as a slicer (even though it will highlight the series in the chart).

Choosing the Correct Approach to Interactive Data Selection

Now that you have taken a tour of the interactive options that Power View offers, it is worth remembering that there is a fundamental difference between slicers and chart filters and tiles:

- Slicers and chart filters apply to the entire Power View report.
- Tiles only affect to the visualization to which that are applied.
- Highlighting will only apply to the selected chart, although it will filter data in other tables and highlight the percentage of this element in other charts.

Filter Granularity

It is worth noting that tiles do not override filters or slicers. They simply apply a further selection at an even lower level of granularity—that of a single visualization. So remember that you could be, in effect, applying the following filters (in the order in which they are given):

- View filter
- Visualization filter
- Slicer
- Tile

This is probably best explained with an example. I propose to create a simple Power View report that will contain all of these elements. It will take a few steps to complete, but if you follow this exercise all the way through, you should certainly not only understand the hierarchy of filtering in Power View, but also be able to handle slicers and tiles with ease.

So, this is what you have to do, beginning with creating the report filter even before adding any visualizations:

1. Create a new Power View report by selecting the Insert ribbon in the Excel workbook containing the CarSales data and subsequently clicking Power View (or by clicking Power View in the Power View ribbon).

2. Display the Field List by clicking Field List in the Power View ribbon (unless it is already visible).

3. In the Field List, expand the Date table.

4. In the Date table, expand the Year Hierarchy.

5. Drag the Year field into the Filters Area (if this is not visible, click Filters Area to display it).

6. Adjust the slider endpoints so that only the years 2012 and 2013 are selected.

We will now create a table that will display costs and sales by client.

7. Drag the ClientName field from the Clients table into the Fields section of the Field List.

8. Drag the CostPrice and SalePrice fields from the SalesData table into the Fields section of the Field List.

We will now add a filter to the table only.

9. Click inside the table which was created in steps 7 through 9.

10. In the Filters area, click "Table".

11. Drag the ClientType field from the Clients table into the filter area.

12. Select the "Dealer" element. This will only show clients who are dealers.

To prove the points about which filters apply to which elements, we need a visualization that will have no filters applied specifically to it, nor any tiles applied. I suggest a simple column chart of sales by country.

13. Click inside the Power View report canvas outside the table that you just created (ensuring that no visualization is selected).

14. Drag the CarAgeBucket field from the SalesData table onto the Power View report.

15. Drag the CostPrice field onto the list of car age ranges that you just created in step 14.

16. In the Design ribbon, click the Column Chart button and select Clustered Column.

The table will become a column chart. Now we will move from filters to interactive selections, adding a slicer first.

17. Click inside the Power View report outside the visualizations that you just created (ensuring that no visualization is selected).

18. Drag the CountryName field from the Country table onto the Power View report.

19. Click Slicer in the Design ribbon. The table of countries becomes a slicer.

Finally we will add tiles to the table of client sales.

20. Select (or click inside) the table that you created in steps 7 through 9.

21. In the Field List, drag Color from the Colors table to the TILE BY box.

And that is it! At the highest level, you have selected only data for 2012 and 2013. Then you filtered the table so that it will only display dealer data. This filter does not apply to the chart. Then you added a country slicer. Selecting one or more countries will affect both the table and the chart; however, selecting an item from the tiles applied to the table will have no effect on the chart. For a final confirmation of how Power View filters data, try clicking on one of the chart columns, and you will see that this too will filter the data elsewhere in the report, complementing both the filters and the slicer selections.

Assuming that all went well—and after, perhaps, a little tweaking to make things look good in Power View—you should have a report that looks something like Figure 6-23.

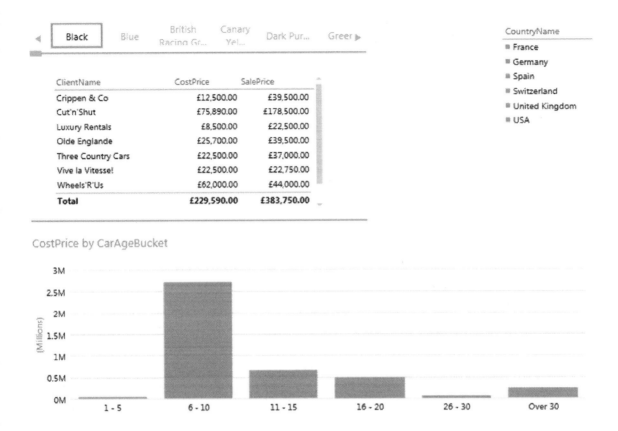

Figure 6-23. *A filtered report ready for slicing, filtering, and tile-based selection*

Now try slicing and highlighting. I will click United Kingdom in the slicer, click the column for the car age range 11-15, and then choose the color Red from the tiles in the table. The result is shown in Figure 6-24.

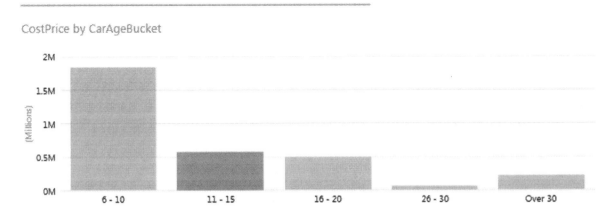

	Blue	British Racing Gr...	Red	Silver		CountryName

ClientName	CostPrice	SalePrice
Bright Orange	£62,000.00	£178,500.00
Cut'n'Shut	£125,000.00	£110,000.00
Total	**£187,000.00**	**£288,500.00**

CountryName
France
Germany
Spain
Switzerland
▓ United Kingdom
USA

CostPrice by CarAgeBucket

Figure 6-24. Slicing, filtering, highlighting, and tiles applied

Believe me, this is just the start of what you can do. In a single click, you can change the country you are slicing the data on. You can examine each car age range in turn, or out of sequence. Then you can see dealer sales by car color, and then cycle through the colors.

Conclusion

In this chapter you have seen how to use the interactive potential of Power View to enhance the delivery of information to your audience. You saw how to add slicers to a report, and then how to use them to filter out data from the visualizations it contains. Then you saw how to add tiles to any table or chart to select a subset of data with a single click. Finally, you learned how to highlight data in charts and tables using charts to isolate specific elements in a presentation.

So all that remains is for you to start applying these techniques using your own data. Then you can see how you too can impress your audiences using all the interactive possibilities of Power View.

CHAPTER 7

■ ■ ■

Images and Presentation

After spending a little time working with Power View, let's assume that you have analyzed your data. In fact, I imagine that you have been able to tease out a few extremely interesting trends and telling facts from your deep dive into the figures—and you have created the tables and charts to prove your point. To finish the job, you now want to add the final touches to the look and feel of your work so that it will come across to your audience as polished and professional.

Fortunately Power View is on hand to help you here, too. It can propel your effort onto a higher level of presentation—without you needing to be a graphic artist—so that your audience is captivated. With a few clicks you can

- Add and format a report title.

- Apply a report background.

- Change the color scheme and fonts used in a report (which, taken together, are called the *theme* of a report).

- Alter the font used in a report.

- Add free-form text and annotations (or text boxes in Power View speak).

- Add images (which Power View calls pictures) to a report.

- Use images in tables.

- Use image-based slicers.

- Apply images to tiles.

This chapter will take you through these various techniques and explain how to use them to add real pizzazz to your analysis. We will use the CarSales.xlsx file as the source data and also the image files, which you can download to the folder C:\HighImpactDataVisualizationWithPowerBI\Images from the Apress web site, as described in Appendix A.

Titles

Let's begin at the start. You have spent quite a while digging into data and have found effective ways of drawing your audience's attention to the valuable information that it contains. However, you need the one, final, cherry on the cake—a title for the report.

Adding a Title

Adding a title is so easy that it takes longer to describe than to do, but nonetheless, here is how you do it:

1. Click in the section at the top of the report with the helpful label Click Here To Add A Title.

2. Type in an appropriate title. I have entered 2013 Key Sales Data.

3. Click outside the title anywhere in the blank report canvas.

Figure 7-1 shows you a before and after snapshot of a title added to a report. Moreover, should you want to modify a title, it is as easy as clicking inside the title box and altering the existing text. You can find this example in C:\HighImpactDataVisualizationWithPowerBI\PVPresentation.xlsx.

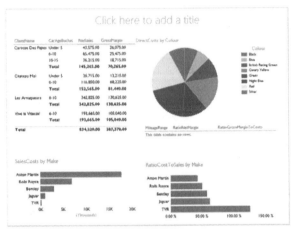

Initial
Report

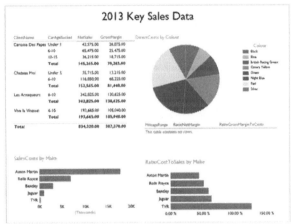

Report with
Title

Figure 7-1. *Adding a title to a report*

Moving and Resizing Titles

Titles are a Power View visualization like any other, and consequently, they can be moved and resized just as if they were a table or a chart. So all you have to do to move a title is to

1. Hover the mouse pointer over the title. The corners and centers of the title box will appear.

2. Place the mouse pointer over the edges of the title box and drag the title to a new position.

To resize a title (should this ever be necessary)

1. Hover the mouse pointer over the title. The corners and centers of the title box will appear.

2. Place the mouse pointer over either the corner or lateral central indicators of the title box and drag the mouse to resize the title box.

Formatting a Title

The title of a Power View report can be formatted specifically so that you can give it the weight and power that you want. To give the title some emphasis

1. Hover the mouse pointer over the title and select the title box (or select the text of the title).

2. Activate the text ribbon, unless it is already active.

3. Select the text attributes that you wish to modify. These are described in the next section.

The aspects of a title that you can change are

- Font

- Font attribute (bold, underline, italic)

- Font size

- Alignment (horizontal and vertical)

■ **Note**   If you really do not want a title and you don't want the Power View prompt Click Here To Add A Title to be visible, then you can delete a title just like you can delete a text box. This is described shortly.

The Text Ribbon

As its name suggests, the text ribbon allows you to modify text display in Power View. It is specifically used with text boxes, such as the title box that we just saw, or free-form text boxes that are explained in the next section.

The buttons available in the text ribbon are described in Figure 7-2.

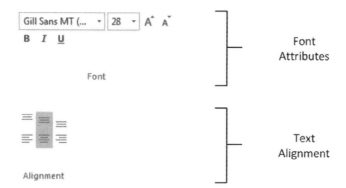

Figure 7-2. *The text ribbon*

Note that you cannot enter a font size; you have to select a size from those available in the font size popup list. You also cannot change the color of the title. The options available for text modification are described in Table 7-1.

Table 7-1. *Text Ribbon Options*

Text Option	Description
Font	Lets you choose the font to apply from those installed on the computer
Font size	Allows you to select a font size from those in the list
Increase font size	Increases the font to the size of the next available size in the list of font sizes
Decrease font size	Decreases the font to the size of the next available size in the list of font sizes
Bold	Switches the font to boldface
Italic	Switches the font to italic
Underline	Underlines the selected text
Align top	Aligns the text at the top of the text box
Align middle	Aligns the text in the middle (horizontally) of the text box
Align bottom	Aligns the text at the bottom of the text box
Align left	Aligns the text at the left of the text box
Align center	Aligns the text in the center (vertically) of the text box
Align right	Aligns the text at the right of the text box

Adding Text Boxes to Annotate a Report

Now that we have seen how to add and modify a title, it is probably a good time to extend the knowledge acquired to the close relative of the title—the text box. A *text box* is a floating text entity that you can place anywhere inside a Power View report. They are especially useful for annotating specific parts of a presentation. To add a text box

1. Switch to the Power View ribbon, unless it is already active.

2. Click on the Text Box button. A new text box is added to the report, and the text cursor will flash inside this box.

3. Type in the text you want to add. I entered **Clear Market Leader** in this example.

4. Click outside the text box, preferably in an empty part of the report canvas, to finish.

5. Move and resize the text box to produce the effect you are looking for.

Figure 7-3 shows a text box added to a chart visualization.

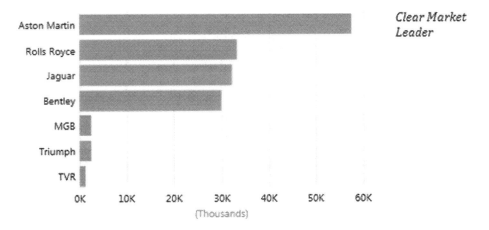

Figure 7-3. *Adding a text box*

A text box can be moved and resized exactly as a title can. Consequently, I will not explain this again; just go back a couple of pages to the section called "Moving and Resizing Titles."

The text inside a text box can be formatted as well. Here, too, the steps to take are identical to those you follow when formatting a title. So once again, just flip back a couple of pages, and it is all explained.

■ **Tip**   Remember that you can highlight only part of the text if you want to format only one or two words. If you select the text box itself, then you will be formatting all the text in the text box.

Deleting Text Boxes

If you want to delete a text box, then be sure to

1.   Hover the mouse pointer over the text box until you see the corner and lateral handles.

2.   Select the text box.

3.   Press the Delete key.

■ **Note**   Merely selecting and deleting the text inside the text box will not remove the text box itself; so to be sure that you do not leave any unnecessary clutter in a report, delete any unwanted and empty text boxes.

The Context Menu

Although we have not mentioned it so far, there is a context menu available when you use Power View. This menu is particularly useful when you are adding the final tweaks to a report, so now is probably a good time to look at what it can do. Right clicking on any visualization, text or image, in a Power View report will display the menu shown in Figure 7-4.

Figure 7-4. *The context menu for visualizations*

If you click on the canvas of a Power View report (that is outside any existing visualization), you will see a slightly different context menu. This is shown in Figure 7-5.

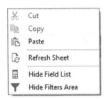

Figure 7-5. *The context menu for reports*

The two available context menus are largely similar. The available options in the context menus are outlined in Table 7-2.

Table 7-2. *Context Menu Options*

Menu Option	Context Menu	Description
Cut	Visualization/Canvas	Removes the selected visualization, text, or image and places it in the clipboard
Copy	Visualization/Canvas	Copies the selected visualization, text, or image to the clipboard
Paste	Visualization/Canvas	Adds the selected visualization, text, or image from the clipboard
Refresh sheet	Visualization/Canvas	Updates the data for the current Power View report
Bring to front	Visualization	Lets you move the selected visualization, text, or image to the top, or forward, above/in front of any others
Send to back	Visualization	Lets you move the selected visualization, text, or image to the bottom, or backward, below/behind any others
Hide/show field list	Canvas	Hides the Field List if it is visible, displays it if it is not
Hide/show filters area	Canvas	Hides the Filters Area if it is visible, displays it if it is not

■ **Note** The Cut, Copy, and Paste options are visible but not accessible in the context menu for the Power View canvas.

Altering the Font Used in a Report

If you work in a corporate environment, then you probably have to follow enterprise guidelines on presentation. Even if this is not the case, you may have preferences when it comes to the choice of fonts that you use. In any case, Power View will let you choose the font used in a presentation. The things that you can change are

- Font Family
- Font Size

Font Family

To change the font used in an entire Power View presentation (that is in every Power View report in an Excel workbook), this is all that you have to do:

1. Switch to the Power View tab (unless it is already active).
2. Click on the downward-facing triangle to the right of Font in the Themes section.
3. Select the font that you wish to apply from those available.

Literally the only thing to remember is that this will affect every Power View report in an Excel workbook. Changing the font this way will not, however, override any font settings made to a specific text box using the font ribbon.

Text Size

You can also change the proportional text size in an entire presentation. Now I really mean *proportional*. Remember that when we created individual tables and charts we set the size of the text in each visualization—at least relative to the other visualizations since we could not set exact font sizes? Well, this can be overridden at the level of the entire presentation, where you can proportionally increase or decrease the size of the text in every visualization, whether it is a table, a chart, or a text box.

To do this

1. Switch to the Power View tab (unless it is already active).
2. Click on the downward-facing triangle to the right of Text Size in the Themes section.
3. Select the proportional text size from those available.

■ **Note** This can produce some quite devastating results and can render a report—or indeed an entire presentation—unreadable. So it is probably best if you use it at an appropriate stage in the creation process, and *before* you have spent valuable time tweaking individual visualizations to get them to appear exactly the way that you want them.

You cannot enter a specific percentage for the text size and have to restrict your choice to the selection on offer. Currently you can choose between

- 200%
- 175%
- 150%

- 125%

- 100%

- 75%

Altering the Theme of a Report

Power View understands that you may not have a lot of time to spend on the presentation of your report. Consequently, many of the visual aspects of a report work using a few simple, yet sophisticated, preset values. Central to these is the notion of the report theme. Basically, what you do is choose a set of colors and fonts from a palette that Power View offers, and the software does the rest.

Rather than discuss the theory, I propose seeing themes in action. So, to apply a theme to a Power View report, whether it is a blank report or an existing one, this is what you do:

1. Click on the Themes button in the Power View ribbon, the available themes will appear in a scrollable list, as shown in Figure 7-6.

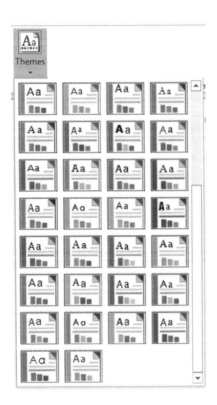

Figure 7-6. *The available themes in Power View*

2. Select a theme by clicking on it.

Yes, it really is as simple as it sounds. However, as the changes can be very subtle, you may not see much change to begin with. What you have probably noticed (assuming that your Power View report has a table, a couple of charts, and a slicer, like the Power View sheet StylesExample in the example workbook entitled PVPresentation.Xlsx) is that the following have changed:

- The **font** used in the entire report—tables, charts, titles, slicers—everything!

- The **color** used as a principal highlight. You will see it change in the line under table titles and above totals as well as in the bullets to the left of slicer items, for instance.

- The **palette of colors** used by charts. This is the basis for bars, columns, pie slices, bubbles, and lines.

- The **report background**.

As an example, Figure 7-7 shows the Power View sheet StylesExample from the sample workbook with the Concourse theme applied.

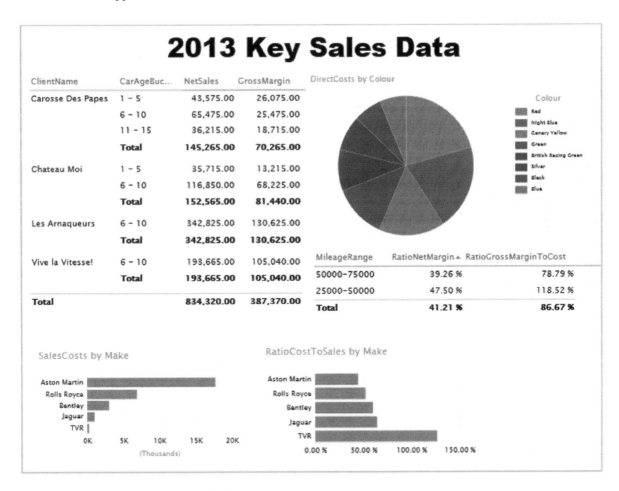

Figure 7-7. *The theme Concourse applied to a Power View report*

Although the color change is not immediately obvious in a book printed in black and white, the change of font family is clear, as is the modification of the font size. In fact, I had to resize the matrix and pie chart very slightly, as well as the column widths in the matrix and table, to achieve an optimum presentation. So, to avoid lots of last-minute retweaking of your reports, I advise you to to decide on a theme earlier rather than later in your creative cycle.

▓ **Note** You have 46 presentation styles to choose from, so the best advice that I can give is that you spend some time trying them out. This way you will see which one is best suited to your presentation style and the type of information that you are delivering.

Deciphering Themes

Testing out the available themes can be great fun, but it does not have to be a process based entirely on trial and error. This is because each image of a theme in the Themes list is, in fact, a preview of what it contains. Each tiny image of a theme indicates the display elements, which are explained in Table 7-3.

Table 7-3. *Themes*

Theme Element	Description
Dark Background Color	The color applied to the canvas if the dark background is selected
Light Background Color	The color applied to the canvas if the light background is selected
Highlight Color	The color used as bullets for slicer elements and general highlighting, as well as being the color used when chart highlighting is applied
Font	The font that will be applied
Chart Color 1	The first color in the chart color palette
Chart Color 2	The second color in the chart color palette
Chart Color 3	The third color in the chart color palette

Exactly how these elements are contained in a theme image is explained in Figure 7-8.

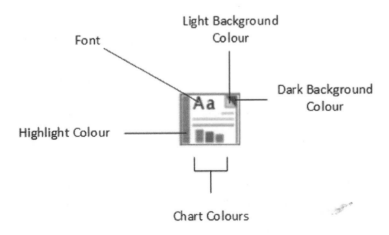

Figure 7-8. *Theme Elements*

The chart color scheme does not stop with three colors, of course, but the colors given in the theme image give you a pretty good idea of the palette that will be used by the theme you have chosen.

If, or hopefully, when, you become a regular user of Power View, you may find that you frequently want to use the same themes over and over. This can, of course, provide consistency and an impression of coherence to your reports. So rather than having to remember that the last time you used the "second column third row" theme in the popup list of themes, it is probably easier to try and remember the theme name. To see a theme name:

1. Hover the mouse pointer over a theme image in the Themes popup, as shown in Figure 7-9.

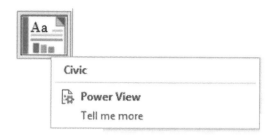

Figure 7-9. *The theme name*

2. If you cannot remember which theme you used, then look closely at the theme images in the Themes list. An active theme has a subtle border around it to indicate that it is selected. An example of this is shown in Figure 7-10.

Figure 7-10. *The active theme*

The themes are in alphabetical order in the Themes menu. They flow from left to right, and the first two rows rejoice in the names Theme 1, Theme 2, and so on.

■ **Note**   If you add a theme to a report containing a slicer, then the slicer will adopt the highlight color from the theme for the square to the left of the slicer element (or the bar if the slicer is an image). However, if you then apply a different theme, the highlight color will not change. If you want to force Power View to apply the new highlight color, you have to switch the slicer back to a table, and then revert back again to a slicer.

Applying a Report Background

Power View does not condemn you to presenting every report with a white background. To avoid monotony you can choose from a predefined set of 12 report backgrounds that you can add to every report in a presentation with a couple of clicks.

To apply a background to a report, all you have to do is

1. On the Power View menu, click the popup triangle for Background (in the Themes section). The choice of available backgrounds will appear as shown in Figure 7-11.

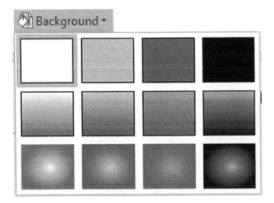

Figure 7-11. *The Background popup menu*

2. Select the background that you want to apply. The sample report that we have been using so far looks like Figure 7-12, if you apply the Dark 1 Solid background (the image on the top right of the set of choices).

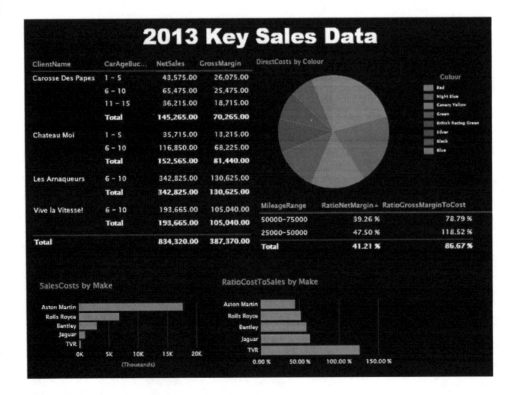

Figure 7-12. *Applying a background to a report*

184

There are three families of background available:

- Solid
- Vertical gradient
- Central gradient

One of each of these is essentially light in tone—it is based on predominantly white coloring. Another set is based on black, so it is consequently dark in tone. The two other sets are based on the two background colors defined in the report theme, one light, the other dark. The actual colors are displayed as the two tiny color triangles at the top right of each theme image in the Theme popup menu.

To explain how the backgrounds are set out, take a look at Figure 7-13.

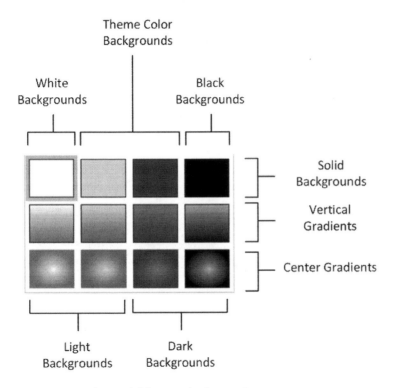

Figure 7-13. *The available report backgrounds*

If you apply any of the dark backgrounds, then Power View will automatically switch the text to white or a light color. Applying a light background will switch all the text in a presentation to black, or a dark color.

If you want a color-based background, then you will have to choose one of the options available in the two central columns in the Background popup menu. However, to choose a color, you must apply a theme to the presentation. As you will discover, there are only a limited set of background colors available.

You can always see which background has been applied by looking at the images in the Background popup menu. The current background has a subtly thicker line around it. The default background is always the top left hand background called Light 1 Solid, which is, in effect, a clear background.

Images

We all know what a picture is worth. Well, so does Power View. Consequently you can add pictures, or images, as they are generically known, to a Power View report to replace words and enhance your presentation. The images that you insert into a Power View report can come from the web or from a file on a disk—either local or on an available network share. Once an image has been inserted it is not linked to the source file. So if the source image changes, you will have to reinsert it to keep it up to date. So, although you can have images from databases appear in tables via PowerPivot, you cannot place these same images outside a table in Power View.

Some of the uses for images in Power View are

- As a background Image for a report.

- Images in tables instead of text. An example could be to use product images.

- Images in slicers. These could be flags of countries, for instance.

- Images in tiles. These could be flags or products.

- Independent images— a logo, for instance, or a complement to draw the viewer's attention to a specific point.

Once we have looked at the types of image formats available, we will see how images can be used in all these contexts.

Image Sources

There are a multitude of image formats that exist. Power View, however, will only accept two of them.

- JPEG—pronounced "JayPeg." This is a venerable standard image file format.

- PNG. This is a standard file format for Internet images.

The former generally have the extension .jpg or .jpeg. The latter generally have the .png extension. Both can deliver reasonable quality images that should certainly suffice for Power View reports.

If you attempt to insert an image that is not in a format that Power View can handle, you will get the alert shown in Figure 7-14.

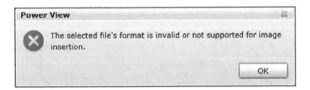

Figure 7-14. *Invalid image format alert dialog*

▓ **Note**   When you attempt to insert an image from a file, the Open dialog will filter the files so that only files with a .jpeg, .jpg, or .png extension are visible. You can force the dialog to display other file formats, but Power View will not be able to load them.

Background Images

One major, and frequently very striking, use of images is as a background to a Report—and possibly even to a whole series of reports. So, let's take a look at how to use images for report backgrounds and some of the things that you can do with them.

Adding a Background Image

Before anything else, you need to add a background image. This is, once again, extremely simple:

1. In the Power View ribbon, select Set Image from the Set Image button. A classic Windows dialog will appear; it lets you choose the source image, as shown in Figure 7-15.

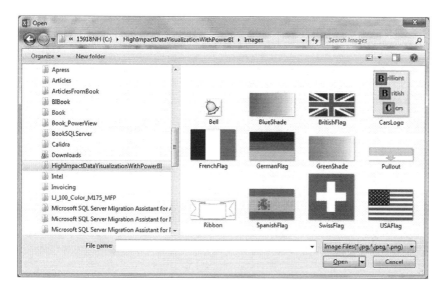

Figure 7-15. *Navigating to a background image file*

2. Navigate to the directory containing the image that you wish to insert. There are several sample images in the folder C:\HighImpactDataVisualizationWithPowerBI\Images which you can install as described in Appendix A.

3. Click on the image file. I will use the example image GreenShade in this example.

4. Click Open.

The selected image will be loaded as a report background. By default it will be adjusted proportionally until it covers the width of the report. The Power View report that we have been developing in this chapter (and that you last saw in Figure 7-12) should look like Figure 7-16.

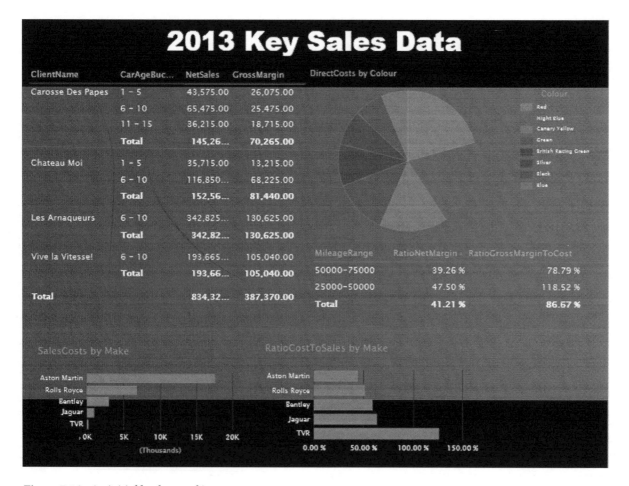

Figure 7-16. *An initial background image*

Fitting a Background Image

Frequently an image can need a little tweaking until it truly enhances a Power View report. To help you control the final display of a background image, Power View offers you several ways to resize the image—both proportionally and non-proportionally—in a report.

For example, to make an image cover an entire report

1. In the Power View menu click the Image Position button.

2. Select Stretch.

The image will be stretched (and possibly distorted) to fit the entire Power View report canvas. This can be seen in Figure 7-17.

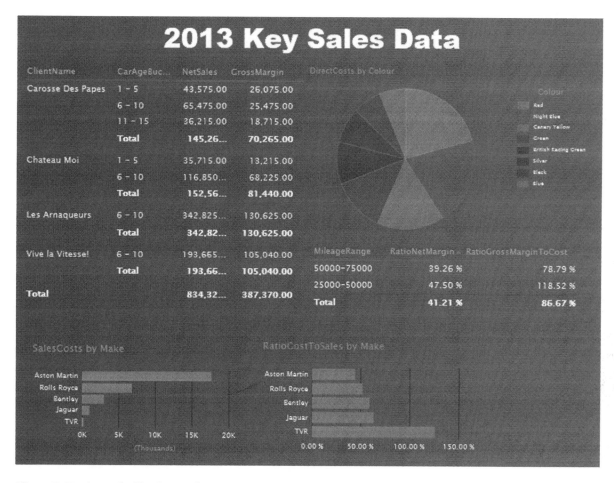

Figure 7-17. *A stretched background image*

There are other options you can use when fitting an image to a report canvas. These are outlined in Table 7-4.

Table 7-4. *Background Image Fit Options*

Image Option	Description
Fit	Enlarges the image proportionally until either the sides or top and bottom of the report canvas are reached
Stretch	Enlarges the image non-proportionally to cover the entire report canvas
Tile	Repeats the image (keeping it at its original size) to cover the entire report canvas
Center	Places the image at the center of the report canvas

Removing a Background Image

To remove a background image, all you have to do is

1. In the Power View ribbon, select Remove Image from the Set Image button.

The existing background image will disappear from the report.

Setting an Image's Transparency

A background image sits on top of the background of the actual report, assuming that you have applied one. This lets you achieve some interesting effects by combining the image with the background. What Power View lets you do, in the interest of greater readability, is set the transparency of the image. Put simply, a largely transparent image will let the background show through, whereas a completely opaque image will not let any of the background underneath the image be visible in the report.

To make this clearer, I suggest altering the transparency of the image that you added to create Figure 7-17.

1. In the Power View button, click Transparency.

2. Select a transparency percentage from those available.

Figure 7-18 shows an example of this, using 0% transparency. The image is as close as possible to the original, and it completely hides any background that was set. If you compare this with the report where the default transparency of 50% was applied (in Figure 7-17), you can see that the underlying dark background is now completely hidden by the background image.

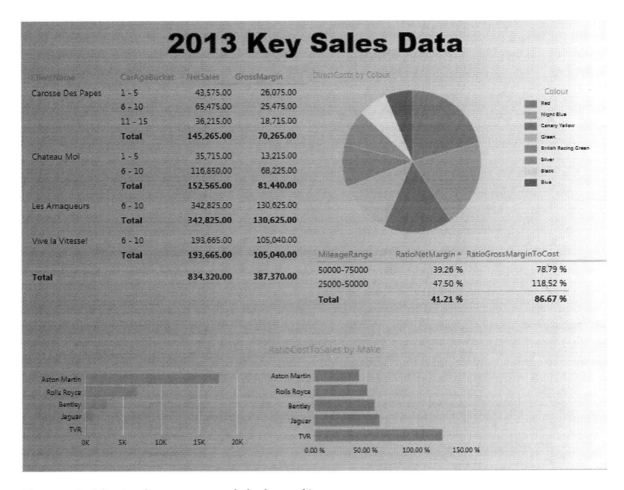

Figure 7-18. Adjusting the transparency of a background image

You cannot choose a transparency setting other than those offered. However, as the selection varies from 0 to 100%, you should always be able to find a setting to suit your needs.

■ **Tip** Even if you hide a background completely (as we have done here), it can have an effect. If you select one of the light backgrounds, then the font color will be dark, and if you choose a dark background, the font color is set to a light color. So selecting the appropriate, but invisible, background can change the font color to make the text more readable. This is what has been applied in Figure 7-18.

The next question that you may be asking is "What purpose can this option possibly serve?" Well, consider the case where you have applied an image over a report where all the presentation's backgrounds are dark, and so the text is, consequently, white. When you apply a fairly clear image, this could make the text hard to read. So adjusting the image's transparency could enable you to "darken" the image, making the text readable.

▓ **Note** It is worth noting that a background image will only be applied to the current report. This is unlike what happens when you set a background, for instance, which will be applied to all reports (Power View worksheets) in an Excel workbook.

Images in Tables

There could be occasions when you prefer to use an image rather than text in a table. This is a technique that, if not over-used, can add some color and variety to a report. As an example of this, let's create a list of clients and their home country using the flag of each country to indicate the geographical zone where the sale occurred. The way to do this is

1. Create a new Power View report.

2. Add a table based on the following three fields:

    a. ClientName

    b. CountryFlag

    c. SalePrice

3. Adjust the table size and column widths to get the best result.

    The resulting table should look like Figure 7-19.

Figure 7-19. *Using images in tables*

As you can see, the effect is instantaneous—and extremely easy to produce.

Resizing Images Used in Tables

The images that are used in tables can be resized globally, but not individually. To adjust the size of all the images, all you have to do is to increase or decrease the width of the column containing the images. This will not, however, cause the row height to change.

Images in Slicers

The use of slicers is one area where images can be a really powerful presentation tool. Suppose that you have a report where you want to add a slicer by country. Now consider how it would look if, instead of the country name, you use the country's flag. Let's see this in action:

1. Choose a report, such as ReadyForSlicer in the sample PVPresentation.xlsx workbook.

2. Drag the CountryFlag field onto the report canvas. A table of flags will appear.

3. Click Slicer in the Power View ribbon.

The table of flags becomes a slicer as shown in Figures 7-20. If you click on any of the flags, you will filter the report to display only data for that country. The slicer is, to all intents and purposes, an ordinary slicer. Consequently you can slice on multiple elements, clear the selection, and, in fact, use all the slicer techniques explained in Chapter 6.

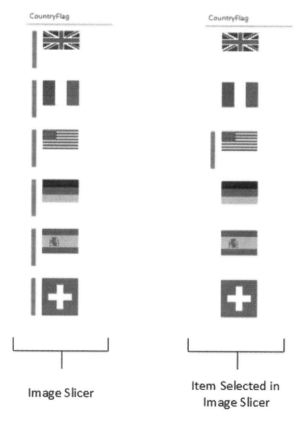

Figure 7-20. *Images in slicers*

Images in Tiles

As I mentioned in Chapter 6 you can also use images in tiles. This is a selection technique that you can often use to great effect. As an example (which still uses the country flags, since we have images for them), I suggest creating a table of clients showing their sales and net margin tiled by country. To create this visualization:

1. In a new or existing Power View report, add a table based on the following fields:

    a. ClientName

    b. SalePrice

    c. NetMargin

2. Drag the CountryFlag field to the TILE BY box in the Layout section of the Field List.

The resulting tiled table should look like Figure 7-21 (Switzerland is the selected country). As you can see, tiles with images can be larger than text-based tiles.

ClientName	SalePrice	NetMargin
Jungfrau	£301,740.00	183,650.00
Three Country Cars	£111,000.00	42,860.00
Voitures Diplomatiques S.A.	£353,000.00	171,520.00
Total	£765,740.00	398,030.00

Figure 7-21. *Using images in tiles*

The tiles act in exactly the same way as tiles based on a text field. You will also notice that, if you use an image in tiles, the tiles will automatically add the name field as a title. Although you cannot make this field disappear, you can reduce its font size if you find it superfluous.

■ **Note**   If you want a more polished final effect, then spend a little time making sure that all the source images are the same size. This way you will avoid one image setting the height for the other images and having empty space above and below the images.

Independent Images

Whether you have added a background image or not, you may still want to add completely free-form floating images to a report. However, before getting carried away with all that can be done with images, remember that Power View is not designed as a high-end presentation package. If anything, it is there to help you analyze and present information quickly and cleanly. Inevitably you will find that there are things that you cannot do in Power View that you are used to doing in, say, PowerPoint. Consequently there are many presentation tricks and techniques that you may be tempted to achieve in Power View using images to try and get similar results. Indeed, you can achieve many things in a Power View report by adding images. Yet the question that you must ask yourself is "Am I adding value to my report?" I am a firm believer that less is more in a good presentation. Consequently, although I will be showing you a few tricks using images, many of them go against the grain of fast and efficient Power View report creation and can involve considerable adjustment whenever the data in a visualization changes. So I advise you not to go overboard using images to enhance your presentations unless it is really necessary.

In any case, let's add a floating, independent image to a Power View report. In this example it will be a company logo—that of Brilliant British Cars, the company whose metrics we are analyzing throughout the course of this book.

1. Click the Picture button in the Power View ribbon. The Open dialog will display as a result.

2. Navigate to the image file that you want to insert (CarsLogo.png in this example, form the samples in C:\HighImpactDataVisualizationWithPowerBI\Images).

3. Click Open.

4. Resize and/or reposition the image.

A Power View report with a logo added is shown in Figure 7-22.

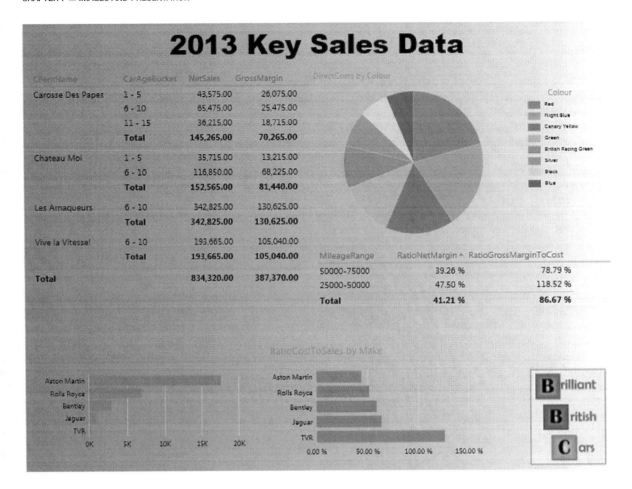

Figure 7-22. *Adding a logo*

■ **Tip**   If you use the corner handles to resize an image, you will keep the image in proportion; that is, the height to width ratio will stay the same. Resizing an image using the lateral handles will distort the image.

Layering Visualizations

As a report gets more complex, you will inevitably need to arrange the elements that it contains not only side by side, but also one on top of the other. Power View lets you do this simply and efficiently.

As an example of this, let's create a chart with another chart superposed on it.

1. Create a bar chart using the following two fields:

    a. Make

    b. RatioCostToSales

2. Order the bar chart by RatioCostToSales, in ascending order.

3. Create a pie chart using the following two fields:

    a. SaleCosts

    b. CountryName

4. Reduce the size of the font in the pie chart, and set the legend to appear on the right.

5. Place the pie chart in the top right-hand corner of the bar chart.

6. With the pie chart selected, choose Arrange ➪ Bring To Front from the Power View ribbon.

Your composite chart should look like Figure 7-23. If you had not set the pie chart to be at the front (in the topmost layer), the vertical lines of the bar chart would have overlaid the pie chart, making it harder to appreciate.

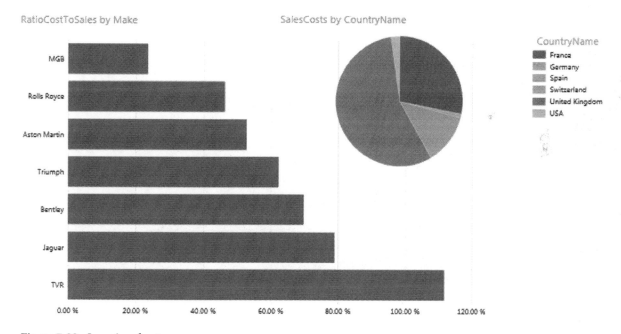

Figure 7-23. *Layering charts*

This technique is particularly useful when you are adding independent images as was described in the previous section. It is also handy when you are combining elements such as images and text boxes, as you will see in the next section.

Some Uses for Independent Images

The limits of what images can do to a report are only those of your imagination, so it is impossible to give a comprehensive list of suggestions. Nonetheless, a few uses that I have found for free-form images include these:

- Company logos, as we have just seen.

- Images added for a purely decorative effect. I would hesitate, however, before doing this at all, as it can distract from the analysis rather than enhance it. Nonetheless, at times, this may be precisely what you want to do (to turn attention away from some catastrophic sales figures, for instance). So add decoration if you must, but please use sparingly!

- To enhance the text in a text box by providing shading that is in clear relief to the underlying image or background.

- As a background to a specific column in a table. Be warned, however, that the image cannot be made to move with a column if it is resized.

- Pullout arrows.

Several of these techniques are shown in Figure 7-24. This example will hopefully clearly indicate the limits of such techniques, as they detract (considerably, in my opinion) from the simplicity and style of an uncluttered Power View report, as well as make it extremely laborious to make any modifications. Nonetheless, it is possible to achieve certain presentation effects using images. So if your boss insists, you can push the boundaries between added effects and visual overload.

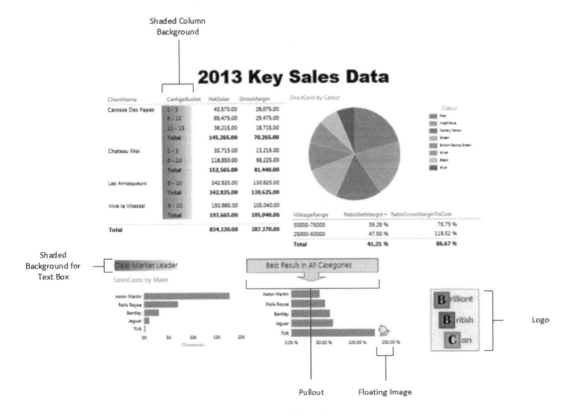

Figure 7-24. *A Power View report somewhat overloaded with images*

■ **Tip** When adding images to a Power View report, you should avoid shaded backgrounds or you may end up spending a lot of time manipulating your images in an attempt to make them conform to the Power View shading.

Image File Format

Earlier in this chapter I mentioned that Power View can only accept two image formats. This is, however, not the limitation that it sounds like it could be, as changing the format of an image file is usually easy.

So—and without going too far off on a tangent about the subject of image file formats—here is a simple technique to try in order to adapt a file to the .png format.

Let's assume that you have received the file for a client logo that you have to include in your Power View presentation. This file has the .gif extension and Power View has refused to load it. Now, if your PC or laptop has a fairly standard Windows installation, you should have Microsoft Paint installed. As there have been many versions of Paint over the years, the instructions given here are fairly generic. So, to create a copy of the client logo file in the .png file format

1. Open Microsoft Paint (for instance, open the Windows menu, enter Paint in the search/run box, and press Enter).

2. In Paint, open the original .gif file.

3. Choose Save As from the File menu. Depending on the version of Paint that you are using you may need to select Save As followed by PNG Picture in the submenu.

4. Ensure that Save As type is set to PNG (*.Png).

5. Modify the file name is you need to and select the appropriate directory.

6. Click Save.

You can now insert the file that you received into a Power View report.

Preparing Images

As I stressed earlier, it is easy to try to use images to produce effects that Power View does not provide out of the box. So, even if this may take a disproportionate amount of time compared to producing your analysis, at times, you simply have to add some visual effects. In other words, here are a few suggestions for those moments when the boss can't spell "overkill."

- For backgrounds, especially if you want a good shading effect, take a look at one of the free graphic design programs that are around. I have a weakness for Pixlr, which I used for many of the sample images that accompany this book.

- If you need to resize an image, remember that there is a Resize option in Paint, and that Pixlr (or several other web sites and free products) can do this too.

- Take a look at the many, many web sites that offer royalty-free stock images. There are so many that I suggest using your favorite search engine for this. Then you can convert them to .png or .jpg as described previously (if this is necessary).

- As you are using Excel, then you could well be a PowerPoint user. Remember that PowerPoint has a vast image library, and that you can export selected images in .png format.

- If your company uses Microsoft Visio, then you may find lots of images to use from among the shapes that come with the product. To export a shape as a .png file, just select it, choose File ➤ Save As, and select Save As Type Portable Network Graphics. You may recognize one or two of the images used in this chapter as coming from Visio, if you look carefully!

Conclusion

In this chapter you have seen how to push the envelope when using Power View to deliver especially compelling presentations. This covers not only the general aspect of a report, such as its background and color scheme, but also the enhancements that you can add by tweaking the font attributes for individual elements.

Finally, you saw how adding images can turbo charge the impression that your analysis can give when you add graphic elements to tables, slicers, and tiles. And, used sparingly, images and free-form text elements can draw your audience's attention to the most salient features of your presentation. So now it is up to you to use these powerful Power View features to deliver some really compelling interactive analyses to your audience.

CHAPTER 8

■ ■ ■

Mapping Data in Power View

Data visualization in Power View is not limited to tables and charts. Another powerful technique that you can use to both analyze and present your insights is to display the data in map form. All that this requires is that your source data contains information that can be used for geographical representation. So if you have country, state, town, or even latitude and longitude in the data set, then you can get Power View to add a map to your report and show the selected data using the map as a background.

Better yet, a Power View map behaves just like any other visualization. This means that you can filter the data that is displayed in a map, as well as highlighting it, just as you can do for charts, tables, and matrices. Indeed, you can even drill down into maps just like you can with matrices and charts. Not only that, but a map is an integral part of a Power View report. So if you highlight data in a chart, a map in the same report will also be highlighted.

The aim of this chapter is to show you some of the ways in which you can add real spice to your reports by using maps. Then, when presenting your analyses, you can interact with the maps and really—no really—impress your audience.

Bing Maps

Before adding a first map I want to explain how mapping works in Power View. The geographical component is based on Bing Maps. So, in order to add a map, you need to be able to connect to the Internet and use the Bing Maps service. Secondly, the underlying data set must contain fields that are recognized by Bing Maps as geographical data. In other words you need country, state, town, or other information that Bing Maps can use to generate the plot of the map. Fortunately Power View will indicate if it recognizes a field as containing data that it can use (hopefully) to create a map, as it will display a tiny icon of a globe in the Field List for every field in the underlying data set that apparently contains geographical data.

To avoid the risk of misinterpreting data you can add metadata to the underlying PowerPivot data model which will define geographical field types. This is explained in Chapter 11 where you will see how to apply data categories to fields. Power View maps will then use these categories to interpret geographical data for mapping.

Preparing data so that any fields used by Bing Maps are not only recognizable as containing geographic data, but are also uniquely recognizable, is vital. You must help Bing Maps so that if you are mapping data for a city named Paris, Bing can see whether you mean Paris, France or Paris, Texas. Chapter 11 explains some of the ways in which you can prepare your data for use by Bing Maps, and consequently use it to add map visualizations to Power View.

Although preparing the data may be necessary, it is certainly a lot simpler than the alternatives that involve finding, loading, and understanding shape files for geographical representation, or manipulating geospatial data in a database such as SQL Server.

■ **Note**   There are some areas of the world that cannot use Bing Maps. So if you attempt to use Power View mapping in these geographical zones, you will not see any map appear when you attempt to create a map.

Maps in Power View

Let's begin by creating a map of Sales by Country. Fortunately the sample data set contains the country where the sale was made. This means that we can use this data to make Power View display a map of our worldwide sales. Here is how to create an initial map:

1. Insert a new Power View sheet. You need to do this because maps tend to need most, if not all, of the available space in a Power View report.

2. Add the following fields to the FIELDS box in the Layout section of the Field List. You will see a table appear in the Power View canvas containing the data.

    a. CountryName

    b. GrossMargin

3. Filter the report to show only data for 2013 (this is described in Chapter 3 if you have started the book at the current chapter).

4. Click Map in the Design ribbon.

5. If this is the first time that you are using the Map function, then Power View will display the alert shown in Figure 8-1.

 PRIVACY WARNING To be displayed on the map, some of your data needs to be geocoded by sending it to Bing. | Enable Content |

Figure 8-1. *The Bing Maps privacy warning*

6. Click Enable Content to allow Bing Maps to be used.

7. The table will be replaced by a map representing the data for each country. You can now resize the map to make it easier to read. It should look something like Figure 8-2.

GrossMargin by CountryName

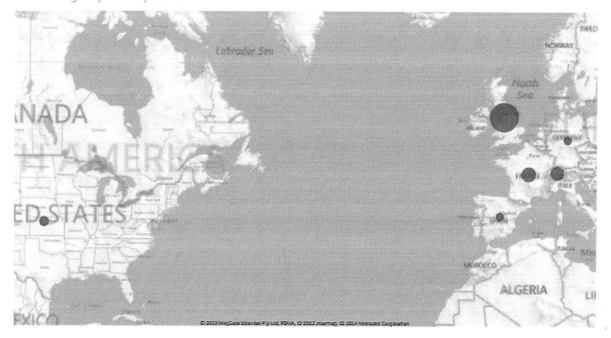

Figure 8-2. *An initial Power View map*

It is probably worth clarifying a few points about maps in Power View before we go any further. The essential points to note are

- A map is a **visualization** like any other. You can resize and move it anywhere on the Power View canvas.

- The map will **apply any filters** that have been set for the report.

- Each data point (or bubble) in a map is **proportional** to the relative size of the underlying data.

- You can hover the mouse pointer over a data "bubble" to **display a popup showing the exact data** that is represented. An example of this is shown in Figure 8-3.

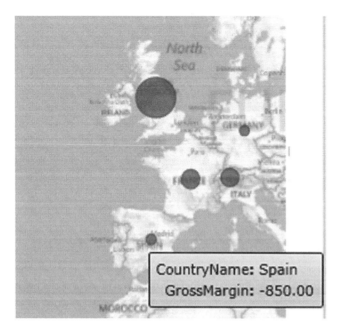

Figure 8-3. *Displaying the exact data in a Power View map*

Adjusting Map Display in Power View

Creating a map is, as you have seen, extremely easy. However the initial map is not necessarily the finalized version that you wish to show to your audience. You may wish to

- Position the map elements more precisely inside the visualization.

- Zoom in or out of the map.

- Remove or add a map title.

- Select a different type of map background.

- Filter the underlying data.

In the next few sections we will look at these various modifications that you can make to Power View maps. Hopefully you will find these tweaks both intuitive and easy to implement. In any case, with a little practice you should find that these modifications take only a few seconds to accomplish.

Positioning the Map Elements

If the area displayed in a map is not quite as perfect as you would prefer, then you can alter the area (whether it is a country or a region) that appears in the map visualization. To do this

1.   Place the mouse pointer over the map. The Zoom and Pan icons will appear at the top right of the map.

2.   Click on the Pan Right icon (the right-facing triangle) to alter the geographical area displayed in the map visualization.

The icons used to pan a map appear in Figure 8-4.

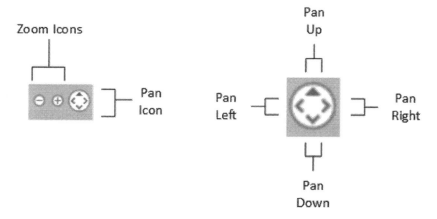

Figure 8-4. *Panning around a Power View map*

> ■ **Tip** You can also click inside a map and drag the mouse to pan around.

Zooming In or Out

It is conceivable that the map that is displayed is not at a scale, which you would prefer. Fortunately this is extremely easy to fix. All you have to do is

1. Place the mouse pointer over the map. The Zoom and Pan icons will appear at the top right of the map.

2. Click on the Zoom Out button (the minus sign) to zoom out, or on the Zoom In button (the plus sign) to zoom in.

> ■ **Tip** You can also move the mouse scroll wheel to zoom in or out of a map.

Removing or Adding a Map Title

A map adds a title automatically to explain what data you are seeing. You can remove (or add back) a title like this:

1. Click on the map visualization to select it.

2. In the Layout ribbon click Title.

3. Select None.

The title will be removed from the map. To add a title back to a map, all you have to do is to carry out the first two steps and then select Above Map instead of None.

Modifying the Map Background

You can choose between any one of five map types when using maps in Power View. By default, a map is displayed as a Grayscale Road Map Background. Yet you can alter the map display in the following way:

1. Click on the map to select it.

2. In the Layout ribbon, click Map Background, and select Aerial (Satellite Photo) Map Background.

Your map will now look like Figure 8-5.

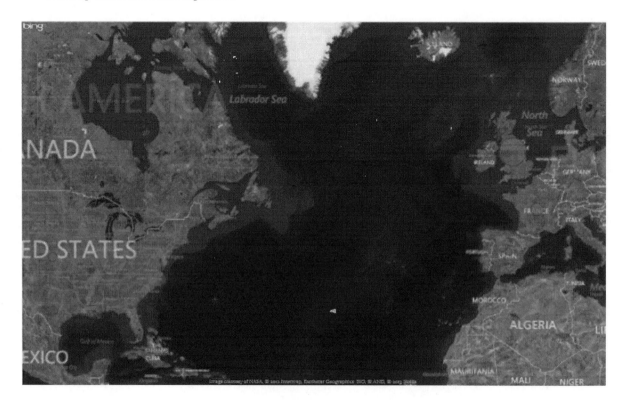

Figure 8-5. *Changing the background of a Power View map*

Power View allows you to choose from five available map backgrounds. These are explained in Table 8-1.

Table 8-1. *Map Background Options*

Map Background Option	Description
Road Map Background	Displays the classic road map with colors.
Grayscale Road Map Background	Shows the road map using monochrome representation of the geographical data and colors for the display data.
Reverse Grayscale Road Map Background	Shows the road map but using dark grayscale for the geographical data and colors for the display data.
Aerial (satellite photo) Map Background	Shows a satellite view of the map.
Grayscale Aerial Map Background	Shows a satellite view of the map using monochrome representation of the geographical data.

Filtering Map Data

A map can be filtered to display only specific data, just like any other Power View visualization. This is virtually identical to the way in which you saw how to filter data in Chapter 3, but as a quick revision, here is how to exclude, say, data for the United States from the list of countries in a Power View map.

1. Display the Filters Area (unless it is already visible).

2. Click on a map; you will see Map at the top of the Filters Area.

3. Click on the word Map. You will see the filters for the fields that are used in the map visualization.

4. Expand the CountryName field.

5. Click (All). A check mark will appear for each country.

6. Uncheck the box for United States.

The data bubble for the United States will be removed from the map, leaving the other countries visible. This is shown in Figure 8-6.

GrossMargin by CountryName

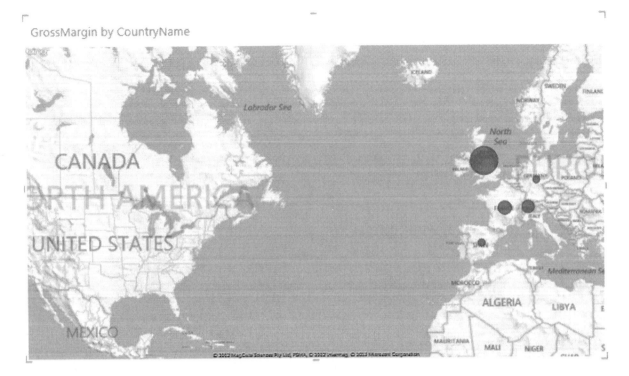

Figure 8-6. *Filtering data for a Power View map*

You can use all the filtering techniques described in Chapter 3 to filter a map. Rather than reiterate all the options here, I suggest that you refer back to that chapter for full details.

▪ **Tip** If you know that you will only want to see the data for a subset of geographical locations, then it can be worth defining a filter to display only the areas that interest you before you switch to a map visualization. This way the initial map will only show the selected locations, which could save you from having to zoom and pan the map.

Multi-Value Series

So far we have seen how you can add a single data series to a map and have the data represented as a data point. Power View can extend this paradigm by allowing you to display the data bubble as a pie that contains a second data series—and consequently display the data broken down by a specific data set per geographical entity.

As an example of this (and to revise the some of the map creation techniques that we have seen so far), let's try to analyze European car sales by age range.

1. Insert a new Power View sheet.

2. Display the Filters Area (if necessary) and add the Year field from the YearHierarchy in the Date table.

3. Adjust the Year slider to select only the year 2013.

4.   Add the following fields to the FIELDS box in the Layout section of the Field List:

   a.   CountryName

   b.   CarAgeBucket

   c.   SalePrice

5.   Filter the table to exclude the United States as described in the previous section.

6.   Click Map in the Design ribbon.

7.   Resize the map visualization.

The map now contains a legend for the CarAgeBucket, and has added the CarAgeBucket field to the COLOR box of the Field List Layout section. Each bubble is now a pie of data. The overall size of the pie represents, proportionally, the sum total data compared to the other pies. The map should now look like Figure 8-7.

Figure 8-7. *Displaying pie charts in a Power View map*

It is worth remarking that if you hover the mouse pointer over the data representation (the pie) for a country, it will expand slightly, and as you pass the pointer over each pie segment, you will see a tooltip giving the details of the data, including which car age range it refers to.

■ **Tip**   The colors of a pie in a Power View map can be modified by selecting a different theme from the Power View menu. This can help the pie stand out against the map background.

Highlighting Map Data

If you have added data to the COLORS box of the Field List, and a legend is displayed, you can highlight segments of data in a map, much as you saw how to do in a chart in Chapter 5. This allows you to draw the audience's attention to specific trends in your data.

1.   Using the map that you created and can see in Figure 8-7, click 6-10 (the second element) in the legend.

The segment of each pie corresponding to the car age range from 6-10 years will be highlighted, as you can see in Figure 8-8.

Figure 8-8. *Highlighting map data*

To remove highlighting from a map, all you have to do is click again on the legend element that you are using to highlight data, or simply click on the title of the legend.

Using a map as a basis for highlighting data follows the same logic that we saw in Chapter 5 for charts. That is, if you highlight a data element in a map, all other objects in the current report will be filtered by that selection.

For example, suppose that you have created the original map of net sales per country shown in Figure 8-6, which you have resized to allow for space to one side and have adjusted to show only European countries. You have also added a table composed simply of the Colour and NetSales fields. This report should look something like Figure 8-9, where you can see a bubble representing the sales figures for European countries where you have clients.

SalePrice by CountryName

Colour	NetSales
Black	756,300.00
Blue	1,381,825.00
British Racing Green	1,090,525.00
Canary Yellow	1,438,939.99
Dark Purple	880,450.00
Green	813,175.00
Night Blue	806,250.00
Red	2,069,515.00
Silver	948,490.00
Total	10,185,469.99

Figure 8-9. *Sales in Europe before highlighting a specific country*

Now, click on the data point for Switzerland. The map will highlight this country's sales, and the table will also be updated to reflect the fact that you are, in effect, filtering out all data except for Switzerland. This report should now look like Figure 8-10.

SalePrice by CountryName

Colour	NetSales
Black	183,450.00
Blue	104,125.00
British Racing Green	41,500.00
Canary Yellow	192,575.00
Dark Purple	38,550.00
Green	44,325.00
Red	36,165.00
Silver	107,800.00
Total	**748,490.00**

Figure 8-10. *Sales in Europe after highlighting Switzerland*

■ **Tip** If you click on a segment of a pie for a country in a report where you have added a field for the Color element of a map as you did to create Figure 8-7, then you will be filtering on both elements that make up the segment—the country *and* the car age range.

Adjusting a Legend

If you are coming to maps in Power View after you have used charts, then you will feel a strong sense of déjà vu when modifying the map legend. Suppose that you want to move the legend from the right side of the map to the bottom of the map. Here is how:

1. Revert to the map displayed in Figure 8-7.

2. Click on the map to select it.

3. In the Layout ribbon, click Legend.

4. Select Show Legend At Bottom.

The map should now look like Figure 8-11.

SalePrice by CountryName, and CarAgeBucket

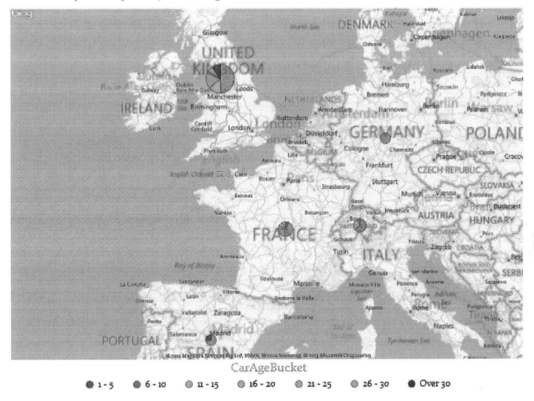

CarAgeBucket

● 1 - 5 ● 6 - 10 ● 11 - 15 ● 16 - 20 ● 21 - 25 ● 26 - 30 ● Over 30

Figure 8-11. *Adjusting the position of the legend in a Power View map*

The options available for positioning a legend are given in Table 8-2.

Table 8-2. *Legend Placement Options for Power View Maps*

Legend Option	Description
None	The legend is removed.
Show Legend At Right	The legend is displayed on the right side the map (this is the default).
Show Legend At Top	The legend is displayed at the top of the map.
Show Legend At Left	The legend is displayed on the left side of the map.
Show Legend At Bottom	The legend is displayed at the bottom of the map.

Adding Tiles to Maps

Another similarity between maps and charts or tables is their capacity for interactive filtering using tiles. Let's suppose that you want to be able to see worldwide car sales by the color of car sold, as well as by car age range. Here is how:

1. Take the map visualization that you created earlier for Figure 8-11.

2. Drag the Colour field from the Colours table to the TILE BY box in the Layout section of the Field List. Alternatively you can click on the popup menu for the Colours field and select Add As Tile By.

Tiles will appear above the map, with the first tile element selected, as shown in Figure 8-12.

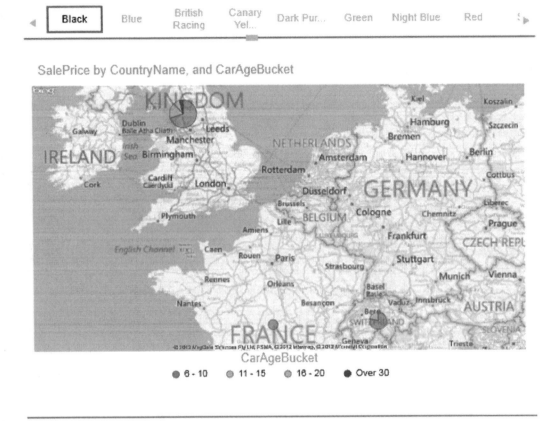

Figure 8-12. Adding tiles to a map

Tiles for maps act in exactly the same way as tiles for tables or charts. Clicking on a tile element will restrict the data in the map to the selected element. This means that the pie segments and the corresponding legend will only display available data. When applied to a map, this has the added effect of swapping the mapped region to show only the geographical areas that have data corresponding to the selected tile. To see this effect, try clicking on the tiles:

- Green

- British Racing Green

- Black

You will see the map "jump" to reflect the selected data. Since we are in the realm of geography, you could also try using the CountryName field to tile the map. This way, when you select a country, there is a real visual effect as the map moves to display the selected country.

In all other respects the tiles will act in the same way as was described in Chapter 6. So if this is your first experience of tiles, I suggest that you refer to the section on tiles in that chapter for further details.

Multiple Maps

Maps can also be displayed as multiples or "trellis" visualizations, just as charts can. To see this in action, let's return to the map of car sales by car age range, as shown in Figure 8-11 earlier, and see how to display multiple maps—one per car color sold.

1. Open the map visualization that you created for Figure 8-11.

2. Drag the Colour field from the Colours table to the VERTICAL MULTIPLES box in the Layout section of the Field List. Alternatively you can click on the popup menu for the Colours field and select Add To Vertical Multiples.

The map will be split into multiple maps, as shown in Figure 8-13. You will note that each individual map has been resized and repositioned automatically to display only data for the relevant geographical area.

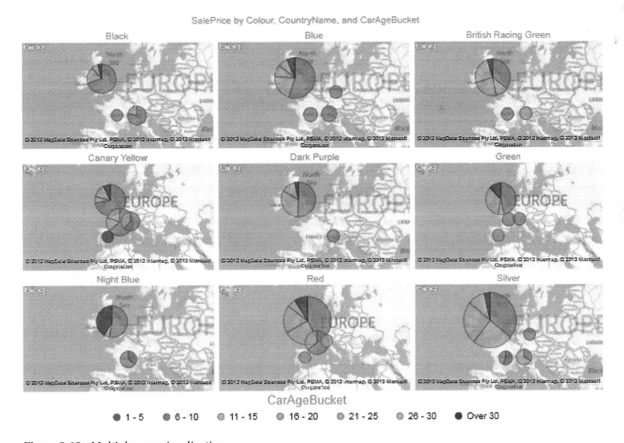

Figure 8-13. *Multiple map visualization*

Multiples, like tiles, behave in exactly the same way for maps as for charts. So, once again, I will not be repeating all the techniques and tricks here; instead I'll refer you to the appropriate sections of Chapter 5 for full details. The only new point that is probably worth taking into consideration is that zooming and panning is now possible for each individual map.

Multiple Maps by Region

One interesting trick when working with multiple maps is to use the same geographical data that is used as the location as the multiple. This is a purely visual effect, but it allows you to see the data per region (country, in this example), while comparing sales per region using the size of the data point.

Here is how you can do this:

1. Open the map visualization that you created for Figure 8-11 earlier.

2. Drag the CountryName field from the Countries table to the VERTICAL MULTIPLES box in the Layout section of the Field List. Alternatively you can click on the popup menu for the CountryName field and select Add To Vertical Multiples.

3. If required, zoom in a little for certain individual maps so that the country fills the available space in the grid.

The map will be split, once again, into multiple maps, as shown in Figure 8-14. This time you can see the country map as a background for the country data. You will also note that the pie charts are proportional to the sales for each country. The only drawback when using this trick is that the title will repeat the field name that you applied to both the COLOR box and the VERTICAL MULTIPLES box. However, you can always remove the title.

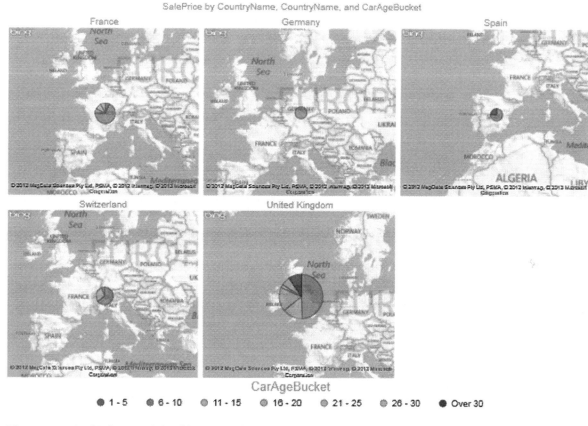

Figure 8-14. *Multiple maps defined by geography*

Drilling Down in Maps

Another extremely interesting interactive aspect of using Power View maps is the ability to drill down into a map to see further levels of detail. This will require, inevitably, source data that contains a geographical hierarchy. Fortunately we have hierarchical data available in the form of country and town, even if these are not specifically defined as a hierarchy in the underlying dataset.

To create a drill-down map, you need to follow the following steps:

1. Insert a new Power View sheet.

2. Create a table based on the following fields.

    a. ClientCountry from the Clients table

    b. NetSales from the SalesData table

3. Convert the table to a map by clicking on the Map button in the Design ribbon.

4. Resize the map to improve visibility.

5. Pan and zoom to place the United Kingdom in the center of the map. You should see something like the map given in Figure 8-15.

NetSales by CountryName

Figure 8-15. *An initial map ready for drill down*

6. Add the Town field from the Clients table to the LOCATIONS box under the ClientCountry field. The map should remain the same, as shown in Figure 8-15.

7. Double-click on one of the bubbles for a country. I suggest the data for the United Kingdom in this example. The map will drill down to show the data for each town where sales occurred.

8. Adjust the map display to show only the area where there is data for a town. You can see this in Figure 8-16.

Figure 8-16. *Drill-down for the United Kingdom*

The map shown in Figure 8-15 has a drill-up icon on the top right, just like a chart or matrix with drill-down enabled. You can see this icon if you place the mouse pointer over the map. Clicking on this will drill back up to the previous level. You can create as many levels of drill-down as your data allows.

Conclusion

Few things add the wow factor to a presentation in the way that a carefully crafted interactive map can. In this chapter, you saw how to add a map to a Power View report and then how to apply the techniques that you learned for other types of visualization to filter and highlight data in maps.

We then explored how to use a Power View map interactively to highlight data in other visualizations in the report. Finally, we saw how you can drill down into map data just as you can with matrices and charts.

Remember also that you can manipulate maps just like any other Power View element. Consequently, you can superimpose a chart on a map. Indeed, you can add slicers, as well, to add to the interactivity. Finally, you can enhance the map with text boxes and pictures to underscore the points that you are making about the data the map contains.

So, used judiciously, maps can become a vital part of your analytical and presentation toolkit. Have fun creating geographical representations of your data, and I hope that your audience is suitably impressed with your newfound skills.

CHAPTER 9

■ ■ ■

PowerPivot Basics

You need one fundamental thing to create stunning visualizations—data. Specifically, you need data in PowerPivot, the Excel add-in that can handle many times the volumes of data that Excel can handle natively—tens of millions of rows if need be. So, to ensure that you are at ease when creating data sets in the Excel Data Model, data sets that are ready for modeling and extending in PowerPivot and for later analysis in Power View, this chapter will take you through the basics of PowerPivot, and will explain how to

- Load data from external sources, specifically SQL Server databases and Excel

- Follow the evolution of changes in the structure of the source data and reflect these modifications in the PowerPivot data set

- Update data in PowerPivot when the source data changes

- Tweak the PowerPivot data set by deleting, renaming, and moving tables and columns

- Select appropriate data types for each column of data

- Apply core formatting to the columns of data

- Sort data

- Filter data

Before we look at these techniques, I need to make one thing extremely clear: PowerPivot is a data repository only. It is *not* designed to directly modify your source data. All changes (whether they are additions, deletions, or modifications) *must* be carried out on the source data first. Then the PowerPivot data set will have to be updated with these changes. So although you cannot edit a cell in a PowerPivot table like you can in Excel, you can perform extensive analysis of huge tables of data with near instantaneous response times.

If you already have a working knowledge of PowerPivot then you may not need much, or any, of the information in this chapter. So feel free to cherry-pick the bits that you need, or even to skip ahead to Chapter 10, if you already know how to load data into PowerPivot and apply data types. Perhaps you are using Power Query to load data into the Excel Data Model, in which case you might just want to skim through this chapter to see if there are any interesting complimentary nuggets of knowledge that you may find useful.

Once again, all the sample files used in this chapter are available on the Apress web site. Once downloaded they should be in the folder C:\HighImpactDataVisualizationWithPowerBI.

The PowerPivot Environment

PowerPivot exists to store and manipulate large quantities of data. So it follows that getting data into PowerPivot is key, and this is what we will be doing shortly. However, I think that it is best if you first familiarize yourself with the tool itself so that you can feel at home in this new environment.

Using PowerPivot

To start using PowerPivot, you need to follow these steps:

1. In Excel, click on the PowerPivot tab. The PowerPivot ribbon will replace the current ribbon.

2. Click the Manage button. You will switch to the PowerPivot environment, which is described in Figure 9-1.

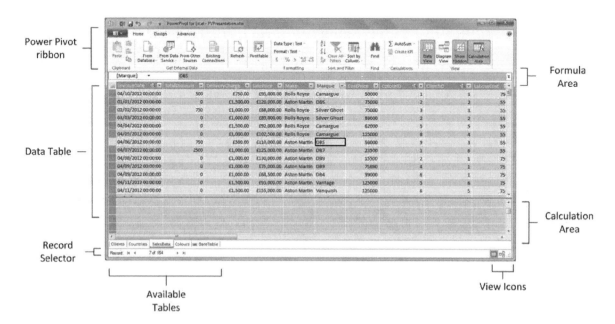

Figure 9-1. *The PowerPivot screen*

■ **Note**　This first image contains some data that already exists in PowerPivot. If you have not yet loaded any data, then you will see a very empty screen!

You could well be thinking that this does not look like very much at all yet. However, be reassured, you will soon see what can be done, and exactly how powerful a tool PowerPivot really is. For the moment, it is essential to remember that you have, so to speak, stepped sideways into a separate environment. Although this new world is hosted by Excel (and you can return to Excel instantaneously), it is best if you consider it a kind of parallel universe for the moment. This universe has its own ribbons and buttons and is in a separate window from Excel.

As an aside, we did see, albeit very briefly, the Excel PowerPivot ribbon. We will not be using it any further in this chapter, however. Once PowerPivot is active, you can switch between PowerPivot and Excel just as you normally would flip between open applications. Switching back to an open PowerPivot window is as easy as choosing the PowerPivot window from the available windows.

The PowerPivot Ribbons

So what, exactly, are you looking at when you start PowerPivot? Essentially, you can see three ribbons, which are all devoted to data management:

- The Home ribbon
- The Design ribbon
- The Advanced ribbon

I prefer to explain the PowerPivot ribbons as we start out, as it should make understanding the PowerPivot environment easier. However, if you prefer to skip this section (or possibly use it as reference later), then feel free to jump ahead to the section called "Loading Data into PowerPivot."

The Home Ribbon

The Home ribbon is used for all core data loading and manipulation such as filtering and sorting. The buttons that it contains are shown in Figure 9-2 and explained in Table 9-1.

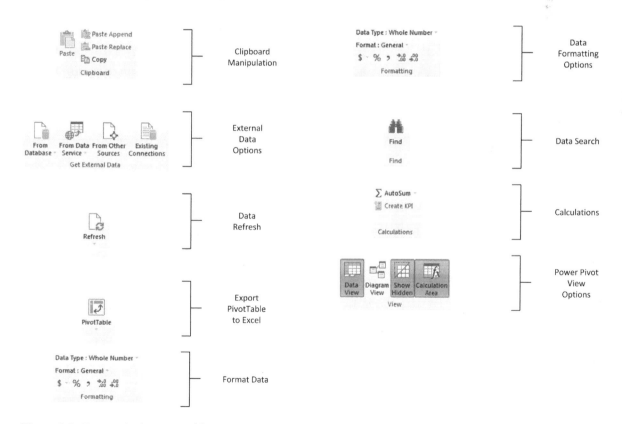

***Figure 9-2.** Buttons in the Home ribbon*

Table 9-1. *The Home Ribbon Buttons*

Button	Description
Paste	Lets you paste data that you have just copied to the clipboard (from Excel, for instance) into a new PowerPivot data table.
Paste Append	Pastes the previously copied data into a table that contains data. The new data is added at the end of the existing data set, which must have been created initially using the Paste command.
Paste Replace	Pastes the previously copied data into a table that contains data. The new data replaces the existing data set, which must have been created using the Paste command.
Copy	Copies the selected data so that you can paste it into another application.
From Database	Starts the process to import data from a Microsoft relational database.
From Data Service	Starts the process to import data from an online or enterprise data service.
From Other Sources	Starts the process to import data from one of the other possible sources of data to which PowerPivot can connect.
Existing Connections	Starts the process to import data using an existing data connection to a data source.
Refresh	Updates the current PowerPivot data table with the latest version of the data in the data source.
Refresh All	Updates all the PowerPivot data tables with the latest version of the data from all the data sources that have been used.
PivotTable	Creates a Pivot Table in Excel using the PowerPivot data set.
Data Type	Indicates, and lets you alter if it is technically possible, the data type for the current column.
Format	Indicates, and lets you modify, the format of numerical or date or time data for the current column.
Sort A-Z	Sorts the data in the current column in ascending (A-Z or 0-9) order.
Sort Z-A	Sorts the data in the current column in descending (Z-A or 9-0) order.
Clear Sort	Removes the effects of the sort operation and leaves the data as it was when imported.
Clear All Filters	Clears all active filters and displays all the data in the table.
Sort By Column	Allows you to set a column that will provide the sort criteria when you are sorting on the current column in Power View.
Find	Searches for metadata (column or table names, for example) in the current table.
AutoSum	Adds a calculated field that aggregates the current column and places the result at the foot of the column. Unless otherwise specified the aggregation is a sum.
Create KPI	Guides you through the creation process to add a Key Performance Indicator (KPI) to the PowerPivot table.
Data View	Switches to the view of the data in a table, and tabs of all the tables in the data set.
Diagram View	Switches to an overview of all the tables and their fields in the data set, with any relationships between the tables.
Show Hidden	Displays or hides any hidden columns (or other elements) that have been flagged as hidden from client tools.
Calculation Area	Displays or hides the calculation area under the data table.

The Design Ribbon

The Design ribbon lets you present the data on screen as well as manage the various properties of the data tables that are joined together. The buttons that it contains are shown in Figure 9-3 and explained in Table 9-2, which follows the image.

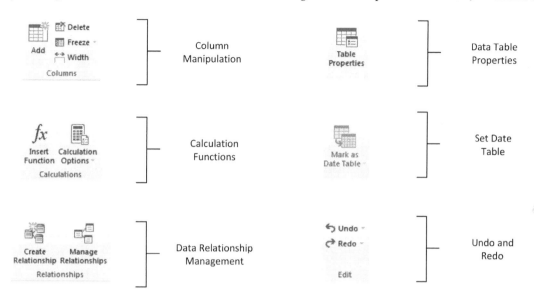

Figure 9-3. *Buttons in the Design ribbon*

Table 9-2. *The Design Ribbon Buttons*

Button	Description
Add	Adds a new column that can contain calculated data.
Delete	Deletes the selected column and all its data or calculations.
Freeze/Unfreeze	Uses the selected column as a column of row titles by sliding it to the left of the data table and then leaving it permanently visible.
Width	Sets the column width in Excel units (based on standard characters in a specific font).
Insert Function	Jumps to the new column to the right of the data and lists all the available functions you can use to define the required calculation.
Calculation Options	Lets you choose between automatic and manual recalculation of the functions that you created or forces a manual recalculation. Functions are introduced in Chapter 10.
Create Relationship	Allows you to define a link, or relationship, between tables.
Manage Relationships	Allows you to modify or delete relationships between tables. Also lets you add new relationships.
Table Properties	Lets you modify the columns used or remap them to the source data, as well as filtering the source data when the table is refreshed.
Mark As Date Table	Defines the table as being a date table that is used for certain specific types of calculation. This is key to using Time Intelligence in PowerPivot.
Undo	Undoes the last action.
Redo	Redoes the last action.

The Advanced Ribbon

The Advanced ribbon lets you prepare the data for effective visualization in Power View and other tools. It might not, however, be displayed initially in your environment. Nonetheless, it is something that we will need to use eventually to prepare the data set for visualization. So, if it is not displayed,

1. Click the File menu to the left of the Home tab.

2. Select Switch To Advanced Mode.

The Advanced ribbon will appear to the right of the Design ribbon.
The buttons that it contains are shown in Figure 9-4 and described in Table 9-3.

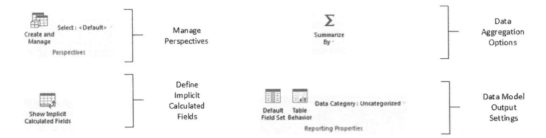

Figure 9-4. *Buttons in the Advanced ribbon*

Table 9-3. *The Advanced Ribbon Buttons*

Button	Description
Create And Manage	Lets you create or modify perspectives (views of the data).
Select:	Lets you switch between perspectives
Show Implicit Calculated Fields	Displays implicit calculated fields that are created when you are creating pivot tables and charts
Summarize By	Lets you select the default autosum function
Default Field Set	Allows you to define a selection of fields (as well as measures and the order in which they all will appear) that can be added in a single click to Power View.
Table Behavior	Contains a set of options that you can set to prescribe certain effects in Power View.

Loading Data into PowerPivot

Ingesting potentially large quantities of data is an inevitable first step when you want to start both analyzing the data and preparing it for display in tools like Power View. In most scenarios you will begin by loading data from one or more sources into the PowerPivot environment. This data can be stored in

*   Excel

*   A relational database such as SQL Server or Access

- A data warehouse such as SQL Server Analysis Services

- A web resource such as the Azure marketplace

- A text file

Now, although we cannot examine every possible source of data, we will look now at the first two options (SQL Server and Excel) as examples of how to import data into PowerPivot. Once you understand the basics, you will find, I am sure, that adding data from other sources is simply an extension of the core techniques.

Loading Data from SQL Server

If you are going to attempt to analyze large quantities of data, then the data might well be stored in a relational database. After all, for a generation these have been the data repository of choice in corporate environments. So what better place to start our journey with PowerPivot than with Microsoft's flagship database, SQL Server?

Before ingesting data from SQL Server you will need to know which authentication type is used in your environment. If you are using Integrated Security, then you are probably lucky, since SQL Server should recognize who you are when you attempt to connect to the database. If it does not, then you will need to get a login name and password from your IT department. Finally, it will help if you have an idea about the data that you are looking for. A SQL Server database can contain hundreds of data tables, so once again, having some upfront guidance from your IT staff could save you time.

In this example we will connect to a SQL Server database called CarSalesData and use Integrated Security. If you have installed the sample database under another name, or you are using SQL Server Security (or if you are connecting to your own database), then you will have to take this into consideration when importing your data. If you will be using the sample SQL Server database, then Appendix A explains how to load it into SQL Server.

1. In the PowerPivot window, activate the Home tab if this has not already been done.

2. Click the From Database button. A popup menu of choices will appear, as shown in Figure 9-5.

Figure 9-5. Database source menu

3. Select From SQL Server. The Table Import Wizard will start up and display the Connect To A Microsoft SQL Server Database pane.

4. Enter the Server name, or click on the popup triangle to get a list of available servers. It can take a minute or two to return the list on a large corporate network.

5. Choose the authentication type (Integrated Security, in this example). If you are using SQL Server authentication, then enter a user name and password.

6. Enter the database name or click on the popup triangle to get a list of available databases on the server. If you are using the sample database, then select CarSalesData. The dialog should look like Figure 9-6.

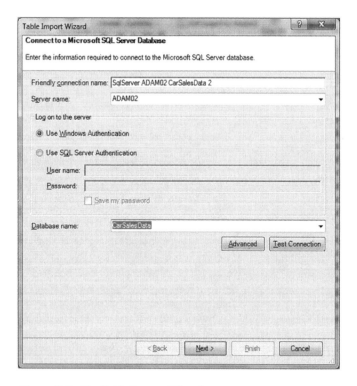

Figure 9-6. *The Table Import Wizard*

    7.   Click Next. The Choose How To Import Data pane of the Table Import Wizard appears. This is shown in Figure 9-7.

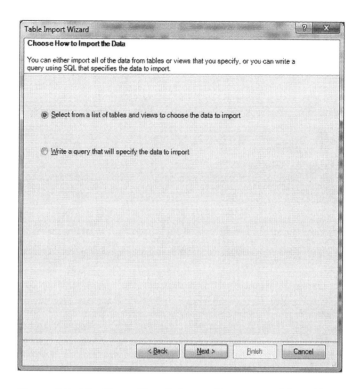

Figure 9-7. The Choose How To Import Data pane of the Table Import Wizard

8. Leave Select From A List Of Tables And Views To Choose The Data To Import selected, and click Next. The Select Tables And Views pane of the Table Import Wizard appears.

9. Select the following tables (or the tables that interest you if you are using your own data):

    a. Clients

    b. Countries

    c. SalesData

    The dialog should look like Figure 9-8.

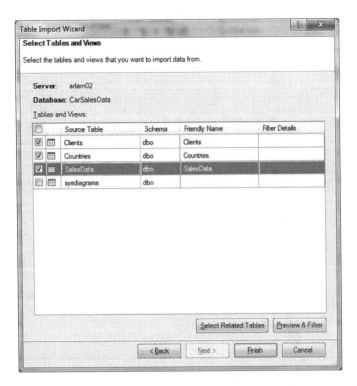

Figure 9-8. *The Select Tables And Views pane of the Table Import Wizard*

10. Click Finish. The tables will be imported into PowerPivot (the dialog will show the import progress), and the Success pane of the Table Import Wizard will be displayed, as shown in Figure 9-9.

Figure 9-9. *The Success pane of the Table Import Wizard*

11. Click Close The PowerPivot window should now contain data, much like in Figure 9-1 at the start of this chapter. Each table that you chose to import is now a "tab" in PowerPivot.

■ **Note** If you chose to select related tables from a database in step 9, then you can click on the Details message in the Success pane of the Table Import Wizard and see the list of all the related tables that were selected, as well as the columns on which they are joined. If the concept of related tables is new to you, then it is explained in greater detail in Chapter 10.

When importing data from a database, it can help to have a rough idea of how many records are in each source table. This way you can compare your approximate figure with the number of rows that PowerPivot has succeeded in importing—and you can track the progress of each import to guess how much time remains for each import. If the import fails for some reason, then you may need to review and redo the import process.

Clearly I tried to show you a flawless import process, and I chose something of a "golden path" to successful data import. This meant I had to make sure I did not get distracted and explain too many non-essential options in the Table Import Wizard. However, there are a few options and techniques that it is probably better to know, so we will go through some of them now.

■ **Note** Generally each data entity that you import into PowerPivot is called a *table*. You may find them referred to as datasheets or (borrowing the Excel term) workbooks as you read about PowerPivot. I will stick to the standard naming convention and call them tables.

Preview and Filter Tables

You may not always want to import an entire table from a database. So, at step 9 in the previous section, you have the option in the Select Tables And Views pane of the Table Import Wizard to subset the elements from each table that you want to import. This includes

- The columns that you want to import

- The subset of records that you want to import, filtered by the elements in one or more columns

Here is how you can *both* take a look at the source data *and* select the data at source so that only a subset of the source table(s) is imported. Obviously, if you exclude records and columns from the start, then you can invalidate your analyses, so you must filter data with care. However, the smaller the data set is in PowerPivot, the faster you will be able to analyze the data. Not only that, but it will load faster and you will be able to save and load the Excel file faster, too.

1. At step (9) in the "Loading Data from SQL Server" section earlier, select the table that you want to subset. It will be highlighted in the wizard.

2. Click Preview And Filter. The Preview Selected Table dialog will appear, as shown in Figure 9-10.

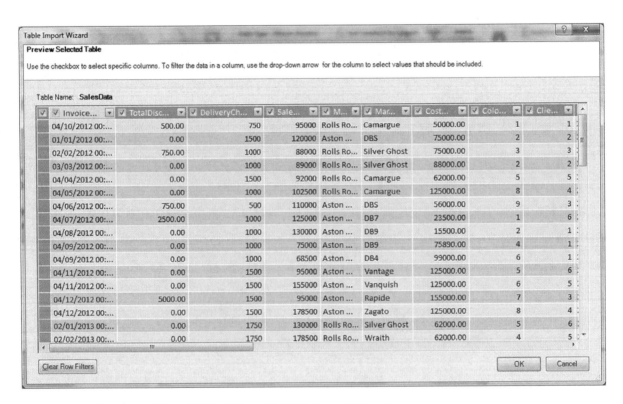

Figure 9-10. *The Preview Selected Table dialog of the Table Import Wizard*

3. Uncheck the columns that you do not want to import. If you cannot see the column titles or data, you can also widen, and narrow, columns by dragging the right column border left or right.

4. Click on the filter popup (the downward facing triangle) for each column where you want to apply a selection to the data contained in the column, and check the elements that you want to import. An example of a filter on the Marque (which is another way of saying vehicle model) column is shown in Figure 9-11.

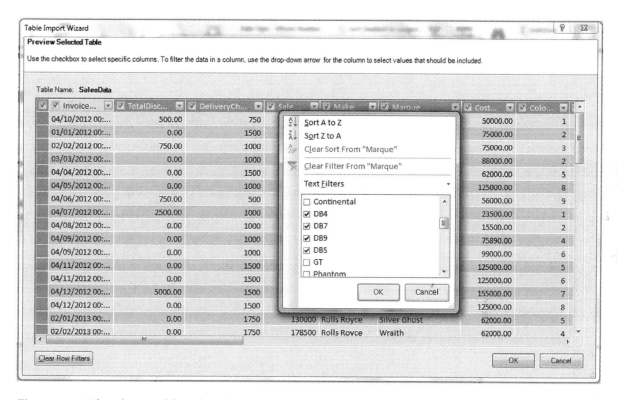

Figure 9-11. *Selected car models in the selected table dialog of the Table Import Wizard*

5. Click OK to return to the Table Import Wizard.

The selected table dialog of the Table Import Wizard also lets you sort the data in the column (in both ascending and descending order) as well as undo a sort operation. If you have applied a complex set of filters you can reset them all by clicking the Clear Row Filters button. Finally, you do not have to accept your filters. You can click the Cancel button and, after confirming that this really is your intention, return to the Table Import Wizard without applying any filters.

Preview and Filter Options

The preview and filter options, which are available in the Preview Selected Table pane of the Data Import Wizard, are not limited to merely including or excluding a selection of values from the data source. You can also either define ranges of numeric values to allow into PowerPivot or set the ranges of values that you wish to exclude. Similarly, you can define text ranges to include or exclude.

These options are available in the Text Filters/Number Filters or Date Filters popup that is displayed when you click on the filter popup for a column when importing data. You can see this in Figure 9-12.

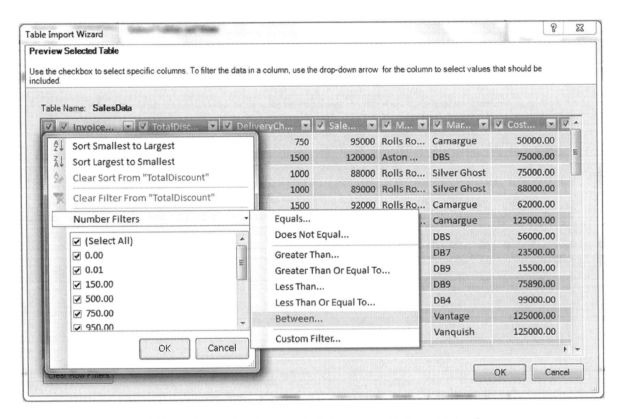

Figure 9-12. *Preview and filter options in the selected table dialog of the Table Import Wizard*

These options are identical to those that you use when filtering data in PowerPivot itself. As I explain them in the "Filtering Data in PowerPivot Tables" section later in this chapter, I will not explain them here, but I suggest that you skip ahead to this section if you need these options when you are importing data.

■ **Tip** You can apply filter options to *all* the tables that you are importing over the same data source without leaving the Data Import Wizard. Just remember to confirm each preview and filter operation for a table, and then click on the next table that you want to subset. Only when all the filter operations are finished do you close the Wizard.

Writing Queries to Select Data

If you have a basic understanding of relational databases—or better, of SQL (the database language used to query SQL Server)—then you can write your own queries to select the data that is imported. A SQL query will select both the rows and the columns of data that will be imported. It can also join tables to select data from several source tables as a single output table.

Fortunately, this does not mean that you have to be a SQL guru to write potentially complex SQL, since the Table Import Wizard has a design pane that will help you create a valid SQL query. Alternatively, if you have existing SQL queries stored as files, you can import them directly to save both time and eventual errors.

To write or design a SQL query that will select the columns and rows of data that you want to use in a PowerPivot table

1. At step 8 in the "Loading Data from SQL Server" section earlier, when the Choose How To Import Data pane of the Table Import Wizard is visible, select Write A Query That Will Specify The Data To Import.

2. Click Next. The Specify A SQL Query pane of the Table Import Wizard will be displayed.

3. If you are a SQL guru, then type or paste in your SQL. If not, then click Design. The Table Import Wizard Design dialog will be displayed (this is explained in more detail in the following pages).

4. Expand the table or view containing the fields that you wish to import in the left-hand pane of the dialog.

5. Select the fields that interest you. The order in which they are selected will be the column order in the PowerPivot table.

6. Click OK. The wizard will write the SQL to filter the data and display it in the dialog. You can then tweak it if you wish.

7. Click Finish to import the data.

Finally you may see a few options when using the Table Import Wizard that I have not yet explained. These are outlined in Table 9-4.

Table 9-4. *Table Import Wizard Options*

Option	Pane	Description
Test Connection	Connect To A Microsoft SQL Server Database	Tests that you can connect to the SQL Server instance that you have selected.
Validate	Specify A SQL Query	Checks that the SQL is accurate.
Select Related Table	Select Tables And Views	Automatically selects any tables that are related (parents or children, for example) to the selected tables. If there are no related tables (or if they are already selected), you will get a message to this effect.

▓ **Tip**   Writing, or tweaking, a SQL query is a great way to specify the order of columns in a PowerPivot table without having to reorder them manually by dragging them around once the data has been imported.

Filtering Data Using the Table Import Wizard Design Dialog

The Table Import Wizard Design dialog is a surprisingly complete and powerful tool for writing fairly complex SQL that will then be used to import data. Although this dialog is fairly intuitive, it is nonetheless a tool that requires a little explanation if you are to use it efficiently.

The Table Import Wizard Design dialog of the Table Import Wizard contains four main parts:

- The Database View pane (on the left) where you can see all the tables and views that you are authorized to access in the database. You can expand the tables and/or views that you want to use here and select and deselect all the fields you want to import. Remember that if you are using data from more than one table, you will have to specify relationships between all the tables and/or views used.

- The Selected Fields pane (the top pane on the right). This pane lists the fields that you have selected and allows you to

    - Change the field order using the up and down icons.

    - Remove a field from the list.

    - Group and aggregate data.

- The Relationships pane (the middle pane on the right). This pane is hidden by default, and you will need to expand it if you are adding or modifying relationships between tables and/or views. it allows you to

    - Detect relationships that already exist in the source database between any of the tables and/or views from which you have selected fields.

    - Add new relationships manually by specifying the fields that make up the relationship.

    - Delete relationships (in the query that you are creating, not in the source database).

    - Change the order of relationships.

- The applied filters pane, which lets you

    - Add filters to subset the data.

    - Delete filters.

    - Modify filters.

These key elements are shown in Figure 9-13.

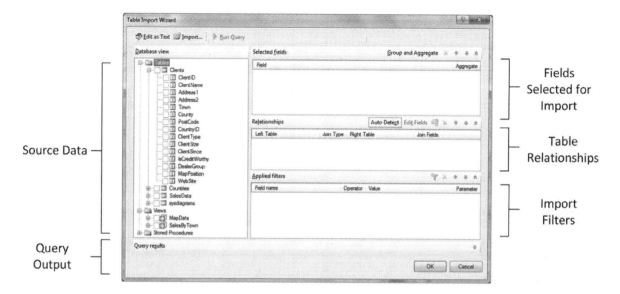

Figure 9-13. *The Table Import Wizard Design dialog of the Table Import Wizard*

So you can see how the Design dialog can work, I suggest a simple example where we will select data from a few fields in two tables in the source database (Clients and Countries). We will join the tables, and then filter to select data only for car dealers.

1. From the PowerPivot screen, choose Existing Connections ➤ Open ➤ Write A Query That Will Specify The Data To Import ➤ Next ➤ Design. This will display the Design dialog.

2. In the Database View pane (on the left) expand the source tables Clients and Countries.

3. Select the ClientName and ClientType fields from the Clients table and select CountryName_EN from the Countries table. You do this by selecting the check box for each required field in the Database View pane. The fields will appear on the right in the upper (Selected Fields) pane.

4. Change the field order. In this example I want the Country Name to be just after the Client Name. Consequently you need to click on the CountryName_EN field in the Selected Fields and click on the Move Up arrow.

5. Open the Relationships pane by clicking on the Expand Pane icon (the double downward-facing chevron). Click AutoDetect. A new relationship will be added to the Relationships pane. PowerPivot knows that these two tables are linked on the CountryID field in each table.

6. Click the Add filter icon (the funnel) above the Applied Filters pane. A new filter will be added showing the first field in the Selected Fields pane.

7. Click on the Field name that is shown. A popup of all the available fields in the tables used in the query appears, as shown in Figure 9-14.

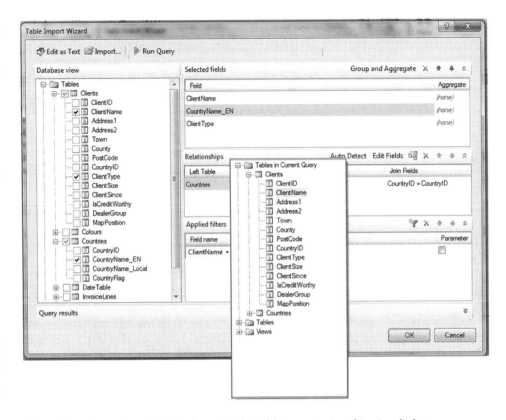

Figure 9-14. *Choosing a field to filter on in the Table Import Wizard Design dialog*

8. Select the ClientSize field.

9. Click on the operator in the second column of the filter and select the Is option.

10. Click in the third column, enter the text **Large** and click the tiny plus symbol. The filter will read ClientSize Is Large.

11. Click OK. The SQL for the query will be displayed in the wizard.

12. Click in the (top) Friendly Name Query box and change the name from Query to something more meaningful, such as ListOfDealers, as shown in Figure 9-15. This will become the table name, saving you from having to rename it later.

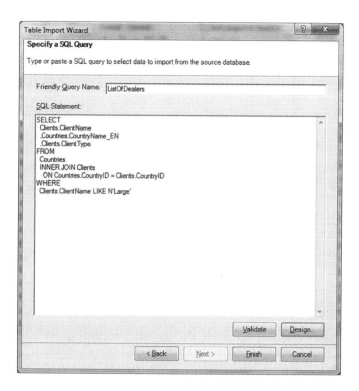

Figure 9-15. *The final SQL created by the Table Import Wizard Design dialog*

13. Click Finish. The query will run and the data will be imported.

There are only a few points to note at this juncture:

- You can create multiple filters. If you do, then all criteria in all the filters will be used simultaneously against the source data to produce (quite possibly) a substantially reduced data set.

- If you choose to define your own relationships between tables, you will need to know which fields to use to create the joins.

- If you are using the Like operator in a filter, then you will need to add a % symbol before and after the text that you are searching for if you want to perform a wildcard search.

- You can always use the designer to create the initial SQL statement and manually tweak it later in the Specify A SQL Query pane of the designer.

List of Tables or Write a Query?

You may be wondering why there are two paths to choose from in the Table Import Wizard in the Choose How To Import The Data pane (which you can see in Figure 9-7 earlier in this chapter). Apart from the reason that we saw immediately in the preceding section—that the Write A Query That Will Specify The Data To Import option allows you to paste in an existing SQL query that you have developed in (say) SQL Server Management Studio—there are other reasons. The differences are outlined in Table 9-5.

Table 9-5. *Write a Query or Select from a List of Tables and Views?*

Option	Description
Write A Query That Will Specify The Data To Import	Imports data from multiple tables joined to produce a single output into a single table
	Allows you to group and aggregate data
	Allows you to reuse existing SQL queries, either by copying and pasting or by importing a file
Select From A List Of Tables And Views To Choose The Data To Import	Allows you to select multiple separate tables that are imported into multiple separate tables
	Lets you apply simple filters based on including or excluding specific values
Either	Allow you to select columns
	Let you define complex filters and data subsets

Importing Other Tables from an Existing Source

Data is nothing if not a moving target, so it is inevitable that you will discover, at times, that you need to import more tables than you originally thought from a data source. This is as easy as the import process that you saw in the previous section, but there is a technique that I want to bring to your attention.

When importing further tables from the same database (or further data from any external source that you are using), reuse the existing connection rather than creating a new one. Now, although you can create a new connection for each source table (even if they are all in the same database), here are some reasons to try to marshal source data so that each table from the same source uses a single, shared connection:

- It makes management of source data much easier when you have dozens of source tables since you can group data by source. This helps you to keep track of the origins of data in your data set.

- It avoids you needing to have dozens of identical connections where only the name changes. This way a single, clearly named connection can replace many others.

- It allows you to refresh all the data from a single source at once if you need to. This is explained in the later section "Data Refresh."

How then, do you reuse an existing connection to import another data table? Here is how:

1. In the Home ribbon click Existing Connections. The Existing Connections dialog will appear.

2. Click Open. The Table Import Wizard will start.

You can now add one or more additional tables—either in their entirety or partially—as you did previously. Adding more tables can be done independently of any tables that you have already imported using a given connection. You should, if possible, avoid re-importing tables that are already in the PowerPivot data set. If you import a table twice, PowerPivot will number it Table 1, Table 2, and so on to indicate the duplication. You can always delete duplicate tables as described a little further on in this chapter.

Modifying Existing Imports

Sometimes column names will change in the source tables from which you have imported data or new columns will be added. Occasionally you will delete columns in an imported table and then want to add them back. Alternatively, you may realize that you no longer need certain columns and want to remove them to save space and declutter the data set. It is also possible that you may have to modify an existing filter on the source data to import more or fewer records. In all of these cases, don't assume that you have to delete the table in PowerPivot and start over. You can easily modify any link to an existing source table and reimport the data. As an example of this, let's suppose that you no longer need the InvoiceNumber column in the SalesData table:

1. Click inside the SalesData table.

2. In the Design ribbon, click the Table Properties button. The Edit Table Properties dialog will be displayed.

3. Scroll through the list of columns to the right, until you can see the column that you wish to modify.

4. Uncheck the InvoiceNumber column. The Edit Table Properties dialog will look like Figure 9-16.

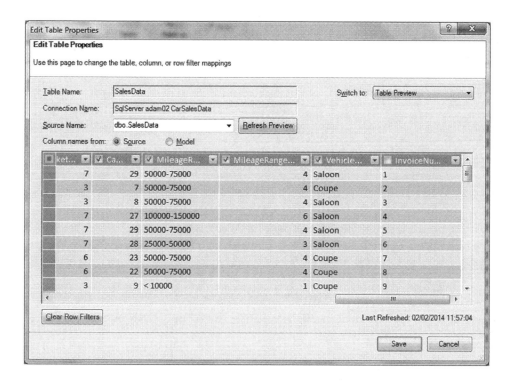

Figure 9-16. *The Edit Table Properties dialog*

5. Click Save. The data will be updated in PowerPivot to reflect the changes you have made to the link to the source data.

This was an extremely simple example of what you can do to tweak the link to source data. As you can imagine, it is far from all that can be done. Some of the techniques that you can apply are described in Table 9-6.

Table 9-6. *The Edit Table Properties Dialog Options*

Option	Description
Source Name	Lets you choose a different table or view in the source database to link to the selected PowerPivot table.
Column Names From	Lets you switch between displaying the columns in the source data or those currently in PowerPivot.
Filter Options	Clicking on the filter popup allows you to subset source data, as described previously.
Column Check Box	Lets you add or remove a column from the data link. Removing a column will delete it from the PowerPivot table.
Clear Row Filters	Removes all filters from all columns. Consequently all the records in the source data will now be imported.

Loading Data from Excel

There is a fighting chance that some of the data that you want to use in PowerPivot is already in Excel. As long as the data is structured as a list (that is, in tabular form), you can add it to a PowerPivot data set in one of two ways:

- Copy and paste (from any Excel workbook)

- Import (from the Excel workbook that contains the PowerPivot data)

Let's now look at both of these possibilities to extend the sample data of car sales that you imported earlier from SQL Server.

Copying and Pasting Data from an Excel Workbook

As long as the source data that you wish to add to PowerPivot is not too voluminous (which you will only discover with experience, and which depends, in any case, on the resources of the PC that you are using), you can simply copy and paste data into PowerPivot from Excel like this:

1. Go to the Excel worksheet containing the data that you wish to copy. In this example it is the sheet named ReferenceData in the Excel file PowerPivotSample.xlsx.

2. Select the data to add to PowerPivot (A1:B10—the table of colors in this example, except for the last line) and copy the table.

3. Switch to the Excel workbook in which you are building a PowerPivot data set (if in another workbook) and switch to PowerPivot. Click Paste in the Home ribbon. The Paste Preview dialog will appear.

4. Enter a table name (Colours in this example).

5. If the data that you copied contains column headers, ensure that the Use First Row As Column Headers. check box is selected. If the data table does not contain column headers, then you can leave this unchecked. The dialog will look like Figure 9-17.

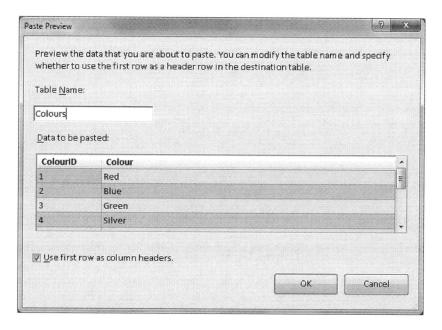

Figure 9-17. Pasting data from Excel

6. Click OK.

The data is copied into PowerPivot and becomes a table with the name you entered.

■ **Note**   You cannot enter a table name that already exists in the PowerPivot data set. If you try this, you will get a warning, and the data cannot be added as a new table.

Appending Data from Excel

If you have copied data from Excel, then the resulting table in PowerPivot is completely static. So if you want to add further data, you need to do it this way:

1. In the source file (PowerPivotSample.xlsx if you are following this example) select the data to add (ReferenceData!A11:B11). Copy these cells.

2. Switch to PowerPivot, select the Colours table, and click Paste Append in the Home ribbon. The Paste Preview dialog will appear, as shown in Figure 9-18.

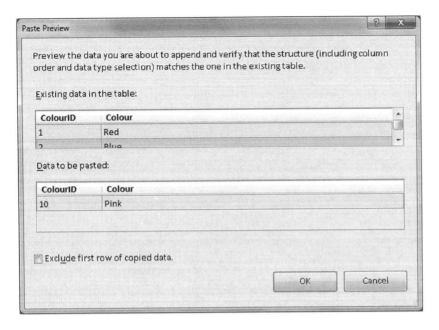

Figure 9-18. *The Paste Preview dialog*

3. Ensure that the format of the copied data is identical to the structure of the destination table, then click OK.

The data that you copied is added to the PowerPivot table at the end of the existing data. If you copied data that includes header rows, then ensure that these do not cause a problem by checking the Exclude First Row Of Copied Data check box.

Updating a Copied Table

In some cases it is easier to replace the entire table in PowerPivot with a new table from Excel. In this case you have to

1. Select the source data in Excel.

2. Switch to PowerPivot and select the destination table.

3. Click Paste Replace in the Home ribbon. The Paste Preview dialog will appear, and you must, once again, check that the source and destination formats are identical.

▓ **Tip** If there is a data type mismatch (that is, if data is perceived as not being compatible), then you will have to correct any anomalies in Excel and attempt the Paste Replace operation again.

Importing Data from an Excel Workbook

If you are fortunate enough to have a table of potential source data in the same Excel file as the one where you are creating your PowerPivot data set, then you can import this table directly into PowerPivot without having to copy and paste. Not only is this operation easier to accomplish, but it places less strain on the resources available on the host PC, and it also makes updating and appending data easier.

If you look at the sample file PowerPivotSample.xlsx, you will see a large table of dates in the ReferenceData worksheet. We will now import this table directly into PowerPivot. In case you were wondering, we need a table of dates to apply what PowerPivot calls "Time Intelligence" to our data, but we'll discuss this more later on in Chapter 10.

1. Select the table of data to import in Excel. In this example it is the range E1:Z1462 in the ReferenceData worksheet of the PowerPivotSample.xlsx file.

2. Click PowerPivot to activate the PowerPivot ribbon in Excel.

3. Click the Add To Data Model button.

The data is added as a new table to PowerPivot. The table is named Table n, but we will see how to change this very shortly.

In the meantime, adding a table from Excel has caused a new ribbon to become visible. This is the Linked Tables ribbon, and its various options (which are shown in Figure 9-19 and describe in Table 9-7) allow you to handle various aspects of linked table data.

Figure 9-19. *Buttons in the Linked Tables ribbon*

Table 9-7. *The Linked Tables Ribbon Buttons*

Button	Description
Update All	Updates the data in all the PowerPivot tables that are linked to Excel worksheets
Update Selected	Updates the data in the current PowerPivot table (which is linked to an Excel worksheet)
Excel Table:	The name of the linked Excel table
Go To Excel Table	Switches to the table in Excel from PowerPivot
Update Mode	Lets you set the way in which data is updated (manually or automatically)

▓ **Note**   You cannot paste data from Excel into a *linked* PowerPivot table, only into a table that was previously *copied* into PowerPivot.

PowerPivot Data Sources

Excel and SQL Server are, fortunately, not the only places from which you can import data into PowerPivot. You can also source your data from

- Other relational databases
- Dimensional data warehouses
- Web- and cloud-based sources
- File-based sources on your local network

Detailing exactly how you can import data from every available source would take up an entire book. Consequently, I only have space here to list several of the available data sources so that you can see those that are easily accessible. Fortunately the process of importing external data follows a broadly similar model, especially if you are connecting to a database, where the techniques described earlier for SQL Server sources can be applied to a greater or lesser extent.

Data can be imported using one of the three buttons in the Get External Data section of the Home ribbon. The first of these, From Database, is described in Table 9-8.

Table 9-8. *Database Sources for PowerPivot*

Database Data Source	Description
Access	Allows you to import data from an MS Access database on your PC or the network
SQL Server	Connects to a Microsoft SQL Server instance to import data
From Analysis Services or PowerPivot	Allows you to import data from an SSAS dimensional data store or another PowerPivot data set

The second button, From Data Service, lets you connect to a web or cloud data source. The options are described in Table 9-9.

Table 9-9. *Data Service Data Sources for PowerPivot*

Data Service Data Source	Description
From Windows Azure Marketplace	Connects to the Windows Azure Marketplace to import data from the available data sources
Suggest Related Data	Attempts to find other useful data sources from the Windows Azure Marketplace
From Odata Data Feed	Imports data in the Odata format

The final button, From Other Sources, lets you connect to a wide variety of data sources including many of the most widely used relational databases and file sources. The options are described in Table 9-10.

Table 9-10. *Other Data Sources for PowerPivot*

Data Type	Description
Microsoft SQL Server	Connects to a Microsoft SQL Server instance to import data
Microsoft SQL Azure	Connects to a Microsoft SQL Server Azure database to import data from the cloud
Microsoft SQL Server Parallel Data Warehouse	Imports data from a Microsoft SQL Server Parallel Data Warehouse appliance
Microsoft Access	Allows you to import data from an MS Access database on your PC or the network
Oracle	Connects to an Oracle Server instance to import data
Teradata	Connects to a Teradata database to import data
Sybase	Connects to a Sybase database to import data
Informix	Connects to an Informix database to import data
IBM DB2	Connects to a DB2 database to import data
Microsoft Analysis Services	Allows you to import data from an SSAS dimensional data store
Report	Imports data from a Microsoft SQL Server Reporting Services report
From Windows Azure Marketplace	Connects to the Windows Azure Marketplace to import data from the available data sources
Suggest Related Data	Tries to find related data from the Azure DataMarket
Other Feeds	Imports data from an atom feed
Excel File	Allows you to import data from an Excel file on your PC or the network
Text File	Allows you to import data from a text file database on your PC or the network

Refreshing Data

Data changes. Nothing is ever permanent, and data less than most things. So just loading your data is rarely the end of the matter. Almost inevitably, you will have to update your data over time as the source data changes.

Now, there is something that we have to be very clear about. PowerPivot is not designed to let you update data in the data set directly. It exists to let you collect and analyze data from disparate sources, but *not* to modify it. So there is no way in which you can add, alter, or delete data in PowerPivot itself, as you can in Excel. However, if your source data changes, you can refresh the copy of the data that you currently hold in PowerPivot with a couple of clicks. This refresh operation completely replaces the existing data in a PowerPivot table to give you a faithful copy of the latest version of the source data.

PowerPivot is indifferent to the source data type, unless it is a linked Excel worksheet. These have to be refreshed separately. However, all other data sources can be refreshed as a whole, if you so choose.

Refreshing Data from External Data Sources

You can refresh tables that contain data from databases, data warehouses, or web-based data sources in three possible ways:

- For a single table
- For all the tables that were loaded using the same connection (which essentially means those from the same external source)
- For all the tables in a PowerPivot data model

Refreshing a Single Table Connected to an External Data Source

Here is how to refresh a single table. I will use the SalesData table that came from an SQL Server database.

1. Select the table whose data you wish to refresh (SalesData, in this example).

2. In the Home ribbon, click the Refresh button. The refresh process starts, and the Data Refresh dialog appears as shown in Figure 9-20.

Figure 9-20. *The Data Refresh dialog*

3. Click Close, assuming that the refresh was flagged as successful.

A data refresh will replace all the data in the table with the latest version from the data source. After the refresh operation, the data will, once again, be a copy of the source data that you chose; that is, it will use the selection of columns and any filters that you set up when you loaded the data initially.

▓ **Note** All refresh operations imply that the structure of the source tables has not been modified. If tables or columns have been renamed or removed, then you will have to tweak the link as described in the earlier section "Modifying Existing Imports."

Refreshing All the Tables in the Data Set Connected to an External Data Source

This technique is extremely useful when you know that a set of linked tables in an external source has changed, and that consequently they all need to be updated in PowerPivot together for the data to remain coherent and valid. To do this

1. In the Home ribbon, click Existing Connections.

2. The Existing Connections dialog appears and lists all the current connections to external data sources.

3. Click on the connection that you want to update. This is shown in Figure 9-21 using the SQLServer Adam02 CarSalesData connection.

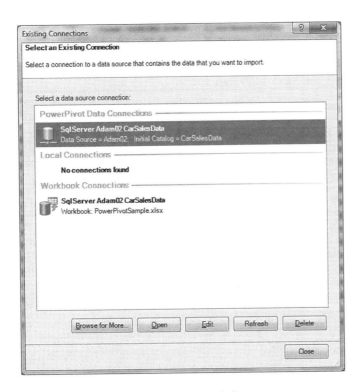

Figure 9-21. The Existing Connections dialog

4. Click Refresh. The Data Refresh dialog will appear (as seen previously in Figure 9-20) and the data will be refreshed. If you are dealing with many tables, or large amounts of data, then this could take a few minutes.

5. Click Close to close the Data Refresh dialog.

6. Click Close to close the Existing Connections dialog.

All the tables where the data originally came from for this data source will be refreshed.

Refreshing All the Tables in the Data Set Connected to an External Data Source

In the case of complex data sets or outdated data, you may well have no choice but to refresh all the tables at once. To do this

1. In the Home ribbon, click the popup menu for the Refresh button and select Refresh All.

2. The Data Refresh dialog appears and lists all the tables whose data is being updated from the data sources.

Refreshing Data from Linked Excel Worksheets

If you have data that you linked to(but have not copied and pasted) from Excel, then you can also update the data either table-by-table or all the tables together.

Refreshing a Single Table Connected to an Excel Worksheet

Here is how to refresh a single table connected to an excel worksheet:

1. Select the table whose data you wish to refresh (DateTable in this example).

2. Ensure that the Linked Table ribbon is activated.

3. Click the Update Selected button.

The data will be refreshed from the source worksheet. Here, too, the current PowerPivot data will be replaced by the data in the source.

Refreshing All the Tables in the Data Set Connected to Excel Worksheets

In the case of complex data sets or outdated data you may well have no choice but to refresh all the tables at once. To do this

1. Click inside any table that is linked to Excel data (remember that there is a tiny chain icon to the left of the table name to indicate that this is a linked Excel table).

2. Ensure that the Linked Table ribbon is activated.

3. Click the Update All button.

▨ **Note** Data that has been copied and pasted from Excel into PowerPivot cannot be updated. You have to copy and replace the data as described previously.

Deleting a Connection

In a complex data set you could end up with dozens of connections. Managing these connections, and deleting unused connections, can help you stay on top of your data. So, if you need to delete a connection

1. Delete all the tables that were imported using this connection.

Deleting all the tables for a connection will remove the connection.

▓ **Note** If you want to see which tables are based on an existing connection, just try and delete the connection by clicking the Delete button in the Existing Connections dialog. A warning dialog will appear telling you which are the tables that you have to delete to remove the connection.

PowerPivot Data Types

When you are importing data from an external source, PowerPivot will try and convert it to one of the six data types that it uses. These data types are described in Table 9-11.

Table 9-11. *PowerPivot Data Types*

Data Type	Description
Date	Stores the data as a date and time in the format of the host computer. Only dates on or after the 1st of January 1900 are valid.
True/False	Stores the data as Boolean—true or false.
Text	Stores the data as a Unicode string of 536,870,912 bytes at most.
Whole Number	Stores the data as integers that can be positive or negative but are whole numbers between 9,223,372,036,854,775,808 (-2^{63}) and 9,223,372,036,854,775,807 ($2^{63}-1$).
Decimal Number	Stores the data as a real number with a maximum of 15 significant decimal digits. Negative values range from -1.79E +308 to -2.23E -308. Positive values range from 2.23E -308 to 1.79E + 308.
Currency	Stores the data as currency—that is, from -922,337,203,685,477.5808 to 922,337,203,685,477.5807 with four fixed precision decimal digits.

For a column of data to be imported successfully, *all* the data in the column must be of the required data type. If any column cannot be converted to the chosen data type, the column will default to text.

Once data has been imported into PowerPivot you can, in certain cases, change the data type. You can, however, only change to a more wide-ranging data type. That is, you can convert most data to text, but alphabetical text cannot be converted to numbers, for instance.

If you are importing data from a relational database, there is a very strong chance that the source data type will map fairly easily to a corresponding PowerPivot data type. So a numeric column will remain as one of the numeric types, and therefore you will be able to aggregate it in PowerPivot. However, other less strongly typed sources (and specifically Excel) can be trickier. It only takes one text field in a million records for the whole column to become a text field in PowerPivot. If this happens, then you cannot force a data type change after the import has finished. You will have to delete the imported table and clean up the source data before re-importing it.

If the data needs any form of cleansing or rationalization then you could be better advised to use Power Query to import int into the Excel data model. This is described in Chapters 12 and 13.

Managing PowerPivot Data

Assuming that all has gone well, you now have a series of tables from various sources successfully added to your PowerPivot data set. You can see these data tables as tabs in the PowerPivot window, much like you see Excel worksheets in an Excel workbook file. It will soon be time to see what we can do with this data, but first, to complete the roundup of overall data management, you need to know how to do a few things like

- Rename tables
- Delete tables
- Move tables
- Move around a table
- Rename a column
- Delete columns
- Move columns
- Set column width
- Freeze columns (set row titles)

Manipulating Tables

Let's begin by seeing how you can tweak the tables that you have imported.

Renaming Tables

Suppose that you wish to rename a table, such as the table of dates that you imported from Excel earlier. These are the steps to follow:

1. Right-Click on the table name tab at the bottom of the PowerPivot window.
2. Select Rename. The current name will be highlighted in the tab.
3. Enter the new name, or modify the existing name.
4. Press Enter.

Deleting a Table

Deleting a table is virtually identical to the process of renaming one—you just right-click on the table name tab and select Delete instead of Rename. As this is a potentially far-reaching operation, PowerPivot will demand confirmation.

Moving a Table

Moving a table is virtually identical to the way in which you move worksheets in an Excel workbook (a process that I am sure that you already know by heart).

1. Click on the table name at the bottom of the PowerPivot window.
2. Drag the table left or right to its new position.

A small black triangle indicates where the table will move. This is shown in Figure 9-22.

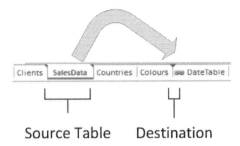

Source Table   Destination

Figure 9-22. *Moving a table*

■ **Note**   Moving a table is something that you are likely to do only because it makes it easier for you to traverse the collection of tables that make up a data set. It will have no effect on the data itself or the way in which PowerPivot uses this data.

The other core table management options are described in Table 9-12.

Table 9-12. *Essential Table Manipulation Options*

Table Option	Description
Delete	Removes the table, its data, and any calculated fields from the PowerPivot data set.
Rename	Renames the table in PowerPivot.
Move	Moves the table relative to the other table tabs.
Description	Lets you add a description to the table that can be used by Power View (and potentially other client tools).
Hide From Client Tools	Leaves the table in Power View, but makes it invisible to Power View (and any other client tools).
Show Calculation Area	Displays the table calculation area under the table data. There is more on this in Chapter 10.

Moving Around a Table

Using the scrollbars to move around a table is one very easy way to look at your data. However, if you have very large tables that contain dozens or hundreds of columns, then it can be easy to spend an excessive amount of time sliding around the data in search of a specific column.

To mitigate the difficulty, PowerPivot lets you

- Select a column name to move to from a list of available columns
- Search for a column

Given the usefulness of these options, it is well worth a rapid detour to see how you can use them.

Selecting a Column from the List of Available Column Names

If you want to leap straight to a column of data (and presuming you know which column contains the data that interests you), all you have to do is

1. Click on the popup (the downward-facing triangle) for the Field List (on the left, immediately above the table grid). An alphabetical list of the fields in the table appears, as shown in Figure 9-23.

Figure 9-23. *The list of columns in a table*

2. Click on the name of the field that contains the data that you want to study.

The cursor will jump to the chosen column in the table. The cursor will remain on the same record it was on before you selected this column.

Searching for Metadata

In the case where you have a pretty good idea of the column name (or table name) that you are looking for, you can get PowerPivot to locate it for you.

1. In the Home ribbon, click Find. The Find Metadata dialog will be displayed.

2. Enter all or part of the field name that you want to locate. I suggest entering the word **InvoiceDate** (without quotes) if you are using the sample data. The dialog will look like Figure 9-24.

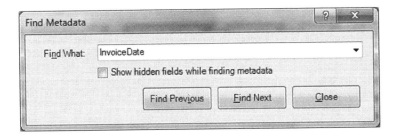

Figure 9-24. *The Find Metadata dialog*

3. Click Find Next (or Find Previous) until you have located the table and/or column that you are looking for.

4. Click Close.

In this example I was looking for column titles, but you can look for any element that PowerPivot contains, whether it is a table, a column, a KPI, or a hierarchy (these latter two are explained in Chapter 11), for instance. Also, if the element is hidden (more of this in the next chapter) you can check the Show Hidden Fields While Finding Metadata check box to have PowerPivot look for hidden elements too.

Also—even if I did mention it in passing in step 2—it is worth noting that you do not have to enter the complete title of a field (or any other valid metadata item). Part of the name will suffice.

■ **Note** The Find Metadata dialog will remember the last few searches. So if you are reusing a previous search, you do not have to type the search element in a second time—you can select it from the popup list that appears if you click the popup menu triangle at the right of the search box.

Manipulating Columns

Now let's see how to perform similar actions—but this time inside a table—to the columns of data that make up the table.

Renaming a Column

Renaming a column is pretty straightforward. All you have to do is

1. Right-click on the title of the column that you wish to rename. In this case it will be CountryName_EN. The column will be selected and the context menu will appear. This is shown in Figure 9-25.

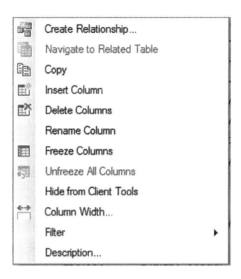

Figure 9-25. *The PowerPivot context menu*

2. Select Rename Column from the context menu. The current column name will be highlighted.

3. Type in the new name for the column (**CountryName**) and press Enter.

And that is it; your column has been renamed. You cannot, however, use the name of an existing column in the same table. If you try, PowerPivot will name the column InvoiceDate2, for example.

Although renaming a column may seem trivial, it can be important. Consider other users first; they need columns to have instantly understandable names that mean something to them. Then there is the Power BI Q&A natural language feature. This will only work well if your columns have the sort of names that are used in the queries—or ones that are recognizable synonyms. Finally, you cannot rename columns in Power View, so you really need to give your columns the names that you are happy seeing in the final output.

■ **Note** Although renaming a column is a piece of cake, the consequences of performing this action can be far-reaching. This could mean that any calculated columns or calculations that refer to this column will now not work (you will see how to create these in the next chapter). Also any visualizations that you have already created that use this column, whether it is using Excel or Power View, will now not work properly. So you should really try and get all your data set elements correctly named *before* you proceed to create calculations and visualizations.

Deleting Columns

Deleting a column is equally easy. You will probably find yourself doing this when you have either brought in a column that you did not mean to import, or you find that you no longer need a column. So, to delete a column

1. Right-click on the title of the column that you wish to delete. The column will be selected and the context menu will appear.

2. Select Delete Columns from the context menu. Unless the column is empty, the confirmation dialog will appear as shown in Figure 9-26.

Figure 9-26. *Deleting a column*

3. Click OK. The column will be deleted from the table.

Deleting unused columns is good practice, as this way you will

- Reduce the memory required for the data set.
- Speed up use of the data in tools like Power View.
- Reduce the size of the Excel file.

■ **Tip** Deleting a column really is permanent. You cannot use the undo function to recover it. Indeed, refreshing the data will not add the column back into the table either. If you have deleted a column by accident, you can choose to close the Excel file without saving and reopen it, thus reverting to the previous version. Otherwise you can tweak the link to the source data and add the column name, as described a few pages previously.

Moving Columns

When you first load data from Excel or SQL Server in this chapter (or from the sources that you are using in your work with PowerPivot) you will noticed that the structure of the tables in PowerPivot reflects exactly the structure of the source tables. All columns appear in PowerPivot in the order in which they appear in the source. Now, as we saw earlier, if you are specifying the data to load using a query or the Table Import Wizard Design dialog, then you can set the order of the columns as you want them in PowerPivot. However, if you prefer to work faster and import a group of tables at once, you have to accept the table structure as is.

However, all is not lost if you want to reorganize the column structure. Doing this can be useful from a data analysis perspective, since it allows you to place columns in an order that makes sense to you. So suppose that you want to move the CostPrice column to the left so that it is now beside, and to the right, of the SalePrice column. This is what you have to do:

1. Click on the column you wish to move (CostPrice). The column will be selected. Ensure that you release the mouse button.

2. Move the mouse pointer over the column title. The cursor becomes a four-headed arrow.

3. Drag the column left or right to its new position. A slim vertical bar will appear to indicate where the column will be moved between existing columns, and you will see a "shadow" of the column header under the mouse pointer.

Figure 9-27 shows how this is done.

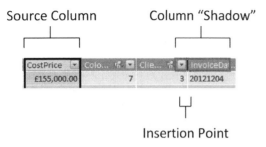

Figure 9-27. *Moving a column*

Setting Column Widths

One final thing that you may want to do to make your data more readable—and consequently easier to manipulate—is to adjust the column width. I realize that as an Excel user you may find this old hat, but in the interests of completeness, here is how you do it:

1. Place the mouse pointer over the right-hand limit of the column title in the column whose width you want to alter. The cursor will become a two-headed arrow.

2. Drag the cursor left or right.

As is the case with Excel, you can select several adjacent columns before widening (or narrowing) one of them to set them all to the width of the column that you are adjusting. You can also double-click on the right-hand limit of the column title in the column whose width you want to alter to have PowerPivot set the width to that of the longest element in the column. Finally you can right-click on a column title and select Column Width. . . to display the Column Width dialog and set the width exactly.

Freezing Columns

When taking an in-depth look at your data you are likely to want to set row titles to the left of the window, just as PowerPivot sets the column titles at the top of the data. There are essentially two ways to do this, depending on whether you wish to use a single column as the row titles or a group of columns.

If all you want to do is to use a single column for the fixed row titles, then all you have to do is

1. Right-click on the title of the column that you wish to use. The column will be selected and the context menu will appear.

2. Select Freeze Columns from the context menu and the selected column will be moved to the left of the table and its contents will be fixed as row titles.

You can now scroll right in the PowerPivot window, and the leftmost column will always remain visible. You will see a slightly thicker column border to the right of the frozen column as a visual indication that the row titles have been set.

If you want to use several columns as row titles

1. Move the columns that you wish to use to the left of the PowerPivot window as a contiguous block.

2. Select the titles of these columns.

3. Right-click on the title of one of the columns and choose Freeze Columns.

You can now scroll right in the PowerPivot window and the chosen columns will always remain visible.

■ **Note**   If you prefer not to use the context (right-click) menu, then the width, freeze, and delete options are also available in the Design ribbon.

To unfreeze all the row titles all you have to do is right-click on any column title—whether it is a frozen row title or an ordinary column—and select Unfreeze All Columns.

Formatting PowerPivot Tables

PowerPivot allows you to apply basic formatting to the data in the tables that it contains. You need to remember, however, that a PowerPivot table is meant to be raw data, and that you should probably not be using this data directly for presentation purposes. After all, that is what Power View is for. However, if you format the data in PowerPivot, then it will appear using the format that you applied in most presentation tools (including Power View). So it is probably worth learning to format data for a couple of reasons:

- You can save time and multiple repetitive operations when creating reports and presentations by defining a format once in PowerPivot. The data will then appear using the format that you applied in multiple visualizations using many different tools.

- It can help you understand your data more intuitively if you can see the figures in a format that has intrinsic meaning.

Here is how to format a column (of figures in this example):

1. Assuming that you have the PowerPivot window open, click on the tab that contains the table where you wish to format data.

2. Click inside the column that you want to format (CostPrice in the sample file).

3. In the Home ribbon, click on the Thousands Separator icon (the comma in the Formatting section). All the figures in the column will be formatted with a thousands separator and two decimals.

The various formatting options available are described in Table 9-13.

Table 9-13. *Currency Format Options*

Format Option	Icon	Description	Example
General		Leaves the data unformatted	100000.01
Decimal Number	,	Adds a thousands separator and two decimals	100,000.01
Whole Number		Adds a thousands separator and truncates any decimals	100,000
Currency	$ ·	Adds a thousands separator and two decimals as well as the current monetary symbol	£100,000.01
Percentage	%	Multiplies by 100, adds two decimals, and prefixes with the percentage symbol	28.78%
Scientific		Displays the numbers in Scientific format	1.00E+05
Increase decimals	⁺⁰	Increases the existing number of decimals	
Decrease decimals	⁻⁰	Decreases the existing number of decimals	

If you wish to return to "plain vanilla" data, then you can do this by selecting the General format. Remember that you are not in Excel, and you cannot format only a range of figures—it is the whole column or nothing. Also there is no way to format nonadjacent columns by Ctrl-clicking to perform a noncontiguous selection. Fortunately you can select multiple adjacent columns, and you can format them in a single operation if, and only if, all the columns are the same data type. Be warned, however, that "same data type" means precisely that. So if one column is a whole number and the one beside it is a decimal, they are considered to be different data types.

■ **Note**   Numeric formats are not available for selection if the data in a field is of text or data/time data type.

Other Currency Formats

By default PowerPivot will apply the currency format that has been set for the PC as a default. If you wish to use another format, then you can do it in this way:

1. Click on the popup (the downward-facing triangle) to the right of the currency format icon. This will display a list of available formats.

2. Select the currency symbol that you want, or click on More Formats to display all the available currency formats, as shown in Figure 9-28, then click OK.

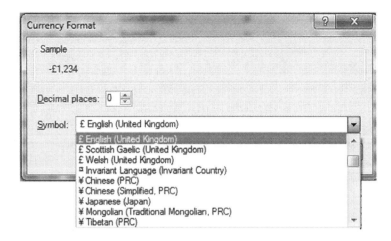

Figure 9-28. *The currency format dialog*

■ **Note**   The thousands separator that is applied, as well as the decimal separator, will depend on the settings of the PC on which the formatting is applied.

Manipulating Data in PowerPivot

Assuming that all has gone well, you now have a set of data tables loaded into PowerPivot, and you have formatted them to suit your taste. The next thing that you may want to do is to take an initial look at the data and see what it contains. PowerPivot contains a set of core functions that are there to help you in this, and that specifically allow you to

- Sort data in PowerPivot tables
- Filter data in PowerPivot tables

Both of these techniques should help you take a first look at your data; let's see how they can be applied.

Sorting Data in PowerPivot Tables

A PowerPivot table could contain millions of rows, so the last thing that you want to have to do is to scroll down through a random data set. Fortunately ordering data in a table is simple:

1. Click inside the column you want to order the data by. I will choose the Make column in the SalesData table.

2. Click the Sort A-Z icon in the Home ribbon to sort it in ascending (alphabetical) order.

The table will be sorted using the selected column as the sort key, and even a large data set will appear correctly ordered in a very short time. If you want to sort a table in descending (reverse alphabetical or largest to smallest order) order, then click on the Sort Z-A icon.

■ **Tip**   If you need a visual indication that a column is sorted, look at the popup icon (the downward-facing triangle) to the right of the column name. You will see a small arrow that faces upward to indicate a descending sort or downward to indicate an ascending sort.

PowerPivot alters the text in the sort icon slightly depending on the data type of the column in which you have clicked. This makes the result even more comprehensible, if anything.

- For a numeric column, the icons read Sort Smallest To Largest and Sort Largest To Smallest.
- For a date column, the icons read Sort Oldest To Newest and Sort Newest To Oldest.

If you want to remove the sort operation that you applied and return to the initial data set as it was imported, all you have to do is click the Clear Sort icon in the Home ribbon.

■ **Note**   You cannot perform complex sort operations; that is, you cannot sort first on one column, then—carry out a secondary sort in another column (if there are identical elements in the first column), as you can in Excel. You also cannot perform multiple sort operations sorting on the least important column and then progressing up to the most important column to sort on to get the effect of a complex sort. This is because PowerPivot always sorts the data based on the data set as it was initially loaded.

Filtering Data in PowerPivot Tables

If you are dealing with millions of rows, then you will probably want to subset the data so that you can take a look at a less overwhelming amount of information. This is where PowerPivot's filtering capabilities can really help you. Suppose that you only want to see the data for a certain make of car in the SalesData table.

1. Click inside the column that you will be using as a basis for filtering the data in the table.

2. Click on the popup icon (the downward-facing triangle) to the right of the column name. The Filter popup will appear, as shown in Figure 9-29, where I want to filter the VehicleType column.

Figure 9-29. *The Filter popup*

3. Uncheck all the boxes for elements that you wish to remove from the filtered data subset.

4. Click OK.

The table will be filtered so that it only displays records that match the filter criteria. You will have a couple of visual indications that a filter is active:

- The popup icon to the right of the column name now contains a small funnel image.

- The row count indicator at the bottom left of the PowerPivot window has changed to show the number of filtered records.

You can filter as many columns as you wish at any one time. Each filter will complement any existing filters and further reduce the amount of visible data. If you want to know quickly what constitutes an active filter, all you have to do is to hover the mouse pointer over the popup icon and a small window will appear displaying the filter settings. An example of this is shown in Figure 9-30.

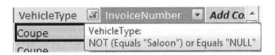

Figure 9-30. *The Filter popup*

▧ **Tip**   If you want to filter quickly on just one data element—for instance, if you want to display only the Aston Martin make—then PowerPivot has a slick way of letting you do this. Simply right-click in the requisite column (Make), click on the required manufacturer name (Aston Martin), and select Filter ➤ Filter By Selected Cell Value. You will see, virtually instantaneously, a data subset only for the records that contain the data in the cell that you chose as your starting point.

When selecting multiple elements to filter on, it is worth remembering that judicious use of the (Select All) option in the filter popup can save you a lot of time. This option selects, or deselects all the elements that are available for filtering. Consequently, if you only want to filter on a few elements—rather than removing a few, as we did in the previous example—then it is probably worth unchecking the (Select All) option so that no elements are selected and then selecting only the items that interest you.

Finally, if you are faced with a long list of elements in the filter popup, then you do not have to scroll down the list to reach an item. If you press the first letter of the item then the list will jump to that element immediately. Then you can use the space bar to select or unselect it, or you can just click the check box to its left.

▧ **Note**   Any filters that you apply are only relevant to your work in the Power Pivot window. They will not be applied to Excel Pivot tables or charts or any visualizations that you create using Power View.

Clearing Filters

As well as applying filters, you will probably need to remove filters from a table. You can do this either for a specific filter, or by clearing all the active filters on a table.

To clear an individual filter:

1.   Click on the popup icon to the right of the column name. In this example, it is for the Marque column in the SalesData table.

2.   In the filter popup, click Clear Filter From "Marque."

The filter is removed, and any data that was hidden by the filter reappears. You will see that the row count indicator at the bottom left of the PowerPivot window has changed to show a larger number of records.

If you want to remove all filters, simply click on the Clear All Filters button in the Home ribbon. All filters will be removed and the entire data set will reappear.

Custom Filters—Text

Rather than choosing lists of items to include or exclude (as we just did), you can also apply more advanced filters to PowerPivot data tables. As with so much in PowerPivot, this is probably best understood if you see an example, so:

1.   Click on the popup icon to the right of the column name (I will use the Make column).

2.   In the filter popup, click on the popup triangle for Text Filters.

3.   Click Equals The Custom Filter dialog appears.

4.   Leave Is Equal To on the left and enter **Jaguar**) in the upper text box on the right. The dialog should look like Figure 9-31.

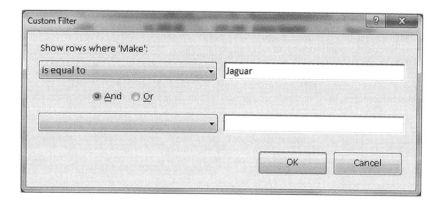

Figure 9-31. *The Filter popup*

5.   Click OK.

The data will be filtered to show only records where the make is Jaguar.

The principal advantage of using advanced filters with text columns is that it can simply be faster to set a filter by typing it in. This also allows you to enter up to two filters by selecting the And option in the Custom Filter dialog and setting the second row in the dialog to filter on another element.

Custom Filters—Numeric

Advanced filters become more useful when applied to numeric data. This is principally because they let you define a range of data—you assign a lower and upper threshold to subset the data if you prefer. To see this in action, let's filter the data for the SalesData table to show only sale prices between £50,000.00 and £100,000.00.

1. Click on the popup icon to the right of the column name (using the SalePrice column here).

2. In the filter popup, click on the popup triangle for Number Filters.

3. Click Greater Than Or Equal To. The Custom Filter dialog appears.

4. Leave Greater Than Or Equal To on the left and enter **50000** in the upper text box on the right.

5. Make sure that And is selected in the center of the Custom Filter dialog.

6. Select Less Than Or Equal To from the lower of the two popups.

7. Enter **100000**) in the lower text box on the right. The Custom Filter dialog should look like Figure 9-32.

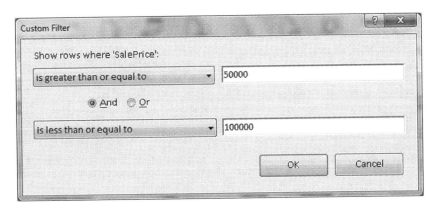

Figure 9-32. *The Custom Filter dialog for a range of numbers*

8. Click OK.

The data will be filtered to show only records where the sale price is between £50,000.00 and £100,000.00. This is not, of course, the only way in which numbers can be filtered. You can look for

- Numbers above a certain limit (by setting the lower threshold only to Greater Than or Greater Than Or Equal To)

- Numbers below a certain limit (by setting the lower threshold only to Less Than or Less Than Or Equal To)

- Numbers outside a specified range, by inversing the use of greater than and less than in steps 3 and 6 in the preceding exercise

- Numbers not equal to a certain value by using the Not Equal To option.

To modify an existing custom filter, all you have to do is click on the popup icon to the right of the column name, click on the popup triangle for Number Filters, and select Custom Filter. The filter that you last specified will reappear and you can tweak it as you see fit.

Custom Filters—Date

Filtering by date is very similar to filtering by numbers. You can select date ranges or all elements where a date is greater or lesser than a certain date. The available options (which include a superb range of instant presets) are outlined in Table 9-14.

Table 9-14. *Date Custom Filters*

Filter Element	Description
Equals	Filters data to include only records for the selected date
Before	Filters data to include only records up to the selected date
After	Filters data to include only records after the selected date
Between	Lets you set an upper and a lower date limit to exclude records outside that range
Tomorrow	Filters data to include only records for the day after the current system date
Today	Filters data to include only records for the current system date
Yesterday	Filters data to include only records for the day before the current system date
Next Week	Filters data to include only records for the next calendar week
This Week	Filters data to include only records for the current calendar week
Last Week	Filters data to include only records for the previous calendar week
Next Month	Filters data to include only records for the next calendar month
This Month	Filters data to include only records for the current calendar month
Last Month	Filters data to include only records for the previous calendar month
Next Quarter	Filters data to include only records for the next quarter
This Quarter	Filters data to include only records for the current quarter
Last Quarter	Filters data to include only records for the previous quarter
Next Year	Filters data to include only records for the next year
This Year	Filters data to include only records for the current year
Last Year	Filters data to include only records for the previous year
Year To Date	Filters data to include only records for the calendar year to date
Custom Filter	Lets you set up a specific filter for two possible date ranges

■ **Note**   All the date presets (those that refer to a week, month, quarter, or year) imply dates relative to the current system date.

Conclusion

Now you can import data into PowerPivot from multiple sources and keep it regularly updated so that you are always looking at the most recent information. Not only that, but you can filter and sort your data, as well as format it and fix row titles to help you look more deeply into the data. All in all, you now have a powerful set of tools in your armory that you can use to begin analyzing extensive data sets.

However, getting an initial data set into PowerPivot is only the first part of the process. You now need to be able to link the tables that you have imported in order to query them efficiently. Then you have to be able to extend the data set with any calculations that you need to convert raw data into accurate analysis. You also need to prepare certain columns to enhance the final display in Power View. These techniques are the subjects of the next two chapters.

CHAPTER 10

Extending the Excel Data Model Using PowerPivot

This chapter further develops the data tables that you imported in the previous chapter. You will discover how to take the data tables that you loaded and convert them into a coherent data set in the Excel Data Model using PowerPivot. This data set will enable you to deliver information, insight, and analysis from the data the tables contain.

Once you have loaded the source data into Power View tables there are essentially three steps to follow to mold the tables into a cohesive whole.

- Establish relationships between the tables so that PowerPivot understands how the data in one table is linked to the data contained in another table. Chaining one table to another will let you use the data to deliver accurate and cogent results.

- Prepare a date table that enables PowerPivot to see how data evolves over time. In the world of data warehousing, such a table is called a date dimension and it is fundamental if there is a date or time element in your analysis.

- Augment the tables with any calculated metrics that you need in the final outputs. These can range from simple arithmetic to complex calculations.

Admittedly, not every data set in PowerPivot will need all these techniques to be applied. In some cases you will only need to cherry-pick techniques from the range of available options to finalize a data set. In any case, it probably helps to know what PowerPivot can do, and when to use which of the techniques outlined in this chapter. So it is up to you to decide what is fundamental and what is useful—and to have a suite of solutions available to deal with any potential issue that you may encounter in your data analysis.

If you want to continue enhancing the data as it appeared at the end of the previous chapter, download the PowerPivotCodeData.xlsx file from the Apress web site. This file will let you follow the examples as they appear in this chapter.

Designing a PowerPivot Data Repository

Congratulations! You are well on the way to developing a high-performance data repository for self-service business intelligence (BI). You have imported data from one or even from several sources into the Excel Data Model. You have taken a good look at your data using PowerPivot and you can carry out essential operations to rename tables and columns, as well as to filter the data. The next step to ensure that your data set is ready for initial use as a self-service BI data repository is to create and manage relationships between tables. This is a fundamental part of designing a coherent and useable data set in PowerPivot.

Before leaping into the technicalities of table relationships, we first need to answer a couple of simple questions:

- What are relationships between tables?

- Why do we need them?

Table relationships are links between tables of data that allow columns in one table to be used meaningfully in another table. If you have loaded the SQL Server data from the example database into PowerPivot (or opened the PowerPivot example PowerPivotCoreData.xlsx file), then you can see that there is a table of sales data that contains a ColourID column, but not the actual color itself. As a complement to this, there is a reference table of colors. It follows that, if we want to say what color a car was when it was sold, we need to be able to link the tables so that the SalesData table can look up the actual color of the car that was sold. This requires some commonality between the two tables and, fortunately, both contain a column named ColourID. So if we are able to join the two tables using this field, then we can see which color is represented by the color ID for each car sold, which figures in the sales data.

Clearly this example is extremely simple. However, it is not unduly contrived, and it represents the way many relational databases store data. So there is every chance that you will see potential links, or relationships, like this in the real-world data that you will import in practice from corporate databases. In any case, if you want to use data from multiple sources in your data analysis, you will have to find a way to link the tables using a common field, like the ColourID field that I just mentioned. The reality may be messier (the fields may not have the same name in the two tables, for instance), but the principle will always apply.

■ **Tip** If you have the necessary permissions as well as the SQL knowledge, then you can, of course, join tables directly in the source database using a query. This way you can create fewer "flattened" tables in Power Pivot from the start.

Data View and Diagram View

Up until now, we have worked exclusively in data view; that is, we have looked at tables and the detail of the data. When moving to the design phase of your data preparation in PowerPivot, it is often easier to switch to diagram view, as this allows you to step back from the detail and look at the data set as a whole. To do this:

1. Click on the Design View button in the Home ribbon. PowerPivot will display the tables in diagram view, as shown in Figure 10-1.

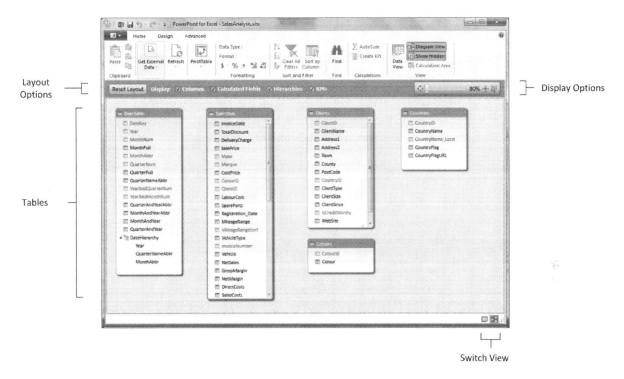

Figure 10-1. *Diagram view*

▪ **Tip**   You can also use the Diagram View icon at the bottom right of the PowerPivot window to switch to diagram view if you prefer.

As you can see from Figure 10-1, you are now looking at most or all of your tables, and although you can see the table and column names, you cannot see the data. This is exactly what we need, because now it is time to think in terms of overall structures rather than the nitty gritty. You can use this view to move and resize the tables. Moving a table is as easy as dragging the table's title bar. Resizing a table means placing the pointer over a table edge or corner and dragging the mouse.

Although repositioning tables can be considered pure aesthetics, I find that doing so is really useful. A well laid out data set design will help you understand the relationships between the tables and the inherent structure of the data.

Diagram View Display Options

The whole point of diagram view is to let you get a good look at the entire data set and, if necessary, modify the layout in order to see the relationships between tables more clearly.

To this end, a few layout options are worth getting to know. They are shown in Figure 10-2.

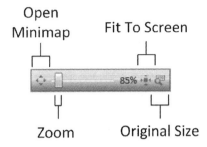

Figure 10-2. *Diagram view display options*

These options are explained in Table 10-1.

Table 10-1. *Diagram View Display Options Explained*

Display Option	Description
Zoom	Allows you to zoom into, or out of, the table display.
Minimap	Shows a high-level overview of the table layout. You can then select the area to view by dragging the mouse over the minimap.
Fit To Screen	Sets the zoom level so that all tables are visible.
Original Size	Displays the tables at their original size.
Reset Layout	PowerPivot displays the tables as they were before any manual adjustment of the layout.

Maximizing a Table

If you have many, many fields in a table, then you may occasionally need to take a closer look at a single table. Fortunately the creators of PowerPivot have thought of this. So, to zoom in on a specific table:

1. Click on the table that you wish to examine more closely.

2. Click the Maximize button at the top right of the table. The table will expand to give you a clearer view of the fields in the table.

    To reset the table to its previous size, click the same icon—now called the Restore button—at the top right of the table.

Creating Relationships

Creating relationships is easy once you know which fields are common between tables. Since we already agreed that we need to join the Colours table to the SalesData table, let's see how to do this.

1. Drag the ColourID field from the SalesData table over the ColourID field in the Colours table.

    A thin arrow will join the two tables as shown in Figure 10-3.

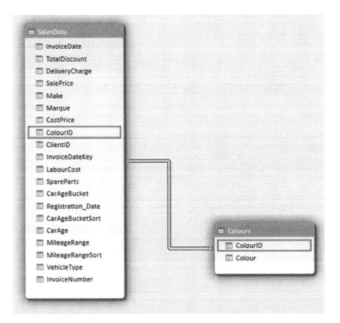

Figure 10-3. *A table relationship*

Creating Relationships Manually

You do not have to drag and drop field names to create relationships. If you prefer, you can specify the tables and fields that will be used to create a relationship between tables. What is more, you do not have to be in diagram view to do this. So, just to make a point and to show you how flexible PowerPivot can be, in this example, you will join the Countries and Clients tables on their common CountryID field:

1. Select the Countries table.

2. Click the Create Relationship button in the Design ribbon. The Create Relationship dialog will appear.

3. On the upper row, where the Countries table is already selected (because you started from the Countries table), select the CountryID field.

4. On the lower row, select the Clients table as the Related Lookup Table. The CountryID field should appear automatically as the field to join on (in the Related Lookup Column field). If PowerPivot has guessed the field, it will display a tiny "i" icon on a round background. If it does not, or if it has guessed incorrectly, you can always select the correct field from the Related Lookup Column popup. The Create Relationship dialog should look like Figure 10-4.

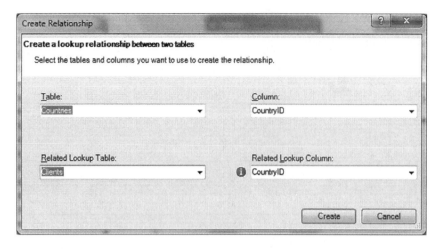

Figure 10-4. *The Create Relationship dialog*

5.   Click Create. The relationship will be created.

■ **Note**   You can create relationships using the manual method in either the data view or the diagram view. Creating relationships manually can be easier when you have hundreds of fields or if you want PowerPivot to guess which fields to use.

Creating Relationships Automatically

If you are importing several tables from a relational database, then you can have PowerPivot to create the relationships during the import process. This approach has a couple of advantages:

- You avoid a lot of manual work.

- You reduce the risk of error (that is, creating relationships between tables on the wrong fields, or even creating relationships between tables that are not related).

This technique is unbelievably easy. You carry out an import from a relational database source (say, using SQL Server). When faced with the list of available tables in the source database (as described in Chapter 9), you

1.   Select the major source table.

2.   Click the Select Related Tables button. Any tables that are linked to the table you have selected will be selected.

3.   Continue the import process as described previously.

Once you have completed the import, switch to diagram view. You will see that the tables you just imported already have the relationships generated in PowerPivot.

■ **Note**   If you choose to select related tables, be aware that doing so only selects tables linked to the table(s) that you have already selected. As a result, you may have to carry out this operation several times, choosing a different starting table every time, to force all the existing relationships to be imported correctly.

Deleting Relationships

In addition to creating relationships, you will inevitably want to remove them at some point. This is both visual and intuitive.

1. Click on the Design View button in the Home ribbon. PowerPivot will display the tables in diagram view.

2. Select the relationship that you want to delete. The arrow joining the two tables will become a double link, and the two tables will be highlighted.

3. Right-click and choose Delete (or press the Delete key). The Confirmation dialog will appear.

4. Click Delete From Model.

The relationship will be deleted and the tables will remain in the data model.

Managing Relationships

If you wish to change the field in a table that serves as the basis for a relationship, then you have another option. You can use the Manage Relationships dialog. This approach may also be useful if you want to create or delete several relationships at once. If you want to use this

1. In the Design tab, click Manage Relationships. The Manage Relationships dialog appears, as shown in Figure 10-5.

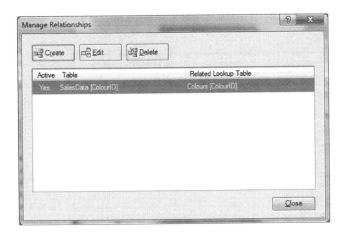

Figure 10-5. *The Manage Relationships dialog*

2. Click the relationship you wish to modify.

3. Click Edit. The Edit Relationship dialog appears (it is virtually identical to the Create Relationship dialog shown in Figure 10-4).

4. Continue modifying the relationship as described previously.

As you can see from this dialog, you also have the option of creating or deleting relationships. Since the processes here are identical to those I have already described, I will not repeat them. If you want to practice using the Edit Relationship dialog, you can use it to complete the data model by adding the following final relationships:

- The SalesData to Clients table on the ClientID field in each table.

- The DateTable table to the SalesData table on the DateKey and InvoiceDate fields, respectively.

The data model will then look like the one given in Chapter 1, Figure 1-13.

■ **Note**   If you delete a set of related tables and subsequently reimport them without importing the relationships, then PowerPivot will *not* remember the relationships that existed previously. Consequently, you will have to re-create any relationships manually. The same is true if you delete and reimport any table that you linked to an existing table in PowerPivot—once a relationship has been removed through the process of deleting a table, you will have to re-create it.

The techniques used to create and manage relationships are not, in themselves, very difficult to apply. It is nonetheless *absolutely fundamental* to establish the correct relationships between the tables in the data set. Put simply, if you try and use data from unconnected tables in a single Power View visualization or Excel pivot table, you will not just get an alert warning you that relationships need to be created, you will also get visibly inaccurate results. Basically, all your analysis will be false. So it is well worth it to spend a few minutes upfront designing a clean, accurate, and logically coherent data set.

Preparing a Date Table

Most business intelligence—indeed, much data analysis—is time-based. Most data sets have date fields in them, and you use these when looking at data over time, but such data is rarely enough to allow you to add what PowerPivot calls time intelligence to a data set.

If you are going to analyze your data using a time dimension (as data warehousing people call it), you will need to add one special thing to your data set: a table that contains a complete and contiguous list of all the dates that you will be using to look at how your data pans out over time.

Since this last sentence was a little dense, let me be clear and state that you *must* add a table to the PowerPivot data set that

- Contains a record for each day in the date/time series—that is, one that extends from the beginning of the year of the first date to the end of the year of the last date for any date field in the table whose data you want to analyze over time.

- Does not contain any gaps in the series of dates. This is vital. Not a single day must be absent from the list of dates.

- Has a date key field that is a date data type.

If you want, you can think of this as a large list of dates that encompasses all the dates for sales, or whatever you are analyzing. This date table can then contain other columns that in turn contain information about each date record. These other columns could, for instance, contain the following:

- Which **Year** the date is

- Which **Quarter** the date is

- What the **Weekday** is

- What the **Month** is

These four examples are only an extremely superficial subset of all the columns that you will probably need in a data table. A good data table will contain every date-based element that you are likely to need in every visualization that you will create using the data model. So you need to foresee every combination of year, day, month, quarter, and possibly week that you are likely to want in every table and chart you will create.

You can then use these complementary columns in visualizations to display the year, quarter, or month (etcetera) and to display them exactly as you have prepared them in the date table. So what you are doing is avoiding the need to format and subset dates in a visualization by preparing the elements that you will use in Power View. Then, once you have such a table, you can link it to the date field in your core data, which will be the basis for time analysis.

So where are you going to get such a table? Well, if you already have such a table in your source data (and corporate data warehouses nearly always contain date tables), then you no longer have a problem. However, if this is not the case, there is nothing to worry about. In PowerPivot there is an easy solution for creating a date table. You simply create the table in an Excel worksheet, and then import it using the techniques I described in the previous chapter.

However, when preparing a date table, the last thing you want to do is enter the month, the quarter, and the day of the week for several hundred rows manually. Table 10-2 contains some selected Excel formulas that will help you create a fairly standard date table easily. Each date element will be a separate column in an Excel table. This table is not meant to be exhaustive, but you can always use this as a starting point and develop it further to correspond more exactly to your requirements. Remember to start with the earliest date that you will be using for all time-based analysis in the table that contains your metrics; then drag the row down in Excel to create as many rows as there are days in the date range that ends at the end of the year corresponding to the last date in your metrics. After you have done this, add the formulas that return the data elements to the first row of the table and copy this row down until you reach the bottom of the date column.

Table 10-2. *Preparing a Date Table*

Column	Formula	Description
DateKey		The unique date.
Year	=YEAR(E2)	The year element.
MonthNum	=MONTH(E2)	The month of the year, as a number. This can be useful for sorting dates.
MonthFull	=TEXT(E2,"mmmm")	The full name of the month.
MonthAbbr	=TEXT(E2,"mmm")	The abbreviated name of the month.
QuarterNum	=ROUNDUP(MONTH(E2)/3,0)	The quarter of the year, as a number. This can be useful for sorting dates.
QuarterFull	="Quarter " & ROUNDUP(MONTH(E2)/3,0)	The full name of the quarter.
QuarterAbbr	="Qtr " & ROUNDUP(MONTH(E2)/3,0)	The abbreviated name of the quarter.
YearAndQuarterNum	=YEAR(E2) & ROUNDUP(MONTH(E2)/3,0)	The year and the quarter in digits. This can be useful for sorting dates.
MonthAndYearAbbr	=TEXT(E2,"mmm") & " " & YEAR(E2)	The abbreviated month of the year and the year.
QuarterAndYearAbbr	=TEXT(E2,"mmm") & "-" & RIGHT(YEAR(E2),2)	The quarter of the year in short form and the year.
MonthAndYear	=TEXT(E2,"mmmm")	The abbreviated month and the year in two digits.
MonthName	=TEXT(E2,"mmmm")	The full name of the month.
MonthNameAbbr	=TEXT(E2,"mmm")	The short name of the month.
QuarterAndYear	="Quarter " & ROUNDUP(MONTH(E2)/3,0) & " " & YEAR(E2)	The quarter and the year fully laid out.

Once you have created a date table, it could look something like Figure 10-6.

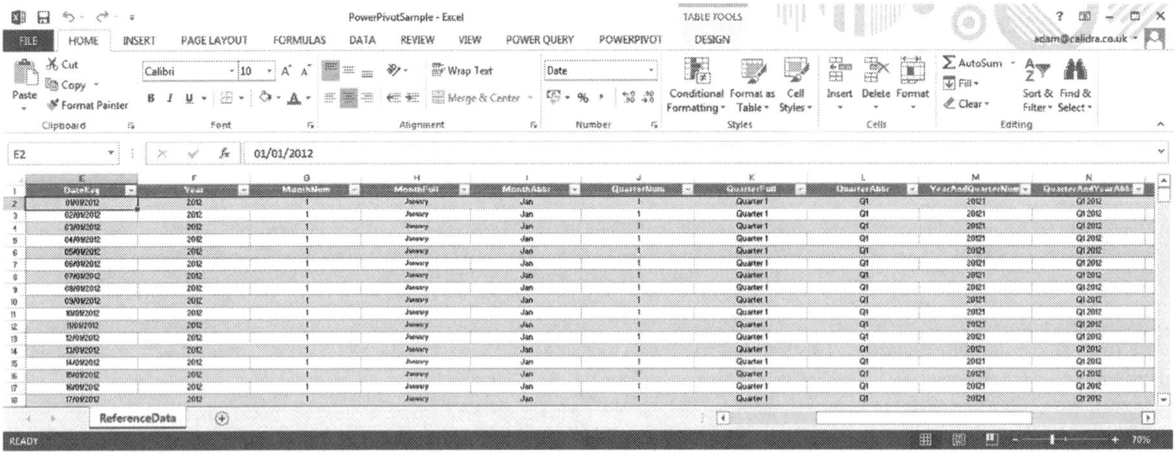

Figure 10-6. *A date table in Excel*

A small date table is in the sample files that you can find on the Apress web site. Once the table is finished, you can then import it into PowerPivot. I will not repeat here how to import a table from Excel; please refer to the previous chapter. Anyhow, once you have imported the date table into Excel, you still have a couple of things to do and then your date dimension will be ready to add time intelligence to your PowerPivot data set.

Marking a Table as a Date Table

PowerPivot now needs to know that the table you have imported is, in fact, a date table that it can use to add time intelligence. This is easier to do than to talk about:

1. Click on the DateTable tab (in data view) or the table itself (in display view).

2. In the Design tab, click the Mark As Date Table button.

3. Switch to the data view.

4. Click on the tab for the DateTable.

5. Select the column that contains the contiguous list of dates. In the example used in this book, it is the DateKey column.

6. To make sure everything has gone well, click on the lower part of the Mark As Date Table button (the small downward-facing triangle) and select Date Table Settings from the popup menu. The Mark As Date Table dialog will appear.

7. The selected (date key) column should appear in the Date popup. If this is not the case, select it from the popup.

8. Click OK.

Now PowerPivot knows that this table is slightly special, and that it contains only a list of dates that can be used to add time intelligence to your analyses. The final thing to do is define a relationship between the DateKey column in the date table and a date field in the table that contains the data you want to analyze over time. In the sample data that we are using, this will be the InvoiceDate field in the SalesDate table. This way the data set knows that you may be looking at sales by invoice date, but that the DateTable will provide the list of days, months, quarters, and years used to display metrics over time.

Calculations

If you are really lucky, then the data that you have imported contains everything that you need to create all the visualizations you can dream up in Power View. Reality, however, is frequently more brutal than that, and it necessitates adding further metrics to one or more tables. These calculated metrics will extend the data available for visualization. This is fundamental when you are using tools such as Power View that do not allow you to add calculated elements to the output, but insist that all metrics—whether they are source data or calculated metrics—exist in the data set. This is less of a constraint and more of a nod toward good design practice, because it forces you to develop calculations once and to place them in a single central repository. It also reduces the risk of error, because users cannot develop their own possibly erroneous metrics and calculations and so distort the truth behind the data.

Calculated Columns

Calculated columns are one of the two ways in which you can extend a data set with derived metrics that you can then use in tools like Power View. There are multiple reasons why you may need further columns. Some reasons, among many, many others, are:

- Concatenating data from two existing columns into one new column

- Performing basic calculations for every row in the table, such as adding or subtracting the data in two or more columns

- Extracting date elements such as the month or year from a date column and adding them as a new column

- Extracting part of the data in a column into another column

- Replacing part of the data in a column with data from another column

- Creating the column needed to apply a visually coherent sort order to an existing column

- Showing a value from a column in a linked table inside the source table

Indeed, the list could go on...

Before you start wondering exactly what you are getting yourself into, I want to add a few words of reassurance about the ways in which a data model can be extended.

- **First**, extending a table with added columns is designed to be extremely similar to what you would do in Excel. Consequently you are building on your existing knowledge.

- **Second**, the functions that you will be using are, wherever possible, similar to existing Excel functions. This does not mean that you have to be an Excel Power User to add a column but that knowledge gained using Excel will help with PowerPivot and vice-versa.

- **Finally**, most of the basic table extension techniques follow similar patterns and are not complex in themselves.

Simple Calculations

To show you what can be done, I will presume that, when working with Power View, you have met a need for a single column of data that contains both the make and model of every car sold. Because the data we imported contains this information as separate columns, we need to add a new column that takes the data from the columns Make and Marque, and joins them together (or concatenates them, if you prefer) in a new column. Here is how it can be done:

1. In the PowerPivot window, make sure that you are in data view.

2. Click on the SalesData tab to select the SalesData table.

3. Scroll to the right of the data in the table and click anywhere in the blank column that appears after the final column of data. This column is currently entitled Add Column.

4. Enter the = (the equals sign). The equals sign will appear in the formula bar above the table of data.

5. Scroll left and click anywhere inside the Make column. The formula bar now reads =[Make].

6. In the formula bar add: **& " " &**. The formula bar now reads =[Make] & " " &.

7. Click anywhere inside the Marque column. The formula bar now reads =[Make] & " " & [Marque].

8. Press Enter. The cursor jumps back to your starting point in the new column at the right of the table. The column is filled automatically with the result of the formula and shows the make and model of each car sold.

9. Right-click on the column header for the new column and select Rename.

10. Enter the word **Vehicle** and press Enter.

The table will now look something like Figure 10-7.

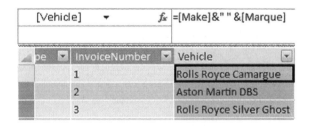

Figure 10-7. *An initial calculated column*

I imagine that if you have been using Excel for any length of time, then you might have a strong sense of déjà vu after seeing this. After all, what you just did is virtually what you would have done in Excel. All you have to remember is that

- Any additional columns are added to the right of the existing columns. You can always move them elsewhere in the table once they have been created.

- All functions begin with the equals sign.

- Any function can be developed and edited in the formula bar at the top of the table.

- Reference is always made to columns, *not* to cells (as you would in Excel). Indeed, you can click anywhere inside a column to obtain a reference to a column, as you did in step 5 in the preceding exercise, or you can type the column name (in square brackets).

- Column names are always enclosed in square brackets.

- You can nest calculations in parentheses to force inner calculations before outer calculations—again, just as you would in Excel.

To extend the basic principle, and also to show a couple of variations on a theme, let's now add a calculation to the SalesData table. More precisely, I will assume that our Power View visualizations will frequently need to display the figure for net sales, which I will define as being the sales figure minus any sales-related costs. To obtain this, by applying a variation on a technique that we used before,

1. Click in the blank column at the right of the SalesData table.

2. Click inside the formula bar.

3. Enter the equals sign.

4. Enter a left square bracket([). The list of the fields available in the SalesData table will appear in the formula bar, as shown in Figure 10-8.

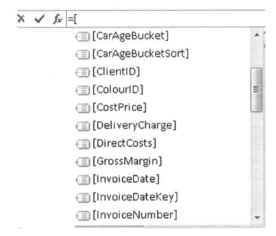

Figure 10-8. *Selecting available columns from a table*

5. Type the first few characters of the column that you want to reference—SalePrice, in this example. The more characters you type, the fewer columns will be displayed in the list.

6. Click on the column name. It will appear in the formula bar.

7. Enter the plus sign (+) or any other mathematical operator you want to use.

8. Continue repeating steps 5 and 6 until you have built the formula you require. In this example, it is

    =[SalePrice] - ([TotalDiscount] + [DeliveryCharge])

9. Click the check box in the formula bar (or press Enter) and the new column will be created. You can now rename and reposition the column.

Using arithmetic in calculated columns in PowerPivot is almost the same as using calculating cells in Excel. Consequently I will not re-explain things you most likely already know. Just use the same arithmetical operators as you would use in Excel and, after a little practice, you should be able to produce calculated columns with ease. If you want to practice a little, begin by adding the columns described in Table 10-3. Adding these columns will prepare the PowerPivot data model, which is used as the basis for all the Power View examples in the previous chapters. These columns are also necessary for some of the formulas that we will use later in this chapter.

Table 10-3. *Calculated Columns in the Sample File*

Calculated Field	Formula	Description
NetSales	=[SalePrice]-([TotalDiscount] + [DeliveryCharge])	Sales minus sales-related costs
GrossMargin	=[NetSales]-[CostPrice]	Sales minus the cost of purchase
NetMargin	=[GrossMargin]-([LabourCost]+[SpareParts])	Sales minus all direct costs
DirectCosts	=[LabourCost]+[SpareParts]	The definition of direct costs
SalesCosts	=[TotalDiscount]+[DeliveryCharge]	Any sales-related costs
Vehicle	=[Make]&" " &[Marque]	The composite column of the make and model/marque

■ **Note** Calculated columns can refer to existing calculated columns. The only trick is to build the columns in a logical order so that you always proceed step by step and do not find yourself needing a column that you have not created yet. Another really helpful aspect of calculated columns is that if you rename a column, PowerPivot will update all formulas that used the previous column name.

Using Formulas in Calculated Columns

Over a few pages you have seen just how easy it is to extend a data model with some essential metrics that you can then use in Power View, or indeed any other end user tool that can take PowerPivot data as its source of information. Yet we have only performed simple arithmetic to achieve our ends. PowerPivot can, of course, do much more than just carry out simple sums. Indeed, it comes with an incredibly powerful data manipulation language called DAX (short for Data Analysis eXpressions).

I am afraid that explaining all the possibilities of DAX would take an entire book, so all I want to do for the rest of this chapter is explain how you can use some core DAX functions in a handful of useful calculations. To begin with—and as an admittedly extremely simple example—I will presume that we need to calculate the age of every car sold relative to the current date. As the source data contains the registration date for each vehicle, this will not be difficult. So, what you have to do is

1. With the SalesData table selected, activate the Design ribbon and click inside any column (not necessarily the empty column at the right of the table).

2. Click Insert Function. The Insert Function dialog will display.

3. From the Select A Category popup at the top of the dialog choose Date And Time.

4. In the Select A Function list click on NOW. The dialog will look like Figure 10-9.

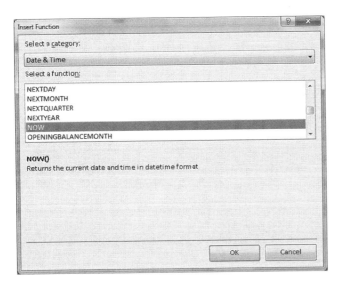

Figure 10-9. *The Insert Function dialog*

5. Click OK. The function is added to the new column and appears in the formula bar. The cursor also jumps directly to the new column at the right of the existing data.

6. Extend the formula so it reads as follows. Remember that you can either enter the Registration_Date field or select it, as described earlier.

    ```
    =(NOW()-[Registration_Date])/365
    ```

7. Press Enter or click the check box in the formula bar. The formula will be added to the entire new column, and you can rename it (I will call it CarAge), move it, and format it as you wish.

Let me be clear, this is not the only way to calculate a time difference using DAX. It is probably not even the best one. It is, however, a simple yet comprehensible introduction to a DAX function which, once again, reminds you just how close a cousin DAX is to the Excel function language. It also shows you an easy way to see exactly what DAX functions are available and what they do, as each function displays a brief explanation when you click on it in the Insert Function dialog.

There is another way to insert functions if you prefer. If you are building a DAX formula in the formula bar, you can call up DAX formulas in the following ways:

- Click on the Fx icon in the formula bar (again, as you would in Excel). This brings up the Insert Function dialog.

- Start typing in the first few characters of the formula—assuming you know that it exists and how it is spelled. This will display a short list of all DAX functions that begin with the characters that you have typed. This is shown in Figure 10-10.

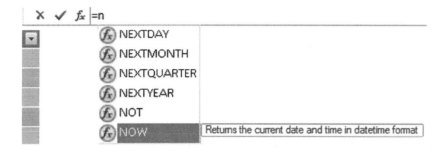

Figure 10-10. Inserting DAX functions in the formula bar

■ **Note**   If you want to abandon a formula while you are creating it, all you have to do is to click the cross icon in the formula bar or press Escape.

To give you another example of a slightly more complex DAX function, but one that is very necessary, consider the following requirement. Our data now has the car age, but we want to group the cars by age buckets. So we will use a nested IF function to do this. Then, to allow us to sort the column in a more coherent way, we will create a Sort By column for the new CarAgeBucket column that we created. I realize that I have not yet explained what a Sort By column is; its use will be explained in the next chapter.

As these columns use the same techniques that you have seen in the last few pages, I will not take you through them step by step but will show you the final, working code as it appears in the sample file. You can then re-create it if you want to as practice. For the sake of clarity, you need to know that the two formulas that follow are based on the following logical DAX functions:

- IF—requires three parameters (just as Excel does): a test, a true result, and a false result.

- AND—allows you to evaluate a number of comma-separated elements, all of which must be true as part of the test in the IF function. Just as in Excel you also have an OR function and a NOT function available.

The code for the CarAgeBucket column is as follows:

```
=IF(
    [CarAge] <=5,"Under 5",
    IF(AND([CarAge]>=6,[CarAge]<=10),"6-10",
        IF(AND([CarAge]>=11,[CarAge]<=15),"10-15",
            IF(AND([CarAge]>=16,[CarAge]<=20),"16-20",
                IF(AND([CarAge]>=21,[CarAge]<=25),"21-25",
                    IF(AND([CarAge]>=26,[CarAge]<=30),"26-30",
                        ">30"
                    )
                )
            )
        )
    )
)
```

The code for the CarAgeBucketSort column is

```
=IF([CarAge]<=5, "1",
    IF(AND([CarAge]>=6, [CarAge]<=10),"2",
        IF(AND([CarAge]>=11, [CarAge]<=15), "3",
            IF(AND([CarAge]>=16, [CarAge]<=20), "4" ,
                IF(AND([CarAge]>=21 , [CarAge]<=25), "5",
                    IF(AND([CarAge]>=26, [CarAge]<=30),"6","7"
                    )
                )
            )
        )
    )
)
```

These formulas could have come straight from an Excel spreadsheet. Indeed, some 80 of the DAX functions are nearly identical to their Excel cousins. So experience and imagination combined have shown me that you have many ways to extend the data you imported by adding calculated columns. Even better, all calculated columns are updated when you refresh the data from the source. The only major caveat is that you have to be careful if you are tweaking the data connection *not* to delete any source columns on which a calculated column depends, or you will get errors in the PowerPivot table.

Just in case you were wondering, you do *not* have to write formulas over multiple lines as I did here. Indeed, the two formulas used earlier could be written as follows:

```
=IF([CarAge] <=5,"Under 5",IF(AND([CarAge]>=6,[CarAge]<=10),"6-10",IF(AND([CarAge]>=11,
[CarAge]<=15),"11-15",IF(AND([CarAge]>=16,[CarAge]<=20),"16-20",IF(AND([CarAge]>=21,
[CarAge]<=25),"21-25",IF(AND([CarAge]>=26,[CarAge]<=30),"26-30","Over 30"))))))
```

And

```
=IF([CarAge] <=5,"1",IF(AND([CarAge]>=6,[CarAge]<=10),"2",IF(AND([CarAge]>=11,[CarAge]<=15),"3",
IF(AND([CarAge]>=16,[CarAge]<=20),"4",IF(AND([CarAge]>=21,[CarAge]<=25),"5",IF(AND([CarAge]>=26,
[CarAge]<=30),"6","7"))))))
```

I chose to write the formulas over multiple lines hoping that by doing so, I'd make the nested logic clearer. You can write your formulas in any way that suits you and that does not cause PowerPivot a problem.

Looking Up Related Data

Most likely, you will frequently want to look up data in another table and have it appear in the table that you are currently enhancing. If you are an Excel user, then you are probably trembling at the thought that there might be a VLOOKUP function in PowerPivot, too. Well, I have good news! The function is no longer as complicated or as lengthy to use to get the lookup in PowerPivot as it can be in Excel. To prove this, imagine that you are using the Clients table and you want to add a calculated column to display the client country that is currently in the Countries table. As the two tables are linked by a table relationship, all you have to do is

1. Scroll to the right of the Clients table and click in the blank column.

2. In the formula bar, add the following code:

   ```
   =RELATED(Countries[CountryName])
   ```

3. Confirm by pressing Enter. The country name for each client will appear in the new column.

4. Rename the column **ClientGeography**.

All that this function does is say, "Use the relationship to the Countries table, and bring back the CountryName field." You do not need to specify how the tables are joined (in this case, on the CountryID fields) as that is defined by the relationship between the tables.

Making Good Use of the Formula Bar

If you only ever enter formulas as simple as those that we just created, then not only will you be extremely lucky, but you can content yourself with a single line in the formula bar. I doubt, however, that this is likely to be the case, as hopefully you will want to do great things with PowerPivot. It follows that you may soon be tired of creating long and complex DAX formulas in a limited space. So here is how to expand the formula bar—pretty much as you would in Excel.

1. Click the Expand icon at the right of the formula bar (the downward-facing chevron).

The formula bar will increase in height to allow you to type and see several lines of text. To reduce the height of the formula bar and reset it to a single line, just click the Reduce icon at the right of the formula bar (which has now become an upward-facing chevron). You'll see this icon in Figure 10-11 momentarily.

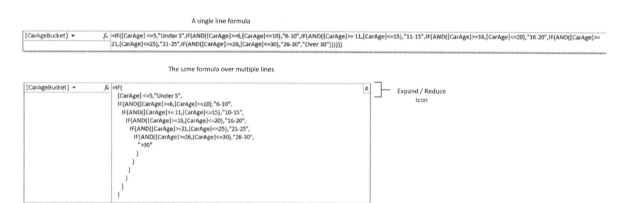

Figure 10-11. Multi-line formulas

If you wish to set the height of the formula bar, all you have to do is drag the top border of the table up or down. The cursor becomes a narrow bar with a small, thin, vertical arrow while you do this—just as if you were adjusting the height of a row in Excel. Interestingly, once you have set the height of the formula bar manually, this is the size that the Expand icon will set it to from this point on in this workbook.

Multiline Formulas

All formulas that you create in PowerPivot will, by default, be on a single line. This can become an extremely wearing way of working, so it is worth knowing that you can tweak long formulas to force them to display over more than one line. All you have to do is force a line return inside the formula bar by pressing Shift-Enter where you want to force a new line. My experience is that PowerPivot will not let you create line breaks everywhere in a formula. Nonetheless, with a bit of trial and error, a more complicated formula, such as the CarAgeBucket column that you created previously, can look like it is in Figure 10-11.

Calculated Fields

Adding calculated columns can provide much of the extra data that you want to output in tools like Power View. It is unlikely, however, that this approach can deliver *all* the analyses that you need. Specifically, calculated columns can only work on a row-by-row basis; they cannot contain formulas that have to apply to all or part of the records in a table. For instance, counting the number of cars sold for a year, a quarter, or a month has nothing to do with the data in a single row in the SalesData table. It does, however concern the table as a whole.

Generally, then, you will almost always need to add a second type of formula to your tables when you have to look at subsets of the data. These formulas are called, simply, calculated fields. These calculations (or measures or metrics—call them what you will) also use DAX. They are, though, applied differently and can produce some extremely powerful results to help you analyze your data.

As with so many aspects of PowerPivot and self-service business intelligence in general, calculated fields are probably best introduced through a few examples. It will, unfortunately, be impossible to do anything other than scratch the surface of calculated fields in a few pages as they are arguably the most powerful element in PowerPivot—one that deserves an entire book to itself. Nonetheless, I hope that this short introduction will whet your appetite, and that you will then continue to learn all about DAX and its more advanced application from the many excellent resources currently available.

A First Calculated Field: Number of Cars Sold

Suppose that you want to be able to display the number of cars sold in Power View. Not only that, but you want this figure to adjust when it is filtered or sliced by another criterion such as country or color. Put simply, you want this metric to be infinitely sensitive to how it is displayed, yet always give the right answer.

So how are we going to achieve this? Here is how:

1. Select the Table to which you wish to add a calculated field. I am choosing SalesData here.

2. Click in a blank cell in the calculation area under the data in the table.

3. Add the following formula to the formula bar:

    `NumberOfCarsSold:=COUNTROWS(SalesData)`

4. Confirm the creation of the formula by pressing Enter or by clicking the check mark icon in the formula bar.

The cell in the calculation area where you placed the calculated field should read `NumberOfCarsSold:=154`. That is, the formula has counted the sales records for the entire table. The name of the formula is NumberOfCarsSold. So, unlike calculated columns, you do not rename calculated fields; you include the name in the formula by entering the name followed by a colon. In this example, the field name did not contain spaces. Had this not been the case, it would have made no difference.

Not difficult, I am sure you will agree. Yet the best is yet to come. Suppose that you now use this field in a Power View table, which is also filtered to show the results for 2013 only, and has tiles. The result is shown in Figure 10-12.

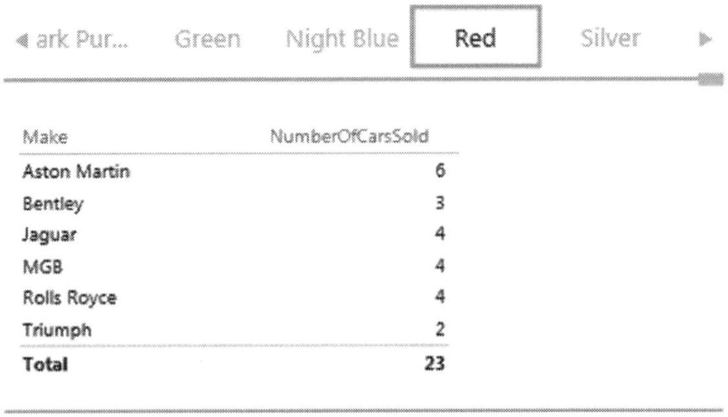

| ◀ ark Pur... | Green | Night Blue | **Red** | Silver | ▶ |

Make	NumberOfCarsSold
Aston Martin	6
Bentley	3
Jaguar	4
MGB	4
Rolls Royce	4
Triumph	2
Total	**23**

Figure 10-12. *Using a calculated field in Power View*

The key thing to take away is that a correctly applied calculated field can be used in Power View or an Excel pivot table or chart and will always show the correct result of any and all filters and selections that you have applied. Also, in pivot tables, the figures will display the correct figure for each intersection of rows and columns. All in all, it is well worth ensuring that you have all the calculated fields that you need for your analytical output in place and that they are working correctly in PowerPivot, because you can then rely on these calculations in the data set in so many different visualizations.

■ **Tip**   Do *not* leave a space between the colon and the equals sign when creating DAX formulas. If you do, PowerPivot will interpret them as text and will not return any result—in addition to leaving you scratching your head for awhile as you wonder why your formula doesn't work.

Basic Aggregations in Calculated Fields

Calculated fields are DAX formulas, so in learning to use calculated fields you will have to become familiar with some more DAX than is generally required for calculated columns. My intention here is definitely not to take you through all that DAX can offer. However, I would like to show you a few basic formulas that can be practically useful in many cases, and as a result give you some initial DAX recipes that should prove of practical use.

As a second example, let's calculate all sales revenue. Although you can just type in a simple DAX formula, I prefer to show you how you can extend the knowledge that you gained when creating calculated columns and apply many of the same techniques to creating calculated fields.

1. Select the SalesData table and click in a blank cell in the calculation area under the data in the table.

2. Enter the calculated field name (**TotalSales**) followed by a colon (**:**) and an equals sign (=).

3. Click the function icon in the formula bar. The Insert Function Dialog will appear.

4. Select Math & Trig as the category and SUM as the function.

5. Click OK.

6. Start typing the table name (**SalesData**). After a couple of characters t[...] fields that it contains will be listed, as shown in Figure 10-13.

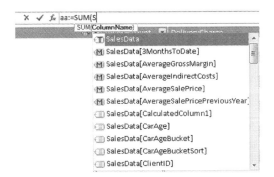

Figure 10-13. *Creating a calculated field*

7. Scroll down and select the SalesData[SalePrice]field.

8. Add a right parenthesis and press Enter (or click the check mark icon in the formula bar). The formula should read: TotalSales:=SUM(SalesData[SalePrice]).

The calculated field will be inserted into the calculation area. This particular function will give you the total of the SalePrice column. However, when you use it in Power View or a pivot table based on the PowerPivot data set, it will be filtered and applied (or sliced and diced if you prefer) to take into account how the data is subset.

One important thing to note when creating calculated fields is that you should almost always use the table name as well as the field name. Also, if a table name contains spaces, then the table name needs to be in single quotes. In all cases the field name has to be enclosed in square brackets.

To practice a little, try creating the average sale price using the following formula:

AverageSalePrice:=AVERAGE(SalesData[SalePrice])

This is still fairly close to an Excel formula, even if it is not identical. Anyway, now that you get the picture, you can use the following formulas (among others) to aggregate your data:

- SUM
- AVERAGE
- COUNT
- MAX
- MIN
- COUNTROWS

For a little practice, then, you could try adding the following calculated fields that are used in the chapters on View:

```
CostToSales:=Sum(SalesData[CostPrice])/SUM(SalesData[SalePrice])
```

```
NetMargin:=SUM(SalesData[NetMargin])/SUM(SalesData[SalePrice])
```

finally

```
GrossMarginToCosts:=SUM(SalesData[GrossMargin])/SUM(SalesData[CostPrice])
```

You may well find that some calculations are displayed (in the calculation area at least) to many decimal places. you find this distracting, then you can format calculated fields in the same way that you format PowerPivot columns. y formats that you apply will be used in Power View by default whenever you use this calculated field.

A final point is that when you insert a table or a field from the popup list that you can see in Figure 10-13, you ll see three types of icon to the left of the table or field: the icon with a T denotes a PowerPivot table; the M icon dicates a calculated field; and the icon without a letter tells you that you are looking at a data field.

More Advanced Aggregations

Now that you have seen how to create basic calculated fields, it is time to move on to some more advanced concepts. More precisely, I want to outline a couple of ways to evaluate data on a row-by-row basis, yet return the result as a function of any filters and slicers. This cannot be done in many cases by using a calculated column and then returning the aggregate of the column data. Think, for instance, of calculating a ratio for each row and then adding up or averaging the results to get the average ratio; it will be arithmetically false.

PowerPivot, fortunately, has some simple yet powerful solutions to this kind of conundrum. One principal tool is the use of the "X" functions—AVERAGEX, COUNTX, SUMX, MAXX, and MINX among others. These functions allow you to specify

- The table in which the calculations will apply
- The row-by-row calculation that is to be applied

As an example, consider the requirement for the average gross margin per sale. Not only do we need this potentially at the finest level of granularity—the individual record—but we may need it sliced and diced by any number of criteria. So here is the formula that you could use in Power View reports:

```
AverageGrossMargin:=AVERAGEX(SalesData,[SalePrice]-[CostPrice])
```

Unlike the AVERAGE function, AVERAGEX takes two inputs (or parameters as they are technically known):

- The *table* to which the formula will be applied
- The *formula* to use, which is just as you would apply it to a calculated column

How It Works

What this formula has done is deduct the CostPrice from the SalePrice for every row in the table, and then return the average dependent on the filters and selections currently applied. This way, you will always get the mathematically accurate result in your visualizations. This is shown in the KPI visualization (Figure 2-30) in Chapter 2.

To make the point (and because they are potentially useful examples for data sets that you might develop), here are a couple more aggregated functions for you to try:

```
AverageIndirectCosts:=AVERAGEX(SalesData, [TotalDiscount] + [DeliveryCharge])
```

and

```
SalePriceAfterIndirectCostsRatio:=(SUM(SalesData[SalePrice]) - (SUM(SalesData[TotalDiscount])
+ SUM(SalesData[DeliveryCharge]))) / SUM(SalesData[SalePrice])
```

The first of these two calculations is largely self-explanatory as it is an extension of the first formula that you saw earlier. The second, however, requires a couple of additional explanations:

- The first point is that it is essential to wrap any field references in an aggregate function, such as SUM, AVERAGE, or COUNT, for an aggregated result to work. This is because the calculation (depending on the filters used) is not applied to only one record, but potentially several records, so data must be aggregated. Hence the use of the SUM function in this example. Should you forget this and not use an aggregate function on numeric fields, PowerPivot will indicate an error, as shown in Figure 10-14. It will also provide a popup message if you hover the pointer over the yellow error symbol. However, I challenge most people to make any sense of the error message.

SalePriceAfterIndirectCostsRatio2..

Figure 10-14. PowerPivot calculated field error message

- The second point is that you can, and indeed, must, nest calculations inside parentheses to force PowerPivot to calculate elements in the correct order. This functions exactly as it does in Excel, so I will not labor the point here.

Describing code may explain some things, but for me, nothing quite explains like a tangible result does. So here, in Figure 10-15, is a Power View table of the three formulas that we developed in this section. The subtle indication that all has been calculated correctly is in the totals, which appeared accurately when the table was created.

2012   **2013**

Colour	AverageGrossMargin	AverageIndirectCosts	SalePriceAfterIndirectCostsRatio
Black	24,333	1,209	98.01 %
Blue	21,787	628	98.91 %
British Racing Green	30,601	917	98.68 %
Canary Yellow	25,002	930	98.40 %
Dark Purple	28,603	634	99.13 %
Green	23,867	832	98.45 %
Night Blue	20,381	840	98.36 %
Red	31,587	1,128	98.50 %
Silver	24,256	778	98.62 %
Total	**25,914**	**889**	**98.57 %**

Figure 10-15. *Some more advanced aggregations using calculated fields*

Time-Dependent Calculations

The penultimate set of functions that I want to explain concern time, or rather, the dates used in analyzing data. PowerPivot calls this *time intelligence* (even though most of the time it refers to is the use of date ranges) and it can be a fundamental aspect of data presentation in business intelligence. After all, what enterprise does not need to know how this year's figures compare to last year's and what kind of progress is being made?

Time intelligence will always require a valid date table, which is one of the reasons why we spent a certain amount of time devoted to this earlier in the chapter. Then the date table has to be joined to the table containing the data that you want to compare over time on a date field. The good news is that once you have a valid date table, and have acquainted yourself with a handful of data and time functions in DAX, you can deliver some extremely impressive results. These kinds of calculations can cover

- YearToDate, QuarterToDate, and MonthToDate calculations

- Comparisons with previous years, quarters, or months

- Rolling aggregations over a period of time, such as the sum for the last three months

- Comparison with a parallel period in time, such as the same month in the previous year

As an introduction to time intelligence in PowerPivot, and also to give you a taste of some of the DAX functions that you are likely to use when analyzing data over time, let's look at some of these calculations.

YearToDate, QuarterToDate, and MonthToDate Calculations

Once you have a date table in place and it is connected to the requisite date field in the table that contains the data you want to aggregate, you can start to deliver some interesting output. Suppose that you want the Quarter to Date and the Year to Date aggregations for car sales. The following two DAX formulas will provide them:

```
SalesQTD:=TOTALQTD(Sum(SalesData[SalePrice]), DateTable[DateKey])
```

```
SalesYTD:=TOTALYTD(Sum(SalesData[SalePrice]), DateTable[DateKey])
```

The formulas used are TOTALQTD (for the Quarter to Date aggregation) and TOTALYTD for the Year to Date aggregation. Both functions take two parameters:

- The *aggregate function* to use (SUM here—although it could be AVERAGE or COUNT or any other aggregate function, depending on the actual metric that you want to deliver) and the table and column that is aggregated.

- The *key field of the date table*. Since the SalesData table is linked to the date table in the data model using the InvoiceDate field, DAX can do the rest.

Interestingly, when you enter the formula correctly, the calculation area cell displays SalesQTD:(blank). This is not any cause for alarm, it is just the way in which some results appear in PowerPivot. Nonetheless, to reassure ourselves, let's see what using these formulas looks like in Power View (Figure 10-16).

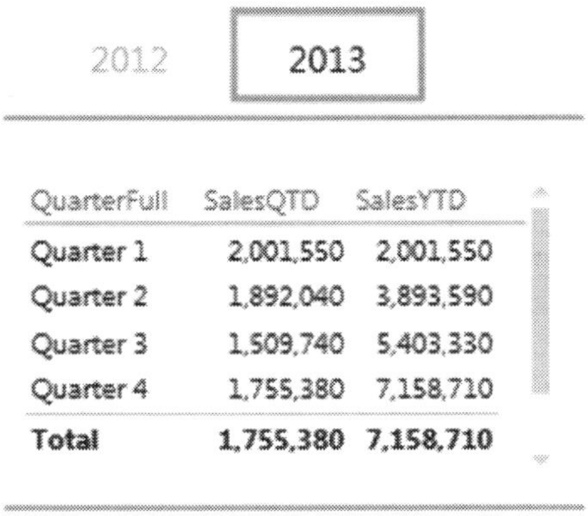

2012	**2013**

QuarterFull	SalesQTD	SalesYTD
Quarter 1	2,001,550	2,001,550
Quarter 2	1,892,040	3,893,590
Quarter 3	1,509,740	5,403,330
Quarter 4	1,755,380	7,158,710
Total	**1,755,380**	**7,158,710**

Figure 10-16. *Quarter to Date and Year to Date functions*

Comparisons with Previous Years, Quarters, or Months

You may have cases when all you want to do is produce the figures for a previous time period so that you can compare the current figures with those for, say, the previous year. There might be several ways of doing this, but here is one fairly simple approach that returns the total car sales for the previous year and the average car sales price for the previous year.

```
SalesPreviousYear:=CALCULATE(SUM(SalesData [SalePrice]), DATEADD(DateTable[DateKey], -1, YEAR))

AverageSalePricePreviousYear:=CALCULATE(
                                  AVERAGE(SalesData [SalePrice]),
                                  DATEADD(DateTable[DateKey], -1, YEAR)
                                  )
```

▪ **Note** I have formatted the code of any complex formulas for greater readability on the page, and hopefully to make the logic of the functions more comprehensible. You might not be able to use the code formatted like this in PowerPivot without simplifying the presentation.

How It Works

Now let me explain. Here we are using a function in DAX called CALCULATE. This function does what its name implies; it calculates an aggregation. However, what is interesting is the way in which its two parameters work:

- The first parameter defines the *function* to use (SUM and AVERAGE here), and the table and column that is aggregated; it could have been potentially a much more complex formula.

- The second parameter is a *filter* to force DAX, in this specific case, to return the data from one year ago. The DATEADD function simply says, "add minus one year to the date column" to get data from a year previously, only it says it as DateColumn / minus 1 / Year.

So what the formula does is to sum or average the data in a column, but only for the previous year, compared to the date field for each row (the InvoiceDate in the sample data, as this is the date field that is linked to the date table in the sample data model). Note that you do not use the InvoiceDate field in these formulas. This is because it is the field that is linked to the DateKey field of the date table. So PowerPivot knows which field to use in the SalesData table as the basis for time comparisons. To labor the point, once again it was essential to create a coherent and complete data model in order to make time intelligence work perfectly.

▪ **Tip**   The DATEADD function lets you replace YEAR with MONTH or DAY if you need to compare with data from days or months previously.

Rolling Aggregations over a Period of Time

We are now getting into the arena of more complex DAX formulas. So, since returning the rolling sum (or average) of a specified period to date necessitates several DAX functions and some in-depth nesting of these functions, I will take this as an example of a more complicated DAX formula. I will begin by outlining some of the functions that are used to deliver a result that is reliable and efficient:

- ISBLANK—This function tests if a calculation returns nothing and allows you to specify what to do if this happens. This is a bit like an IF function that only tests for blank data.

- BLANK()—Returns a blank (or Null). This is useful for overriding unwanted results and replacing them with a blank.

- DATESBETWEEN—Lets you select a range of dates. The three parameters are the date key field from the date table, then the starting date, then the ending date.

- FIRSTDATE—Allows you to get the first date from a range. Since we are using this momentarily to go back a defined number of months, it will get the first day of the month.

- LASTDATE—Allows you to get the last date from a range. Since we are using this momentarily to go back a defined number of months, it will get the last day of the month.

You can now create two calculated fields (3MonthsToDate and Previous3Months) using some fairly sophisticated logic to ensure that only blank cells are returned if there is no previous year's data using the following formulas:

```
3MonthsToDate:=IF(
            ISBLANK(SUM(SalesData[SalePrice])),
                BLANK(),
                CALCULATE(
                        SUM(SalesData[SalePrice]),
                        DATESINPERIOD(
```

```
                                        DateTable[DateKey],
                                        LASTDATE(DateTable[DateKey]),-3,MONTH
                                    )
                        )
                )
Previous3Months:=IF(
                ISBLANK(
                        CALCULATE(
                                SUM(SalesData[SalePrice]),
                                DATEADD(DateTable[DateKey],-1,MONTH)
                                )
                        ),
                        BLANK(),
                        CALCULATE(
                                SUM(SalesData[SalePrice]),
                                DATESBETWEEN(
                                        DateTable[DateKey],
                                        FIRSTDATE(DATEADD(DateTable[DateKey],-4,MONTH)),
                                        LASTDATE(DATEADD(DateTable[DateKey],-1,MONTH))
                                )
                        )
                )
        )
```

How It Works

The formula 3MonthsToDate essentially evaluates the code that is in boldface. This says, "Add up the sales for a time period ranging from three months ago to now," using the InvoiceDate field as the date to evaluate. The IF function detects if there are sales for the current date, and if there are none (ISBLANK), then the calculation is not attempted, and a BLANK is returned.

The formula Previous3Months is pretty similar, except that the time period uses the DATESBETWEEN function to set a range of dates—from the first day of the month four months ago to the last date in the preceding month.

Comparison with a Parallel Period in Time

The following two calculated fields (YearOnYearDelta and YearOnYearDeltaPercent) return the increase or decrease in sales compared to a previous year and also that change expressed as a percentage. These calculated fields extend the logic of the last few formulas using functions that you have already met. The code is as follows:

```
YearOnYearDelta:=IF(
                ISBLANK(
                        SUM(SalesData [SalePrice])
                        ),
                BLANK(),
                IF(
                    ISBLANK(
```

```
                            CALCULATE(
                                    SUM(SalesData [SalePrice]),
                                    DATEADD(DateTable[DateKey], -1, YEAR)
                                    )
                        ),
                    BLANK(),
                    SUM(SalesData[SalePrice])
                    - CALCULATE(
                                SUM(SalesData [SalePrice]),
                                DATEADD(DateTable[DateKey], -1, YEAR)
                                )
                )
            )

YearOnYearDeltaPercent:=IF(
                    ISBLANK(
                            SUM(SalesData [SalePrice])
                            ),
                    BLANK(),
                    IF(
                        ISBLANK(
                                CALCULATE(
                                        SUM(SalesData [SalePrice]),
                                        DATEADD(DateTable[DateKey], -1, YEAR)
                                        )
                            ),
                        BLANK(),
                        (
                            SUM(SalesData[SalePrice])
                            - CALCULATE(
                                        SUM(SalesData [SalePrice]),
                                        DATEADD(DateTable[DateKey], -1, YEAR)
                                        )
                        )
                        /CALCULATE(
                                    SUM(SalesData [SalePrice]),
                                    DATEADD(DateTable[DateKey], -1, YEAR)
                                    )
                    )
                )
```

How It Works

These two formulas are a lot easier than they look, believe me.

The formula for YearOnYearDelta is really only

```
SUM(SalesData[SalePrice])
- CALCULATE(SUM(SalesData [SalePrice]), DATEADD(DateTable[DateKey], -1, YEAR))
```

All the code says is "Subtract last year's sales from this year's sales." Everything else is wrapper code to prevent a calculation if either this year's or last year's data is zero.

Equally, for the formula YearOnYearDeltaPercent, the core code is this:

```
SUM(SalesData[SalePrice]) - CALCULATE(SUM(SalesData [SalePrice]),DATEADD(DateTable[DateKey], -1,
YEAR)) / CALCULATE(SUM(SalesData [SalePrice]),DATEADD(DateTable[DateKey], -1, YEAR))
```

In other words, "Subtract last year's sales from this year's sales and divide by last year's sales." Everything else in the complete formula that is given in full earlier exists to prevent divide-by-zero errors or unwanted results for the first year where there is no previous year's data!

We have seen several DAX functions in this short section and have put together some fairly complex formulas. So I think that it is a good idea to see how they look when you apply them. In this case, I will use an Excel pivot table to show the results, as you can see in Figure 10-17. I am presuming that as an Excel user, you probably already know quite a lot about pivot tables, but if you need a one-minute introduction into how to create pivot tables from PowerPivot, skip to the end of this chapter where this is explained.

Row Labels	TotalSales	SalesPreviousYear	3MonthsToDate	Previous3Months	YearOnYearDelta	YearOnYearDeltaPercent	AverageSalePricePreviousYear
⊖2012	3185500		944,000	2,824,000			
Jan	203500		203,500				
Feb	177000		380,500	203,500			
Mar	172500		553,000	380,500			
Apr	246000		595,500	553,000			
May	256500		675,000	799,000			
Jun	259500		762,000	852,000			
Jul	279000		795,000	934,500			
Aug	350000		888,500	1,041,000			
Sep	297500		926,500	1,145,000			
Oct	249000		896,500	1,186,000			
Nov	333500		880,000	1,175,500			
Dec	361500		944,000	1,230,000			
⊖2013	7158710	3,185,500	1,755,380	7,897,960	3973210	1.247279862	81,679
Jan	737500	203,500	1,432,500	1,241,500	534000	2.624078624	67,833
Feb	610750	177,000	1,709,750	1,681,500	433750	2.450564972	59,000
Mar	653300	172,500	2,001,550	2,043,250	480800	2.787246377	57,500
Apr	642800	246,000	1,906,850	2,363,050	396800	1.61300813	82,000
May	691240	256,500	1,987,340	2,644,350	434740	1.694892788	85,500
Jun	558000	259,500	1,892,040	2,598,090	298500	1.150289017	86,500
Jul	520050	279,000	1,769,290	2,545,340	241050	0.863978495	93,000
Aug	455000	350,000	1,533,050	2,412,090	105000	0.3	116,667
Sep	534690	297,500	1,509,740	2,224,290	237190	0.797277311	74,375
Oct	638250	249,000	1,627,940	2,067,740	389250	1.563253012	83,000
Nov	614880	333,500	1,787,820	2,147,990	281380	0.843718141	83,375
Dec	502250	361,500	1,755,380	2,242,820	140750	0.389349931	90,375
⊖2014		7,158,710		2,290,070			62,250
Jan		737,500		2,290,070			73,750
Feb		610,750					67,861
Mar		653,300					59,331
Apr		642,800					64,280
May		691,240					62,840
Jun		558,000					62,000
Jul		520,050					52,005
Aug		455,000					56,875
Sep		534,690					59,410
Oct		638,250					70,917
Nov		614,880					55,898
Dec		502,250					62,781
Grand Total	10344210	10,344,210		10,344,210	0	0	67,170

Figure 10-17. Pivot table output for time intelligence functions

Other Possibilities

As a final nod to the myriad possibilities that DAX offers, here is how to rank sales by the age of cars in the CarAgeBucket field:

```
SalesRankByAge:=RANKX(ALL(SalesData[CarAgeBucket]),SalesData[TotalSales],,,Dense)
```

How It Works

As its name implies, RANK will rank the first field using the order returned by the descending output of the second field.

Putting It All Together

Finally, if you have created all the calculated fields that are described in this chapter, the calculation area could look something like Figure 10-18.

NumberOfCarsSold: 154	AverageIndirectCosts: 1,031	SalesPreviousYear: 10,344,210.00
TotalSales: 10,344,210	SalePriceAfterIndirectCostsRatio: 98.47 %	AverageSalePricePreviousYear: 67,170.19
AverageSalePrice: 67,170.19		3MonthsToDate: (blank)
	SalesQTD: (blank)	Previous3Months: 10344210
AverageGrossMargin: 26,060.68	SalesYTD: (blank)	YearOnYearDelta: 0
		YearOnYearDeltaPercent: 0
RatioCostToSales: 61.20 %	SalesRankByAge: 1	
RatioNetMargin: 34.64 %		
RatioGrossMarginToCosts: 60.89 %		

Figure 10-18. Calculated fields in the calculation area

A Few Comments and Notes on Using Calculated Fields

Calculated fields are an immense subject. The breadth and depth of the calculations that can be delivered using DAX are little short of astounding. Consequently, it is impossible in an introductory chapter to do anything other than give you a taste of what can be done and hopefully provide a few useful starter functions for you to adapt to your own requirements.

As you move on with DAX, a few things might help you on your way. The first concerns the use of calculated columns. Sometimes they are such an easy solution that it is a shame not to create them. However, they are stored in the table and do take up space. This means more space on disk and more space in memory. This is particularly true for a table containing tens of millions of rows. Calculated fields, on the other hand, are only calculated at run time, and so they take up virtually no space. So, if you are considering creating many calculated columns, perhaps some of them could become calculated fields instead.

Another trick worth knowing is that you can, of course, delete calculated fields by simply using the Delete key (or by right-clicking and choosing Delete). You will need to confirm this choice. However, you can also cut and paste calculated fields, one at a time, in the calculation area. This is a useful technique when you want to rearrange the fields into a more visibly coherent order.

Finally, and particularly if you are creating dozens of calculated fields, remember that you can increase the visible size of the calculation area. Simply drag the line separating the calculation area from the table data up or down.

Calculation Options

I imagine that you have not had to worry about recalculation of PowerPivot workbooks if you have been using relatively small data sets like the sample data for this book. If, however, you are using vast amounts of data (and, after all, this is what PowerPivot was designed for), then recalculation could become a subject that you need to master.

By default PowerPivot will recalculate all calculated columns and calculated fields when there is a change in the data set. These are the main operations that can trigger a recalculation:

- Data from an external data source (of any kind) have been updated.

- Data from an external data source have been filtered.

- You have changed the name of a table or column.

- You have added, modified, or deleted relationships between tables.

- You have altered any formula for a calculated column or a calculated field.

- You have added new calculated columns or calculated fields.

In the case of a large data set, recalculation can take some time. If this slows you down, you can inhibit automatic recalculation and then recalculate the data set when it suits you. To do this

1. In the Design ribbon, click the Calculation Options button. You will see the popup shown in Figure 10-19.

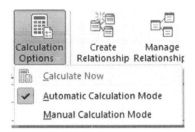

Figure 10-19. *Calculation options*

2. Select Manual Calculation Mode.

Now all you have to do is remember to force a manual recalculation when you have finished a set of changes to the formulas, for instance. This is done by selecting the Calculate Now option from the Calculation Options menu. These options are explained in Table 10-4.

Table 10-4. *Calculation Options.*

Calculation Option	Description
Calculate Now	Recalculates every calculation in the PowerPivot data set if the calculation mode has been set to manual calculation
Automatic Calculation Mode	Sets the calculation mode to manual calculation
Manual Calculation Mode	Sets the calculation mode to automatic calculation

▓ **Note**   It is vital that you recalculate your PowerPivot formulas before saving a worksheet or deploying it using Power BI (of which you will learn more later in Chapter 14).

Creating Pivot Tables from PowerPivot

As I wrote in Chapter 1, I am presuming that you are already familiar with Excel to some extent and that it is quite possible that you are a relatively advanced user. I realize, nonetheless, that you might not have used all that Excel has to offer. So just in case, here is an extremely rapid introduction to creating pivot tables from PowerPivot data.

The art and science of creating and modifying pivot tables in Excel could easily be, indeed is, the subject of many good books. I have no intention of reiterating vast swathes of things that you probably already know. Suffice it to say that when you create a pivot table or chart using a PowerPivot data set, you are using the existing Excel PivotTable tools. I hope that by merely indicating a starting point, I will enable you to continue to use this irreplaceable analytical tool.

Creating a Pivot Table

Assuming that your data set has all the requisite calculations in place, the time has come to create a simple pivot table. This can be a great way to test any calculations that you have developed and to see if they produce the results that you expect.

1. In the PowerPivot window (and you can be in either design view or data view), activate the Home ribbon.

2. Click the Pivot Table button. The Create Pivot Table dialog appears.

3. Select New Worksheet to create the pivot table in a new, independent worksheet. A new worksheet will be created and activated; that is, you will leave the PowerPivot window. This worksheet will contain an empty pivot table and will display the Field List containing the available fields from the PowerPivot data set, as shown in Figure 10-20.

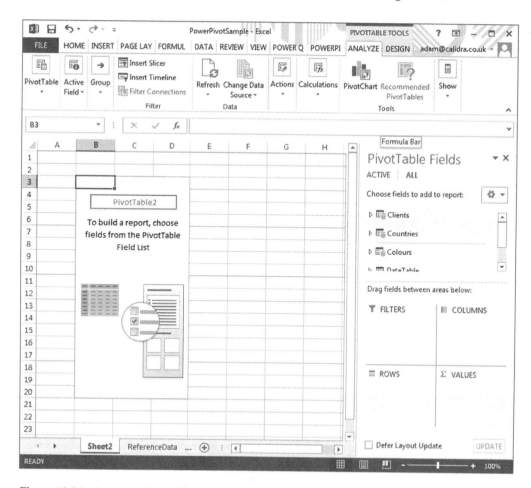

Figure 10-20. *An empty pivot table using the PowerPivot data set*

4. Expand the Countries table and drag the CountryName_EN field to the ROWS area.

5. Expand the Colours table and drag the Colours_EN field to the COLUMNS area.

6. Expand the SalesData table and drag the NumberOfCarsSold field to the VALUES area. The pivot table will look like Figure 10-21.

NumberOfCarsSold	Column Labels ▾										
Row Labels ▾	Black	Blue	British Racing Green	Canary Yellow	Dark Purple	Green	Night Blue	Red	Silver	Grand Total
France	1	1		1	6		2	3	4	2	20
Germany		1								1	2
Spain					1		1		1		3
Switzerland	3	2		1	2	1	1		1	2	13
United Kingdom	8	16		10	12	10	11	10	20	11	108
USA		1		2	1		1		1	1	1	8
Grand Total	12	21		14	22	12	15	14	27	17	154

Figure 10-21. *A simple pivot table*

This is, admittedly, the simplest pivot table I have ever made. However it serves to make the point that PowerPivot data sets can be the basis for pivot tables as well as Power View visualizations. Also, and at some risk of laboring the point, pivot tables are essential for testing your DAX formulas.

The PowerPivot Ribbon

Although we have not needed it so far, now is quite a good time to outline the buttons contained in the PowerPivot ribbon. These buttons are shown in Figure 10-22 and are then described in Table 10-5.

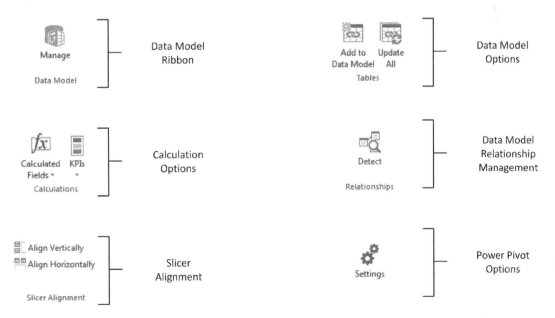

Figure 10-22. *Buttons in the PowerPivot ribbon*

Table 10-5. *The PowerPivot Ribbon Buttons*

Button	Description
Manage	Switches to the PowerPivot window and the data model
Calculated Fields	Allows you to create calculated fields in the data model
KPIs	Lets you create and modify Key Performance Indicators (KPIs)
Align Vertically	Aligns slicers to the pivot table vertically
Align	Aligns slicers to the pivot table horizontally
Add To Data Model	Adds the Excel table to the PowerPivot data model
Update All	Updates all the PowerPivot tables that are linked to Excel tables of data
Detect	Detects relationships from the data used in a pivot table
Settings	Lets you choose the language used by PowerPivot

If you need to add calculated fields to the data model while working in a pivot table, you can do this without switching to the PowerPivot window. Simply click on the Calculated Fields button and define the field. Similarly, you can create KPIs (which you will see in the next chapter) by clicking the KPI button.

Copying Data from PowerPivot

So far when I explained how to subset and order data or when I showed you how to create calculated columns I suggested that it was in order to get a look at the information that you were using. This is certainly true, but it is only one of the reasons for spending time working on your data. Another valid reason is that you want to use the power and speed of PowerPivot to prepare a data set that you will copy into another application, such as Excel, for further customization.

This operation is as easy as it is fast, and the only limitations are

- The memory of the PC on which you are working
- The capacity of the destination application

So, if we presume that you want to copy a subset of data from PowerPivot into Excel, and you have checked the row counter to ensure that you have not gone over the million row Excel limit, all you have to do is

1. Order the columns; filter and sort the data to obtain exactly the subset you want.

2. Click on the top-left corner of the grid for the PowerPivot table. The data subset will be selected.

3. Click Copy in the Home ribbon.

4. Switch to Excel, and select the destination worksheet.

5. Click Paste.

The data is now standard Excel data, ready to be used as you see fit.

Conclusion

In this chapter you have taken the raw data that you successfully imported into PowerPivot and developed it into a coherent and reliable data set. You did this by linking tables to create a cogent whole from the separate tables. Then you saw how to prepare the data set for time intelligence by adding a date table. Finally, you saw how to start adding formulas to the data set to prepare all the metrics that your Power View reports could need.

The data is now almost ready for output. All it needs is a few tweaks to prepare it for Power View (and, to a lesser extent, for Excel pivot tables). This will be the subject of the next chapter.

CHAPTER 11

■ ■ ■

PowerPivot for Self-Service BI

After reading the last two chapters you now understand how to create a valid PowerPivot data model. This data set will allow you to slice and dice your data in many different ways and can be used as-is with many tools such as Excel pivot tables and, of course, Power View.

Indeed, there is little to prevent you now from starting to use the data model that you have created in pivot tables or, better still, to deliver stunning Power View visualizations. However, while we are on the subject of finalizing the data model, there are a handful of tweaks that you may want to apply to the tables in the data set. These modifications are not always necessary, and in many cases might not be required at all. Yet there could be an equal number of times when you will need to spend a couple of minutes preparing the data so that any output (and specifically Power View reports) can deliver what you expect immediately and flawlessly.

The kind of tweaks that we are looking at include these:

- Setting a default field set (a predefined subset of columns that can be used by default in tables and charts)

- Setting default table behavior to prevent aggregation

- Defining the default aggregation for a column

- Indicating that a table has a unique identifier, and which field this is

- Indicating that a column contains images

- Indicating that the text in a column is a URL pointing to an image (and so, in effect, it represents an image)

- Indicating to output tools such as Power View that the data in a column is a URL

- Preparing hierarchies

- Setting Key Performance Indicators (KPIs)

- Hiding certain columns form the end user

- Indicating that the data in a field is a specific geographical type so that Power Map or Power View can use the data to display maps correctly

- Optimizing the file size

None of the techniques that you will see in this chapter are particularly complicated. Few of them take any time at all to apply. Yet, used effectively, they can enhance the output that you present to your audience.

If you want to follow the examples in this chapter, use the sample file PowerPivotSampleDataset.xlsx. This file is available on the Apress web site and contains the data set prepared according to the instructions given in the previous two chapters. You can install this file as described in Appendix A.

Default Field Set

Some data tables will contain hundreds of fields (or columns, if you prefer); others will contain only a few. Many will contain a subset of columns that you will want to use frequently in Power View visualizations. PowerPivot allows you to define a default field set for each table that "remembers" the frequently used columns so that you can use them all at once in a table or chart, without having to add them individually and potentially laboriously. This subset is called the default field set, and it will also be the list of columns that is returned by the Power BI Q&A (natural language query) functionality, which you will learn more about in Chapter 15.

What is more, a default field set is easy to apply in Power View, because all you have to do is click on the table in the Power View Field List. Power View will immediately create a table using *only* the columns in the default field set, in the order in which you defined them when you created the field set. Once this is done, nothing is stopping you from removing any unwanted columns from the table; this is often faster than adding columns individually. Here, then, is how you create a default field set.

1. Ensure that the Advanced ribbon is displayed. This is described in Chapter 9.

2. Click on the tab for the table for which you want to define a default field set. I will take SalesData as an example.

3. Click on the Default Field Set button in the Advanced ribbon. The Default Field Set dialog will be displayed.

4. Add the fields you foresee as being useful as a core group in Power View. I suggest the fields Make, Marque, CarAgeBucket, and SalePrice. To add fields, just double click on a field name in the left-hand pane.

5. Click OK.

6. Save the Excel/Power Pivot file.

You will not see any immediate change in Power View. However, the next time that you click on the SalesData table in the Power View Field List, a table containing the fields Make, Marque, CarAgeBucket, and SalePrice will be created, in this order.

▓ **Note** You cannot create a table in Power View using the default field set by dragging the table name on to the Power View canvas.

If you prefer, rather than double-clicking in step (4) above, you can select a field name in the left-hand pane and click the Add button in the Default Field Set dialog. In addition, to remove a selected field, all you have to do is click on a field name in the right-hand pane and click the Remove button in the Default Field Set dialog. If you want to change the order of the fields that make up the Default Field Set, then all you have to do is click on the field name in the right-hand pane and click the Move Up or Move Down buttons. An existing default field set can be modified at any time by following the steps given earlier.

Table Behavior

Sometimes the data in a table may be accurate and complete, but it will not display exactly as you hoped it would. For example, you may want to sort on a column but find that it needs custom sort criteria so that another column actually provides the sort order. Alternatively, you may want to prevent grouping on certain columns—so that PowerPivot does not presume that all your clients named John Smith are the same person, for instance. These and other options are possible and easy to apply so that your final output projects the effect you require in a clear and transparent way. Together these options are known as *modifying the table behavior* and are applied where necessary to individual tables.

Sort Column

An initial aspect of table behavior that you could find yourself wanting to apply frequently is defining a sort column. Take, for instance, the CarAgeBucket column in the SalesData table in the sample PowerPivotSampleDataset.xlsx data file. If you sort this column directly, the unique values <5 and >30 will appear at the top of the sorted data. Clearly this is not what you want to see, because a viewer would count on the "greater than the fixed upper limit" range to be at the *bottom* of the ascending sort, not at the top. This kind of logical anomaly can be solved by using another column to provide the sort order. Fortunately this was foreseen in the previous chapter when we created not only the CarAgeBucket column but also the CarAgeBucketSort column. So here is how you apply the CarAgeBucketSort column to sort the CarAgeBucket column correctly.

1. Click on the tab name of the table in which you wish to set a custom sort for a column. Let's take as an example the SalesData table in the sample data. This table presents a slight problem when sorting on the CarAgeBucket column, because the values in this column do not sort coherently.

2. Click anywhere inside the CarAgeBucket column, and click the Sort By Column button in the Home tab. The Sort By Column dialog is displayed.

3. In the By popup on the right, select the CarAgeBucketSort column. The dialog will look like Figure 11-1.

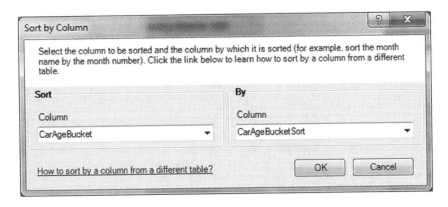

Figure 11-1. *Applying a Sort By column to another column*

4. Click OK.

Now if you sort the data using the CarAgeBucket column as the sort key, the data will actually be sorted using the data in the CarAgeBucketSort column.

■ **Note**   Columns such as CarAgeBucketSort and MileageRangeSort are ideal candidates to be hidden from the user, as they are not really directly useful so they can be considered more a part of the data set infrastructure. Hiding columns is explained later in this chapter.

If you are preparing the PowerPivot data set for use in the Power View chapters of this book, you will need to add Sort By Columns for the fields in Table 11-1.

Table 11-1. *Columns in the Data Set Requiring Sort By Columns*

Table	Column	Sort By Column
SalesData	CarAgeBucket	CarAgeBucketSort
SalesData	MileageRange	MileageRangeSort
Date Table	QuarterAndYearAbbr	YearAndQuarterNum
Date Table	QuarterAndYear	YearAndQuarterNum
Date Table	MonthAndYearAbbr	YearAndMonthNum

Row Identifier

The remaining aspects of table behavior that you can change to enhance output all require that the table contain a unique identifier for each row of data. If your data comes from a relational database, then it probably already has what is known as a *unique primary key*. This is the case for the Countries and Clients tables, so these are the ones that we will use to show the remaining table behavior options.

Before applying any other table properties, we need to tell PowerPivot which column contains the unique key. This is called setting the row identifier.

1. Click on the tab for the table for which you want to set the table behavior. I will take Countries as an example. If you are in diagram view, click on the table.

2. In the Advanced tab, click Table Behavior. The Table Behavior dialog will appear.

3. In the Row Identifier popup, select CountryID. This will cause the three remaining options to become active (and consequently no longer grayed out). The dialog will look like in Figure 11-2.

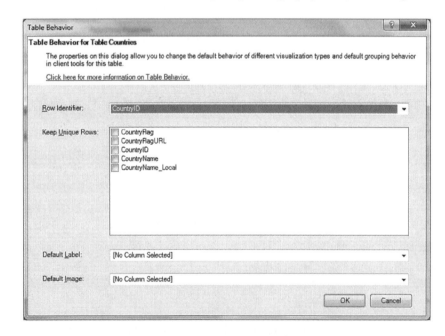

Figure 11-2. *Setting a row identifier for a table in PowerPivot*

4. Click OK.

Once you have successfully set the row identifier, you can proceed to set other table behavior options, as you will see in the next few paragraphs.

■ **Note** If the column that you chose as the row identifier does not contain unique data, then you will get an error message and will not be able to set table behavior. This is something that will have to be dealt with in the source data itself.

Keep Unique Rows

One table behavior option that can be extremely useful is the ability to prevent PowerPivot (and consequently Power View) from aggregating data for a column. As an example, imagine that you have two clients with the same name. They could be subsidiaries in different states or countries. Anyway, you do not want Power View to display a single total when you analyze data by client. If you tell PowerPivot to keep unique rows for the column that contains the client names, then you can achieve this aim.

1. Click on the tab for the table for which you want to stop data aggregating—this will be the Clients table. If you are in diagram view, then click on the table.

2. Define the row identifier for the table (ClientID in this example) as described previously. Do not close the Table Behavior dialog. If you have previously done this, then in the Advanced tab, click Table Behavior.

3. In the Keep Unique Rows section of the dialog, check ClientName.

4. Click OK.

Now when you use the ClientName field in Power View, each client will appear separately, even if more than one client has the same name.

Default Label

Power View treats all text fields as labels. Such egalitarianism may be laudable in many circumstances, but it can diminish certain visual effects when you are using tiles, for instance. So one option is to set a default label field. Put simply, any default label field will be given prominence in certain Power View visualizations.

Let's take Countries as an example here, because it contains two fields that might be used in visualizations. However, let us presume that we need the CountryName field (the renamed CountryName_EN field) to stand out when visualizations are created. Here is how you can set a field to be a default label.

1. Click on the tab for the table for which you want to define the column containing the default image (Countries). If you are in diagram view, then click on the table.

2. In the Advanced tab, click Table Behavior.

3. Ensure that the Row Identifier has been set as CountryID.

4. From the Default Label popup select CountryName.

5. Click OK.

Now, when you create cards in Power View, you get the sort of difference that you can see in Figure 11-3.

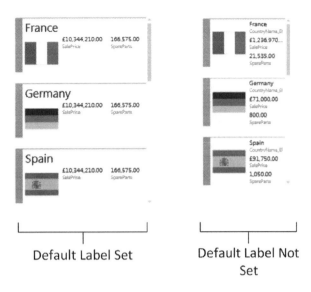

Default Label Set   Default Label Not
                                              Set

Figure 11-3. *Cards in Power View when the default field label is used*

Set a Default Aggregation (Summarize By)

In PowerPivot itself, and in client tools such as Power View, you will inevitably be aggregating numeric data. Normally, this means summing up the data in a table or matrix. In some cases, however, you may find that you want a different aggregation to be applied when you are analyzing your data. Now, you can certainly override any default aggregations when creating Power View visualizations, as we saw in Chapter 2. But it can get very wearing to override the default time and time again in dozens of visualizations in possibly hundreds of reports. So to avoid this waste of energy, define the default aggregation for any field in a PowerPivot data set.

1. Click on the tab for the table for which you want to define the default aggregation. If you are in diagram view, then click on the table.

2. Click on the column or field whose default aggregation you wish to alter.

3. In the Advanced tab, click Summarize By. A popup list of potential aggregations will appear. This is shown in Figure 11-4.

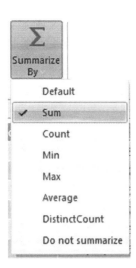

Figure 11-4. *Defining a default aggregation*

    4.   Click on the aggregation you wish to apply as the default.

From now on, the selected aggregation will be applied whenever you use this metric in a Power View table, matrix, or chart. This does not mean that you are stuck forever with the default aggregation that you set, just that it will be used by default until you apply another in a specific visualization.

■ **Note**   Setting a default aggregation can just well mean indicating that *no* aggregation must be applied. This is essentially required when a column contains a numeric value that has no meaning if it is summarized. One example is a column containing years; another is a column of IDs. In these cases, you should choose Do Not Summarize as the aggregation.

Preparing Images for Power View

PowerPivot will not display images, but it can reference or contain images so that Power View can use them to impress your audience. You can make PowerPivot return images to Power View in two ways. Both require a column of data containing either of the following:

- The image as binary data in the source table in a relational database
- A URL to files on an accessible network

Both require a small amount of preparation. Indeed, the two methods are very slightly different depending on how the image is stored. Yet the result is well worth the small amount of effort required to deliver some impressive results, as I am sure you will agree.

Before walking through the techniques for specifying to PowerPivot that fields contain either images or references to images, I think that it is best to explain what the source data must be.

- **Binary data** in a database has to be a file stored as binary data. In SQL Server, for instance, this is data of VARBINARY type. Loading such files into a database could require technical database knowledge and is outside the scope of this book. For further details on this, please consult my book *SQL Server 2012 Data Integration Recipes* (Apress 2012).

- **Image URLs** must be a text reference containing the complete path reference to the binary file that contains the image.

In any case, these are requirements that must be dealt with at the level of the data. Remember that you cannot alter the data itself in PowerPivot.

Binary Images

I will once again take the Countries table as an example here, as it contains binary images that were previously loaded into the database table—and that consequently have been imported into PowerPivot. To tell PowerPivot that a field actually contains an image:

1. Click on the tab for the table for which you want to define the column containing the image (Countries). If you are in diagram view, click on the table.

2. Click on the column that you know contains the binary data for the image (CountryFlag, in this example).

3. Switch to the Advanced tab (unless it is already active).

4. In the Datacategory popup at the right of the ribbon, select Image.

That is all you have to do. From now on, Power View will recognize this field as an image and display the image in visualizations.

Image URLs

In some cases you may have data that does not contain the image but refers to it, either in a network share or on the web. In these cases your source data will (must) have a column that contains the complete path to the image file, including the file name. However, you will need to tell PowerPivot that the text that is imported is not just a label but contains the path to an image. Here is how this can be done for an image on disk:

1. Click on the tab for the table for which you want to define the column containing the image (Countries). If you are in diagram view, then click on the table.

2. Click on the column that you know contains the UNC path to the binary data for the image (CountryFlagURL, in this example).

3. Switch to the Advanced tab (unless it is already active).

4. In the Datacategory popup at the right of the ribbon, select Image URL.

Default Image

As you know, Power View treats all labels as equal; it does the same with images. However, you can choose to decide that some images are more equal than others, and consequently, you give them preeminence when they are displayed. To do this:

1. Click on the tab for the table for which you want to define the column containing the default image (Countries). If you are in diagram view, click on the table.

2. In the Advanced tab click Table Behavior.

3. Check that a row identifier is defined—here it should be CountryID.

4. From the Default Image popup, select CountryFlag or CountryFlagURL.

5. Click OK.

PowerPivot now knows that this image is the default image it should use in output and visualizations.

Preparing Hyperlinks for Power View

Another visualization technique that can impress your audience is to include hyperlinks in Power View reports. Once again, all that this requires is a little preparation.

1. Click on the tab for the table for which you want to define the column containing the hyperlink (Clients). If you are in diagram view, click on the table.

2. Click on the column that you know contains the binary data for the image (ClientWebSite in this example).

3. Switch to the Advanced tab (unless it is already active).

4. In the Datacategory popup at the right of the ribbon, select Web URL.

If you use this field in Power View, it will not just display the URL—it becomes a hyperlink.

■ **Note** You could find that PowerPivot actually recognizes most URLs for what they are and sets them as Web URL (suggested) in the Datacategory popup.

Creating Hierarchies

Hierarchies can be an extremely powerful complement to your data set. Although they are rarely strictly necessary, they can make your data set both easier to understand and easier to use.

A *hierarchy* is a set of columns in a table that guide the user through a predefined path from the highest level to the lowest level. As this is probably best understood with an example, consider how you might describe cars when you are analyzing sales. You probably want to start with the make of car, and then the model. Let's create a hierarchy based on these two elements.

1. Switch to the diagram view in PowerPivot.

2. Right-click on the table title (SalesData, in this example) and select Create Hierarchy. A new hierarchy is created under the last field in the table.

3. Right-click on the new hierarchy (which will currently be called Hierarchy*n* where n is a number) and select Rename.

4. Enter a suitable name (CarDetails, in this example) and press Enter. You will see the new name replace the default name.

5. Drag the first field that you want to add to the hierarchy under the name of the hierarchy. I will use Make. This will become the first level of the hierarchy.

6. Drag the second field that you want to add to the hierarchy under the first level of the hierarchy. I will use Marque (the vehicle model). This hierarchy will look like Figure 11-5.

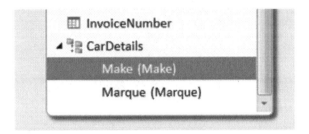

Figure 11-5. *A hierarchy in PowerPivot*

7. Save the Excel/PowerPivot file.

Using a hierarchy (in Power View, for instance) is easy. All you have to do is drag the hierarchy onto the Power View canvas; when you do a table containing all the fields that you defined in the hierarchy will be created in the order in which you created them. So a single click can convert this table into a matrix with a predefined progression through the data, or into a drill-through chart. If you want to use only one of the fields from a hierarchy, then (in Power View again) you just expand the hierarchy and drag the field that you want onto the Power View canvas.

■ **Tip** Once you are used to creating hierarchies in PowerPivot you might like to accelerate the process slightly using the following technique. Start by right-clicking on the first field that you want to appear in a new hierarchy before you select Create Hierarchy. A new hierarchy will then be created using this field. You can then rename the hierarchy and add other fields as described previously.

You can create a hierarchy of many levels in PowerPivot. However, as this technique is primarily to help and guide the user, I would advise that you not overdo it. You can also rename any level in a hierarchy just as you rename a field. PowerPivot will always place the original field name in brackets after the hierarchy name so that you can see which field was the source.

Modifying Hierarchies

Hierarchies are as easy to modify as they are to create. You can add or remove levels, change the order of levels in a hierarchy, or remove the hierarchy entirely.

Adding a Level to a Hierarchy

To add a level to a hierarchy all you have to do is

1.   Click on the name of the field that you want to add to the hierarchy.

2.   Drag the new level onto the hierarchy either between existing levels or above or below the top or bottom existing levels.

When you drag a field onto an existing hierarchy, the cursor becomes a thick black line that indicates where the added level will be placed. This is shown in Figure 11-6.

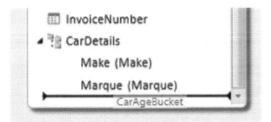

Figure 11-6. *Adding a level to a hierarchy in PowerPivot*

Removing a Level from a Hierarchy

To remove a level from a hierarchy all you have to do is

1.   Right-click on the level that you wish to remove inside the hierarchy at the bottom of the table.

2.   Select Remove From Hierarchy.

3.   Confirm your choice by clicking Remove From Hierarchy in the confirmation dialog that appears.

■ **Note**   Removing a level from a hierarchy has no effect on the data field, which remains in the field list.

Altering the Levels in a Hierarchy

You do not have to re-create an entire hierarchy to modify the levels that you previously created. Suppose that you wish to change the order of the elements in a hierarchy.

1.   Right-click on the level that you wish to reorder inside the hierarchy at the bottom of the table.

2.   Select Move Up or Move Down.

If you prefer to use the mouse, then you can simply drag a level in a hierarchy up and down to reorder the hierarchy. The cursor will become a thick black line to indicate where the level will be moved to.

Deleting a Hierarchy

To delete a hierarchy

1. Right-click on the level that you wish to delete inside the hierarchy at the bottom of the table.

2. Select Delete.

3. Confirm your choice by clicking Remove From Model in the Confirmation dialog.

You can, of course, use the Delete key to remove a previously selected level in a hierarchy, provided that you confirm your action.

■ **Note**   Deleting a hierarchy has no effect on the data fields on which it was based, which remain in the Field List.

Hiding the Original Field

If you are using a field in a hierarchy, you probably do not want to see the field name twice in Power View—once as a field and once again in the hierarchy. PowerPivot has a quick trick to help out here:

1. Right-click on the hierarchy level whose original field you want to hide.

2. Select Hide Source Column Name.

The field will remain in the hierarchy and in the table, but it will no longer appear in Power View as a separate field.

Hiding Hierarchies from the Diagram View

You may not always want your hierarchies to be visible in the diagram view. In this case you can choose to hide—or display—hierarchies like this:

1. In the Display Options bar above the diagram uncheck the Hierarchies check box.

All hierarchies will be hidden in all tables in the data model. To make the hierarchies reappear, simply ensure that the Hierarchies check box is ticked.

Key Performance Indicators (KPIs)

PowerPivot is designed to handle very large amounts of data. Power View is built to allow you to view the salient points in the data. Nonetheless, it can get hard to track and remember many key numbers in a large data set where you have tens, if not hundreds, of important figures to follow.

This is where Key Performance Indicators (KPIs) step in. KPIs, are visual indicators of essential metrics in your data. You set the KPI to indicate whether your sales are on target, for instance. Or you can set a KPI (as we will do now) to keep an eye on gross margins. Then you will display the KPI as a very visual alert in Power View, as you saw in Chapter 2, Figure 2-30.

Creating a KPI

So what we will do here is create a KPI using the AvgGrossMargin calculated field from the sample data. We will then tell PowerPivot that we are aiming for a gross margin of £15,000.00, and that we will accept a range of £11,000.00 to £16,000.00 as acceptable. Anything below £11,000.00 is unacceptable and will trigger a visual warning; anything over £16,000.00 will be flagged as good news.

1. Switch to data view (unless you are already in this view).

2. Select the SalesData tab.

3. Click on the calculated field AvgGrossMargin in the calculation area at the bottom of the datasheet. If it is not there, refer to the "Calculated Fields" section of Chapter 10 to learn how to create it.

4. Click the Create KPI button in the Home tab. The Key Performance Indicator (KPI) dialog will appear. The AvgGrossMargin field will be set at the top of the dialog as the KPI base field (value).

5. Click the Absolute Value radio button.

6. Enter a value of **15000** in the Absolute Value field (it probably shows 100 at the moment).

7. Click anywhere in the middle of the dialog. The Status Thresholds (the funnel indicators separating the red, yellow, and green bands) will change.

8. Drag the upper status threshold to the right of the target until the value is 16000. Alternatively, you can enter the figure in the yellow box above the upper threshold.

9. Drag the lower status threshold to the right until the value is 11000. Alternatively, you can enter the figure in the yellow box above the lower threshold.

10. Select the fifth icon style from the left (a red cross, a yellow exclamation point, and a green tick mark). The dialog should look like Figure 11-7.

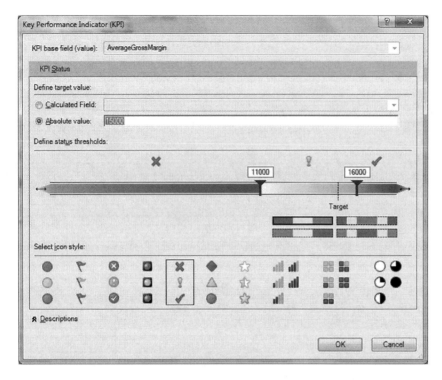

Figure 11-7. *The Key Performance Indicator (KPI) dialog*

11.   Click OK.

The KPI has been created, and a small icon with three colors appears to the right of the calculated field that you used as the basis for the KPI. You can now use the Status, Value, and Goal fields in Power View table and matrix visualizations.

___

■ **Note**   KPIs require that the input data be from a calculated field. You cannot just use a column of data for this.

___

KPI Options

When building this first KPI we bypassed some variations on a theme that you may find interesting. It follows that there are a couple of techniques that you could be tempted to apply when developing your own KPIs.

First, there is the question of the number of status thresholds, and consequently, the number of status icons that you can use. The choice is fairly simple:

- Three status icons (using two status thresholds)

- Five status icons (using four status thresholds)

Once you have decided whether to use three or five icons, you can choose how the base field relates to the target:

- Three icons going from red to green, or green to red. Red to green implies that a lower number is poor, and a higher number is better. Green to red implies the reverse, and that the higher the number, the worse the result. If you have chosen one of the single-color KPI images, then the bar that indicates the thresholds will show a progressive shading instead of colors.

- Five icons using red at the extremes or red at the center. Red at the extremes indicates that the further from the center the result is, the worse things are. Red at the center implies the opposite. Once again, if you have chosen one of the single-color KPI images, then the bar that indicates the thresholds will show a progressive shading instead of colors.

You make these four choices by clicking on one of the four status threshold icons in the Key Performance Indicator (KPI) dialog. Figure 11-8 shows the status threshold pane of the Key Performance Indicator (KPI) dialog for a five icon choice. As you can see, you can then adjust the four thresholds that define the five ranges that will be represented by the appropriate icon.

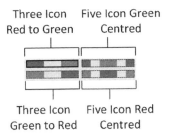

Figure 11-8. *The Key Performance Indicator (KPI) options*

The icon selections are described in Table 11-2.

Table 11-2. *KPI Options*

Indicator	Type	Comments
Circles	Three	Simple colored circles
Flags	Three	Colored flags
Indicators in a circle	Three	Symbols in a colored circle
Traffic Light	Three	Uses a traffic light style
Symbols	Three	Colored symbols
Shapes	Three	Colored shapes
Stars	Three	Stars of a single color that fill up to indicate the status
Bars	Five	Progressively increasing bars of a single color
Squares	Five	Progressively filled-in squares of a single color
Pies	Five	Progressively filled-in pies of a single color

KPI Descriptions

Creating KPIs is easy, as you have just seen. Remembering the details later can be harder, however. Because of this, PowerPivot lets you add comments to each KPI you create. You can add comments while you are creating a KPI or at a later date, of course. Here, however, I will show you how to add comments to an existing KPI.

1. Right-click on the calculated field that you used as the KPI base field.

2. Select Edit KPI Settings. The Key Performance Indicator (KPI) dialog will appear.

3. Click on Descriptions at the bottom of the dialog. The dialog will display the Descriptions page.

4. Enter any comments that you feel useful in describing what your KPI was designed to do. This is shown in Figure 11-9.

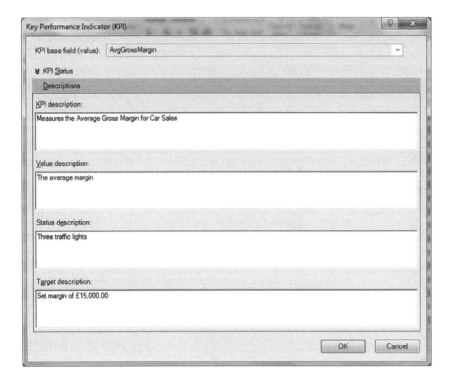

Figure 11-9. *The Key Performance Indicator (KPI) dialog Descriptions pane*

5. Click OK to complete the modification.

To return to the main (status) pane of this dialog, all you have to do is click on KPI Status at the top of the dialog.

■ **Note**   The KPI description will be used as a tooltip in Power View.

Calculated KPI Targets

On some occasions you could have a variable rather than a fixed target for a KPI that you are creating. Creating one of these is a virtually identical process to the one that you followed previously in the "Creating a KPI" section, but here are a few minor differences:

- In step 5, earlier in the chapter, click Calculated Field rather than the Absolute Value radio button.

- In step 6, select a calculated field. The data model contains a field named AverageSalePricePreviousYear, and I suggest using this field.

- In steps 8 and 9, set percentage rather than absolute values. You can either enter the values or drag the threshold indicators left and right to do this.

Once you have done completed these steps, the KPI dialog should look like Figure 11-10, where I have also changed the icon style.

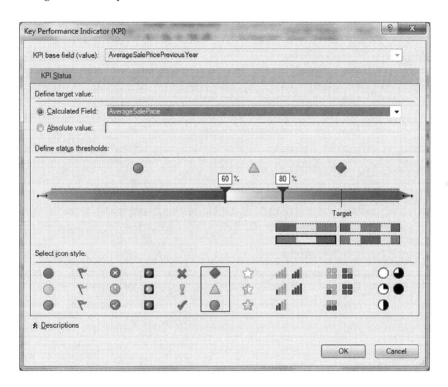

Figure 11-10. *The Key Performance Indicator (KPI) options for calculated KPI targets*

Modifying a KPI

Of course, you may need to tweak a KPI once you have created it. This is why it is so important to be aware of the KPI icon that can appear to the right of calculated fields. This icon is shown in Figure 11-11.

AvgGrossMargin: 26,060.68

Figure 11-11. *The Key Performance Indicator (KPI) icon for a calculated field*

To modify a KPI, all you have to do is

1. Right-click on the calculated field that you used as the KPI base field.

2. Select Edit KPI Settings. The Key Performance Indicator (KPI) dialog will appear.

3. Make any adjustments you need to the KPI elements and confirm with OK.

Deleting a KPI

IF a KPI has become redundant, you can delete it:

1. Right-click on the calculated field that you used as the KPI base field.

2. Select Delete KPI.

■ **Note** The KPI will be deleted without any confirmation or warning. Deleting a KPI will not affect the calculated field(s) it was based on.

Perspectives

It is easy, with a little practice, to develop quite complex PowerPivot data models that contain dozens of tables and hundreds of columns. This is fabulous for defining a "single version of the truth"—the Eldorado of business intelligence. The downside is that the sheer complexity and breadth of a large model can become difficult for end users to navigate.

So the PowerPivot team came up with a solution. The answer is to create and use perspectives. A *perspective* is a subset of the tables and columns that are particularly relevant to a group of users. Once a set of perspectives has been created, users can switch from one to another and thus only see the data that is relevant to a specific type of analysis.

Creating a Perspective

Here is how you can create a perspective:

1. In the Advanced tab, click the Create And Manage button. The Perspectives dialog appears.

2. Click New Perspective. A column appears containing a check box for every table and field in the data set.

3. Replace the current new column name (NewPerspective) with something more appropriate. I will name it ExecutiveGroup.

4. Expand all the tables that contain fields you want to retain, and check the boxes for those fields. In this example I will choose

    a. CountryName from the Countries table

    b. Make, Marque, and SalePrice from the SalesData table

    c. Colour from the Colours table

    d. ClientName from the Clients table.

The Perspectives dialog will look like Figure 11-12.

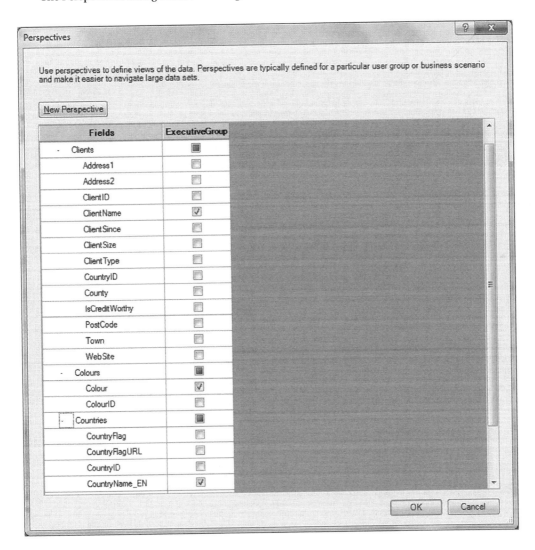

Figure 11-12. *The Perspectives dialog*

5. Confirm with OK.

Applying a Perspective

Nothing has happened when you created a perspective—yet. So now it is time to use the perspective that you just created.

1. In the Advanced tab, click the popup labeled Select:. You will see all the available perspectives, including the standard, default perspective, as shown in Figure 11-13.

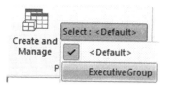

Figure 11-13. *Applying a perspective*

2. Select the perspective that you just created (ExecutiveGroup).

Any tables that were not selected as part of the perspective will temporarily be hidden, and any columns in the visible tables that you did not select will also be hidden from view. So you, or your users, can perform any required analyses on a simpler data model. Of course, you can return to the initial, default perspective at any time by selecting it from the list of available perspectives.

■ **Note**   Power View can currently only use the default perspective.

Data Categories

A few pages ago we indicated to PowerPivot that certain fields were to be treated as images. Well, these are not the only hints that you can give to PowerPivot concerning the data a field contains. You can choose to apply to your data to several data categories, and this can only help Power View or Power Map (more on that in Chapter 13) display the sort of results that you really want.

Because we have already seen how to apply data categories in the context of images, I will not repeat the process, but will explain, in Table 11-3, what the remaining data categories are and when you should use them.

Table 11-3. *Data Category Options*

Data Category	Type	Comments
Address	Geography	Indicates to Power View maps and Power Map that this field can be used by Bing maps
City	Geography	Indicates to Power View maps and Power Map that this field can be used by Bing maps
Company	Organization	A custom category
Continent	Geography	Indicates to Power View maps and Power Map that this field can be used by Bing maps
Country/Region	Geography	Indicates to Power View maps and Power Map that this field can be used by Bing maps
County	Geography	Indicates to Power View maps and Power Map that this field can be used by Bing maps
Date	Date	Tells Power View that the column contents are a date
Image	Image Reference	Tells Power View that the column contents are to be displayed as an image
Image URL	Image Reference	Tells Power View that the column contents are to be displayed as an image
Latitude	Geography	Indicates to Power View maps and Power Map that this field can be used by Bing maps
Longitude	Geography	Indicates to Power View maps and Power Map that this field can be used by Bing maps
Organization	Organization	A custom category
Place	Geography	Indicates to Power View maps and Power Map that this field can be used by Bing maps
Postal Code	Geography	Indicates to Power View maps and Power Map that this field can be used by Bing maps
Product	Product	A custom category
State or Province	Geography	Indicates to Power View maps and Power Map that this field can be used by Bing maps
Web URL	Hyperlink	Tells Power View that data in this field is a hyperlink and that it can be clicked to open the URL

Hiding Columns from Client Tools

If you have spent a few minutes preparing your data set so that it is ready to be used in Power View (or many other visualization tools), then you could be looking at many, many columns of data. Some of these columns might be necessary for the data visualization to work effectively, but you and your users might not need to see them in Power View. Such columns have become part of the infrastructure of the data but are not required in the tables and charts that you will be creating.

So, if you want to remove extraneous clutter from your data set and hide columns that (and this list is not exhaustive)

- Are only used to sort other columns by
- Appear in hierarchies, and so are redundant if they appear in the field list as well
- Contain intermediate calculations (as you saw in Chapter 10)

then you can simply hide these columns from Power View and the end user. To do this:

1. Right-click on any column that you want to hide from the user.
2. Select Hide From Client Tools in the context menu.

The selected column will be grayed out in the table, and it remains in the data set. It will not, however, be visible in Power View or the PowerPivot table Field List.

■ **Tip** You can Ctrl-click to select multiple fields, even from several tables, before right-clicking and choosing to hide the fields from client tools.

If you are using this chapter to prepare the PowerPivot data model that is used as the basis for all the Power View examples in the previous chapters, then you will need to hide a certain number of columns from Power View. These columns are given in Table 11-4. Be aware, though, that you will need to create some of these columns in the data model before you can hide them from the user. This is explained in the previous chapter.

Table 11-4. Columns to Hide to Prepare the Data Model

Table	Column
SalesData	CarAge
SalesData	CarAgeBucketSort
SalesData	MileageRangeSort
SalesData	RegistrationDate
Colours	ColourID
Countries	CountryID
Clients	ClientID
Clients	Address1
Clients	Address2
Clients	CountryID
Clients	IsCreditWorthy
Clients	Website

Preparing Data for Natural Language Querying

When you delve into Chapter 15 you will see, amongst other things, how you can query the data in a PowerPivot data model using natural language querying – that is without needing to learn a computer language to return data. However as humans (and not computers) we tend to use many words to describe the same thing, or even to use idiosyncratic vocabulary when defining data models.

PowerPivot lets you add synonyms for the names of objects (that is essentially columns and tables) to a data model. This helps the natural language querying engine interpret requests with greater accuracy. If you want to extend the data model with synonyms

1. Click the Synonyms button in the Advanced tab. Power Pivot switches to Diagram View and displays the Synonyms pane on the right.

2. Click on a table or field name in the Synonyms pane.

3. Enter a comma-separated list of synonyms for the table or field name.

Some synonyms are in bold. These are autogenerated by PowerPivot, and cannot be modified.

___

■ **Note**   Synonyms are only available in Office 365 Professional Plus or the Click-to-Run version of Office 2013 Professional Plus. Also you must be signed in to Office 365 with an organizational account.

___

Optimizing File Size

Although it is not something which springs to mind when initially creating a PowerPivot data model, file size can be important. It is altogether too easy to create huge data models in PowerPivot, if only because the existing Excel worksheet limits are no longer a constraint. In practice, though, you are probably better off trying to create the most compact data model that you can.

There are several reasons for this:

- A large data model – despite compression – will take up more memory, more space on disk and be slower to load and save.

- A data model which contains lots of tables, duplicate data or unneeded columns will be hard to understand for end users.

To end this chapter, here are a few techniques and ideas to help you create lean and efficient data models in Power Pivot. This list is not exhaustive, by any means, but it should point you in the right direction.

- *Avoid unneeded tables* – If a table contains a subset of data in an existing table, use the main table only.

- *Avoid unneeded columns* – If a column will likely never be used, remove it. If a column is a duplicate of data in another column, but formatted or shaped differently, try and choose only the most useful variant of the data.

- *Avoid unwanted data* – Do not import redundant data in the first place, and tweak your connections to source data to exclude unwanted data to avoid re-importing it by mistake when updating.

- *Structure the dataset cleverly* – Try to create calculated fields rather than calculated columns, if you can.

- *Avoid unneeded data* – Use filters when importing data to exclude unnecessary records.

- *Use short data strings* – Break long, complex columns of data into smaller columns. This allows for better in-memory compression, as more elements are identical in a column, which helps the compression algorithm to work more efficiently.

- *Apply appropriate data types* – Try and use the most suitable data type for each column. For instance, use a date type when you don't need data and time – it takes up less space.

- *Use reference tables* – do not duplicate the same data inside a table when you can use a lookup table, and save lots of space.

On a more general note, you can also reduce the size of Excel worksheets by removing

- Unused worksheets

- Images and Clip art

- Formatting

- Backgrounds

File size optimization is a never-ending cycle of trial and error. However, if you are aware of the basic techniques that can be used, then you should be able to build more efficient data models from the ground up.

Conclusion

So that is all there is to preparing a data set for top of the range Power View reports. As long as you have set any relevant table behavior options to define default field sets and columns containing images, for instance and applied Sort By columns and data categories, then your data should appear correctly and with greater panache. To finish, add a few Key Performance Indicators, ensure that any columns that are not really required by users are hidden, and make sure all useful hierarchies are set up; if you do all this, your audience will be really impressed. If as well you have prepared the data for natural language querying and have structured it so that there is no data redundancy, then you have really done a good job.

CHAPTER 12

■ ■ ■

Discovering and Loading Data with Power Query

Before you can present any analysis or insight, you need source data. Your source data could be in many places and in many formats. Nonetheless, you need to access it, look at it, and quite possibly clean it up to some extent. You may also need to join separate data sources before you can shape the data into a coherent data set using PowerPivot, deliver the results using Power View or Power Map, and then share it using Power BI.

Discovering, loading, cleaning, and modifying source data is where Power Query comes in. Using this, the latest addition to the Microsoft self-service business intelligence stack, you can carry out

- **Data Discovery**—Find and connect to a myriad of data sources containing potentially useful data. This can be from both public and private data sources.

- **Data Loading**—Select the data you have examined and load it into Power Query for shaping.

- **Data Modification**—Modify the structure of each data table that you have imported, filter and clean the data itself, and then join any separate data sources (we will look at this in detail in Chapter 13).

Although I have outlined these three steps as if they are completely separate and sequential, the reality is that they often blend into a single process. Indeed there could be many occasions when you will examine the data *after* it has been loaded into Power Query—or join data tables *before* you clean them. The core objective will, however, always remain the same: find some data and then load it into Power Query where you can tweak, clean, and shape it.

This process could be described simplistically as "First, catch your data." In the world of data warehousing, the specialists call it ETL, which is short for **E**xtract **T**ransform **L**oad. Despite the reassuring confidence that the acronym brings, this process is rarely a smooth logical progression through a clear-cut series of processes. The reality is often far messier than that. You may often find yourself importing some data, cleaning it, importing some more data from another source, combining the second data set with the first one, cleaning some more, and then repeating many of these operations several times.

In this chapter and the following one then, I will try and show you how the process can work in an ideal world. I hope that this will make the various steps that comprise an ETL process clearer. All I am asking is that you remain aware that all the options and possibilities that Power Query offers make it a multifaceted and tremendously capable tool. The science is to know *which* options to use. The art is to know *when* to use them.

In this chapter we will begin by seeing how to find and load data from a variety of sources. Once again I will be using a set of example files that you can find on the Apress web site. If you have followed the instructions in Appendix A, then these files will be in the C:\HighImpactDataVisualizationWithPowerBI folder. Now, although I will be re-creating the source data set that we have used up until now in this book, I will also be going beyond that and importing data that is not used in the Power View, PowerPivot, and Power Map chapters. This is because the sheer variety of techniques that can be applied to load and transform data goes beyond those that you can demonstrate with a simple data set. Consequently, at times, the examples I use will not necessarily lead into a structured data set, but I will use them as just that—examples—to show you a specific solution to a particular ETL problem.

The Power Query Interface

You access Power Query using the Power Query tab and ribbon that appear in Excel once you've downloaded the Power Query add-in and installed it (as described in Chapter 1). Similar to the way we worked with PowerPivot, you begin working in Excel, using the options available in the Power Query ribbon, and then you progress to the Power Query window where you will carry out most of your work.

The Power Query ribbon essentially lets you find data and connect to it. It will also show a list of all the queries that you have developed in the current workbook and let you manage queries. It will be your starting point for both developing new queries and using or modifying existing queries.

The Power Query Ribbon

The Power Query ribbon contains the elements that are explained in Figure 12-1.

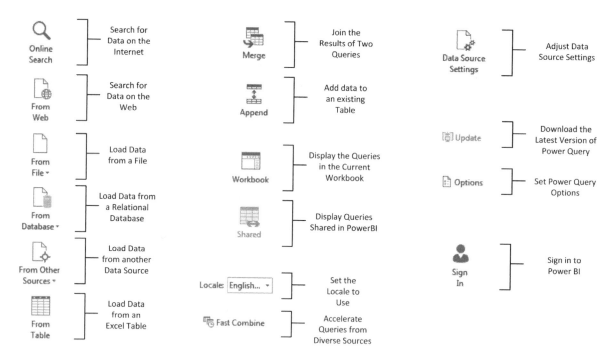

Figure 12-1. *The Power Query ribbon*

Table 12-1. *Power Query Ribbon Options*

Option	Comments
Online Search	Search for data from public sources.
From Web	Import tabular data from web pages.
From File	Import data from CSV, text, XML, and Excel files.
From Database	Import data from relational databases.
From Other Sources	Import data from a variety of sources.
From Table	Import data from an Excel table to the current workbook.
Merge	Join two queries to add columns from one query output to another.
Append	Add data from an identically structured query output to the selected query.
Workbook	Display—or hide—the list of queries in the current workbook.
Shared	Display any shared queries.
Locale	Define the regional settings used by Power Query.
Fast Combine	Bypass security to accelerate data loads.
Data Source Settings	Manage data source settings.
Update	Update Power Query with the latest version.
Options	Choose Power Query options.
Sign In	Sign in to Power BI to access shared queries and data.

Data Sources

Power Query groups potential data sources into the following categories:

- **Web Pages**—This option lets you see all available data that is formatted as tables in a web page. Then you can import tables of data from these pages.

- **File Sources**—Include Excel (both from the current worksheet and other workbooks), CSV (comma separated values) files, text files, and XML files.

- **Databases**—A fairly comprehensive collection of relational databases that are current in the workplace and in the cloud, including (among others) SQL Server, MS Access, and Oracle. The full list is given later on in this chapter.

- **Other Sources**—A considerable and ever-growing range of data sources from Facebook to MS Exchange. The full list is given later on in this chapter.

You can also list the contents of folders on any available local disk or network share (even if it is not always a data source) and then leverage this to import files. Similarly (if you have the necessary permissions), you can list the databases and data available on the database servers you connect to. This way Power Query can provide not only the data, but also the metadata—or data about data—which can help you get the job done.

Unfortunately the sheer range of data sources from which Power Query can read data is such that we do not have space here to examine the minutiae of every one. As a consequence, we will take a rapid tour of *some* of the most frequently used data sources in the next few pages. You will probably be using some types of data source much more than others including, I hope, those that are outlined here. What is more, many of the data sources can be used in a similar way, and the Power Query interface does a wonderful job of making the arcane connection details as unobtrusive as possible. As a result, once you have grasped the way in which Power Query connects to data sources in general, it should not be difficult for you to use some of the more rare connections types without detailed explanation.

File Sources

Sending files across networks and over the Internet or via email has become second nature to most of us. As long as the files that you have obtained conform to some of the widely-recognized standards currently in use (of which you will learn more later), you should have little difficulty in loading them into Power Query.

The file sources that Power Query can currently read and from which it can load data are given in Table 12-2.

Table 12-2. *File Sources*

File Sources	Comments
Excel	Allows you to read Microsoft Excel files (versions 97 to 2013) and load worksheets, named ranges, and tables
CSV	Lets you load text files that conform to the CSV (comma separated values) format
XML	Allows you to load XML data
Text	Lets you load text files using a variety of separators

Databases

Much corporate data currently resides in relational databases. It follows that being able to look at this data is essential for much of today's business intelligence. In the real world, connecting to corporate data will require, at the very least, you to have a logon name and possibly a password that will let you connect. I imagine that it will also require permissions to read the tables and views (which, without going into the grisly details, are essentially the same thing for Power Query). So the techniques described here are probably the easy bit. The hard part is having to be pleasant with the guardians of corporate data so that they concede that you actually *need* the data and should be allowed to see it.

The databases that Power Query can currently connect to, and can preview and load data from, are given in Table 12-3.

Table 12-3. *Database Sources*

Database	Comments
SQL Server	Lets you connect to a Microsoft SQL Server on-premises database and import records from all the data tables and views that you are authorized to access
Windows Azure SQL Database	Lets you connect to a Microsoft SQL Server cloud-based database and import records from all the data tables and views that you are authorized to access
Access Database	Lets you connect to a Microsoft Access file on your network and load queries and tables
Oracle Database	Lets you connect to an Oracle database and import records from all the data tables and views that you are authorized to access
DB2 Database	Lets you connect to an IBM DB2 database and import records from all the data tables and views that you are authorized to access

(continued)

Table 12-3. (*continued*)

Database	Comments
MySQL	Lets you connect to a MySQL database and import records from all the data tables and views that you are authorized to access
PostgreSQL	Lets you connect to a PostgreSQL database and import records from all the data tables and views that you are authorized to access
Sybase	Lets you connect to a Sybase database and import records from all the data tables and views that you are authorized to access
Teradata	Lets you connect to a Teradata database and import records from all the data tables and views that you are authorized to access

Connecting to Oracle, DB2, MySQL, PostgreSQL, Sybase, or Teradata will require not only that the database administrator has given you the necessary permissions, but also that connection software (known as drivers or providers) has been installed on your PC. Given the "corporate" nature of the requirements, I suggest that you talk directly to your IT department to get this set up.

Other Sources

Up until now we have seen some of the more traditional sources of data that you might need for your analysis. As the world changes, the available sources evolve, and the current trend is toward less "structured" (and controlled) data sources and toward more varied and often less corporate sources.

Power Query can connect to, and read data from, a whole host of these less classic sources. Those to which it can currently connect are listed in Table 12-4.

Table 12-4. *Other Sources*

Source	Comments
SharePoint List	Loads a SharePoint List as a data table. You will need SharePoint permissions to access SharePoint data.
OData Feed	Connects to an OData feed to read and load the data it contains. OData is a standardized protocol for creating and consuming data, especially over the Internet.
Windows Azure Marketplace	Lets you load data that you are authorized to access on the Windows Azure Marketplace. This will require a Windows Azure Marketplace subscription.
Hadoop File	Reads Hadoop ("Big Data") files.
Windows Azure HDInsight	Reads cloud-based Hadoop files in the Microsoft Azure environment.
Windows Azure Blob Storage	Reads from a cloud-based unstructured data store.
Windows Azure Table Storage	Reads from Windows Azure tables.
Active Directory	Reads data from the Enterprise Active Directory. This will probably require custom access rights.
MS Exchange	Reads data from the MS Exchange Email system.
Facebook	Reads Facebook data.

These data sources are so varied, and often personal, that I will not be going through them here. Suffice it to say that the connection principles and approach are as identical as possible to those that you will see in the next few pages. So it is up to you to try connecting to this brave new world and using the data it offers.

Loading Data

It is time to start looking at the heavy lifting aspect of Power Query, and how you can use it to load data from a variety of different sources. As always, I will begin on the bunny slopes with a simple example of "scraping" data from a web page. Then, given the plethora of available data sources, and so we can better give the process some structure, we will begin by loading the five tables that make up the data set you used in the chapters on Power View and PowerPivot. However, each table will come from one of the classic data sources that currently can be found in most workplaces:

- **CSV**—This file type will be the source of the Countries table.

- **Text**—Here we will use the Date table.

- **XML**—We will use an XML file containing the Colours data.

- **Excel**—We will use the SalesData table from both an Excel file on disk and an open file.

- **Access**—Finally we will load the Clients table from an Access database file.

After we have loaded these five tables, we will look into getting data from a relational database—SQL Server will be the example here—as databases are, in my experience, a frequent source of core data for analysis, and we can apply several tricks and techniques to database sources. Finally, we will look at a technique for loading multiple files of the same format, as this can be a frequent requirement.

Web Pages

As a first and extremely simple example, let's grab some data from a web page. Since I want to concentrate on the method rather than the data, I will use a web page that has nothing to do with the sample data in the book, and that we will not be using at all, other than as a simple introduction to the process of loading data using Power Query.

1. In Excel, click on the Power Query tab to activate the Power Query ribbon.

2. Click From Web. The From Web dialog will be displayed.

3. Enter the following URL (it is a Microsoft help page for Power Query that contains a few tables of data): `http://office.microsoft.com/en-gb/excel-help/guide-to-the-power-query-ribbon-HA103993930.aspx`. Of course, if you have a URL that you want to try out, then feel free! The dialog will look something like Figure 12-2:

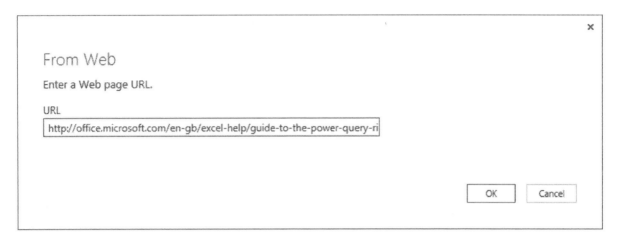

Figure 12-2. *The From Web source dialog*

4. Click OK. The Navigator window will appear to the right of the Excel worksheet. After a
few seconds during which Power Query is connecting to the web page, the list of available
tables of data in the web page will be displayed, as shown in Figure 12-3.

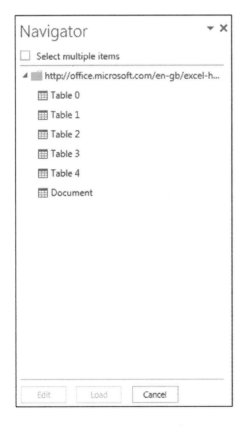

Figure 12-3. *The Navigator window*

5. Hover the mouse pointer over one of the tables in the Navigator window. The Peek popup (also known as the fly-out) will appear to show you what the data in the chosen table looks like. This is shown in Figure 12-4:

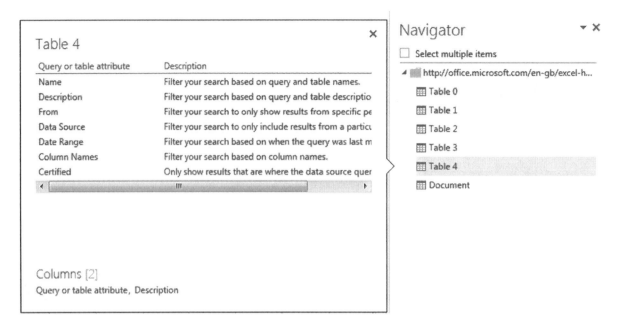

Figure 12-4. *The Peek popup*

6. Select Table 4 in the Navigator window.

7. Click Edit at the bottom of the window (or double-click the table name). The Power Query window will open displaying the table of data loaded into Power Query. It should look like Figure 12-5. We will be looking at this window in detail later in this chapter.

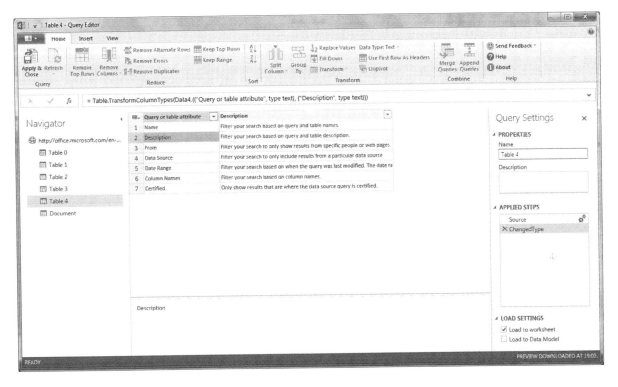

Figure 12-5. *The Power Query window*

8. Click Apply & Close in the Power Query Home ribbon. The Power Query window will close and copy the data into a new Excel worksheet. Once back in Excel you will see not only the data but also the WorkBook Queries window.

In a few simple steps you have seen just what Power Query can do and how it is done. You have found data and loaded it into Excel—a complete ETL process in a few clicks. In a very short time, you have seen lots of things happen and a whole new world open up in front of you. Consequently, I think that it would be a good idea to explain some of these new elements before going any further.

The Navigator Window

The Navigator window will appear when connecting to many, but not all, data sources. It is there to let you

- Take a quick look at the available data tables in the data source.

- Look at the data in individual tables.

- Select one or more data tables to load into Power Query and from there into Excel or PowerPivot.

Depending on the data source to which you have connected, you might see only a few data tables in the Navigator window, or hundreds of them. In any case, what you can see are the structured data sets that Power Query can recognize and is confident that it can import. Equally dependent on the data source is the level of complexity of what you will see in the Navigator window. If you are looking at a database server, for instance, then you may start out with a list of databases, and may need to dig deeper into the arborescence of the data by expanding databases to list the available data tables and views.

The Peek Popup

The Peek popup (also known as the fly-out) is, as its name implies, a preview of the data in a table. It provides

- A brief overview of the top few records in any of the datasets that you want to look at. Given that the data you are previewing could be hundreds of columns wide and millions of rows long, there could be scroll bars for the data table visible inside the Peek popup.

- A list of the available columns in the data table. These are shown at the bottom of the Peek popup.

■ **Note**   The Peek popup is a brilliant data discovery tool. Without having to load any data, you can take a quick look at the data source and any data that it contains that can probably be loaded by Power Query into Excel or PowerPivot. You can then decide if it is worth loading, and so you do not waste time on a data load that could be superfluous.

The Peek popup will only show you a tiny snippet of the available data. This is deliberate because it is only designed to provide a preview. One useful trick, if you have a table containing many columns, is to click on a column name at the bottom of the Peek popup. The chosen column will appear in the window so that you can see the data it contains.

The WorkBook Queries Window

Power Query will not forget how it loaded data. Each separate load process is remembered as a "query" and appears in the WorkBook Queries window, which is normally to the right of the current workbook. Each query in the WorkBook Queries window has a name and a last activated date, as well as an indication of whether it loads data into Excel or PowerPivot or remains a query process, but without actually loading the data anywhere from Power Query.

The WorkBook Queries window also has a Peek popup. So if you hover the cursor over a query, you will see what the data returned by this query will look like. If you want to go back to a query to continue modifying it, all you have to do is double-click on it, and you will open the Power Query window and see the data as you left it. Figure 12-6 shows the WorkBook Queries window in more detail.

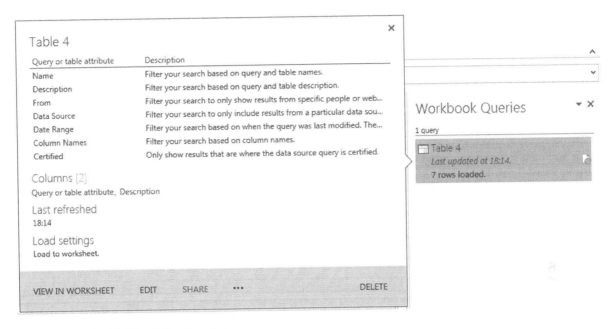

Figure 12-6. *The WorkBook Queries window*

Since you will be using the various possibilities of the WorkBook Queries window in your day-to-day work using Power Query, Table 12-5 explains the available options in the context menu that appears when you right-click on a WorkBook query.

Table 12-5. *Query Options*

Option	Description
Edit	Opens the Power Query window where you can modify the query. Double-clicking will also carry out this action. This is also possible by clicking on Edit in the Peek popup.
Refresh	Runs the query and reprocesses the data.
Duplicate	Makes a copy of the query.
Reference	Creates a new query that references the selected query.
Delete	Deletes the query. You will be asked for confirmation. This is also possible by clicking on Delete in the Peek popup.
Merge	Lets you join the data from two queries. This is described in the section "Merge."
Append	Lets you add identically structured data from another query to the selected query.
Share	Lets the user share this query (and its output) using Power BI. This is described in Chapter 15.
Show the Peek	Displays the Peek popup.

If you wish to rename a query, you can do this from inside the Power Query window.

■ **Note** If you have returned data to a worksheet, and then you delete the worksheet, you will also delete the query—without any warning.

CSV Files

The scenario is as follows: you have been given a comma-separated text file (also known as a CSV file) containing a list of data. You now want to load this into Power Query so that you can look at the data and consider what needs doing (if anything) to make it useable. Here is what you have to do:

1. In the Power Query ribbon, click From File and select From CSV in the popup menu. The Browse dialog will appear.

2. Navigate to the folder containing the file and select the file (C:\HighImpactDataVisualizationWithPowerBI\Countries.csv, in this example).

3. Click OK. The Power Query window will open and display the contents of the table. This is shown in Figure 12-7.

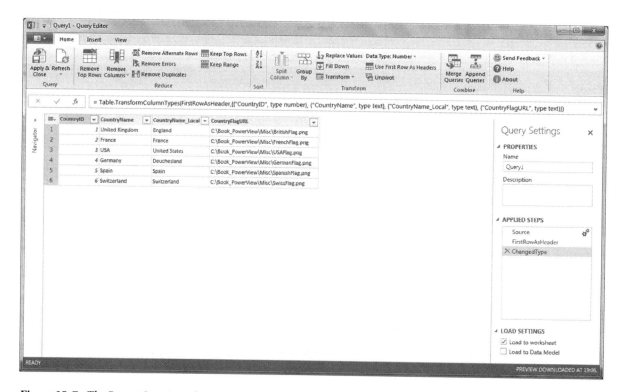

Figure 12-7. *The Power Query window*

4.   Uncheck the Load To Worksheet box at the bottom right of the Power Query Query
     Settings pane at the right of the Power Query window, because we do not want to load the
     data yet.

5.   Enter a name for this query in the Name box of the Power Query Query Settings pane.
     I suggest **Countries** as the query name.

6.   Select Apply & Close from the Power Query Home ribbon. You will return to Excel. You
     should now see the query appear in the WorkBook Queries window at the right of the
     Excel window.

And that, for the moment, is that. You have loaded the file into Power Query and, in the next chapter, you will soon learn how to shape the data and load it into either Excel or PowerPivot. If you really want to jump ahead to this discussion now, all is explained in the sections "Dataset Shaping" and "Data Cleansing and Modification" in Chapter 13.

What Is a CSV File?

Before we move on to other file types, there are a few comments I need to make about CSV files. There is a technical specification of what a "true" CSV file is, but I won't bore you with that. What's more many programs that generate CSV files do not always follow the definition exactly. What matters is that Power Query can handle files that

- Have a .csv extension (it uses this by default to apply the right kind of processing).

- Use a comma to separate the elements in a row. This too is a default that can be overridden, as you will see at the end of the next chapter.

- End with a line feed, carriage return, or line feed/carriage return.

- Can, optionally, contain double quotes to encapsulate fields. These will be stripped out as part of the data load process. If there are double quotes, they do not have to appear for every field, nor even for every record in a field that can have occasionally inconsistent double quotes.

- Can contain "irregular" records, that is, rows that do not have every element that is found in a standard record. However the first row (whether or not it contains titles) must cover every element found in all the remaining records in the list. Put simply, any other record can be shorter than the first one but cannot be longer.

- Do not contain anything other than the data table. If the file contains header rows or footer rows that are not part of the data, then Power Query cannot load the data table without further work. There are workarounds to this all-too-frequent problem, and one is given in the following chapter.

Text Files

If you have followed the process for loading a CSV file in the previous section, then you will find it considerably similar to loading a text file. This is not surprising. Both are text files, and both should contain a single list of data. The core differences are these:

- A text file can have something other than a comma to separate the elements in a list. You can specify the delimiter when defining the load step.

- A text file should normally have the extension .txt (though this, too, can be overridden).

- A text file *must* be perfectly formed. That is, every record (row) must have the same number of elements as every other record.

- A text file, too, *must not* contain anything other than the data table if you want a flawless data load first time.

- If a text file encounters difficulties, it should import the data as a single column that you can then try and split up into multiple columns as described in chapter 13.

Here, then, is how to load a text file into Power Query:

1. In the Power Query ribbon, click From File and select From Text in the popup menu. The Browse dialog will appear.

2. Navigate to the folder containing the file and select the file (C:\HighImpactDataVisualizationWithPowerBI\DateTable.txt, in this example).

3. Click OK. The Power Query window will open and display the contents of the table.

4. Enter a name for this query in the Name box of the Power Query Query Settings pane. I suggest **DateTable**.

5. Uncheck the Load To Worksheet box at the bottom right of the Power Query window, as we do not want actually to load the data yet; then select Apply & Close from the Power Query Home ribbon to return to Excel. You will see that this query has been added to the list of queries in this worksheet.

Where Power Query is really clever is that it can make a very educated guess as to how the text file is designed. That is, it can nearly always guess the field separator (the character that isolates each element in a list from the other elements) and so not only will it break the list into columns, but it will also avoid importing the column separator.

XML Files

XML, or Extensible Markup Language, is a standard means of sending data between IT systems. Consequently you have every chance of having to load an XML file one day. Although an XML file is just text, it is text that has been formatted in a very specific way, as you can see if you ever open a XML file in a text editor such as notepad. To load an XML file,

1. In the Power Query ribbon click From File and select From XML in the popup menu. The Browse dialog will appear.

2. Navigate to the folder containing the file and select the file (C:\HighImpactDataVisualizationWithPowerBI\ColoursTable.xml, in this example).

3. Click OK. The Power Query window will open and display the contents of the XML file.

4. Display the Power Query Navigator window on the left of the Power Query window (unless it is already visible).

5. Click on the Colours table (the second element) in the Navigator window. The contents of the table will be displayed. The Power Query window should look like Figure 12-8.

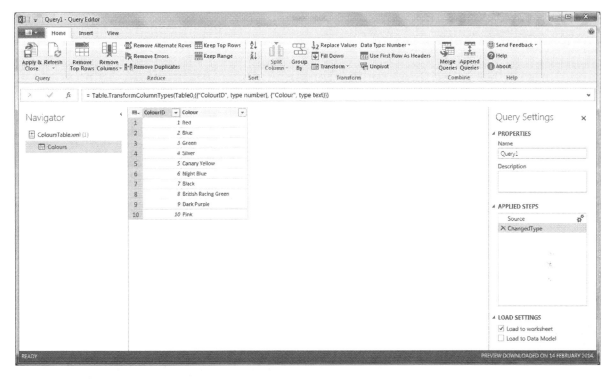

Figure 12-8. *The Power Query window after loading an XML file*

6. Uncheck the Load to Worksheet box at the bottom right of the Power Query window, since we do not want actually to load the data yet; then select Apply & Close from the Power Query Home ribbon to return to Excel.

The actual internal format of an XML file can get extremely complex. Sometimes an XML file will contain only one data table, sometimes it will contain many data separate tables. On other occasions it will contain one table whose records contain nested levels of data that you need to handle by expanding or aggregating. These techniques are described later in this chapter in the context of database sources.

Excel

If you are using Power Query you are probably already a major Excel user and have many, many spreadsheets full of data that you want to rationalize and use for analysis and presentation. So, let's see how to load the contents of an Excel file. To begin with, I will show you how to get data from another workbook:

1. In the Power Query ribbon click From File.

2. In the Popup list, select From Excel. The Browse dialog will appear.

3. Navigate to the directory containing the file that you want to look at (C:\HighImpactDataVisualizationWithPowerBI, in this example).

4. Select the source file (SalesData.xlsx, in this example) and click OK. The Navigator window will appear, showing the worksheets, tables, and ranges in the workbook file.

5. Hover the mouse pointer over one of the tables in the Navigator window. The Peek popup will appear to show you what the data in the chosen table looks like.

6. Click on the Sales2012_2013 table. The Power Query window will appear.

7. Uncheck the Load To Data Model box at the bottom right of the Power Query window, since we do not want actually to load the data yet, then Select Apply & Close from the Power Query Home ribbon to return to Excel.

As you can see from this simple example, having Power Query read Excel data is really not difficult. However, you might still be wondering about a couple of things that you saw during this process, so here are some anticipatory comments:

The Navigator window will display

- Worksheets

- Named Ranges

- Named Tables

Sometimes these can, in effect, be duplicate references to the same data, so you should really use the most precise data source that you can. For instance, I advise using a named table or a range name rather than a worksheet source, as the latter could easily end up containing "noise" data, which would make the load process more complex than it really needs to be.

Power Query will list, and use, data connections in a source Excel workbook *if* the data connection is active and has returned data to the workbook. Once a link to Power Query has been established, you can delete the data table itself in the source Excel workbook—and still use Power Query to load the data over the data connection in the source workbook.

Power Query will not take into account any data filters on an Excel data table. Consequently you will have to reapply any filters (of which you'll learn more later) in Power Query if you want to subset the source data.

Excel Data from the Current Workbook

Loading a table from an existing worksheet into Power Query is, if anything, easier than the process that you just saw, but is, nonetheless, slightly different. Here is what you have to do:

1. Select the table of data in Excel that you want to process in Power Query.

2. Click the From Table button in the Power Query ribbon. The From Table dialog will appear, as shown in Figure 12-9.

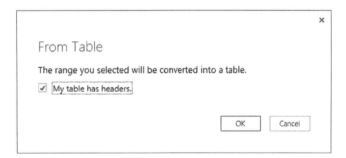

Figure 12-9. *Loading data from the current spreadsheet—the From Table dialog*

3. If your table has headers, leave the check box selected (or uncheck it if there is not a header row).

4. Click OK. The Power Query window will open.

The source list will be converted into an Excel table and its data loaded into Power Query.

Microsoft Access Databases

Another well-used data repository that proliferates in many corporations today is Microsoft Access. It is a powerful relational desktop database and can contain multiple tables, each containing millions of records. So we need to see how to load data from this particular source.

1. In the Power Query ribbon, click From Database and select From Access Database in the popup menu. The Browse dialog will appear.

2. Navigate to the folder containing the file and select the file (C:\HighImpactDataVisualizationWithPowerBI\CarSales.accdb, in this example).

3. Click OK. The navigator window will appear listing all the tables and queries in the Access database.

4. Click on the Colours table and click Edit. The Power Query window will open and display the contents of the table. The table name will become the query name.

5. Uncheck the Load To Worksheet box at the bottom right of the Power Query window, since we do not want actually to load the data yet, then Select Apply & Close from the Power Query Home ribbon to return to Excel. You will see that this query has been added to the list of queries in this worksheet.

I am sure that you can see a pattern emerging here. Indeed, this pattern will continue as you progress to loading tables from relational databases in a few pages time.

■ **Note** Power Query cannot see linked tables, only imported tables or tables that are actually in the Access database. It can, however, read queries overlaid upon native, linked, or imported data.

Loading Multiple Tables

An Access database can contain hundreds of tables or queries (which, like database views, can be considered as if they are tables). So what if you want to import several tables at once? No problem:

1. Follow steps 1 through 3 of the procedure in the preceding section.

2. Once the Navigator window is open and has finished loading the list of tables, check the Select Multiple Items box at the top of the window. A check box will appear to the left of every table and query in the Navigator.

3. Select all the data tables and queries that you want to load into Power Query.

4. Continue with the load as described previously.

Each table or query in Access will become a separate Power Query query and will be listed in the WorkBook Queries window. Each query will take the name of the table it has loaded into Power Query. If you want to see the contents of the query in the Power Query window and continue transforming the data, then all you have to do is to double-click on the query.

Loading the List of Tables

Another option that you may find useful is loading the list of tables and queries into Power Query rather than the data. There are two potential reasons for this:

- The database contains hundreds of data tables and/or queries, and you want to keep the list of this metadata (as it is called).

- Once you have saved the metadata as a query, you can then use it to preview the tables and apply data transformations (which follow in the next chapter) from inside the "metadata" query.

Here is how to do this:

1. Follow steps 1 through 3 in the earlier "Microsoft Access Databases" section.

2. Click on the database name in the Navigator window, not on a table or query name.

3. Click Edit. The Power Query window will open and display the contents of the Access database.

How you can use this list of tables to load data is handled later in this chapter in the section "Database Metadata". For the moment, let's just say that it is a smart way to get a handle on your data.

Relational Databases

Enterprise relational databases still hold much of the world's data, so you really need to know how to tap into the potentially vast mines of information that they contain. The bad news is that there are many, many databases out there, each with their intricacies and quirks. The good news is that once you have learned to load data from one of them, you should be able to use any of them.

As Power BI and Power Query are core Microsoft technologies, I will use the Microsoft enterprise relational database—SQL Server—as an example to show the principles of database access. The first advantage of this setup is that you probably do not need to install any software to enable access to SQL Server (though this is not always the case, so talk this through with your IT department). A second advantage is that the techniques are pretty similar to those used and applied by Oracle, DB2, and the other databases to which Power Query can connect. Furthermore, you can load multiple tables or views (each as a separate query) from a database. To see this in action (and presuming you have created the database CarSalesData as described in Appendix A), take the following steps:

1. In the Power Query ribbon, click the From Database button. The list of potential database sources will appear.

2. Click From SQL Server Database. The Microsoft SQL Database dialog will appear.

3. Enter the server name in the Server text box. The dialog will look like Figure 12-10.

Figure 12-10. *The Microsoft SQL Database dialog*

4. Enter the database name; if you are using the sample data, it will be CarSalesData.

5. Click OK. Power Query will connect to the server and will display the Navigator window containing all the tables and views in the database that you have permission to see on the server you selected.

6. Check the Select Multiple Items check box.

7. Click on the chek boxes for the SalesData and Countries tables. These two tables will appear in the Selected Items box in the Navigator. The Navigator window will look like Figure 12-11.

Figure 12-11. *The Navigator window when selecting multiple items*

8. Click on a table name in the Selected Items box. I will choose SalesData in this example.

9. Click Edit in the Navigator window. The Power Query window will open and display the contents of the SalesData table. The table name will become the query name.

10. Uncheck the Load to Worksheet box at the bottom right of the Power Query window, as we do not want actually to load the data yet; then select Apply & Close from the Power Query Home ribbon to return to Excel. You will see that this query has been added to the list of queries in this worksheet.

Since this is very similar to the way in which you loaded data from Access, I imagine that you are getting the hang of things by now. As always, though, there are a few comments to make.

First, let's cover the initial connection to the server. The options are explained in Table 12-6.

Table 12-6. Database Connection Options

Option	Comments
Server	You cannot browse to find the server and need to type or paste the server name. If the server has an instance name, you need to enter the server and the instance.
Database	If you know the database, then you can enter (or paste) it here. This will restrict the number of available tables in the Navigator window and will make finding the correct table or view easier.
SQL Statement	If you enter an SQL SELECT statement that is *fully qualified*—that is, it contains the database reference if you have not added this already in the dialog—then Power Query will open the Power Query window and load the table directly.

■ **Note** These options will vary depending on the make of database you are connecting to.

Second, remember that the world of relational databases is huge; much, much more could be said at this point. I am afraid that I simply do not have the space to devote to all the subtleties of how you can use the available relational database sources, however. One important point to note is that you can use stored procedures (with SQL Server or Oracle, for instance) to return data. These are complex pieces of business logic that are stored in a database. To call a SQL Server stored procedure, you would enter the following elements into the Microsoft SQL Database dialog:

- Server: <your server name>

- Database: <the database name>

- SQL Statement: EXEC <enter the schema (if there is one, followed by a period) and the stored procedure name>

This way, either you or your IT department can create complex and secure ways to allow data from the corporate databases to be read into Power Query from enterprise databases.

Finally, you can create multiple workbook queries at once if you have selected multiple items by clicking the Load button. This will create a query for each selected table which you can modify and extend later.

Database Metadata

There could well be occasions when you want to connect to a database, but not yet load the data. Perhaps you want merely to memorize the connection parameters, or alternatively, you want to examine the data more thoroughly. This is possible if you load not a table, but the database metadata, into Power Query, like this:

1. Using the From Database button, load the Access database C:\HighImpactDataVisualizationWithPowerBI\CarSales.accdb into the Navigator window.

2. Click not on a table, but on the database name (CarSales.accdb) in the Navigator window.

3. Click Edit. The database metadata will be loaded into the Power Query window.

4. Expand the Navigator window of the Power Query window. You should see something like Figure 12-12.

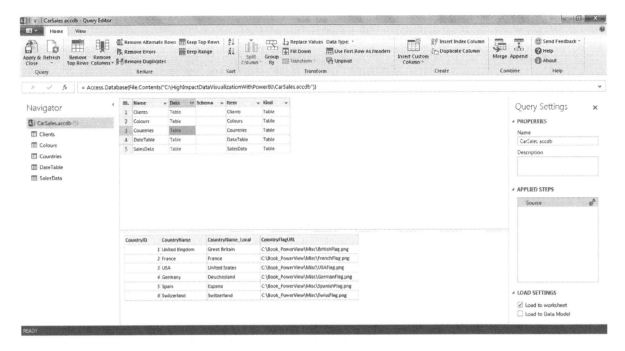

Figure 12-12. *Database metadata*

From here, you can look at the tables in the database and choose any single table that you wish to load by clicking on it in the Navigator window (or by right-clicking and selecting Drill-down in the table data). Creating a query like this, and then copying it to load the data tables, saves you from having to reconnect to the source repeatedly.

■ **Note**   Here I was using MS Access as a demonstration. The same principles apply to all relational databases which Power Query can connect to.

Data Discovery or Data Load?

You have now seen how to load data from several different sources, although far from all of them. What you have been able to see, I hope, is that Power Query applies a common interface to the art and science of loading data, whatever the source.

Yet you may remember that, at the start of this chapter, I mentioned that Power Query is for discovering data as well as loading it. This covers the following points:

- You can, for many data sources, peek at the data before you actually load it. This can save a considerable amount of wasted time by avoiding loading the wrong data.

- When it comes to data outside the corporate environment, Power Query can help you search for data.

Peeking at Data

Only data sources containing multiple data tables can be previewed. If a source contains, by definition, only one data table, then you cannot "peek" at it but can only load it into Power Query and take a look at it there. As we have seen, Excel files, Access database files, and relational databases allow you to see the structure of the available data before you even see the data itself. However, I wanted to warn you first that the following file types cannot be previewed:

- **CSV Files**—By definition, a CSV (**c**omma **s**eparated **v**alues) file can only contain a single "table" of data. Indeed, if it contains anything else, you could have difficulties loading the file. So it simply loads directly.

- **Text Files**—A text file is one that contains a single list of data where each element—or column, if you wish—is separated by a tab character, a pipe (|) character , or a semicolon, among others. This file, by definition, cannot contain anything else. So it simply loads directly, too.

- **Tables in the current Excel workbook**—Because you can see any existing tables in the current workbook, you do not need to preview them.

- **XML files**—Even though an XML file may contain multiple tables, it cannot be previewed. You will have to examine it in Power Query.

Searching for Data

There are already many thousands of publicly available data sources, and the number is growing at an incredible rate. It could well be that you need data from the public domain to add to your corporate data to provide comparisons, or perhaps you need it just on its own to make a point. Power Query can search for available public data and attempt to get you the information that you are looking for. As an example of this

1. In the Power Query ribbon, click the Online Search button. The Online Search window will appear at the right of the spreadsheet window.

2. Click inside the Search box at the top of the Online Search window and enter a search term. I will use **Exchange Rates**.

3. Press Enter or click the Magnifying Glass icon to the right of the Search box. A list of available data sources will appear in the Search box, and the Search ribbon will appear. Hover the pointer over one of the results and the fly-out will appear to give you a preview of the data. This could look something like Figure 12-13.

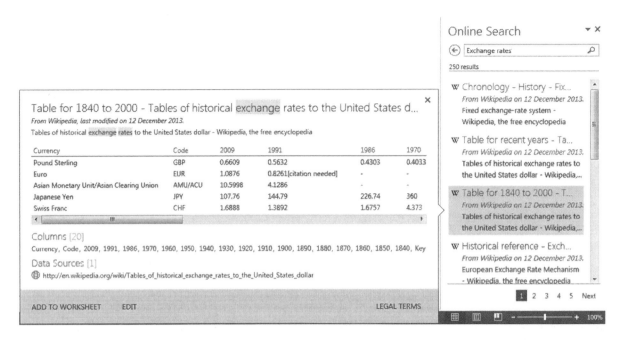

Figure 12-13. *The Search window*

The list of data sources could cover many pages of the Online Search window. You can flip from page to page by clicking the page number figures at the bottom of the window. Hovering the mouse pointer over a data source will display the fly-out showing the data. You can then load the data that interests you by right-clicking on it and selecting Edit.

Another facet of the Search facility is its ability to scan corporate data sources that have been made available using Power BI (this is explained in Chapter 15). If you or your colleagues have made searches available, and you have access rights, then Power Query will attempt to find these too.

The Search ribbon also lets you refine your search. Essentially you can

- Choose one of the Scope buttons to expand or restrict the search to public and/or enterprise data.

- Refine the search by searching specifically for words in the name or description of a search.

The Search ribbon is shown in Figure 12-14 and its options explained in Table 12-7.

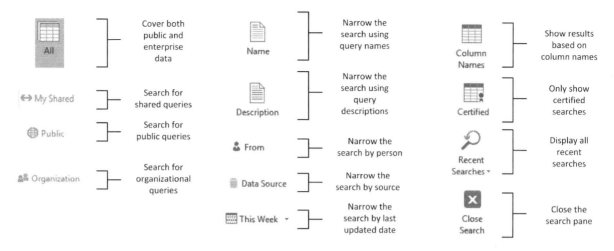

Figure 12-14. The Search ribbon

Table 12-7. Search Ribbon Options

Option	Description
All	Searches across all areas—public and organizational
My Shared	Only uses searches for queries that you have shared in Power BI.
Public	Searches for public data only
Organization	Searches for organizational data only
Name	Filters the search using the search name
Description	Filters the search using the search description
From	Filters the search to specific people or web sites
Data Source	Filters the search to specific sources of data
This Week	Filters the search to queries updated in a specific time frame
Column Names	Show results based on column name filtering
Certified	Only displays certified searches
Recent Searches	Lists any recent searches
Close Search	Closes the search window

■ **Note**   Shared and organizational shared queries are explained in Chapter 15.

Conclusion

In this chapter you have seen how the latest addition to the Power BI toolset, Power Query, can help you find and load data from a variety of sources. These sources can be more traditional—such as Access, Excel, or text files—or they could come from big data repositories or social media sources. Indeed, data could even be found in public data repositories or from commercial cloud-based sources. Power Query will even help you find available data (from both inside and outside the enterprise) and remember any recent searches you have made. Yet this is only the first part of the story. Now you need to learn how to shape and tweak the data to prepare it for further use. This is the subject of the next chapter.

CHAPTER 13

■ ■ ■

Transforming Data with Power Query

In the previous chapter we saw some of the ways in which you can find and load data into Power Query. Inevitably this will be the first part of any process that you create to extract, transform, and load data. Yet it is quite definitely only a first step. Once the data is in Power Query, you will need to know how to adapt it to suit your requirements in a multitude of ways.

The transformations that you can apply to the raw data are many and varied. They can include the following:

- Renaming, removing, and reordering columns

- Subsetting columns to extract part of the available data in a column

- Excluding records

- Pivoting data to make it easier to handle

- Transforming text, numeric, and date columns to present the data differently

- Calculating columns

- Sorting the data

- Merging data from separate queries

- And many more

These modifications, or transformations, if you prefer another term, are the subject of this chapter. Learning to apply these transformations will enable you to take data as you find it and push it as a coherent and structured data table into Excel or into the Excel Data Model so it is ready for finalizing with PowerPivot.

In this chapter I will also be using a set of example files that you can find on the Apress web site. If you have followed the instructions in Appendix A, then these files will be in the folder C:\HighImpactDataVisualizationWithPowerBI.

Modifying Data

Once you have one or more queries in Power Query that can connect to data sources and bring the data into this environment, you can start thinking about the next step—transforming the data so that it is ready for use. Depending on the number of data sources that you are handling and the extent of any modifications that are required, this could vary from the simple to the complex. To give a process some structure, I advise that you try to break down any steps into the following main threads:

- **Shape the dataset**—This covers filtering out records to reduce the size of the dataset, as well as removing any extraneous columns. It may also involve adding columns that you create by splitting existing columns, creating calculated columns, or even joining queries.

- **Cleanse and modify the data**—This is also known as data transformation (the *T* in ETL). It encompasses the process of converting text data to upper- and lowercase as well as (for instance) removing non-printing characters. Rounding numbers and extracting date parts from date data are also possible (among many other eventual transformations).

The next part of this chapter will take you through some of the techniques that you will need to know to cleanse and shape your data.

The Power Query Window

Before we go any further, I would like to explain the Power Query window, since it is something that you will be using a lot in this chapter from this point on. You saw it briefly in Figure 12-5 in the previous chapter, but Figure 13-1 is a more detailed overview.

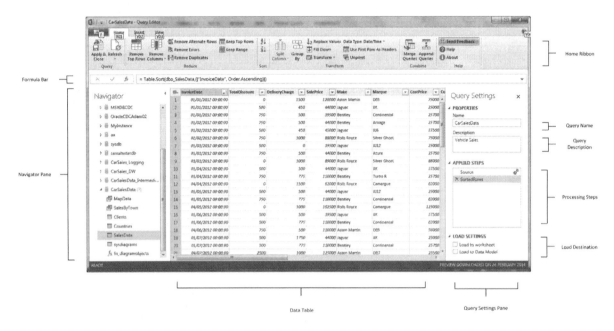

Figure 13-1. *The Power Query window*

The key elements are as follows:

- **The Navigator**—In a way similar to the Navigator window in Excel, this will show you the source data tables in the current data source.

- **The Data**—This is the essence of what you are dealing with, at each stage in the process. Note that the data will change with each step that you add to the list of process steps. Indeed, when you click on a process step, the data in the Data table will be updated to reflect the state of the data in the process up to and including the selected step.

- **The Query Settings pane**—This contains the detailed list of process steps that you have applied to this particular data table, and it also allows you to (re)name the query and add a description.

When it comes to the data itself, a multitude of synonyms can be used to describe the constituents of the data. I will use the following terms in this chapter:

- Data set and data table describe the whole block of data.

- Record and row denote a line of data.

- Column and field denote the vertical separation of data.

- Cell and element describe the intersection of a row and a column.

▦ **Note**   Clicking on a table in the Navigator is a way of telling Power Query that you want to swap the current source table with a new one. This is not a problem if you have not yet added any steps to transform the data. If you do it once you have created a complex process, however, be aware that it can invalidate all your work. It can be extremely useful, though, if you have a new data source that is identical to an old one and you need to reference it at the top of the sequence of processing steps.

Remember that working in the Power Query window essentially blocks your access to Excel. Consequently, you will have to close the Power Query window (and either save or discard your modifications) to continue using Excel.

The Power Query Ribbons

Power Query uses (in the March 2014 version, at least) three ribbons. Two of them will be fundamental to what you will be learning in the course of this chapter:

- The Home ribbon
- The Insert ribbon

The Home Ribbon

Since we will be making intense use of the Power Query Home ribbon to transform data, it is important to have an idea of what it can do. I explain the various options in Figure 13-2 and in Table 13-1.

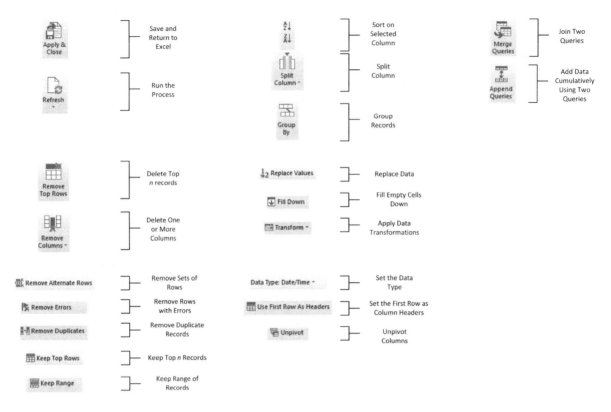

Figure 13-2. *The Query Editor Home ribbon*

Table 13-1. *Query Editor Home Ribbon Options*

Option	Comments
Apply & Close	Finishes the processing steps; saves and closes the query.
Refresh	Refreshes the source data and reprocesses all the steps.
Remove Top Rows	Removes a specified number of rows from the top of the data table.
Remove Columns	Removes one or more columns.
Remove Alternate Rows	Removes a defined number of rows every *n* rows, starting at a specified row.
Remove Errors	Removes all rows where that contain processing errors.
Remove Duplicates	Removes all duplicate rows, leaving only unique rows.
Keep Top Rows	Removes all but the specified number of rows at the top of the table.
Keep Range	Keeps a range of rows beginning at a specified row.
Sort	Sorts the table using the selected column as the sort key.

(continued)

Table 13-1. (*continued*)

Option	Comments
Split Column	Splits a column into one or many columns at either a specified delimiter or after a specified number of characters.
Group By	Groups the table using a specified set of columns and aggregates any numeric columns for this grouping.
Replace Values	Carries out a search and replace operation on the data in a column or columns. This will only affect the complete data in a column.
Fill Down	Copies the data from cells above into empty cells.
Transform	Carries out certain operations on the data, such as converting to uppercase.
Data Type	Applies the chosen data type to the column.
Use First Row As Headers	Takes the first row as being the column titles.
Append	Adds the (identically structured) data from another query to the current query.

The Insert Ribbon

A surprisingly useful set of functions are available in the Insert ribbon. The various options it contains are explained in Figure 13-3 and Table 13-2.

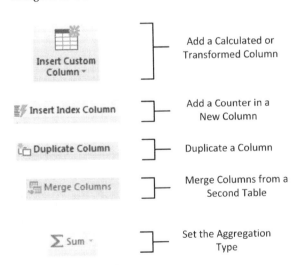

Figure 13-3. *The Query Editor Insert ribbon*

Table 13-2. *Query Editor Insert Ribbon Options*

Option	Comments
Insert Custom Column	Adds a new column using a custom formula
Insert Index Column	Adds a column containing a sequential numbering scheme
Duplicate Column	Duplicates a selected column
Merge	Joins a second query table to the current query results and either aggregates or adds data from the second to the first
Aggregation	Calculates the sum or product of multiple numeric columns

Dataset Shaping

So you are now looking at a data table that you have loaded into Power Query. For argument's sake, let's assume that it is the C:\HighImpactDataVisualizationWithPowerBI\SalesData.xlsx file from the sample data. What can you do to this data now that it is in Power Query?

Using First Row as Headers

As you can see from the source file, one immediate need for this particular data source is to tell Power Query to take the first record and have it function as the column headers. This is fundamental for two reasons:

- You avoid leaving the columns named Column1, Column2, and so on. Leaving them named generically like this would make it needlessly difficult for a user to understand the data.

- You avoid having a text element (which should be the column title) in a column of figures, which can cause problems later on. This is because a whole column needs to have the same data type in order for another data type to be applied. Having a header text in the first row prevents this for numeric and data/time data types, for instance.

Fortunately, applying the first row as headers is simple:

1. Click Use First Row As Headers in the Transform section of the Power Query Home ribbon.

After a few seconds, the first record will disappear, and the column titles will become the elements that were in the first record. The APPLIED STEPS list on the right will now contain a FirstRowAsHeader element, indicating which process has taken place. This step will be highlighted.

▓ **Note**   Power Query will often be able to apply this step automatically when the source is a database and can often guess correctly when the source is a file. However, it cannot always guess accurately, so sometimes you will have to intervene.

In the rare event that Power Query gets this operation wrong and presumes that a first row is column titles when it is not, you can reset the titles to be the first row by deleting the FirstRowAsHeader element in the Applied Steps window. To do this, merely click on the cross (x) to the left of the step name that appears if you hover the pointer over the step.

Renaming Columns

In cases where your source data does not have either column names in the source data or a first row that can be promoted to column names, you can rename any or all the columns in the data table. To do this

1. Right-click on the column name. The whole column will become highlighted.

2. Select Rename from the context menu. The column name will stay highlighted.

3. Enter the new name, or edit the existing name.

4. Press Enter, or click outside the column title.

The column will be renamed and the column will no longer be highlighted. The APPLIED STEPS list on the right will now contain another element, RenamedColumn. This step will be highlighted.

■ **Note**   I admit that renaming columns is not actually modifying the form of the data table. However, when dealing with data, I consider it vital to have all data clearly identifiable (in other words, with a column name). Consequently, I consider this modification to be fundamental to the shape of the data, and also as an essential best practice when importing source data.

Reordering Columns

Power Query will load data as it is in the data source. Consequently, the column sequence will be defined by the source data (or by a SQL query if you used a source database, as described earlier). This need not be definitive, however, and you can reorder the columns if that helps you understand and deal with the data. To change column order

1. Click on the header of the column you want to move.

2. Drag the column left or right to its new position. You will see the column title slide laterally through the column titles as you do this, and a thicker grey line will indicate where the column will be placed once you release the mouse button. ReorderedColumns will appear in the APPLIED STEPS list.

Figure 13-4 shows this operation.

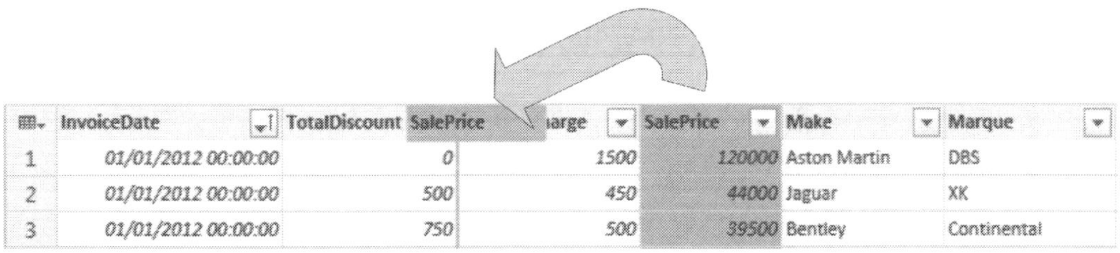

⊞▾	InvoiceDate	▾ᵢ	TotalDiscount	SalePrice	ᵢarge	▾	SalePrice	▾	Make	▾	Marque	▾
1	01/01/2012 00:00:00		0		1500		120000		Aston Martin		DBS	
2	01/01/2012 00:00:00		500		450		44000		Jaguar		XK	
3	01/01/2012 00:00:00		750		500		39500		Bentley		Continental	

Figure 13-4. *Reordering columns*

Removing Columns

So how do you delete a column or series of columns? Like this:

1. Click inside the column you want to delete, or if you want to delete several columns at once, Ctrl-click on the titles of the columns you want to delete.

2. Click the Remove Columns button in the Home ribbon. The column(s) will be deleted and RemovedColumns will be the latest element in the APPLIED STEPS list.

When working with imported data sets over which you have had no control, you may frequently find that you only need a few columns of a large data table. If this is the case, you will soon get tired of Ctrl-clicking on many, many columns to select those you want to remove. Power Query has an alternative method. Just select the columns you want to keep and delete the others. To do this:

1. Ctrl-click on the titles of the columns you want to keep.

2. Click the lower part of the Remove Columns button in the Home ribbon (the downward-facing triangle). Select Remove Other Columns from the menu. All unselected columns will be deleted and RemovedOtherColumns will be the added to the APPLIED STEPS list.

■ **Note** Both these options are also available from the context menu if you prefer. This will show Remove (or Remove Columns if there are several columns selected) when deleting columns.

Removing Records

When you first look at data or when you are testing data cleansing and experimenting with selection processes, use a smaller data set to really speed up the development of a complex data extractions and transformation process. This is essentially sampling the data in order to work on a reduced data set. You may even want to analyze a reduced data set to extrapolate theses and inferences and save analysis on a full data set for later, or even using a more industrial-strength toolset such as SQL Server Integration Services.

To allow you to sample the data, Power Query proposes the following options out of the box:

- Keep the top *n* records.

- Keep all *but* the top *n* records.

- Keep a specified range of records.

- Remove *n* records every *y* records.

Most of these techniques are very similar, so let's start by imagining that you want to keep the top 50 records in the sample (Sales2012_2013) dataset.

1. In the Home ribbon, click the Keep Top Rows button. The Keep Top Rows dialog will appear.

2. Enter 50 in the Number Of Rows box. The dialog will look like Figure 13-5.

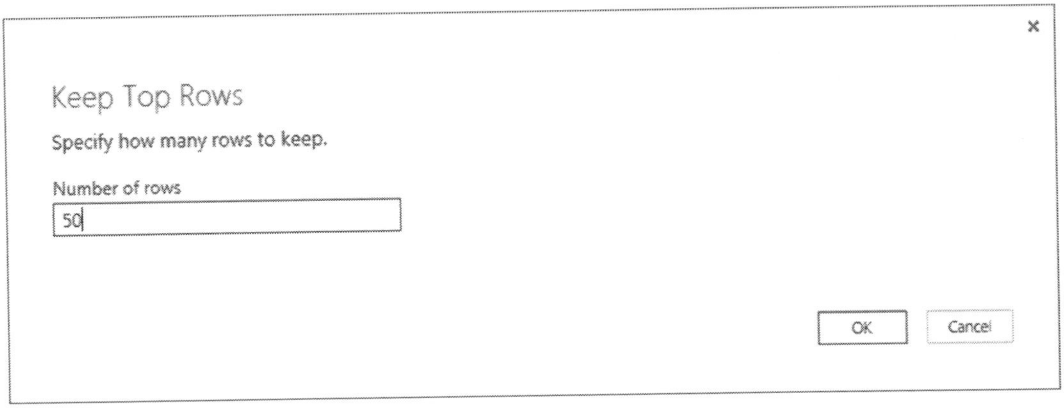

Figure 13-5. *The Keep Top Rows dialog*

3. Click OK. All but the first 50 records will be deleted and KeptFirstRows will be the added to the APPLIED STEPS list.

Removing the top n rows is a virtually identical process, so I will not go through it in detail. All you have to do is click the Remove Top Rows button in the Home ribbon in step 1 earlier, then continue with steps 2 and 3. The APPLIED STEPS list will read RemovedFirstRows in this case.

To keep a range of records, you will need to specify a starting record and the number of records to keep from then on. For instance, suppose that you wish to lose the first 10 records but keep the following 25. This is how to go about it:

1. In the Home ribbon, click the Keep Range button. The Keep Range dialog will appear.

2. Enter **11** in the First Row box.

3. Enter **25** in the Number Of Rows box. The dialog will look like Figure 13-6.

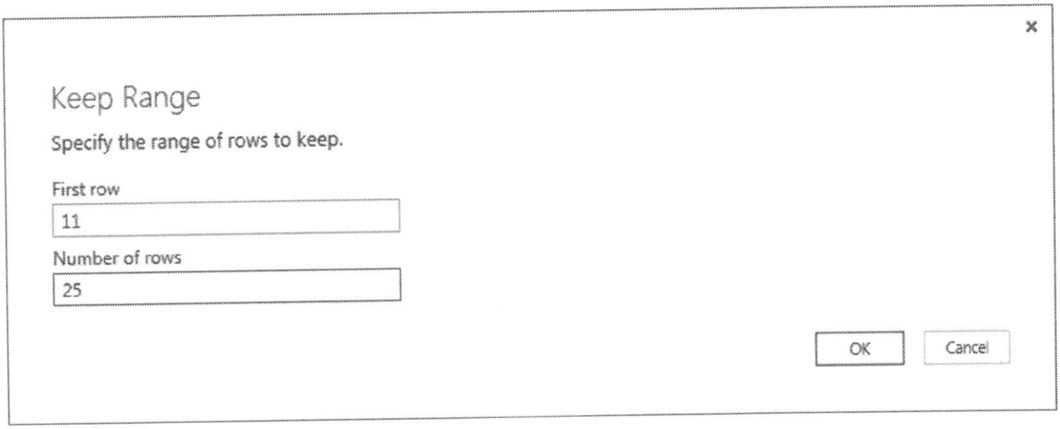

Figure 13-6. *The Keep Range dialog*

4. Click OK. All but the records 1-10 and 36 to the end will be deleted and RowRange will be the added to the APPLIED STEPS list.

As a sampling technique, removing one or more records every few records is a good way of subsetting the source data. To do this, you need to

1. Click Remove Alternate Rows in the Home ribbon. The Remove Alternate Rows dialog will appear.

2. Enter **10** as the First Row To Remove.

3. Enter **2** as the Number Of Rows To Remove.

4. Enter **10** as the Number Of Rows To Keep. The dialog will look like Figure 13-7.

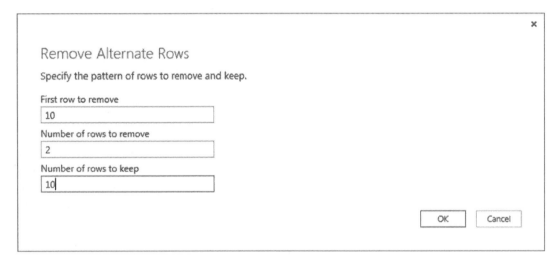

Figure 13-7. The Remove Alternate Rows dialog

5. Click OK. All but the records matching the pattern you entered in the dialog will be removed. AlternatedRows will be then added to the APPLIED STEPS list.

If you are really determined to extract a sample that you consider to be representative of the key data, then you can always filter the data before subsetting it to exclude any outliers. Filtering data is explained in a couple of pages.

Removing Duplicate Records

An external source of data might not be quite as perfect as you might hope. One of the most annoying features of poor data is the presence of duplicates. These are insidious since they falsify results and are not always visible. If you suspect that the data table contains strict duplicates (that is, where every field is identical in two or more records), then you can remove the duplicates like this:

1. Click the Remove Duplicates button in the Home ribbon. All duplicate records will be deleted and DuplicatesRemoved will be the added to the APPLIED STEPS list.

> ■ **Note**   I must stress that this approach will only remove identical duplicates. If two records have just one character or number different but everything else is identical, then they are not considered duplicates by Power Query.

So if you suspect or are sure that the data table you are dealing with contains duplicates, what are the practical solutions? This can be a real conundrum, but there are some basic techniques you can apply:

- Remove all columns that you are sure you will not be using later in the data-handling process. This way Power Query will only be asked to compare essential data across potentially duplicate records.

- Group the data on the core columns; this is explained a little further on in this chapter.

Removing Errors

Assuming that you do not need records that Power Query has flagged as containing an error, you can have all such records removed in a single operation:

1. Click inside the column containing errors, or if you want to remove errors from several columns at once, Ctrl-click on the titles of the columns that contain the errors.

2. Click Remove Errors in the Home ribbon. Any records with errors flagged in the selected columns will be deleted. RemovedErrors will be the added to the APPLIED STEPS list.

You have to be very careful here not to remove valid data. Only you can judge, once you have taken a look at the data, if an error in a column means that the data can be discarded safely. In all other cases, you would be best advised to look at cleansing the data or simply leaving records that contain errors in place. The range and variety of potential errors is as vast as the data itself. You could see errors due to invalid data types, for instance.

Filtering Data

The most frequently used way of limiting a data set is, in my experience, the use of filters on the table that you have loaded. Now, I realize that you may be coming to Power Query after years with Excel, or after some time using PowerPivot, and that the filtering techniques that you are about to see probably look very like the ones you may have used in those two tools. However, as it can be fundamental to include and exclude the appropriate records when loading source data, I prefer to handle Power Query filters reasonably thoroughly, even if this means I have to use a certain amount of repetition. If you need further detail, Chapter 9 contains a more in-depth explanation of how to apply filters.

Here are two basic approaches for filtering data in Power Query:

- Select one or more specific values from the unique list of elements in the chosen column.

- Define a range of data to include or exclude.

The first option is common to all data types, whether they are text, number, or data/time. The second approach varies according to the data type of the column you are using to filter data.

Selecting Specific Values

Selecting one or more values present in a column of data is as easy as this:

1. Click on the popup menu for a column. I will use Make in the sample data set in this example. The filter menu appears.

2. Check all elements that you want to retain, and uncheck all elements that you wish to exclude. In this example, I will keep Bentley and Rolls Royce as shown in Figure 13-8.

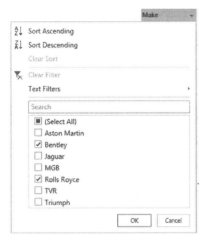

Figure 13-8. *A Filter menu*

3. Click OK. The APPLIED STEPS box will add FilteredRows.

■ **Note**   You can deselect all items by clicking the (Select All) check box; then reselect all the items by checking this box again. It follows that if you want to keep only a few elements, it may be faster to unselect all of them first, and then only check the ones that you want to keep.

Finding Elements in the Filter List

Scrolling up and down in a filter list can get extremely laborious. A fast way of limiting the list to a subset of available elements is to

1. Click on the popup menu for a column. I will use Marque in the sample data set in this example. The filter menu appears.

2. Enter a letter or a few letters in the Search box. The list will shorten with every letter or number that you enter. If I enter **ar**, then the filter popup will look like Figure 13-9.

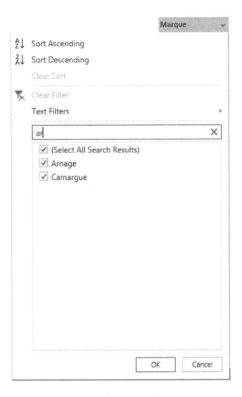

Figure 13-9. *Searching the filter menu*

Filtering Text Ranges

If a column contains text, then you can apply specific options to filter the data. These elements are found in the filter popup of any text-based column in the Text Filters submenu. The choices are given in Table 13-3.

Table 13-3. *Text Filter Options*

Filter Option	Explanation
Equals	Sets the text that must match the cell contents
Does Not Equal	Sets the text that must not match the cell contents
Begins With	Sets the text at the left of the cell contents
Ends With	Sets the text at the right of the cell contents
Contains	Lets you enter a text that will be part of the cell contents
Does Not Contain	Lets you enter a text that will not be part of the cell contents

Filtering Numeric Ranges

If a column contains numbers, then there are also specific options that you can apply to filter the data. You'll find these elements in the filter popup of any text-based column in the Number Filters submenu. The choices are given in Table 13-4.

Table 13-4. *Numeric Filter Options*

Filter Option	Explanation
Equals	Sets the number that must match the cell contents.
Does Not Equal	Sets the number that must not match the cell contents.
Greater Than	Cell contents must be greater than this number.
Greater Than Or Equal To	Cell contents must be greater than or equal to this number.
Lesser Than	Cell contents must be less than this number.
Lesser Than Or Equal To	Cell contents must be less than or equal to this number.
Between	Cell contents must be between the two numbers.

Filtering Date and Time Ranges

If a column contains dates or times (or both), then specific options can also be applied to filter the data. These elements are found in the filter popup of any text-based column in the Date/Time Filters submenu. The choices are given in Table 13-5.

Table 13-5. *Date and Time Filter Options*

Filter Element	Description
Equals	Filters data to include only records for the selected date
Before	Filters data to include only records up to the selected date
After	Filters data to include only records after the selected date
Between	Lets you set an upper and a lower date limit to exclude records outside that range
Tomorrow	Filters data to include only records for the day after the current system date
Today	Filters data to include only records for the current system date
Yesterday	Filters data to include only records for the day before the current system date
Next Week	Filters data to include only records for the next calendar week
This Week	Filters data to include only records for the current calendar week
Last Week	Filters data to include only records for the previous calendar week
Next Month	Filters data to include only records for the next calendar month
This Month	Filters data to include only records for the current calendar month
Last Month	Filters data to include only records for the previous calendar month
Next Quarter	Filters data to include only records for the next quarter
This Quarter	Filters data to include only records for the current quarter
Last Quarter	Filters data to include only records for the previous quarter
Next Year	Filters data to include only records for the next year

(continued)

Table 13-5. (*continued*)

Filter Element	Description
This Year	Filters data to include only records for the current year
Last Year	Filters data to include only records for the previous year
Year To Date	Filters data to include only records for the calendar year to date
All Dates In Period	Filters data to include only records where the date range corresponds to the selected period (month or quarter of the year)
Custom Filter	Lets you set up a specific filter for two possible date ranges

Extending Data

Transforming data does not only consist of reducing it. Often you may have to extend the data to make it useable. This normally means adding further columns to a data table, and the techniques to do this cover

- Duplicating columns.

- Splitting columns.

- Adding custom columns that possibly contain calculations or extract part of a column's data into a new column, or even concatenate columns.

- Adding "index" columns to ensure uniqueness or memorize a sort order.

Duplicating Column

Sometimes you just need a simple copy of a column, with nothing added and nothing taken away. This is where the Duplicate Column button comes into play.

1. Click inside (or on the title of) the column that you want to duplicate.

2. Click the Duplicate Column button in the Insert ribbon. After a few seconds a copy of the column is created at the right of the existing table. DuplicatedColumn will appear in the APPLIED STEPS box.

3. Scroll to the right of the table and rename the existing column; it will currently be named Copy Of *whatever the original column was called.*

Splitting Columns

Sometimes a source column contains data that you really need to break up into smaller pieces across two or more columns. The classic cases where this happens are

- A column contains a list of elements, separated by a specific character (known as a delimiter).

- A column contains a list of elements, but the elements can be divided at specific places in the column.

- A column contains a concatenated text that needs to be split into its composite elements (a bank account number or a Social Security number are examples of this).

The following short sections explain how to handle such eventualities.

Splitting Column by a Delimiter

Here is another requirement that you may have occasionally. The data that has been imported has a column that needs to be further split into multiple columns. Imagine a text file where columns are separated by semicolons, and these subdivisions each contain a column that holds a comma-separated list of elements. Once you have imported the file, you then need to further separate out the contents of this column that uses a different delimiter. Take the text file DelimitedSubList.txt as an example in the sample data; here is what you can do:

1. Load the sample file C:\HighImpactDataVisualizationWithPowerBI\DelimitedSubList.txt as described in Chapter 12 in the "Text Files" section.

2. Promote the first row to become the column title.

3. Click the Split Column button in the Home ribbon.

4. Select By Delimiter in the popup menu. The Split A Column By Delimiter dialog appears.

5. Select Comma from the list of available options in the Select Or Enter Delimiter popup.

6. Click At Each Occurrence Of The Delimiter. The dialog should look like Figure 13-10.

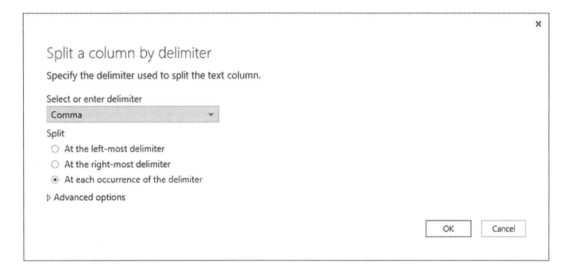

Figure 13-10. *Splitting a column using a delimiter*

7. Click OK. SplitColumnDelimiter will appear in the APPLIED STEPS box.

The initial column will remain, but be renamed .1. As many additional columns as there are delimiters will be created each will be named (*Column.n*) and will be sequentially numbered.

This particular process has several options, and their consequences can be fairly far-reaching as far as the data is concerned. So, initially, Table 13-6 contains a description of the available options followed by a few comments.

Table 13-6. *Delimiter Split Options*

Option	Description
Colon	Uses the colon (:) as the delimiter.
Comma	Uses the comma (,) as the delimiter.
Equals Sign	Uses the equals sign (=) as the delimiter.
Semi-Colon	Uses the semicolon (;) as the delimiter.
Space	Uses the space ( ) as the delimiter.
Tab	Uses the tab character as the delimiter.
Custom	Lets you enter a custom delimiter.
Left-Most Delimiter	Splits the column once only at the first occurrence of the delimiter.
Right-Most Delimiter	Splits the column once only at the last occurrence of the delimiter.
At Each Occurrence of the Delimiter	Splits the column into as many columns as there are delimiters.
Number of Columns to Split Into	Allows you to set a maximum number of columns into which the data will be split in chunks of the given number of characters. Any extra columns will be placed in the rightmost column.

Splitting Columns by Number of Characters

Another variant on this theme is when text in each column is a fixed number of characters and needs to be broken down into constituent parts at specific intervals. Suppose, for instance, that you have a field where each group of (a certain number of) characters has a specific meaning, and you want to break it into multiple columns. Alternatively, suppose you want to extract the leftmost or rightmost n characters and leave the rest. This is where splitting a column by the number of characters can come in useful. As the principle is very similar to the process that we just saw, I will not repeat the whole thing again. All you have to do is choose By Number Of Characters at step 4 in the previous exercise. Options for this type of operation are given in Table 13-7.

Table 13-7. *Options When Splitting a Column by Number of Characters*

Option	Description
Number Of Characters	Lets you define the number of characters of data before splitting the column.
Once, As Far Left As Possible	Splits the column once only at the given number of characters in from the left.
Once, As Far Right As Possible	Splits the column once only at the given number of characters in from the right.
Repeatedly	Splits the column as many times as necessary to cut it into segments every defined number of characters.
Number Of Columns To Split Into	Allows you to set a maximum number of columns into which the data will be split in chunks of the given number of characters. Any extra columns will be placed in the rightmost column.

There are a couple of things to note when splitting columns:

- When splitting by a delimiter, Power Query will make a good attempt at guessing the maximum number of columns into which the source column must be split. If it gets this wrong (and you can see what its guesstimate is if you expand the Advanced Options box), you can override the number here.

- If you select a Custom Delimiter, Power Query will display a new box in the dialog where you can enter a specific delimiter.

- Every record does not have to have the same number of delimiters. Power Query will simply leave the rightmost column(s) blank if there are fewer split elements for a row.

▓ **Note**   You can only split columns if they are text data. The Split Column button will remain grayed out if your intention is to try and split a date or numeric column.

Custom Columns

Another way to extend the original data table is to add more columns. Although these are known as custom columns in Power Query, they are also known more generically as derived columns or calculated columns. Although they can do many things, which we will not look at in this chapter, their essential role is to

- Concatenate, or join, if you prefer, existing columns.

- Add calculations to the data table.

- Extract a specific part of a column.

- Add flags to the table based on existing data.

The best way to understand these columns is probably to see them in action; I've provided an initial example that should explain the basics, and you can see further techniques in Table 13-8. You can then extend these principles in your own processes.

Initially, then, let's perform a column join and create a column named Vehicle, which concatenates the Make and Marque columns with a space in between.

1. In the Insert ribbon, click Insert Custom Column. The Insert Custom Column dialog will be displayed.

2. Click on the Make column in the column list on the right, then click on the Insert button; =[Make] will appear in the Custom Column Formula box at the left of the dialog.

3. Enter & " " & in the Custom Column Formula box after =[Make].

4. Click on the Marque column in the column list on the right, then click on the Insert button. The dialog will look like Figure 13-11.

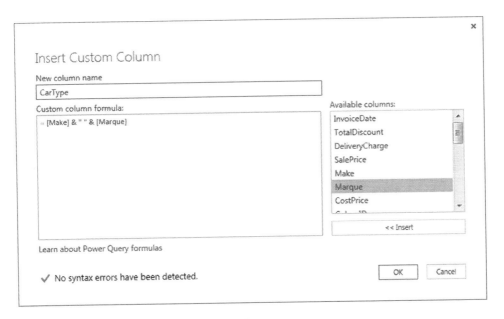

Figure 13-11. *The Insert Custom Column dialog*

5. Click inside the New column name box and enter a name for the column. I will call it **CarType**.

6. Click OK. The new column will be added at the right of the data table and will contain the results of the formula. InsertedColumn will appear in the APPLIED STEPS box.

You can always double-click on a column to insert it into the Custom Column Formula box if you prefer. To remove a column, simply delete the column name (including the square brackets) in the Custom Column Formula box.

■ **Note**   You must always enclose a column name in square brackets—just like you saw in Chapter 10 when using PowerPivot.

Rather than take you step by step through other examples, I prefer to show you some of the formulas that you can use to calculate columns and extract data into a new column. These code snippets are given in Table 13-8. As an Excel user, you can probably see a distinct similarity with how you build formulas in Excel, except that here, as in PowerPivot, you use column names rather than cell references.

Table 13-8. *Custom Column Code Examples*

Output	Code Snippet	Explanation
Column Calculations	`= [SalePrice]-[CostPrice]`	Subtracts the Cost Price from the Sale Price to give the Gross Margin
Column Arithmetic	`=[SalePrice] * 1.2`	Adds the UK sales tax (20%) to the Net Sale Price
Left	`Text.Start([Make],3)`	Will return the first three characters from the Make column
Right	`Text.End([Make],3)`	Will return the last three characters from the Make column
Up to a specific character	`Text.Start([Make],Text.PositionOf ([Make]," "))`	Will return the leftmost characters up to the first space

If you have already read Chapter 10, then you are probably wondering why you carry out operations like this in Power Query when you can do virtually the same thing in PowerPivot. Well, it is true that there is some overlap; so you have the choice of which to use. You can perform certain operations at multiple stages in the data preparation and analysis process. It will all depend on how you will be using the data and with what tool you will be carrying out the analyses.

▓ **Note**   If you have read the chapters on PowerPivot in this book, then you may well be wondering if you should be using PowerPivot or Power Query to carry out operations like the ones described just now. After all, both tools can perform them equally well. Indeed, Excel can also carry out many of these operations. So essentially—you choose! Do whatever seems best according to the circumstances specific to each data analysis operation with the tool that seems the most appropriate. Having said this, if you can make all data manipulation processes using Power Query, your solution may be more coherent.

Index Column

An index column is a new column that numbers every record in the table sequentially. This numbering scheme will apply to the table as it is currently sorted and will begin at zero. An index column can be useful in the following cases (and this list is not intended to be exhaustive in any way; you will almost certainly find other uses as you work with Power Query):

- Re-apply a previous sort order.
- Create a unique reference for every record.

Whatever need transpires, here is how to add an Index column:

1. Click Insert Index Column in the Insert ribbon. The new, sequentially numbered column is added at the right of the table, and InsertedIndex is added to the APPLIED STEPS box.

2. Scroll to the right of the table and rename the index column; it is currently named Index.

Data Cleansing and Modification

If your data has been "shaped," then it probably now only needs a few final modifications to make it ready for consumption. The sort of things that you may be looking to do can include the following:

- Change the data type for a column—by telling Power Query that the column contains numbers, for example.

- Replace the values in a cell with other values.

- Transform the column contents—by making the text uppercase, for instance.

- Fill data down across empty cells to ensure that records are complete.

- Sort the entire table by a specific column.

Changing Datatype

A truly fundamental aspect of data modification is ensuring that the data is of the appropriate type; that is, if you have a column of numbers that are destined to be calculated at some point, then the column should really be a numeric column. If it contains dates, then it should be set to one of the date or time datatypes. I realize that this can seem arduous and even superfluous; however, if you want to be sure that your data can be sliced and diced correctly further down the line, then setting the right data types is vital. An added bonus is that if you validate the data types early on in the process of loading data, you can see from the start if the data has any potential issues—dates that cannot be read as dates, for instance. This allows you to decide what to do with poor or unreliable data early in your work with a data set.

The good news here is that for many data sources, Power Query will apply an appropriate data type. Specifically, if you have loaded data from a database, then Power Query will recognize the data type for each column and apply a suitable native data type. Things can get a little more painful with file sources, specifically .CSV, text, and Excel files, as well as some XML files. In the case of these file types, Power Query will often try and guess the data type, but there are times when it will not succeed. If it has made a stab at deducing data types, then you will see a ChangedType step in the APPLIED STEPS box. Consequently, if you are obtaining your data from these sources, then you could well be obliged to apply data types to many of the columns manually. So, to change data type for a column or a group of columns, once you have loaded the file SalesData.xlsx

1. Click inside the column whose data type you wish to change. If you want to modify several columns, then Ctrl-click on the requisite column titles. In this example, you could select the CostPrice and TotalDiscount columns.

2. Click the Data Type button in the Transform section of the Power Query Home ribbon. A popup menu of potential data types will appear.

3. Select an appropriate data type. If you have selected the CostPrice and TotalDiscount columns, then Number is the type to choose.

After a few seconds the data type will be applied, and ChangedType will appear in the APPLIED STEPS pane. The data types that you can apply are outlined in Table 13-9.

Table 13-9. *Data Types in Power Query*

Data Type	Comments
Binary	Defines the data as binary, and consequently, it is not visible directly.
Date	Converts to a date data type.
Date/Time	Converts to a date and time data type.
Date/Time/Timezone	Converts to a date and time data type with the time zone.
Duration	Sets the data as being a duration. These are used for date and time calculations.
Logical	Sets the data type to Boolean (True or False).
Number	Applies a numeric data type.
Text	Sets to a text data type.
Time	Sets to a time data type.

Inevitably there will be times when you try to apply a data type that simply cannot be used with a certain column of data. Converting a text column (such as Make in this sample data table) into dates will simply not work. If you do this, then Power Query will replace the column contents with Error. This is not definitive or dangerous, and all you have to do to return the data to its previous state is to delete the ChangedType step in the APPLIED STEPS pane.

It can help to alter data types at the same time for any columns where you think that this operation is necessary. There are a couple of good reasons for this approach:

- You can concentrate on getting data types right, and if you are working methodically, you are less likely to forget to set a data type.

- Applying data types for many columns (even if you are doing this in several operations, to single or multiple columns) will only add a single step to the APPLIED STEPS box.

▨ **Note**   Don't look for any data formatting options in Power Query; there aren't any. This is deliberate, since this tool is designed to load data. Companion tools such as PowerPivot or Power View carry out the formatting.

Replacing Values

Some data that you load will need certain values to be replaced by others in a kind of global search and replace operation, just as you would in a document. For instance, perhaps you need to standardize spellings where a make of car (to use the current sample dataset as an example) has been spelled incorrectly. To carry out this particular data cleansing operation

1. Click on the title of the column that contains the data that you want to replace. The column will become selected. In this example, I will use the Marque column.

2. Click the Replace Values button in the Transform section of the Home ribbon. The Replace Values dialog will appear.

3. In the Value To Find box, enter the text or number that you want to replace. I will use **Ghost** in this example.

4. In the Replace With box, enter the text or number that you want to replace. I will use **Fantôme** in this example. This dialog should now look like Figure 13-12.

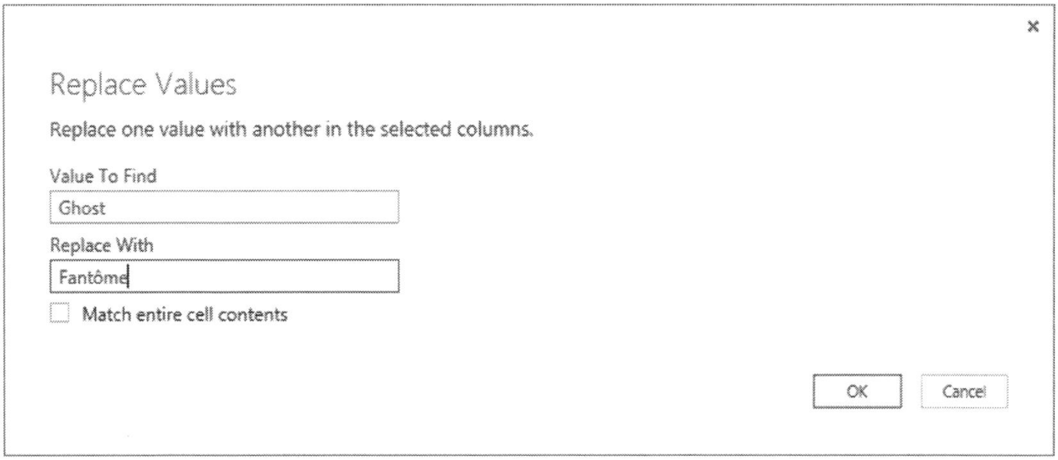

Figure 13-12. *The Replace Values dialog*

5. Click OK. The data will be replaced in the entire column. ReplacedValues will be added to the APPLIED STEPS box.

I only have a couple of comments for this operation:

- The Replace Values process searches for every occurrence of the text you are looking for in each record of the selected column. It will not look for the entire contents of the cell unless you specifically request this by checking the Match Entire Cell Contents check box.

- If you click on a cell containing the contents that you want to replace (rather than the column title, as we just did), before starting the process, Power Query will automatically place the cell contents in the Replace Values dialog.

As a final, and purely spurious comment, I must add that I would never, of course, suggest rebranding a Rolls-Royce, as it would be close to automotive sacrilege.

Transforming Column Contents

Power Query has a powerful toolbox of automated data transformations that allow you to standardize the contents of a column in several ways. These include

- Setting the capitalization of text columns

- Rounding numeric data or applying math functions

- Extracting date elements such as the year, month, or day (among others) from a date column

Let's see a simple transformation operation in action. As an example, I will get Power Query to convert the Make column into uppercase characters.

1. Click anywhere in the column whose contents you wish to transform (Make, in this case).

2. Click the Transform button in the Transform section of the Home ribbon. A popup menu will appear.

3. Select Text Transforms ➤ UPPERCASE, as shown in Figure 13-13.

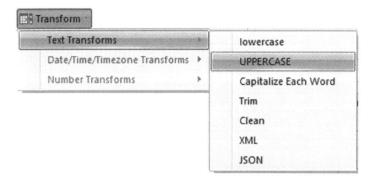

Figure 13-13. *Transform operations*

The contents of the entire column will be converted to uppercase. TransformedColumn will be added to the APPLIED STEPS box.

You will have noticed that only the Text Transforms option was available in the Transforms popup menu in Figure 13-13. This is because transforms are totally dependent on the data type of the selected column. This is yet another confirmation that applying the requisite data type is an operation that should be carried out early in any data transformation process. So, you will only be able to select a numeric transformation if the column is a numeric data type, and you will only be able to select a date transformation if the column is a date data type. Assuming that you have column of the appropriate data type, then a range of transformations is available. These options are given in Table 13-10.

Table 13-10. *Data Transformations*

Transformation	Data Type	Comments
Lowercase	Text	Converts all the text to lowercase
Uppercase	Text	Converts all the text to uppercase
Capitalize Each Word	Text	Converts the first letter of each word to a capital
Trim	Text	Removes all spaces before and after the text
Clean	Text	Removes any non-printable characters
XML	Text	Parses each cell as an XML document
JSON	Text	Parses each cell as a JSON document
Round	Number	Rounds each number to the specified number of decimal places
Round Up	Number	Rounds each number up
Round Down	Number	Rounds each number down
Absolute Value	Number	Makes the number absolute (positive)
Factorial	Number	Gives the factorial of numbers in the column
Logarithm	Number	Returns the Base 10 or natural logarithm of the numbers in the column
Power	Number	Returns the square, cube, or specified power of the number in each cell

(*continued*)

Table 13-10. (*continued*)

Transformation	Data Type	Comments
Square Root	Number	Returns the square root of the number in each cell
Date	Date/Time	Converts the data to a date without the time element
Time	Date/Time	Converts the data to the time element without the date part
Day	Date/Time	Extracts the day from the date
Month	Date/Time	Extracts the number of the month from the date
Year	Date/Time	Extracts the year from the date
Day of Week	Date/Time	Extracts the day of the week as a number (with Monday as Day 1)

Filling Down

Imagine a data source where the data has come into Power Query from a matrix-style structure. The result is that some columns only contain a single example of an element and then a series of empty cells until the next element in the list. If this is difficult to imagine, then suppose that you have loaded the sample file CarMakeAndModelMatrix.xlsx, and are looking at the table shown in Figure 13-14.

▦.	Make	Marque	Sales
1	Aston Martin	DB4	391000
2	null	DB7	500740
3	null	DB9	915070
4	null	DBS	230000
5	null	Rapide	225000
6	null	Vanquish	746500
7	null	Vantage	320850
8	null	Zagato	178500
9	Bentley	Arnage	44000
10	null	Azure	239250
11	null	Continental	991250
12	null	Turbo R	347500

Figure 13-14. *A matrix data table*

All these blank cells are a problem since we need a full data table—or rather, they would be, if Power Pivot did not have a really cool way of overcoming this particular difficulty. To solve this problem

1. Click in the column that contains the empty cells; make sure you click where you want to replace the empty cells with the contents of the first non-empty cell above.

2. Click Fill Down in the Transform section of the Home ribbon. FillDown will be added to the APPLIED STEPS box.

The table will now look like Figure 13-15.

■.	Make ▼	Marque ▼	Sales ▼
1	Aston Martin	DB4	391000
2	Aston Martin	DB7	500740
3	Aston Martin	DB9	915070
4	Aston Martin	DBS	230000
5	Aston Martin	Rapide	225000
6	Aston Martin	Vanquish	746500
7	Aston Martin	Vantage	320850
8	Aston Martin	Zagato	178500
9	Bentley	Arnage	44000
10	Bentley	Azure	239250
11	Bentley	Continental	991250
12	Bentley	Turbo R	347500

Figure 13-15. *A data table with empty cells replaced by the correct data*

■ **Note**   This technique is built to handle a fairly specific problem and will only really work if the imported data is grouped by the column containing the missing elements.

Sorting Data

Although not strictly a data modification step, sorting an imported table will probably be something that you want to do at some stage. To sort the data

1. Click inside the column you wish to sort by.

2. Click Sort Ascending (the A/Z icon) or Sort Descending (the Z/A icon) in the Home ribbon.

   The data will be sorted in either alphabetical (smallest to largest) or reverse alphabetical (largest to smallest) order. If you want to carry out a complex sort operation (that is, first by one column, and then by another if the first column contains the same element over several rows), you do this simply by sorting the columns one after another. Power View will add a tiny 1, 2, 3, and so on to the right of the column title to indicate the sort sequence.

■ **Note**   An alternative technique for sorting data is to click on the popup menu for a column (the downward-facing triangle at the right of a column title), and select Sort Ascending or Sort Descending from the popup menu.

Managing the Transformation Process

Pretty nearly all the transformation steps that we have applied so far have been individual elements that can be applied to just about any data table. However, when you are carrying out even a simple data load and transform process, you are likely to want to step through several transformations in order to shape, cleanse, and filter the data to get the result you want. This is where the Power Query approach is so clever, because you can apply most data transformation steps to just about any data table. The art is to place them in a sequence that can then be reused any time that the data changes to reprocess the new source data and deliver an up-to-date output.

The key to appreciating and to managing this process is to get well acquainted with the APPLIED STEPS list in the Query Settings pane. This list contains the details of every step that you applied, in the order in which you applied it. Each step retains the name that Power Query gave it when it was created, and each can be altered in the following ways:

- Modified
- Renamed
- Deleted
- Moved

Many steps can also be modified, so you are not stuck with the choices that you initially apply.

■ **Note** Remember that, before tweaking the order in which the process is applied, clicking on any process step will cause the table in the Power Query window to refresh to show you the state of the data up to and including the selected step. This is a very clear visual guide to the process and how the ETL is carried out.

Modifying a Step

How you alter a step will depend on how the original transformation was applied. This will become second nature after a little practice and will always involve first clicking on the step that you wish to modify and then applying a different modification. If you invoke a ribbon option, such as altering the data type, for instance, then you change the data type by simply applying another data type directly from the ribbon. If you used an option that displayed a dialog (such as splitting a column, among others), then you can right-click on the step in the APPLIED STEPS list and select Edit Settings from the context menu. This will cause the original dialog to reappear; in it you can make any modifications that you consider necessary.

A final step that makes it easy to alter the settings for a process is to edit the formula that appears in the formula bar each time you click on a step. We will look at this method toward the end of this chapter.

■ **Note** If you can force yourself to organize the process that you are writing with Power Query, then a little forethought and planning can reap major dividends. For instance, certain tasks such as setting data types can all be carried out in a single operation. Not just that, but if you need to alter a data type for a column at a later stage, I suggest that you click on the ChangedType step before you make any further alterations. This way you will extend the original step, rather than creating other steps, which can make the process more confusing and needlessly voluminous.

Renaming a Step

Because Power Query names steps using the name of the transformation that was applied, and then, if another similar step is applied later, uses the same name with a numeric increment, you may prefer to give more user-friendly names to process steps. This is done as follows:

1. Right-click on the step that you want to rename.
2. Select Rename from the context menu.

3. Type in the new name.

4. Press Enter.

The step will be renamed and the new name will appear in the APPLIED STEPS list in the Query Settings pane.

Deleting a Step or a Series of Steps

Deleting a step is all too easy, but doing so can have serious consequences. This is because an ETL process is often an extremely tightly coupled series of events, where each event depends intimately on the preceding one. So deleting a step can make every subsequent step fail. Knowing which events you can delete without drastic consequences will depend on the types of process that you are developing as well as your experience with Power Query. In any case, this is what you should do if you need to delete a step:

1. Right-click on the step that you want to delete.

2. Select Delete. The Delete Step dialog might appear, as in Figure 13-16.

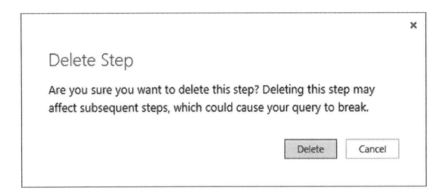

Figure 13-16. *The Delete Step dialog*

3. Confirm by clicking the Delete button. The step will be deleted.

If—and it is highly possible—deleting this step causes issues for the rest of the process, you will see that the data table is replaced by an error message. This message will vary depending on the type of error that Power Query has encountered.

When describing this technique I was careful to state that you *might* see the Delete dialog. If you are deleting the final step in a sequence of steps, then you will probably not see it, since there should not be any potentially horrendous consequences; at worst you will have to re-create the step. If you are deleting a step in the middle of a process, then you might want to think seriously about doing so before you cause a potentially vast number of problems. Consequently, you are asked to confirm the deletion in these cases.

■ **Note** If you realize at this point that you have just destroyed hours of work, then (after drawing a deep breath) click on the File menu in the Power Query window (the downward-facing triangle at the top left) and select Discard And Close. You will, however, lose all work up until the last time you clicked Apply And Close. Don't count on using an Undo function as you can in Excel!

An alternative technique is to place the pointer over a process step and click the plus (+) icon that appears. You may still have to confirm the deletion.

If you realize that an error in a process step has invalidated all your work up until the end of the process, rather than deleting multiple elements one by one, click Delete Until End from the context menu at step 2 in the preceding exercise.

Adding a Step

You can add a step anywhere in the sequence. All you have to do is to click on the step that *precedes* the new step that you want to insert *before* clicking on the icon in any of the ribbons that corresponds to the new step. As is the case when you delete a step, Power Query will display an alert warning you that this action could cause problems with the process from this new step on.

Altering Process Step Sequencing

It is possible—technically—to resequence steps in a process. However in my experience, this is not always practical, since changing the order of steps in a process can cause as much damage as deleting a step. Nonetheless, you can always try it like this:

1. Right-click on the step that you want to resequence.

2. Select Move Up or Move Down from the context menu.

I remain pessimistic that this can work miracles, but it is good to know that it is there.

An Approach to Sequencing

Given the array of available data transformation options, you may well be wondering how best to approach a new ETL project using Power Query. I realize that all projects are different, but as a rough and ready guide, I would suggest attempting to order your project something like this:

- **First**, of course, load the data into Power Query.

- **Second**, promote or add correct column headers. For example, you really do not want to be looking at step 47 of a process and wondering what Column29 is, when it could read ClientName.

- **Third**, remove any columns that you will not be needing. The smaller the data set, the faster the processing. What is more, you will find it easier to concentrate on, and understand, the data if you are only looking at information that you really need. Any columns that have been removed can be returned to the data set simply be deleting or editing the step that removed them.

- **Fourth**, alter the data types for every column in the table. Correct data types are fundamental for many transformation steps, and are essential for filtering, so it's best to get them sorted out early on.

- **Next**, filter out any records that you do not need. Once again, the smaller the dataset, the faster the processing. This includes deduplication.

- **Then**, carry out any necessary data cleansing and transforms.

- **Finally,** carry out any necessary column splits or adding custom columns.

Once again, this is not a definitive guide, but I hope that it will help you to see the wood for the trees.

Changing the Data Structure

Sometimes your requirements go beyond the techniques that we have seen so far when discussing data cleansing and transformation. Some data structures need more radical reworking, given the shape of the data that you have acquired. I include in this category the following:

- Unpivoting data

- Grouping records

- Merging datasets

Each of these techniques is designed to meet a specific, yet frequent, need in data loading, and all are described in the next few pages.

Unpivoting Tables

From time to time you may need to analyze data that has been delivered in a "pivoted" or "denormalized" format. Essentially, this means that information that really should be in a single column has been broken down and placed across several columns. An example of the first few rows of a pivoted data set is given in Figure 13-17 and can be found in the sample file C:\HighImpactDataVisualizationWithPowerBI\PivotedDataSet.xlsx.

▦.	InvoiceDate	Aston Martin	Bentley	Jaguar	MGB	Rolls Royce	Triumph	TVR
1	02/01/2013 00:00:00	75890	25700	88200	4500	62000	8500	null
2	09/01/2013 00:00:00	31125	null	null	null	null	null	null
3	10/01/2013 00:00:00	17500	null	null	null	null	null	null
4	02/02/2013 00:00:00	75890	25700	63200	8500	62000	17000	37500
5	11/02/2013 00:00:00	22500	null	null	null	null	null	null
6	02/03/2013 00:00:00	75890	25700	88200	4500	75890	8500	null
7	12/03/2013 00:00:00	17500	null	null	null	null	null	null
8	13/03/2013 00:00:00	null	null	null	null	31125	null	null
9	14/03/2013 00:00:00	17500	null	null	null	null	null	null

Figure 13-17. *A pivoted data set*

To analyze this data correctly, we really need the makes of the cars to be switched from being column titles to becoming the contents of a specific column. Fortunately, this is not hard at all:

1. Load the data from the C:\HighImpactDataVisualizationWithPowerBI\PivotedDataSet. xlsx file (there is only one worksheet) into Power Query using the techniques described earlier in this chapter. Ensure that the first row is set to be the table headers.

2. Select all the columns that you want to unpivot. In this example, this means all columns except the first one.

3. Click the Unpivot button in the Home ribbon (or right-click with the columns selected and choose Unpivot from the context menu). The table will be reorganized, and the first few records will look as they do in Figure 13-18. Unpivot will be added to the APPLIED STEPS box.

▦.	InvoiceDate	Attribute	Value
1	02/01/2013 00:00:00	Aston Martin	75890
2	02/01/2013 00:00:00	Bentley	25700
3	02/01/2013 00:00:00	Jaguar	88200
4	02/01/2013 00:00:00	MGB	4500
5	02/01/2013 00:00:00	Rolls Royce	62000
6	02/01/2013 00:00:00	Triumph	8500
7	09/01/2013 00:00:00	Aston Martin	31125
8	10/01/2013 00:00:00	Aston Martin	17500
9	02/02/2013 00:00:00	Aston Martin	75890
10	02/02/2013 00:00:00	Bentley	25700
11	02/02/2013 00:00:00	Jaguar	63200
12	02/02/2013 00:00:00	MGB	8500
13	02/02/2013 00:00:00	Rolls Royce	62000

Figure 13-18. *An unpivoted data set*

The data is now presented in a standard tabular way, and so it can be used for analysis with PowerPivot and presentation with Power View.

Grouping Records

At times, you will need to subset your original data in a quite extreme way—by grouping the data. This is very different from filtering data, removing duplicates, or cleansing the contents of columns. When you group data, you are altering the structure of the data set to "roll up" records where you

- Define the attribute columns that will become the unique elements in the grouped data table

- Specify which aggregations will be applied to any numeric columns that will be included in the grouped table

Grouping is frequently an extremely selective operation. This is inevitable, since the more attribute (that is non-numeric) columns you choose to group on, the more records you are likely to include in the grouped table. However, this will always depend on the particular data set you are dealing with, and grouping data efficiently is always a matter of flair, practice, and good, old fashioned trial and error. As an example, you could try out the following:

1. Load the SalesData2012_2013 worksheet from the Excel workbook C:\ HighImpactDataVisualizationWithPowerBI\SalesData.xlsx into Power Query.

2. Select the following columns (by Ctrl-clicking on the column headers):

   a. Make

   b. Marque

3. Click the Group By button in the Power Query Home ribbon. The Group By dialog will appear.

4. In the New Column Name box enter **TotalSales**.

5. Select Sum as the operation.

6. Choose SalePrice as the source column in the Column popup list.

7. Click the plus (+) icon to the right of the new column elements that you just entered, and repeat the operation, only this time, use the following:

    a. New Column Name: AverageCost

    b. Operation: Average

    c. Column: CostPrice

8. The dialog should look like the one in Figure 13-19.

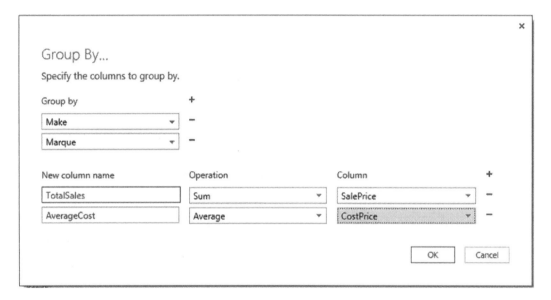

Figure 13-19. *The Group By dialog*

9. Click OK. All columns other than those that you specified in the Group By dialog will be removed, and the table will be grouped and aggregated, as shown in Figure 13-20. GroupedRows will be added to the APPLIED STEPS box. I have also sorted the table by the Make and Marque columns to make the grouping clearer.

▦.	Make	1 ↓↑	Marque	2 ↓↑	TotalSales	▼	AverageCost	▼
1	Aston Martin		DB4		391000		81667.5	
2	Aston Martin		DB7		500740		21203.125	
3	Aston Martin		DB9		915070		48143.888889	
4	Aston Martin		DBS		230000		65500	
5	Aston Martin		Rapide		225000		140000	
6	Aston Martin		Vanquish		746500		87200	
7	Aston Martin		Vantage		320850		36250	
8	Aston Martin		Zagato		178500		125000	
9	Bentley		Arnage		44000		25700	
10	Bentley		Azure		239250		25700	
11	Bentley		Continental		991250		49035.714286	
12	Bentley		Turbo R		347500		32960	

Figure 13-20. Grouping a data set

■ **Note** You do not have to Ctrl-click to select the grouping columns. You can add them one by one.

Merging Data

Until now we have treated each individual query as if it existed in isolation. The reality, of course, is that you will frequently be required to use the output of one query in conjunction with the output of another to join data from different tables in various ways. Assuming that the results of one query share a common field with another query, you can "join" queries into a single data table. Power Query calls this a merge operation, and it enables you, among other things, to

- Look up data elements in another "reference" table to add lookup data. This could be where you want to add a client name where only the client code exists in your main table, for instance.

- Aggregate data from a "detail" table (such as invoice lines) into a higher-grained table such as a table of invoices.

Here, again, the process is not difficult. The only fundamental factor is that the two tables, or queries, that you are merging must have a shared field that is unique in the table into which you are loading data from the more detailed table. Let's look at a couple of examples.

Adding Reference Data

First, let's try looking up reference data that we will add to the data in a query.

1. Prepare two queries (neither of which load data into either Excel or the data model) using the techniques that we have seen previously:

   a. The *first one* should use the SalesData.xlsx Excel workbook. Name this query **Sales**.

   b. The *second one* should use the Clients.txt text file. Name this query **Clients**.

2. Once the two queries have been prepared, reopen the query named Sales.

3. In the Power Query window, click the Merge button in the Home ribbon. The Merge dialog will appear.

4. In the upper part of the dialog—where an overview of the output from the current query is displayed—click the ClientID column title. This column will be highlighted.

5. In the popup under the upper table, select the Clients query. The output from this query will appear in the lower part of the dialog.

6. In the lower table, select the column title for the column—the join column—that maps to the column that you selected in step 4. This column will also be selected. You may be asked to set privacy levels for the data sources. If this is the case, set them to Public.

7. Click Only Include Matching Rows. The dialog will look like Figure 13-21.

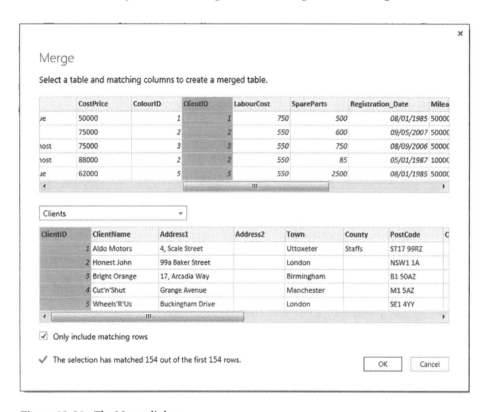

Figure 13-21. *The Merge dialog*

8. Click OK. A new column will be added to the right of the existing data table.

9. Scroll to the right of the existing data table and click on the Expand icon to the right of the column name (it has probably been named New Column). The popup list of all the available fields in this data table (or query, if you prefer) will be displayed, as shown in Figure 13-22. For the moment, all columns are selected.

Figure 13-22. *The fields available in a joined query*

10. Ensure that the Expand radio button is selected.

11. Clear the selection of all the columns by unchecking the (Select All Columns) check box.

12. Select the following columns:

    a. ClientName

    b. ClientSize

    c. ClientSince

13. Click OK. The selected columns from the linked table are merged into the main table, and the link to the reference table (New Column) is removed.

14. Rename the columns that have been added and apply and close the query.

You now have a single table of data that contains data from two linked data sources. Reprocessing the Sales query will also reprocess the dependent clients query and result in the latest version of the data being delivered.

Aggregating Data During a Merge Operation

If you are not just looking up reference data but need to aggregate data from a separate table and then add the results to the current query, then the process is largely similar. This second approach, however, is designed to suit another completely different requirement. Previously, you saw the case where the current query had many records that mapped to a single record in the lookup table. This second approach is for when your current (or main) query has a single record where there are multiple linked records in the second query. Consequently, you need to aggregate the data in the second table to bring the data across. Here is a simple example, using some of the sample data from the C:\HighImpactDataVisualizationWithPowerBI folder.

1. Use the Excel source file InvoicesAndInvoiceLines.xlsx. Load the two worksheets it contains (Invoices and InvoiceLines) into two queries in Power Query. Remember to click Select Multiple Items in the Navigator and to uncheck Load To Data Model to make the operation clean and quick.

2. Open the query named InvoiceLines (the queries took the worksheet names automatically). Check Use First Row As Headers.

3. Set the data type for the field SalePrice to Number and then click Apply And Close.

4. Open the query named Invoices. Check Use First Row As Headers.

5. Click the Merge button in the Home ribbon. The Merge dialog will open.

6. Click on the column header for the ID column.

7. In the popup, select the InvoiceLines query, and then select the InvoiceID column for the lower table. Check Only Include Matching Rows; then click OK.

8. Scroll to the right of the existing data table and click on the Expand icon to the right of the new column. The popup list of all the available fields in the InvoiceLines query will be displayed.

9. Select the Aggregate radio button.

10. Select the Sum Of SalePrice field and click OK.

Power Query will add up the total sale price for each invoice and add this as a new column. Naturally, you can choose the type of aggregation that you wish to apply (before clicking OK), if the sum is not what you want. To do this, place the cursor over the column that you want to aggregate (see step 10 in the preceding exercise) and click on the popup menu at the right of the field name. Power Query will suggest the following options:

- Sum
- Average
- Minimum
- Maximum
- Count (all)
- Count (Not Blank)

The merge process that you have just seen, while not complex in itself, suddenly opens up many new horizons. It means that you can now create multiple separate queries that you can then use together to expand your data in ways that allow you to prepare quite complex data sets.

Here are a couple of comments I have to make about the merge operation:

- Only queries from the active workbook can be used when merging tables.

- Selecting Only Include Matching Rows will filter the data in the main (or primary) table and exclude any records that do not have a match on the selected column in the second table. If you do *not* check this option, then you will get blank cells in the new columns from the second table where no match can be found.

▓ **Note**   Refreshing a query will cause any other queries that are upstream of this query to be refreshed also. This way you will always get the most up-to-date data from all the queries in the process.

Appending Data

Not all source data is delivered in its entirety in a single file, or as a single database table. You may be given access to two or more tables or files that have to be loaded into a single table in Excel or PowerPivot. In some cases, you might find yourself faced with hundreds of files, all text, CSV, or Excel format, and the requirement to load them all. Well, Power Query can handle these eventualities too.

Adding the Contents of One Query to Another

In the simplest case, you could have two data sources that are structurally identical (that is, they have the same columns in the same order), and all that you have to do is add one to another to end up with a query that outputs the amalgamated content of the two sources. This is called *appending data*, and it is easy, provided that the two data sources have *identical* structures; this means

- They have the same number of columns.

- The columns are in the same order.

- The data types are identical for each column.

- The columns have the same names.

As long as all these conditions are met, you can append the output of queries (which Power Query calls Tables) onto another. The queries do not have to have data that comes from identical source types, so you can append the output from a CSV file to data that comes from an Oracle database, for instance. As an example, we will take two text files and use them to create one single output.

1. Create queries to load each of the following text files into Power Query—without the final load step, which would output them to Excel or the Excel Data Model. Both files are in the folder C:\HighImpactDataVisualizationWithPowerBI\MultipleTextFiles. Name the queries **Colors_01** and **Colors _02**:

   a. Colors_01.txt

   b. Colors_02.txt

2. Open one of the queries (I will use Colors_01, but either will do).

3. Click the Append Queries button in the Power Query Home ribbon. The Append dialog will appear.

4. From the Select The Table To Append popup, choose the query Colors_02.

5. Click OK.

The data from the two output tables will be placed in the current query. You can now continue with any modifications that you need to apply. You will notice that the column names are not repeated as part of the data when the tables are appended one to the other.

Adding Multiple Files from a Source Folder

Now let's consider another possibility. You have been sent a load of files, possibly downloaded from an FTP site, and you have placed them all into a specific directory. However, you do not want to have to carry out the process that we just saw and load files one by one if there are several hundred files. So here is a way to get Power Query to do the work of trawling through the directory and only loading files that correspond to a file name specification you have indicated.

1. In the Power Query ribbon, click the From File button; then select From Folder in the menu. The Folder dialog will be displayed.

2. Click the Browse button and navigate to the folder that contains the files to load. In this example, it is C:\HighImpactDataVisualizationWithPowerBI\MultipleTextFiles. You can also paste in, or enter, the folder path if you prefer. The Folder dialog will look like Figure 13-23.

Figure 13-23. The Folder dialog

3. Click OK. The Power Query window will open and the contents of the folder will be listed as a table. This is shown in Figure 13-24.

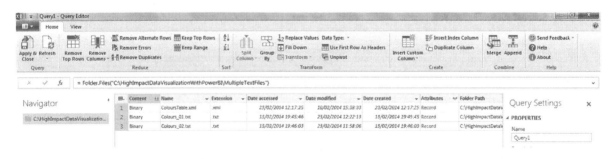

Figure 13-24. The folder contents in Power Query

4. As we want to load only text files, and avoid files of any other type, click on the filter popup menu for the column title Extension and uncheck all elements except .Txt.

5. Click on the Expand icon to the right of the first column title; this column will be called Content, and every row in the column will contain the word Binary. Power Query will load all the files and display the result. This is shown in Figure 13-25.

▦.	ColourID	Colour
1	1	Red
2	2	Blue
3	3	Green
4	4	Silver
5	5	Canary Yellow
6	ColourID	Colour
7	6	Night Blue
8	7	Black
9	8	British Racing Green
10	9	Dark Purple
11	10	Pink

Figure 13-25. *All files loaded from a folder*

6. If (but only if) each file contains header rows, then scroll down through the resulting table until you find a title element. In this example it is the word ColourID in the ColourID column.

7. Right-click on ColourID and select Text Filters ➤ Does Not Equal. All rows containing superfluous column titles will be removed.

8. Click Apply And Close.

Now, if ever you add more files to the source directory, and then click Refresh in the Home ribbon, *all* the source files will be reloaded including any new files added to the directory.

■ **Note** If your source directory only contains the files that you want to load, then step 4 is unnecessary. Nonetheless, I always add steps like this in case files of the "wrong" type are added later, which would cause any subsequent process runs to fail. Equally, you can set filters on the file name to restrict the files that will be loaded.

Data Destinations

We are close to the end of our whirlwind tour of Power Query. One final question is this: "What do we do with the data?" You have a choice of two solutions:

- Load the data into an Excel worksheet.

- Load the data into the Excel Data Model.

I suggest that you only load the data into an Excel worksheet when you have a relatively small data set and you want to carry out spreadsheet-type calculations. That is, you want to move, copy, and paste data in rows or cells and add subtitles, charts, and possibly even pivot tables with slicers and other tools. In most other cases, I expect that you will be loading the data into the Excel Data Model where you will extend it using PowerPivot from where you will be using Power View and Power Map to present your results.

The Power Query View Ribbon

Until now we have concentrated our attention on the Power Query Home and Insert ribbons. This is for the good and simple reason that this is where all the action takes place. There is, however, a third Power Query ribbon—the View ribbon. The buttons that it contains are shown in Figure 13-26, and the options are explained in Table 13-11.

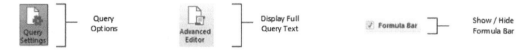

Figure 13-26. *The Power Query View ribbon*

Table 13-11. *Power Query View Ribbon Options*

Option	Comments
Query Settings	Displays or hides the Query Settings pane at the right of the Power Query window
Advanced Editor	Displays the Advanced Editor dialog containing all the code for the steps in the query
Formula Bar	Shows or hides the formula bar

Effective Use of the Formula Bar

Until now, in this chapter, we have not really paid much attention to the code that Power Query adds to the formula bar every time that you add a new process step. Indeed, if you are adding steps that are handled using the ribbon, or if you never need to modify a process step, then you may never need to use the formula bar. However, when adding certain operations for which there is no button in the ribbon, or if you want to make a minor adjustment to an existing process step, then it can really help to look at how Power Query has written the code that carries out the step.

Looking at the formulas takes us into the realm of programming Power Query, and the M language which it uses. Now, I have no intention of doing anything more than showing you how to add simple code snippets and tweak existing code. However, I can recommend an excellent book by Chris Webb, *Power Query for Power BI and Excel* (Apress 2014) if you want to learn the M language; I strongly advise you to get this if you want to continue down this path.

Each formula is different, and the query language can take some getting used to. However, here are a few examples to get you started. Note that each step refers to the previous query step using the name it was given, such as ReorderedColumns, or ReplacedValue.

Replacing Values

Replacing text in a column uses the following code:

```
= Table.ReplaceValue(ReorderedColumns,"Ghost","Fantôme",Replacer.ReplaceText,{"Make"})
```

It is easy to alter the find and replace elements (Ghost and Fantôme, in this example) with other elements.

Transforming

Transforming text in a column uses the following code:

```
= Table.TransformColumns(ReplacedValue,{{"Make", Text.Upper}})
```

You can change the column name (Make) or alter the code from upper to lower to alter the process.

Grouping

When you grouped data previously, this was the formula that Power Query created:

```
= Table.Group(Source, {"Make", "Marque"}, {{"TotalSales", each List.Sum([SalePrice]), type number},
{"AverageCost", each List.Average([CostPrice]), type number}})
```

Suppose that you now decide that you need to add another column to the grouping criteria—the column AgeRangeBucket. You do not need to delete the step and rebuild it. Simply altering the code to add the column as shown in the following code snippet will do the trick:

```
= Table.Group(Source, {"Make", "Marque","AgeRangeBucket"}, {{"TotalSales", each List.
Sum([SalePrice]), type number}, {"AverageCost", each List.Average([CostPrice]), type number}})
```

Extending a Filter

You saw earlier that you can filter by data in a column. However you cannot, at least when using the interface, use a single filter step and filter across multiple columns. For instance, suppose that you have filtered the files in a directory to show only files with the extension .txt that begin with Colour. This will give you two query steps using the following code:

```
= Table.SelectRows(Source, each ([Extension] = ".txt"))
```

And

```
= Table.SelectRows(FilteredRows, each Text.StartsWith([Name], "Colour"))
```

You could replace the two steps with a single step containing the following code:

```
= Table.SelectRows(Table.SelectRows(Source, each [Extension] = ".txt"), each Text.StartsWith([Name],
"Colour"))
```

Here we have nested the filters (the Table.SelectRows command) one inside the other.

I will stop here, because to continue would require a complete explanation of every code snippet used in this chapter. So all I can advise you to do is take a close look at the code that Power Query generates each time you add a step to an ETL process, and, if you feel like it, try tweaking the code to see how it works.

■ **Tip** As is the case with Excel and PowerPivot, you can expand and collapse the formula bar in Power Query.

Conclusion

This chapter showed you how to shape your source data into a valid data table from one or more potential sources. If necessary you can filter the data so that only the key elements flow into Excel; from there you can present it to your audience using the Microsoft self-service BI tools.

You have seen, in this chapter and the previous one, what is essentially a three-stage process: first you find the data, then you load it into Power Query, and finally from there (as you saw in this chapter), you cleanse and modify it. The techniques that you can use are simple but powerful and can range from changing a data type to merging multiple data tables. Now that your data is prepared and ready for use, you can add it to the Excel Data Model and start analyzing with Power Pivot, Power View, and Power Map.

CHAPTER 14

Power Map

An extremely recent addition to the panoply of self-service BI tools that Excel now makes available is Power Map. As its name implies, it is a powerful mapping tool that can generate some exceedingly cool geospatial representations of your data. Specifically, it can

- Create various types of map to represent geospatial data

- Add multiple layers of information to each map to show different data representations

- Add a time dimension to a map and display how the data evolves over time

- Chain several maps together into a dynamic visualization that can then be exported as a multimedia file

Power Map will use the data that you have prepared in the Excel Data Model, or it can add data from a spreadsheet table to a data model for geographical representation. So once again, it can be important to spend a certain amount of time creating and finalizing an accurate and coherent data model before you try and display—or discover—new insights using Power Map.

You may well be wondering why you have the choice between adding a map to Power View or using Power Map to display your data. Well, they have two quite different uses. Power View maps let you use all of the interactive filtering and slicing techniques that you learned in earlier chapters; however, if you want to create rich multilayered visualizations or the stunning exportable "movies," then you will need to use Power Map. In any case, once you master both approaches, you will be able to choose the Excel add-in that best suits your needs.

Power Map is now part of Excel and should be available in the Insert ribbon. If you cannot see the Map button, then please ensure that you have followed the instructions in Chapter 1.

This chapter will use a sample file named PowerMapSample.xlsx, which is in the C:\HighImpactDataVisualizationWithPowerBI folder, assuming that you have downloaded the sample files as described in Appendix A.

Bing Maps

Power Map, just like maps created with Power View, uses Bing Maps to provide the geographical data. Consequently, you will need to allow Power Map access to Bing Maps or maps simply cannot be created. Power Map currently needs an Internet connection to function correctly.

■ **Note** Some areas of the world cannot use Bing Maps. If you attempt to use Power Map in these geographical zones, nothing will appear when you attempt to create a map.

Running Power Map

Time to get started! Clearly the first thing that we need to do is to launch Power Map, which is similar to the way that you learned to launch Power View. What you have to do is

1. In Excel, click Insert to activate the Insert ribbon.

2. Click the Map button. The Power Map window will open, looking (most probably) like Figure 14-1.

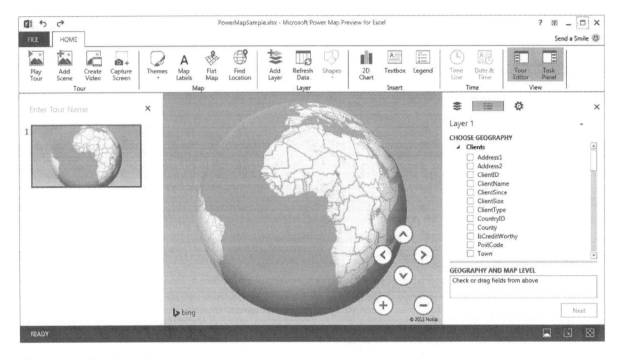

Figure 14-1. *The Power Map window*

▪ **Note** Power Map needs data to work. Consequently, it is important that you have either an Excel Data Model in the workbook from which you launch Power Map, or a table of data that you have selected before you run Power Map.

The Power Map Window

Even if the Power Map window and many of the elements that you will use are largely intuitive, I prefer to continue with the logic applied throughout this book, and explain the Power Map window and the objects that it contains from the outset. This way (I hope), the terms and elements that you will be using will be as clear as possible.

The Power Map window consists of the following five main elements:

- **The map visualization**—This is the core of Power Map and where your audience will see your analysis and the geographical representation of your insights.

- **The Task panel**—This is the area where you select data (both geographical data and the metrics that you want to overlay on the map) as well as modify many of the presentation aspects of the map.

- **The Tour Editor**—This panel is where you can put together an automated slideshow, or film, of the data for your audience.

- **The Power Map ribbon**—This is where you will find many of the available options for adding elements or enhancing the map that you are creating and modifying.

- **The Power Map information bar**—This indicates the state of any mapping calculations and progression of any timelines.

The main elements of the Power Map window are shown in Figure 14-2.

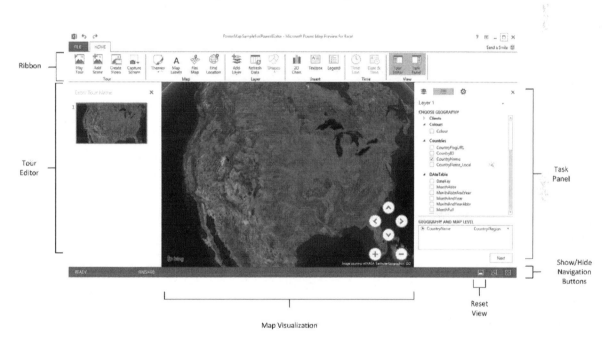

Figure 14-2. *The principal elements of the Power Map window*

The Power Map Ribbon

One of the key features of the Power Map window is the Power Map ribbon. The buttons that it contains and their uses are outlined in Table 14-1.

Table 14-1. *The Power Map Ribbon*

Button	Description
Play Tour	Plays a Power Map tour
Add Scene	Adds a new scene to a Power Map tour
Create Video	Exports a Power Map tour as a stand-alone video
Capture Screen	Creates a screen capture of the map
Themes	Alters the Power Map presentation style
Map Labels	Adds country, region, and town labels to the map
Flat Map	Switches between a flat (2-dimensional) and curved (3-dimensional) map
Find Location	Finds a location on the map by entering a map reference or a town or county name
Add Layer	Adds another separate layer to the map
Refresh Data	Refreshes the source data
Shapes	Chooses the bar chart shape
2-D Chart	Adds an independent 2-D chart based on the data in a layer on the map
Textbox	Adds a floating textbox
Legend	Adds one or more legends
Time Line	Shows or hides the time line
Date And Time	Shows or hides the date and time
Tour Editor	Displays or hides the Tour Editor
Task Panel	Displays or hides the Task panel

Region Maps

As a first, and admittedly very simple map, suppose that you want to see the cumulative sales for the various countries where Brilliant British Cars has hawked its wares in 2012—2013. This example will introduce the core mapping concepts that you will build on later in this chapter to develop some more complex geographical visualizations.

1. In the Task panel, expand the Countries table and check the CountryName field. This field will be added to the GEOGRAPHY AND MAP LEVEL box. The map of the globe could swivel to display the area of the world where the majority of the data can be found.

2. Click Next in the Task panel. The Task panel will switch to the metrics pane.

3. In the lower part of the Task panel, select Region from the TYPE popup list. The countries where there are sales will appear colored in on the map.

4. Expand the SalesData table. Check the SalePrice field. This will be added to the VALUE box and will indicate that the aggregation that has been applied is Sum. The countries will be shaded at different levels of intensity on the map to represent the proportion of sales by country. Power Map will also add a legend.

5. Click the plus (+) icon a few times to zoom in on the map.

6. Resize the legend by dragging the circle icon in the bottom right (or left) of the legend.

7. Reposition the legend by dragging the legend window bar (probably green) at the top of the legend when you place the cursor over the legend. The map might look something like Figure 14-3.

Figure 14-3. *A simple regional sales map*

This short example did quite a few things and introduced several concepts. To make some of the ideas easier to reapply in the future, here is a quick overview of the key points to note.

Power Map Source Data

As I mentioned in the introduction to this chapter, Power Map uses the Excel Data Model (or data from a worksheet added to the data model) as the source for the data that you will deliver as a map. It is important, then, to consider Power Map as you consider Power View—that is, as a final output medium, and not as a data management solution. You will probably need to import data with either Power Query or PowerPivot, and will then almost certainly have to mold the data set into a coherent data model before you start using Power Map. When you launch Power Map it will display the current data model, and this is what you will be using to create your maps.

■ **Note**   You can add data to the data model when you launch Power Map. This implies that you must select the data first, and then choose the Add Selected Data To Power Map option from the Map button in the Excel Insert ribbon. However, I only advise doing this if you have a complete set of data in an Excel spreadsheet—and an empty data model in Excel; otherwise you will inevitably need to switch to PowerPivot and adjust the data model at some point. Consequently—in my opinion—it is much easier to follow the regular process and set up a correct data model before you launch Power Map.

Refreshing Data

If your data has changed (and remember that it could have changed in a source database or a shared worksheet on a network drive), you could both need and want to refresh the data so that Power Map will redraw the visualization to display the latest version of events. To do this

1.   Click the Refresh Data button in the Power Map ribbon.

The data will be updated from the source, and the map(s) will be redrawn. If the path to the source data involves a Power Query process and a PowerPivot data model, then the entire chain of data will be updated.

Geographical Data Types

In this first Power Map example we added a single geographical data field. What is more, this field was recognized instantly for what it was—country names. In the real world of mapping data, however, you may not only have to add several fields but also specify which type of geographical data each field represents. Put simply, Power Map needs to know what the data you are supplying represents. Not only that, it needs to know what it is looking at without ambiguity. Consequently, it is up to you to define the source data as clearly and unambiguously as possible. This can involve one or more of several possible approaches.

Define the Data Category in the Data Model

As we saw in Chapter 11, you can define a data category for each column of data in PowerPivot. Although this is not an absolute prerequisite for accurate mapping with Power Map, it can help reduce the number of potential anomalies.

Add Multiple Levels of Geographical Information

Power Map lets you add several levels of geographical information from a data model. For instance (and as you will see in a few pages time), you can add not just a country, but also a town if you want. The advantage of adding as many relevant source data fields as possible is that by working in this way, you are helping Power Map dispel possibly ambiguous references. For instance, if you add only a field for Town, Power Map might not know if you are referring to Birmingham Alabama or England's second city. If, however, you add a Country field and a Town field, then Power Map has a much better chance of detecting the correct geographical location. This principle can be extended to adding states, counties, and other geographical references. So remember, you can add multiple source fields, but you should only select the one that you want to display in a map.

Select the Correct Geographical Data Type in Power Map

Power Map will indicate in the GEOGRAPHY AND MAP LEVEL box the geographical data type that it is using for each selected field. If you have applied the right data category in the data model, then your life is made easier, because the correct geographical data type will be displayed. If you have *not* attributed a data category, then Power Map will try and guess the correct geographical data type. On most occasions, it will guess right; occasionally, however, you will need to override its choice to ensure that the mapping is applied correctly. Selecting another geographical data type is as easy as clicking on the popup (the downward-facing triangle) for each geographic data field in the GEOGRAPHY AND MAP LEVEL box whose data type you wish to change and selecting the appropriate data type.

The available geographical data types are explained in Table 14-2.

Table 14-2. *Geographical Data Types*

Data Type	Comments
Latitude	Indicates that the source data contains the latitude
Longitude	Indicates that the source data contains the longitude
City	Tells Power Map that the data is a town or city
Country/Region	Tells Power Map that the data defines a country or region
County	Indicates that the source data defines a county
State/Province	Indicates that the source data defines a state or province
Street	Provides street-level data
Zip	Contains a zip (postal) code
Address	Contains a full address
Other	Indicates other geographical data that can be interpreted by Bing Maps

Using the Task Panel

The Task panel is where much of the work is done both to specify the data that will be displayed in a map and to tweak the available options for the map. To be sure that you are at ease with this key facet of the Power Map interface, let's take a more in-depth look at what it has to offer.

Showing and Hiding the Task Panel

If you have finished, temporarily or permanently, with the Task panel, you can hide it (or make it reappear) by clicking the Task Panel button in the Power View ribbon. Alternatively, to make it disappear entirely, you can click the Close icon (the small X) at the top right of the panel.

Task Panel Panes

A Task panel can flip between three main panes:

- The Data pane (geographical and metrics)
- Display settings
- Layer modification

You can move between the available panes by clicking on the icons shown in Figure 14-4.

Figure 14-4. *Task panel pane selection*

For the next few pages we will be looking only at the Data pane; I will introduce the others a little further on in this chapter. Since we are looking at the Data pane of the Task panel, you need to know something important—how to switch from geographical data to data for metrics and vice versa.

Whenever you create a new map in Power Map, you begin by adding the geographical data, as we did in the first example, earlier. Fairly logically, Power Map defaults to displaying the geographical data view of the Data pane when you start to build a geographical representation of your data. As you saw in step 2 of the previous example, once the geography data is in place, you switch to the metric Data pane by clicking Next at the bottom of the Task pane. So what do you do to return to the geographical data view should you need to modify this data? The answer is that you click on the Geography icon in the Data pane, which is shown in Figure 14-5:

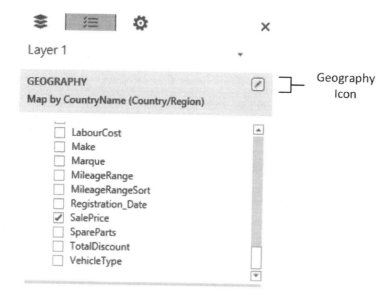

Figure 14-5. *Switching back to the Geography pane of the Task panel*

Clicking on the Geography icon will take you back to the initial task pane from which you started out. Once this view is selected, you can modify the geographical data to suit your requirements. As before, clicking Next will switch to display the data for any metrics that you want to show on the map.

The Task Panel Data Views

You saw the data views of the Task panel briefly in steps 2 and 3 of the earlier example. As this reference was only in passing, here is a more complete overview of what the two views in this pane actually do.

- The **Geography** view lets you select the source of the geographical data from the data set.

- The **Metric** view allows you to select which source data metrics will be shown in the map.

Both of these data elements can be taken a lot further than the first example showed. However, I think that it is easier to understand the possibilities using examples, as a result, we will see how to develop the use of both geographical data and display metrics a little further on.

In the meantime, the two views are explained in Figure 14-6.

Geography View   **Metric View**

Figure 14-6. *The Task panel, explained*

Removing a Field

Inevitably there will be times when you will want to remove a field from the Task panel. The technique is the same whether you are deleting a field from the Geography view or the Metric view.

1. Click on the popup for the field (or the data type for geographical fields).

2. Select Remove from the popup menu.

The field will be removed from the map (but not from the underlying data model) and the map will be redrawn to reflect the modification. Alternatively, you can uncheck the field in the Field List of the Task panel if you prefer.

■ **Note**   This operation cannot be undone—so if you have removed the wrong field, you will just have to add it back again.

Moving Around in Power Map

When you first add geographical data, Power Map will adjust the map to display the geographical area with the greatest concentration of data. However, you may need to tweak the continents, countries, or counties that are displayed to make your point. If the area displayed in a map is not quite as perfect as you would prefer, then you can alter the area that appears in the map visualization. This involves

- *Zooming in and out*—to get closer to the detail of the data—or inversely taking a bird's eye view.

- *Panning around*, which essentially means moving to the area that interests you.

- *Altering the pitch*; this can enhance the visual experience by changing the 3-D view of the map.

The icons used to zoom and pan around a map are explained in Figure 14-7.

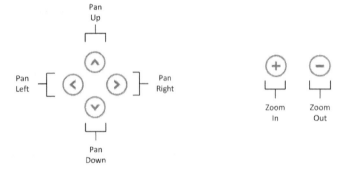

Figure 14-7. *Zoom and Pan icons*

You can hide the Zoom and Pan icons by clicking the Show/Hide Navigation Buttons icon at the bottom right of the Power Map window. This icon is shown in Figure 14-2, earlier.

Moving Around a Map

Moving around a map (without altering the pitch) is, as you would probably expect, extremely easy:

1. Click on the Pan Right icon (the right facing symbol) to alter the geographical area displayed in the map visualization.

■ **Tip**   You can also click inside a map and drag the mouse to pan around, or you can use the cursor keys to move up, down, left, or right without altering the pitch.

Zooming In or Out

It is conceivable that the map that is displayed is not at a scale that you would prefer. Fortunately this is extremely easy to adjust to get the effect that you want. All you have to do is

1. Click on the Zoom Out button (the minus sign) to zoom out or click on the Zoom In button (the plus sign) to zoom in.

░ **Tip** You can also move the mouse scroll wheel or use the Pg Up and Pg Dn keys to zoom in or out of a map.

Changing the Pitch of a Map

Power Map lets you change the pitch, or viewing angle, of a map. This can be particularly useful when displaying complex column charts, for example. All you have to do is

1. Press Alt and drag the map.

░ **Tip** If you prefer to use the keyboard, press Alt and use the Up and Down cursor keys to alter the pitch of a map.

Flat Map and 3-D Globe

Although the Power Map default is to show a three dimensional globe, you can flip to a flattened view if you prefer. This view will show more data and will allow you to avoid having parts of the map disappear over the horizon. To switch between 3-D and flat mapping:

1. Click the Flat Map button in the Power Map ribbon.

░ **Tip** Using a flat map does not prevent you from changing the pitch of the map to obtain some really cool effects.

Going to a Specific Location

Sometimes all you want to do is move to a particular location. You can do this in a couple of ways. If you can see the place where you want to take a closer look, simply double-click on it and Power Map will zoom in. If you want to jump straight to a particular region or town, then

1. Click Find Location in the Power Map ribbon. The Find Location dialog will appear.

2. Enter the place you want to find. The Find Location dialog will look like Figure 14-8.

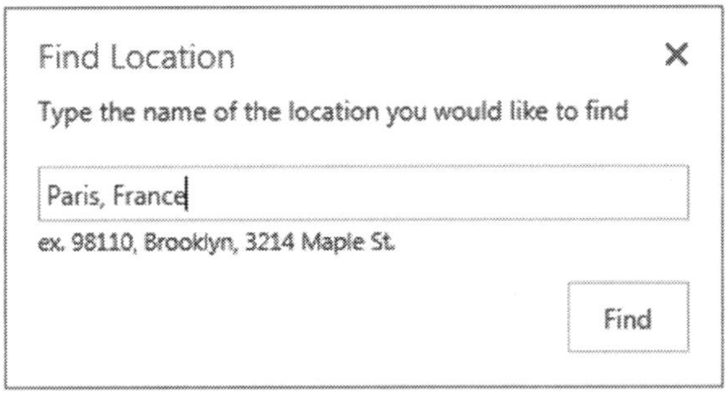

Find Location ✕

Type the name of the location you would like to find

Paris, France|

ex. 98110, Brooklyn, 3214 Maple St.

Find

Figure 14-8. *The Find Location dialog*

3. Click Find. Power Map will jump to the location.

4. If Power Map has found the place that you were looking for, you can close the Find Location dialog by clicking on the Close icon (the X at the top right). If not, enter a new location and click Find, again.

■ **Tip** You can move the Find Location dialog around the screen—and essentially away from the center of the map—to get a better view of the area that it has found. Remember that you can zoom in and out while searching for a specific place to ensure that you have found the right one. This can help to ensure that you are not looking at Paris, Texas, when you really wanted the French capital.

Power Map Aggregations

When you used the SalePrice field in the first example in this chapter as the basis for shading the regions in the map, Power Map automatically used the default aggregation for the field that you chose. This probably comes as no surprise, since it is exactly what Power View does. Similarly, Power Map does not limit you to using the default aggregation for a numeric field or a count for an attribute field. To select another aggregation

1. Switch to the Geography view of the Data pane of the Task panel (unless it is already active).

2. Click on the popup icon (the downward-facing triangle to the right of the selected metric name) for the metric. The popup list should look like Figure 14-9.

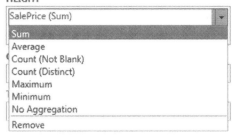

Figure 14-9. *Aggregations*

3.   Click on the required aggregation.

The map will be updated to reflect the new metric. The available aggregations are outlined in Table 14-3.

Table 14-3. *Aggregation Types*

Aggregation	Description
Sum	Returns the total of the numeric field.
Average	Returns the average of the numeric field.
Count (Not Blank)	Counts all the non-blank records.
Count Distinct	Counts all unique values in the data.
Maximum	Returns the maximum value from a numeric field.
Minimum	Returns the minimum value from a numeric field.
No Aggregation	No aggregation is applied.

Map Types

Power Map is not limited to shading in countries—far from it. In the current version there are four main map types. These are described in Table 14-4, and we will move on to take a look at each map type to see how they can best be used in the next few sections.

Table 14-4. *Map Types in Power Map*

Chart Type	Description
Column	Adds a Column chart to the map
Bubble	Adds a Bubble (or Pie) chart to the map
Heat Map	Adds a heat map indicator (concentric colored circles) to the map
Region	Shades geopolitical entities by country or region

The Various Map Types, by Example

Now that you understand the basic elements of Power Map, it is time to move on to the various ways in which data can be displayed and overlaid onto a geographical background. I feel that the best way to do this is to explain the data used, step by step, to give you an idea of what you can achieve. So, on that note, here are the four types of mapping data that Power Map can display. Let me just add that these map types are not explained in any particular order; it is up to each user to apply the type of visualization that makes their point most clearly and effectively.

Bubble Maps

A very simple, yet effective, way of displaying data is to use a bubble map. This is simply a circular representation of the data for each data point, where the relative size of each dot (or bubble, or point; there are many synonyms used to describe this) gives an idea of the proportional extent of the underlying data.

Bubble maps in Power Map come in two distinct flavors:

- Simple bubbles.
- Bubbles with multiple "subdivisions" or categories. These look like pie charts superimposed upon the map.

Let's look at each in turn. To begin with, here is how to create a simple bubble map:

1. Starting with the PowerMapSample.xlsx file, click Map in the Insert tab to launch Power Map.

2. Select the CountryName field from the Countries table and click Next.

3. Select CostPrice from the SalesData Table.

4. Remove the Legend by clicking on the close icon (the small X) at the top right of the legend.

5. Select Bubble as the type. Your map should look like Figure 14-10.

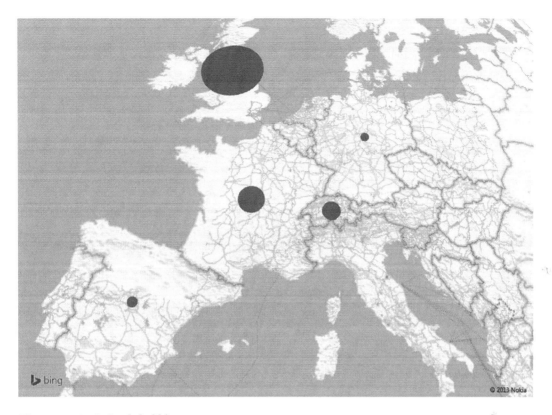

Figure 14-10. *A simple bubble map*

Now let's extend this by adding a further breakdown—and consequently further information—by adding categories to the map.

1. In the bubble map you just created, click Legend in the ribbon to add a legend.

2. Resize and place the legend where it does not hide any data.

3. In the Task panel, click on the Make field in the SalesData table. Make will be added to the CATEGORY box.

4. Hover the cursor over one of the segments for the pie in the United Kingdom. A popup will appear explaining what the segment represents.

The map should now look like the one in Figure 14-11. As you can see, each bubble is now a pie chart.

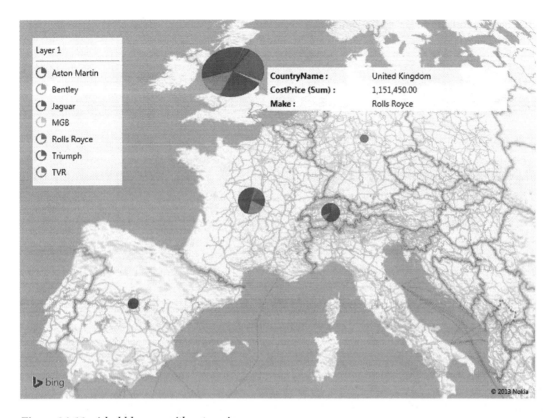

Figure 14-11. *A bubble map with categories*

I have a couple of comments to make here. First, you can only add a single category to a map. So, if you need multiple categories (such as make and model) to subdivide the data further, then you need to add a calculated column to the data first. Second, the aesthetics of having a legend or not will entirely depend on your requirements and circumstances.

An alternative to analysis by sector in a pie-style bubble map is to compare multiple values. As an example, let's suppose that you want to see the proportional costs (Parts, Labour, and Discount) for each country.

1. Starting with the PowerMapSample.xlsx file, click Map in the Insert tab to launch Power Map.

2. Select the CountryName field from the Countries table and click Next.

3. Select the following fields from the SalesData table:

    a. SpareParts

    b. LabourCost

    c. TotalDiscount

4. Select Bubble as the type.

5. Click Flat Map in the Power Map ribbon to remove the 3-D view.

6. Resize and reposition the legend.

7. To anticipate a little (and to ring the changes), click the Themes button and select the first theme on the second row. The map should look like Figure 14-12.

Figure 14-12. *A bubble map containing multple values*

I will explain the use of themes in more detail a little later on in this chapter. Nonetheless, I wanted to add a little variety to the presentation. As you can see, you have displayed the costs, and their proportional representation, for each country.

Column Maps

To take the example a little further, but still using very simple data, let's now see how you can use columns to display the data for each geographical element. Here again there are two main options:

- Clustered columns
- Stacked columns

In both cases the height of the column represents the scale of the data. In the case of clustered columns, you can see the data points side by side; in the case of stacked columns, you can get an idea not only of the relative values but also of the totals for each geographical point.

Clustered Columns

I will begin by showing you how a clustered column could look.

1. Follow steps 1-4 for the first bubble map I showed you earlier.

2. Drag the Make field to the CATEGORY box.

3. Select Column as the type from the TYPE popup.

4. Click on the clustered column icon (the left-hand one) that appeared above the CATEGORY popup when you switched to Column in step 3.

5. Tweak the presentation using the zoom and pan buttons for greater effect. Specifically try altering the pitch to get a more persuasive fly-over effect.

The map should look like Figure 14-13.

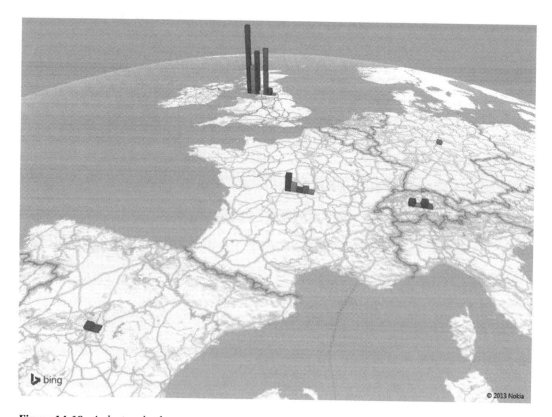

Figure 14-13. *A clustered column map*

___

■ **Note** Here again, you may, or may not, want a legend. It is entirely up to you.

___

Stacked Columns

An alternative to clustered columns is to use stacked columns. Which you choose to use will depend on your requirements and the available data. I would merely suggest that when you have multiple data points, stacked columns can be easier to read and can avoid clutter in the presentation. As an example of this, let's see sales for each town by make.

1. Starting with the PowerMapSample.xlsx file, click Map in the Insert tab to launch Power Map.

2. Select the CountryName field from the Countries table.

3. Select the Town field from the Clients table.

4. Click Next.

5. Select CostPrice from the SalesData table.

6. Drag the Make field to the CATEGORY box.

7. Resize and reposition the legend.

8. Select Column as the type from the TYPE popup.

9. Adjust the zoom and panning to get the best effect, focusing on the United Kingdom.

The map should look like Figure 14-14.

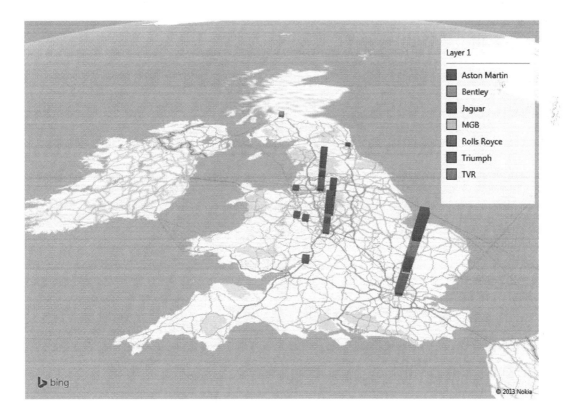

Figure 14-14. *A stacked column map*

Heat Maps

The term *heat map* can mean many different things to different people. In Power Map it means a colored bubble where the intensity and shading of the color represents the scale of values that is represented. To see this, let's look at the costs of sales for UK towns.

1. Follow steps 1 to 7 that you used to create a stacked column map.

2. Select Heat Map as the type from the TYPE popup.

3. Adjust the zoom, panning, and pitch to get the best effect, once again centering the map on the United Kingdom.

The map should look similar to Figure 14-15.

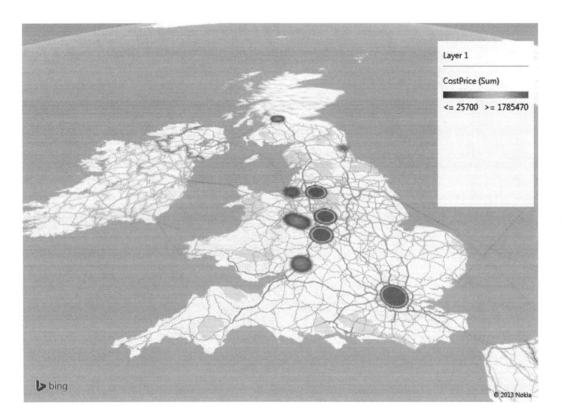

Figure 14-15. A simple heat map

▓ **Note**   A heat map is somewhat more limited than some of the other map types. For instance you cannot choose a category, neither can you add multiple metrics.

Region Maps

The first map that we created in this chapter was a region map, and the example that you created covers much of what you can do when you use this map type. Nonetheless, there is an interesting variation on a theme that deserves to be explained—using categories with region maps.

Suppose, for instance, that you want to see the sales by country, but you also want the colors of car sold to shape the data. Here is how:

1. Starting with the PowerMapSample.xlsx file, click Map in the Insert tab to launch Power Map.

2. Select the CountryName field from the Countries table and click Next.

3. Select SalePrice from the SalesData Table.

4. Drag the Colour field from the Colours table to the CATEGORY box.

5. Delete the legend.

6. Select Region as the type from the TYPE popup.

7. Adjust the zoom and panning to get the best effect.

8. Click on Spain to highlight the borders of the country.

9. Hover the cursor over any country to display the sales breakdown by color of car sold. The map should look something like Figure 14-16.

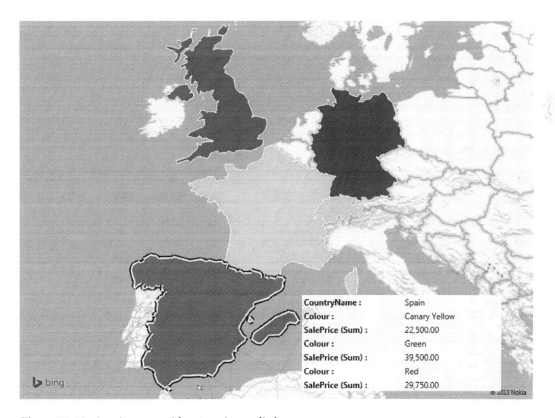

CountryName :	Spain
Colour :	Canary Yellow
SalePrice (Sum) :	22,500.00
Colour :	Green
SalePrice (Sum) :	39,500.00
Colour :	Red
SalePrice (Sum) :	29,750.00

Figure 14-16. A region map with categories applied

When you see the result in a black and white book, the effect is probably less immediate. On screen, however, the change is profound as each country is now a different color. If you look at the popup for each country, you will see that the top selling category for each country has forced the choice of color for the country. In a couple of pages, you will see how to choose these colors so that you can, for this example, set the display color to match the sale color.

As a final remark, you can only select a region for which data exists.

■ **Tip** In some cases you may want to just apply different colors to each country without using the color to represent anything meaningful. To achieve this (and assuming that the source data is set up to allow it), drag the CountryID field to the CATEGORY box of the Task panel. Since each country will have a different ID, each country will be displayed in a different color. This can be a good trick when you are setting up a background layer for a map; you'll learn more about this toward the end of the chapter.

Presentation Options

Great! We have now seen how to create maps using Power Map, and we've also taken a look at the major types of geographical visualization that you can put together with this powerful extension to your self-service BI armory. Now it is time to move on to look at some of the presentation options that are available and that will help you:

- Adjust the way in which metrics are displayed

- Change the colors used for charts, bubbles, and heat maps

- Tweak the size of charts, bubbles, and heat maps

The Settings View

The first thing to retain is that all the map options that I listed earlier are adjusted from the Settings view of the Task panel. As a result, you will have to make sure that the Task panel is visible before you can proceed. The second point is that the settings will vary slightly depending on the type of map that you have chosen. So, as an example, let's suppose that I want to display a heat map of sales of spare parts by country, but I also want to make the heat "bubbles" larger and alter the shading. Here is how:

1. Starting with the PowerMapSample.xlsx file, click Map in the Insert tab to launch Power Map.

2. Select the CountryName field from the Countries table.

3. Select the Town field from the Clients table.

4. Click Next.

5. Select CostPrice from the SalesData Table.

6. Resize and reposition the legend.

7. Select Heat Map as the type from the TYPE popup.

8. Adjust the zoom and panning to get the best effect, focusing on Europe.

9. Click on the Settings icon in the Task panel (this icon is shown in Figure 14-4).

10. Set the Colour Scale to 125% (or drag the slider to the right to get the effect that you need).

11. Set the Radius Of Influence to 500% (or drag the slider to the right to get the effect that you need). The Task panel should look like Figure 14-17.

Figure 14-17. *The Task Panel Settings view*

The map should look like Figure 14-18.

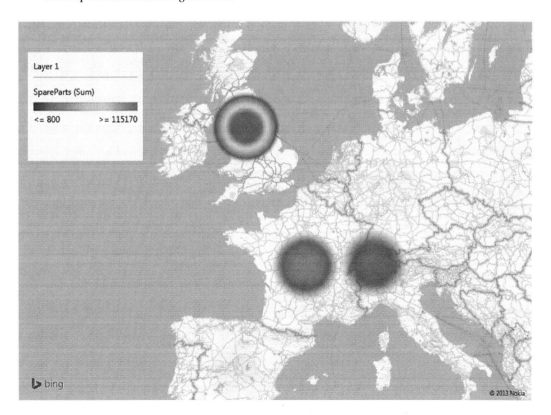

Figure 14-18. *A heat map after adjusting some of the available options*

▨ **Note**   You can switch to the Settings view from both the Geography and the Metrics panes.

Now that you have seen the principles, it is probably easiest to outline the options for each map type rather than give examples for each variation on a theme. As there are certain common options, I will begin with those first. Any shared settings are given in Table 14-5.

Table 14-5. *Common Map Settings*

Option	Explanation
Show Zeroes	Displays attributes even when the value is zero
Show Negatives	Displays attributes even when the value is a negative number
Show Nulls	Displays attributes even when the value is null
Lock Current Scale	Freezes the current scale

Bubble Map Settings

Bubble maps allow you to tweak the settings outlined in Table 14-6.

Table 14-6. *Bubble Map Settings*

Option	Explanation
Size	Sets the size of the bubble or pie.
Color	For a bubble map *without* categories or multiple metrics, this option lets you choose the color of each data point.
Thickness	For a bubble map *with* categories or multiple metrics, this option gives the pie a slight 3-D effect.

Column Map Settings

Column maps allow you to alter the options given in Table 14-7.

Table 14-7. *Column Map Settings*

Option	Explanation
Height	Sets the height of the column.
Thickness	Sets the width of the column.
Color	Lets you select each metric from the popup list and attribute the color that you choose from the color palette.

Column Shapes

If you are changing the settings for a Column map, then you may find one specific option useful. This is the choice of the shape of the actual column. So, assuming that you have created a Column map (such as the one in Figure 14-14), here is how you can alter the shape of the columns:

1. Click the Shapes button in the Power Map ribbon. The Shapes popup will appear.

2. Click on the shape you want to use. The selected shape will be applied to all the columns.

The available shapes are described in Figure 14-19.

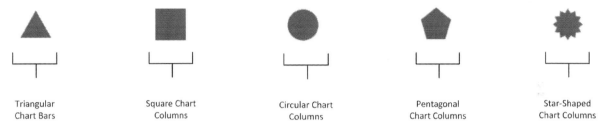

| Triangular Chart Bars | Square Chart Columns | Circular Chart Columns | Pentagonal Chart Columns | Star-Shaped Chart Columns |

Figure 14-19. *Column shapes*

▓ **Note**   The Shape settings apply equally well to clustered columns as to stacked columns.

Region Map Settings

Region maps allow you to tweak the options shown in Table 14-8.

Table 14-8. *Region Map Settings*

Option	Explanation
Color	Lets you choose the color used for the shading.

Heat Map Settings

Heat maps allow you to adjust the options outlined in Table 14-9.

Table 14-9. *Heat Map Settings*

Option	Explanation
Color Scale	This option allows you to adjust the balance (from the center to the periphery) of the color shading.
Radius Of Influence	Lets you set the size of the heat bubble.

Power Map Themes

Certain types of data require a different type of geographical presentation. Sometimes you may want a simple political map that shows countries and towns. At other times you may need a satellite image. At still others, you may want to see some physical geography such as forests and rivers in your presentation. This is where Power Map themes come into play. Power Map comes with eight types of map, in both monochrome and color. Some themes contain generic road maps and some contain high fidelity satellite images. The theme that you choose to apply is independent of the way in which data is plotted, so you can consider it as a geographical backdrop, if you prefer. As we saw when creating the bubble map shown in Figure 14-12, applying a theme is as easy as selecting the required theme from the popup that appears when you click the Themes button in the Power Map ribbon. Themes are described in Figure 14-20 and Table 14-10.

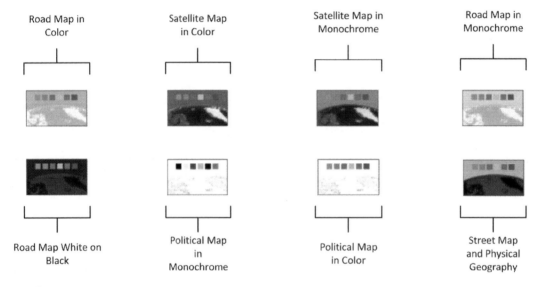

Figure 14-20. *Power Map themes*

Table 14-10. *Power Map Themes explained*

Theme	Description
Theme 1	Road map in color.
Theme 2	Satellite map in color.
Theme 3	Satellite map in monochrome.
Theme 4	Road map in monochrome.
Theme 5	Road map white on Black.
Theme 6	Political map in monochrome.
Theme 7	Political map in color.
Theme 8	Street and physical geography map in color.

Text Boxes

A picture (or even a map) may be worth many words, but on occasion, you still need a few comments to make a point. Consequently (or inevitably) you can add one or more text boxes to your Power Map visualizations to drive home the message. So, let's suppose you're the national Sales Manager for the UK and you want to crow about your success. Here is how you might add a text box to Figure 14-14.

1. Once you have created the Power Map which displays the data, click the Text Box button in the Power Map ribbon. The Edit Text Box dialog will appear.

2. Click inside the TITLE box and enter a title. I will add **UK Sales Key To Success!** in this example.

3. Click inside the DESCRIPTION box and enter a description. I will use **More Sales Of More Makes To More Customers!** as an example.

4. Click inside the TITLE box and select the font, font size, and font attributes that you want to apply. I will choose Tahoma, 20pt, bold.

5. Click inside the DESCRIPTION box and select the font, font size, and font attributes that you want to apply. I will choose Andalus, 14, italic. The content preview box will display the text as it will appear. The Edit Text Box dialog should look like Figure 14-21.

Figure 14-21. *The Edit Text Box dialog*

6. Click OK. The Edit Text Box dialog will close, and the text box will appear on the map.

7. Reposition the text box by dragging its title bar (the colored bar that appears when the pointer is placed over the text box).

8. Resize the text box by dragging its resize handles (the circles that appear at the top left and bottom right when the pointer is placed over the text box).

9. Click on the map to deselect the text box. The text box might look something like Figure 14-22.

UK Sales Key to Success!

More sales of more makes to more customers!

Figure 14-22. *A text box in Power Map*

You can see this text box used in a map in Figure 14-24, a little further on in this chapter. To alter the properties of a text box, all you have to do is right-click on a text box and select Edit from the context menu. The Edit Text Box dialog will be displayed, and you can alter the text of the title and/or the description as well as modify the font attributes.

To remove a text box you can

- Right-click on a text box and select Remove from the context menu.
- Place the cursor over the Text Box so that the title bar and resize handles appear and then click the Close icon in the top right corner of the text box.

The various options available for text boxes are explained in Table 14-11.

Table 14-11. *Text Box Options*

Aggregation	Description
Font Family	Lets you choose the font family from those available.
Font Size	Lets you choose the font size from those available.
Bold	Makes all the text in the text box appear in boldface.
Italic	Makes all the text in the text box appear in italics.
Font Color or Shade	Lets you apply a color or shade of gray (depending on the theme) to the text.
Text	Enter the text here.
Description	Add more descriptive text under the text box title.
Bring Forward	Brings the text box forward relative to other elements in the current layer.
Send Backward	Sends the text box backward relative to other elements in the current layer.
Bring to Front	Brings the text box to the top of all other elements in the current layer.
Send to Back	Sends the text box to the back of all other elements in the current layer.

Timelines

Up until now all the metrics that we have seen have been static. They have been a snapshot taken at a specific moment. Power Map, however, can add another dimension to geographic visualization by adding a time element. If the source data contains a time field (or better still, a date table as part of the data model) then you can

- Show the evolution of data over time, both automatically and manually.

- Display the data for a specific date or time in a single click.

This is done by adding a Timeline element to the map that you are creating. Adding a timeline will add a *Time decorator*, as Power Map calls it, to the visualization. This object allows you to display the exact date and/or time when the data was in a certain state. What is more, you can set the map to display the data changes over a range of dates (or times) that you specify if you want to concentrate on a subset of data. You can also define the playback settings for a timeline to set the duration of the display. This is probably best appreciated through an example, so let's see first how to add a timeline to a map and then look at some of the cool effects that you can add once you have implemented a timeline.

Adding a Timeline

Rather than add a timeline to an existing map, I prefer to re-create a map so that you can see the whole process. What you do is

1. Starting with the PowerMapSample.xlsx file, click Map in the Insert tab to launch Power Map.

2. Select the CountryName field from the Countries table.

3. Select the Town field from the Clients table.

4. Click Next.

5. Select CostPrice from the SalesData Table.

6. Resize and reposition the legend.

7. Select Column as the type from the TYPE popup.

8. Add Make to the CATEGORY.

9. Click the Stacked Column icon above the CATEGORY box.

10. Expand the Date Table, and check the MonthAndYearAbbr field. This will be added to the TIME box in the Task panel. The timeline slider and a Time Decorator will appear on the map.

11. Adjust the zoom and panning to get the best effect—focus on the United Kingdom.

12. Right-click on the Time Decorator and select Edit. The Edit Time Decorator dialog will appear.

13. Select June 2010 (the month and year format) from the Time Format popup. The Edit Time Decorator dialog will look like Figure 14-23.

Figure 14-23. *The Edit Time Decorator dialog*

14. Click Accept to close the Edit Time Decorator dialog.

15. Add the text box described in the previous section.

16. Resize and reposition the Time Decorator just as you learned to do with a Text Box.
    The map should look something like Figure 14-24.

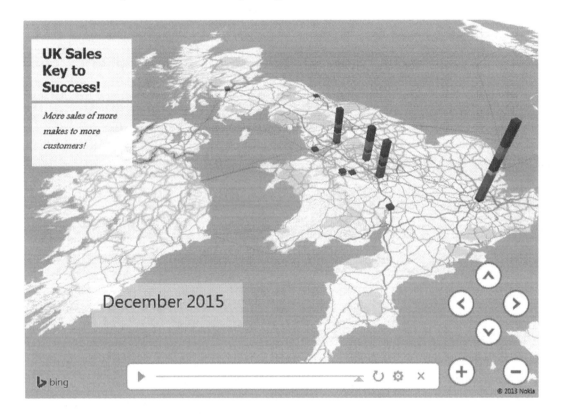

Figure 14-24. *A map with a timeline added*

And that is it. You have a map that can display the evolution of your data over time. Interestingly, when you add a timeline, the map does not change; this is because a timeline's default setting is to show the data at the *end* of the time period. Now, in the next section, we will see how you can use the timeline to enhance your presentation.

> ▒ **Note**   Modifying the font attributes for a Time Decorator is, to all intents and purposes, identical to tweaking a text box, so I will not repeat the options here, but refer you back to Table 14-9.

Using a Timeline

So, what can we do now that your map has a timeline, and what does it bring to the party? Perhaps the first thing is to understand the timeline itself. Figure 14-25 explains the various parts of a timeline.

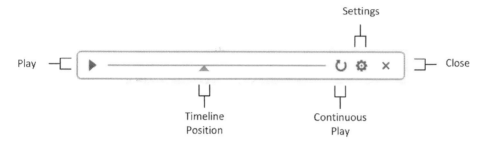

Figure 14-25.   *Timeline elements*

Playing the Timeline

Probably the first thing that you will want to do is see the evolution of your data over time. To do this, click the Play icon in the timeline (the triangle on the left). The data will initially disappear from the map, and then it will reappear, developing progressively over time until the final date is reached. Not only that, but the Time Decorator will scroll through the dates and/or times to show the linear evolution of the data over time.

Pausing the Timeline

When a timeline is playing, the Play icon becomes a Pause icon. Yes, you guessed it, clicking on this will halt the playback so that you can take a closer look at the data.

When a timeline is paused (or even if it is still playing), you can still move around the map as well as zoom and pan. With a little practice, and once you know your data, you can apply these techniques to draw your audience into the heart of what you are communicating.

Selecting Points along the Timeline

Although a timeline is linear, you do not have to apply it in a linear fashion. You can drag the timeline position icon (the triangle under the timeline) to any point along the timeline to show the data at a chosen point in time. As you slide the timeline position icon left and right, the Time Decorator will change to show the exact date and/or time that you have selected.

Figure 14-26 shows you a bird's eye view of how the timeline used in this example progresses from start to finish.

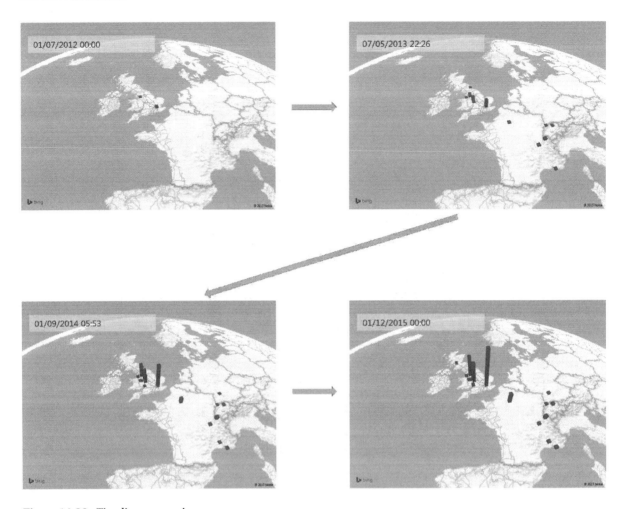

Figure 14-26. *Timeline progression*

Setting Timeline Duration

I mentioned earlier in passing that you can modify the duration of a timeline. You may find yourself needing to do this since the default is only 6 seconds, which could be much too short in many cases. To do this:

1. Click the Settings icon in the timeline (the cog at the right). The Scene Options settings pane of the Task panel will be displayed.

2. Enter a scene duration or use the up and down triangles for the Scene Duration box to set a number of seconds for the playback time. I have set 45 seconds in this example, as you can see in Figure 14-27.

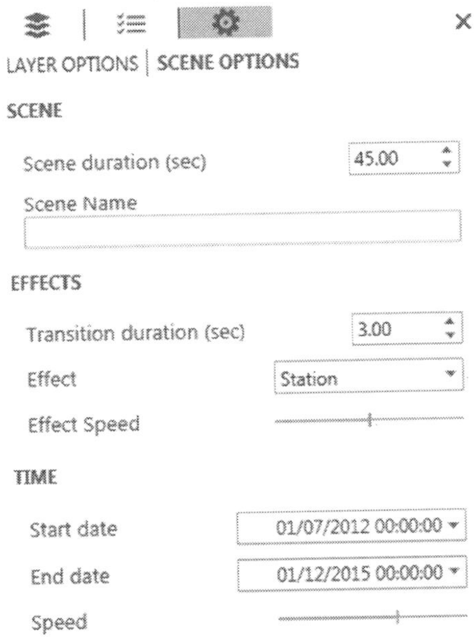

LAYER OPTIONS | SCENE OPTIONS

SCENE

Scene duration (sec)   45.00

Scene Name

EFFECTS

Transition duration (sec)   3.00

Effect   Station

Effect Speed

TIME

Start date   01/07/2012 00:00:00 ▾

End date   01/12/2015 00:00:00 ▾

Speed

Figure 14-27. Timeline options

That is all that you have to do. When you next play the timeline the display will last for 45 seconds.

■ **Tip**　If you prefer a more intuitive approach, drag the vertical bar in the Speed section left or right to set the playback speed, which is another way of defining the playback time.

Hiding the Time Decorator

You can choose one of the following ways to remove a Time Decorator:

- Click the Date And Time button in the Power Map ribbon.
- Right-click on a Time Decorator and select Remove from the context menu.
- Place the cursor over the Time Decorator so that the title bar and resize handles appear; then click the Close icon in the top right corner of the Time Decorator.

Hiding the Timeline

Hiding a timeline is very similar to hiding a Time Decorator. There are two possible techniques:

- Click the Timeline button in the Power Map ribbon.
- Click the Close icon in the right-hand corner of the Timeline.

Setting the Date Range for Playback

A final aspect of a timeline is that it can become a kind of date filter, in that you can set the start and end dates for the display. To do this

1.   If the Scene Options settings pane of the Task panel is not visible, click the Settings icon in the timeline (the cog at the right).

2.   Click the popup triangle at the right of the Start Date and select a date.

3.   Click the popup triangle at the right of the End Date and select a date.

It is really that easy. If you now play back the timeline, you will see that the metrics begin with the Start Date and the timeline progression stops at the End Date.

Date and Time Formats in the Time Decorator

In step 13 of the process where we added a timeline earlier in the chapter, you set a date format to override the default date and time format. Several date and time formats were available. These are explained in Table 14-12.

Table 14-12. Date and Time Formats

Description	Format
Short date and time	01/04/2015 12:00
Short date	01/04/2015
Long date	01 April 2015
Long date and time	01 12:00
Long date and time with seconds	01 April 2015 12:00:10
Short date and time with seconds	01 April 2015 12:00:10
Day and month	01 April
Short date in ISO format with fractions of a second	01 April 2015T12:00:10.0000000
Weekday, short date and time with seconds and time zone reference	Wed, 01 April 2015 12:00:10 GMT
Short date in ISO format with seconds	01 April 2015T12:00:10
Time	12:00
Time with seconds	12:00:10
Month and year	April 2015

Using Layers

For the remainder of this chapter we will start creating more complex—and I hope more impressive—map-based visualizations. More complex, and consequently more telling, map visualizations use layers in Power Map. Each layer is a separate map that uses different metrics and possibly different geographical elements. However, using multiple layers is merely an extension of the techniques that you have learned so far. As an example, let's produce a map that uses the following:

- **Layer 1**—Sales by country
- **Layer 2**—A heat map of profit per town
- **Layer 3**—A stacked column of town sales by color

Let's see this in action. The process is a little long since we are creating three maps in one, but we are essentially revising techniques that we have already used. The result is, I hope you will agree, well worth it:

1. Starting with the PowerMapSample.xlsx file, click Map in the Insert tab to launch Power Map.

2. Select the CountryName field from the Countries table. Click Next.

3. Check the SalePrice field in the SalesData Table.

4. Select the Region Map type.

5. Place the cursor over the layer name (Layer 1) at the top of the Task panel.

6. Click the Rename icon that appears at the right of the layer name (a pencil).

7. Enter the name **CountrySales** and press Enter.

    The first layer is now created, and displays sales for each country. The next layer will be a heat map of profit per town.

8. Click the Layers icon at the top of the Task panel. The Layers pane is displayed, as shown in Figure 14-28.

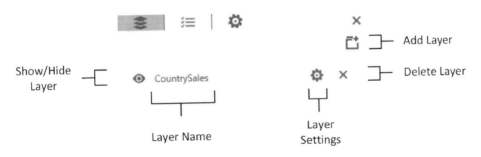

Figure 14-28. *The Layers pane of the Task panel*

9. Click the Add Layer icon.

10. Rename the layer **ProfitByTown** as described in steps 6 and 7.

11. Add the Town and CountryName fields, then Click Next.

12. Add the GrossProfit field.

13. Choose HeatMap as the type.

14. Resize and reposition the legend to the left of the map.

The second layer is now created. All that remains is to create a clustered column map of sales by make for the third and final layer and to tweak the presentation.

15. Click the Add Layer icon.

16. Rename the new layer **SalesByMake** as described in steps 6 and 7.

17. Add the Town and CountryName fields, then Click Next.

18. Add the SalePrice and Make fields.

19. Choose Column as the type and ensure that the clustered column icon is selected.

20. Resize and reposition the legend to the left of the map under the existing legend.

21. Zoom, pan, and swivel the map to display the data to best effect.

Now we need to adjust a couple of settings to enhance the readability of the map.

22. Click the Settings icon in the Task panel and tweak the height and thickness of the column.

23. Click on the popup icon (the downward-facing triangle) to the right of the layer name and select the layer ProfitByTown.

24. Tweak the Color Scale and Radius Of Influence settings to make the profit more visible.

That is it. The multilayered map should look something like Figure 14-29.

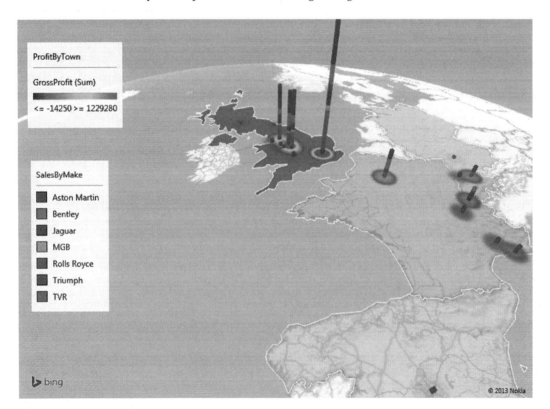

Figure 14-29. A multilayered map

As you have seen, each layer is quite simply a standard Power Map just like all those that you have developed thus far. The trick is to add further maps (in practice they will nearly always be of different types) to get the desired effect.

■ **Note**   When creating layered maps, I find that it really helps to have an idea of what I want initially. However nothing will stop you from creating different layers and experimenting as you go.

I just have a few final comments to make about using layers.

- You can hide, or display, an existing layer by clicking the Show/Hide Layer icon in the Layers pane of the Task panel.

- To delete a layer, simply click the Delete icon in the Layers pane of the Task panel. Power Map will show an alert that warns you that this operation cannot be undone.

- You can also display the settings for a layer from the Layers pane of the Task panel by clicking the Settings icon for the relevant layer.

■ **Tip**   You can adjust the map presentation by zooming and panning at any time. However, Power Map will always create a new layer from a global map, so I find it easier to adjust the map display right at the end of the process, once and for all.

2-D Charts

In some cases you may want to enhance a purely geographical representation of data with a more classic visualization. Power Map can let you do this, without distracting from its core aim, by letting you add a two-dimensional chart to a map. This chart will apply to an existing layer of that map and will use the data that the selected layer already represents on the map.

As an example, when shading is used, such as in the case of Region maps, I find that a chart can give a more accurate grasp of the underlying figures. So, let's see how to add a 2-D chart to a map that contains two layers:

- A Region map of sales by country

- A Stacked Bar map of sales by town and make

Here is the way to go about creating such a visualization:

1. Follow steps 1-8 and 15-22 from the procedure in the "Using Layers" section to create a two-layer map of

    a. sales by country

    b. sales by town and make

2. Select the SalesByCountry layer.

3. Click the 2-D Chart button in the Power Map ribbon. A chart will be added.

4. Select the Horizontal chart type from the popup list of available chart types at the right of the chart name.

5. Resize the chart and position it so that the country data is not obscured.

The map should now look like Figure 14-30.

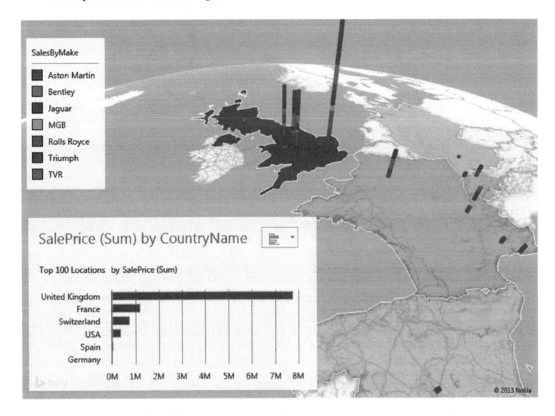

Figure 14-30. A map with a 2-D chart superimposed

2-D Chart Types

There are only four available 2-D charts:

- Column charts
- Stacked column charts
- Bar charts
- Stacked bar charts

As these chart types are identical to the Power View charts described in Chapter 4, I will not describe them again here.

Hiding the Map Data

If you really do not want the data to appear in the map at all, but you do want it to show in a chart, then there is a trick that will allow this. It is a fudge, I admit, but a useful one!

1. Create the map shown in Figure 14-30.

2. Select the SalesByMake layer, and click the Settings icon.

3. Click the Color popup for the CostPrice (Sum) field.

4. Click More Colors. The Color palette will appear.

5. Select a light shade of gray.

6. Click OK. This shade will appear in both the chart and as the shading for the countries on the map. The result should look like Figure 14-31.

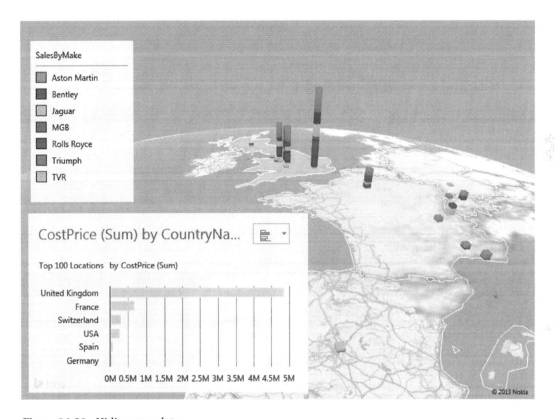

Figure 14-31. *Hiding map data*

The trick here is to find a shade (it need not be gray) that will scarcely show a difference on the map but will be visible in the 2-D chart.

Power Map Tours

Up until now we have treated each map that we have created as a completely separate entity. Indeed, we have acted as if an Excel workbook could only contain a single map, even if it was composed of multiple layers. Nothing could be further from the truth, because you can add as many separate maps to an Excel workbook as you like. However, you will not see separate worksheets as you did when using Power View; Excel handles maps in a slightly different way. Each map is called a *tour*, and you can choose which map (or tour) you wish to use when you launch Power Map.

Creating Power Map Tours

To see this in action, we will create (or re-create) a couple of independent maps in a single Excel workbook and see how to manage these elements:

1. Starting with the sample file PowerMapSample.xlsx, create the map you first made for Figure 14-3 at the start of this chapter.

2. Assuming that the Tour Editor is visible on the left (and if it is not, click the Tour Editor button in the Power Map ribbon to display it), click inside the TOUR NAME box and enter a name. I suggest **SalesByRegion**.

3. Click on FILE ➤ Close to close Power Map.

4. From inside Excel, click Map in the Insert ribbon. The Launch Power Map dialog will be displayed, as shown in Figure 14-32.

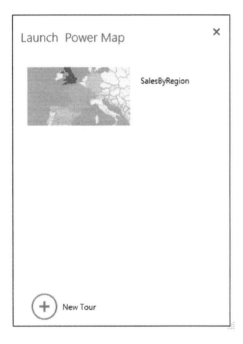

Figure 14-32. *The Launch Power Map dialog*

5. Click the New Tour icon (the plus sign in a circle). A new, blank map will be created.

6. Create the map shown in Figure 14-10.

7. Name this tour **GrossProfit**.

8. Click on FILE ➤ Close to close Power Map.

That is it. You now have two separate maps inside the Excel workbook. Whenever you click the Map button in the Excel Insert ribbon, you will see the existing tours. You can launch a tour directly simply by clicking on the preview of the tour which is visible in the Launch Power Map dialog.

Deleting a Power Map Tour

Sometimes you will want to delete a tour. This is how to do so:

1. From inside Excel, click Map in the Insert ribbon; the Launch Power Map dialog will be displayed.

2. Hover the pointer over one of the tours. An X will appear to the upper right of the map image, as shown in Figure 14-33.

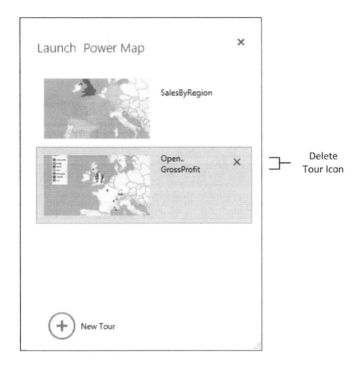

Figure 14-33. *Deleting a tour*

3. Click on the X. Excel will display a confirmation dialog as in Figure 14-34.

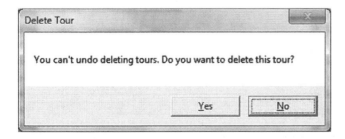

Figure 14-34. *Confirm tour deletion*

4. Click OK. The tour will be deleted.

Power Map Movies

A final, but extremely impressive, Power Map function is the way that you can create and replay "movies" of geographical data. This technique can extend maps (with or without layers and timelines) to create a sequence of views of the data that can be played back either from within Power Map, or as separate multimedia files. A multimedia file created by Power Map does not even need Excel to work.

A Power Map movie is a Power Map tour that can contain several scenes. Each scene is a copy of an existing scene that is then modified to display a different visualization. You can also add transition effects so that each scene flows into the following scene. As always, this is best visualized by using an example. Let's imagine that you want to begin with an initial map of European sales and then take a closer look at UK sales. Our example Power Map movie will only have two scenes, whereas in reality, you can create much more complex scenarios. Here is how to do it:

1.   Create a map of Country Sales as you did at the start of this chapter (you can see this in Figure 14-3).

2.   Set the map type to Flat Map in the Power Map ribbon.

3.   Add a timeline using the MonthAndYear field from the Date table and tweak the Time Decorator for best effect.

4.   Click the Settings icon in the Task panel and select Scene Options.

5.   Enter a scene name in the Scene Name box and press Enter. I suggest **European Sales** as the name.

6.   In the Scene Duration (sec) box, set the duration to **10**.

7.   Set the Effect to Circle from the effects popup list.

   You have finished the first scene. Now we will add a second scene.

8.   In the Power Map ribbon, click Add Scene. A second scene thumbnail will appear in the Tour Editor on the left. This scene will be a copy of the initial scene (or the selected scene if there are already several scenes in the movie).

9.   Ensure that the second scene is selected, and rename it **UK Sales by Make**.

10.   Set the scene duration to 30 seconds.

11.   Remove the MonthAndYear field from the data to delete the timeline.

12.   Add the Town field to the geographical data.

13.   Add the Make field to the metric data.

14.   Zoom in on the UK only.

15.   Remove the legend.

16.   Click the Settings icon in the Task panel and select Scene Options.

17.   Set the duration to **20** seconds.

18.   Set the effect to Push In.

19.   Set the map type to Curved (Not Flat) Map.

20.   Click Play Tour in the Power Map ribbon.

Power Map will play the two scenes and run one into the other. It will play the timeline from the first scene and then remove the legend and timeline as well as change the map type and the data displayed to show the second scene.

This movie was only a tiny sample of what you can do with Power Map to create fluid and extremely impressive automated visualizations. You can create movies containing as many scenes as you want. Set the following for each one:

- A duration in seconds

- A transition effect

- The map type and data

- A timeline

- Multiple map layers

As always, it is your data and the points that you want to emphasize that will make or break a good Power Map movie. Just remember that less is frequently more when creating effects, and that you can add and remove legends and text boxes to each separate scene if you want to clarify certain aspects of the data. You can even use text boxes to create your very own silent movie.

You can pause a movie at any time by clicking the Pause icon that appears in the status bar at the bottom of a movie. Clicking this icon again (it will have become a Play icon) will continue with the playback. You can jump from scene to scene by clicking the Next and Previous icons in the movie status bar. Pressing the Esc key will cancel a movie and return you to Power Map.

Transitions

When creating this example, you tried out a couple of transitions. A transition is always the visual effect that introduces a scene—and that will link a scene to its predecessor. The available transitions are explained in Table 14-13. You can alter the speed of a transition using the Effect Speed slider.

Table 14-13. *Transition Options*

Aggregation	Description
Circle	The map will pivot around a central axis for the duration of the scene.
Dolly	The map will move to the center of the frame.
Figure 8	The map will move its central point around an imaginary horizontal figure eight, as if tracing an infinity symbol.
Fly Over	The map will move from top to bottom as if a camera were flying over the map.
Push In	The map will zoom in progressively.
Station	The map will not move.

Exporting a Movie

Once you have created and perfected a movie, you are not limited to using Power Map to display your artwork. You can export a Power Map movie as a Windows multimedia file (in MP4 format) so that it can be played back without a user needing Excel 2013 or Office 356. To create a movie file:

1. Create a movie as described earlier.

2. Click Create Video from the Power Map toolbar. The Create Video dialog will be displayed, as shown in Figure 14-35.

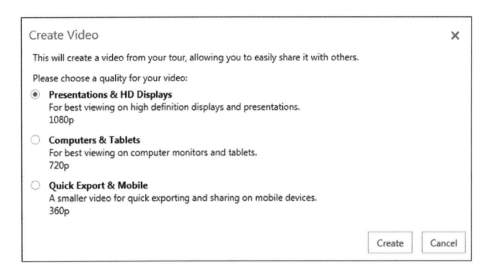

Figure 14-35. *The Create Video dialog*

3. Select the appropriate resolution as a function of the output device that you expect to be used.

4. Click Create. The Save Movie dialog will appear.

5. Enter a file name, select a destination directory, and click Save.

6. The Creating Video message box will appear as in Figure 14-36.

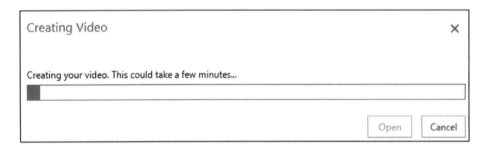

Figure 14-36. *Exporting a Power Map movie*

7. Click Close.

You can now open the Power Map movie file in a multimedia player—or you can double-click on it in Windows Explorer to play back the movie. A version of the movie described here can be found at C:\HighImpactDataVisualizationWithPowerBI\SampleMovie.Mp4, assuming that you have downloaded the sample files from the Apress web site.

Conclusion

This, then, is Power Map. You can now push the creation of geospatial data representation to places that previously you could not achieve without using specialized software. Now, with just Excel, you can achieve some stunning effects and data displays. In this chapter you saw how to create maps, alter map types, and even add multiple varieties of maps and overlay them to produce succinct and clear insight into your data. Finally, you saw how to merge distinct visualizations into a movie that you can export as a file and send to colleagues.

Now all that remains is to pull the pieces together and see how to share your insights and presentations with colleagues in a single place—the cloud. This will be the subject of the next chapter.

CHAPTER 15

■ ■ ■

Self-Service Business Intelligence with Power BI

You are now approaching the end of your journey into the world of self-service business intelligence (BI). Up until now in this book you have seen how to use the four Excel add-ins that make up the Excel BI toolkit to prepare and visualize your data. Now, all that remains is to learn how to share your insights with your colleagues. This is where Power BI comes into the frame.

So what can you do with Power BI? Well, you can

- Share your Excel BI workbooks in the cloud. This will allow your co-workers to view and interact in real time with Power View reports in a browser window.

- Use the new Power BI app for mobile devices to view and interact with Power View reports on tablet devices.

- Configure any workbooks that you have loaded into a Power BI site so that they connect to on-premises data and so they refresh the PowerPivot data that they contain from on-site databases at regular intervals. This way you can be sure that your colleagues are always using the most recent available data.

- Share complex queries.

- Access on-premises data from Power Query.

- Enable Excel BI workbooks for interactive natural language querying so that you and your co-workers can get results without having to learn a query language.

Power BI is an amalgam of new and existing technologies. Consequently it is a fairly vast subject. It follows that I do not have the space here to cover all the aspects of the product. Specifically, because it is based on SharePoint online, I will not be discussing all the details of how to create and manage a SharePoint site in the Microsoft cloud, as this would take up an entire volume.

In addition, Power BI is somewhat multifaceted. It can do many things, and not all users will need to avail themselves of all that it offers. In this chapter, I try to describe as much of its potential and possibilities as is reasonable. However, if there are aspects that you do not need, feel free to skip a section or two and to come back to other parts of the chapter at a later date.

For the purposes of this chapter, I am presuming that you have a working Power BI site, as described in Chapter 1. As always, all the sample files are available on the Apress site, and you can download them to the C:\HighImpactDataVisualizationWithPowerBI folder if you want to follow the examples given in this chapter.

Using Excel Workbooks in Power BI

It is all very well and good if you actually have a Power BI site, but what is it and what can you use it for? A Power BI site is essentially a collaboration environment optimized for self-service business intelligence. Given the whole self-service ethos that underlies Power BI, I think that the easiest way to understand self-service BI is to see the steps in the lifecycle of an Excel BI worksheet. This will show the process, from initial load, through interaction, to deletion. Hopefully this will give you an idea of why Power BI is so different, so visual, and so tremendously useful in practice.

Adding a Workbook

When you add Excel workbooks to your SharePoint Online portal, you will automatically be making them visible in the Power BI site. This is because the Power BI site is simply a view of the documents that have been uploaded to the portal. The Power BI site will, however, *only* show Excel files. As an (admittedly very simple) example, let's add a sample workbook directly to the Power BI Site.

1. In the Power BI Site, click Add. The popup will appear as in Figure 15-1.

Figure 15-1. *Adding a file to the Power BI site*

2. Click Upload File. The Add A Document dialog will be displayed, as in Figure 15-2.

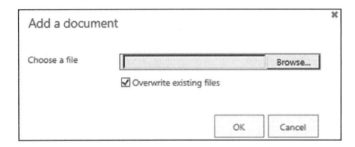

Figure 15-2. *The Add A Document dialog*

3. Click Browse and navigate to the Excel workbook that you want to add to the Power BI site. I will use the file KeySalesData.xlsx in this example.

4. Click OK. The workbook will be added to the portal and will appear in the Documents section of the Power BI site. An example of this is shown in Figure 15-3 where you can see that a few workbooks have already been loaded.

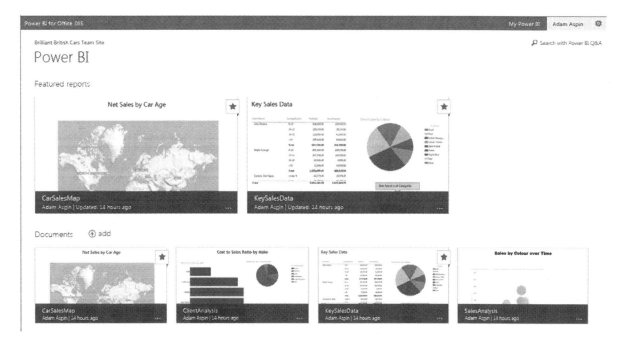

Figure 15-3. *The Power BI site with documents added*

The file that we loaded contains a Power View report; this report was the active worksheet when the file was saved. Consequently, the report is visible as a thumbnail in the Power BI site. If the workbook contains Power Map visualizations, for instance, then these cannot be displayed as thumbnails.

A Power BI site will only accept Excel files, and even then, only Excel files for versions 2010 and 2013. If you try and load any other type of file, you will get the error message that you can see in Figure 15-4 to remind you of this.

Figure 15-4. *Error message if you attempt to load a non-valid file into Power BI*

Enabling Team Site Excel Files

You can add files to the team site in much the same way, and these can be files of many different types. What's interesting is that any valid Excel workbooks will appear automatically in the Power BI site even if you add them as "standard" documents. In addition, any Excel workbooks that you add to the Power BI site will appear alongside the other team site documents.

Any team site is a standard SharePoint Online site. I will not be explaining SharePoint in detail here, since it is outside the scope of this book. That said, there is one minor tweak that you need to be aware of. An Excel file added to the team site (but not specifically to the Power BI site) may appear in the Power BI site, but it is not yet fully ready for use. You can recognize this file instantly, as it does not *yet* have a thumbnail image, just a generic SharePoint illustration. Consequently, you need to enable workbooks like this for Power BI. Once you have done this, the Power View sheet that was active when the workbook was saved will become the thumbnail image for the file in the Power BI site. This can be done as follows:

1. In the Power BI site, click the ellipses (the three dots) in the bottom right corner of the workbook you want to enable for Power BI.

2. Select Enable from the popup menu. The Enable dialog will appear, as shown in Figure 15-5.

Figure 15-5. *The Enable dialog*

3. Click Enable. After a short time the confirmation dialog will appear, as shown in Figure 15-6.

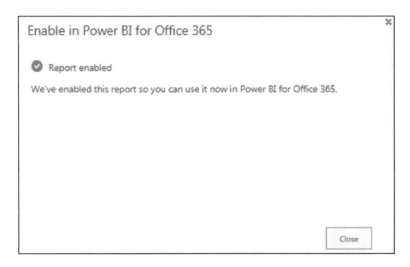

Figure 15-6. *Confirmation that a workbook is enabled for Power BI*

4. Click Close. The workbook is now enabled, and the active worksheet will appear as a thumbnail.

Adding a Workbook to Featured Reports

A Power BI site could contain dozens, or hundreds, of Excel BI workbooks. If this is the case, then you will clearly need some way of prioritizing key information. This is where Featured Reports come into their own. This option lets you display a select few workbooks above their peers as larger thumbnails in the upper part of the page.

To add a workbook to the Featured Reports section of the site (and this has to be done individually for each separate workbook):

1. Click the ellipses (the three dots) in the bottom right corner of the workbook you want to add to Featured Reports. A popup menu will appear as in Figure 15-7.

Figure 15-7. *The workbook popup menu in the Power BI site*

2. Select Add To Featured Reports. After a few seconds the report will appear in the top half of the Power BI site window; it will also remain among the "unfeatured" documents in the bottom half of the window.

■ **Note**   Of course, if you make too many workbooks into Featured Reports then you will lose the impact you can achieve when you only give a few reports this level of preeminence. If you add several workbooks to the Featured Reports section, a scroll bar will appear, allowing you to scroll laterally through the reports. The most recently added reports will always be on the left.

Should you ever want to remove a workbook from the Featured Reports section, all you have to do is

1. Click the ellipses (the three dots) in the bottom right corner of the workbook in the Featured Reports section and select Remove From Featured Reports.

The report will remain in the Power BI site, but will only be displayed alongside the non-featured workbooks at the bottom of the Power BI site window.

Marking a Workbook as a Favorite

Another way of making certain workbooks stand out from the crowd is to mark them as favorites. This has the added advantage of making them also appear in your personal collection of specific workbooks—the My Power BI site, which is only accessible for individual users. To mark a workbook as a favorite (and you will see how this fits in with the My Power BI site later in the chapter),

1. Click the ellipses (the three dots) in the bottom right corner of the workbook in either the Documents section or the Featured Reports section and select Favorite. The workbook will look something like Figure 15-8.

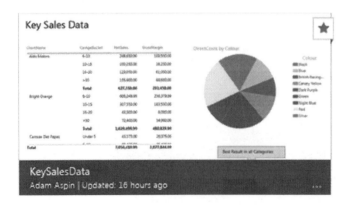

Figure 15-8. *A workbook marked as a favorite*

You will see a star appear at the top right of the workbook. A little later on, you will also see that this workbook now appears in the My Power BI site. Should you ever want to unflag a workbook as a favorite, all you have to do is

1. Click the ellipses (the three dots) in the bottom right corner of the workbook in either the Documents section or the Featured Reports section and select Unfavorite.

The star will be removed and this workbook will no longer appear in the My Power BI site.

Interacting with a Workbook

The whole point in creating a Power BI site is to share the information contained in the Excel workbooks that are on the site. Depending on what you want to do, you have three potential levels of interaction:

- View spreadsheets in the Excel web app where you can see data and interact with Power View sheets by modifying existing filters, applying slicers, or highlighting data.

- Edit spreadsheets in Excel online. This is a more traditional approach and only really applies to "classic" spreadsheets. You cannot modify Power View reports or the data model in PowerPivot this way.

- Edit spreadsheets in Excel—assuming you have a local copy of Excel or a valid Office 365 account that will install a local copy of Excel. Doing this will allow you to update a data model in PowerPivot as well as add or tweak Power View reports.

To give you a more in-depth idea of which approach is best to use in which circumstances, let's take a look at some examples of interacting with a self-service BI workbook.

Interacting with Power View in the Excel Web App

Using the Excel web app is an ideal way for end users to interact with Power View reports. They can modify existing filters and see the results of their changes instantaneously in the report. Existing view-level and visualization-level filters can be modified using the techniques described in Chapter 3. You can also apply slicers and use highlighting as outlined in Chapter 6.

■ **Note** You cannot add or remove fields or add new filters in the Excel web app. Nor can you access the underlying data model.

Interacting with an Excel BI workbook is as easy as clicking on it in the Power BI site. You will then see not only the Power View report that was used for the thumbnail on the Power BI site, but will gain access in your web browser to all the other Power View reports contained in the workbook. If you have loaded the sample report KeySalesData.xlsx into your Power BI site as described earlier, click on it to see something like Figure 15-9.

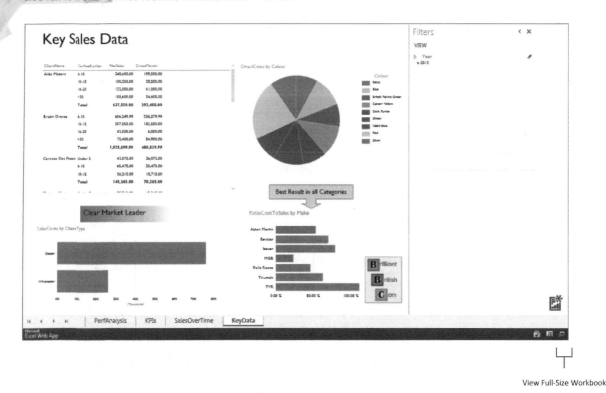

Figure 15-9. *Interacting with a Power View report in the Excel web app*

Once you have accessed a Power View report in the Excel web app, you can interact with Power View (within the constraints and limits described previously) much as you can in Excel. When you have finished with Power View, simply click the browser's Back button to return to your Power BI site.

Editing Excel in the Excel Web App

An Excel workbook (but not Power View reports, Power Map tours, or the underlying data model) can be modified if you edit a workbook in the Excel web app. Since describing Excel in SharePoint Online is outside the realm of this particular book, I will not go into this in any detail. For the sake of completeness, however, note that clicking on the View Full-Size Workbook icon at the bottom right of the web browser window (as shown in Figure 15-9) will switch to edit mode in the Excel web app and open the workbook in a new browser window (shown in Figure 15-10).

Figure 15-10. *Editing a Power View report in the Excel web app*

One useful function that now becomes available is data refresh. Assuming that you have set up a data gateway (described later in this chapter), you can refresh the source data in the workbook as follows:

1. Click on the Data menu. You will see the options shown in Figure 15-11.

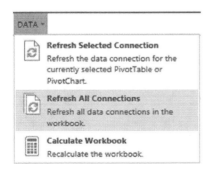

Figure 15-11. *The Excel web app data menu*

2. Click Refresh All Connections. The Query And Refresh Data dialog will appear as shown in Figure 15-12.

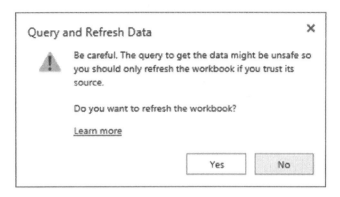

***Figure 15-12.** The Query And Refresh Data dialog of the Excel web app*

3.   Click Yes. The data in the workbook will be refreshed, and all Power View reports will be updated.

One you have updated the data model in the spreadsheet in the Excel web app, all you have to do is close the current browser tab to return to the previous browser window.

Should data refresh fail, you will see the dialog shown in Figure 15-13.

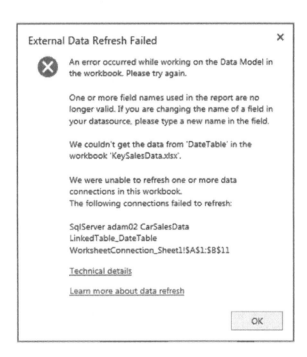

***Figure 15-13.** Data refresh failure alert in the Excel web app*

If this occurs, you will have to debug or rebuild your data connection. The techniques for doing this are described later in this chapter.

Editing a BI Workbook in Excel

If you are the author of a Power BI workbook, or if you have been given the appropriate permissions, you can edit the workbook directly on the Power BI site using Excel. For this, of course, you need to have a valid Office 365 subscription or a copy of Excel Professional installed on your local PC.

1. In the Power BI site, click on the thumbnail of the workbook that you wish to edit, unless you have already done this.

2. Click on the View Full-Size Workbook icon (described earlier and shown in Figure 15-9).

3. Click on the Edit Workbook popup (the downward-facing triangle.). The Edit Workbook menu will appear as shown in Figure 15-14.

Figure 15-14. *The Edit Workbook menu in the Excel web app*

4. Select Edit In Excel. After a few seconds the dialog in Figure 15-15 will appear in the web browser.

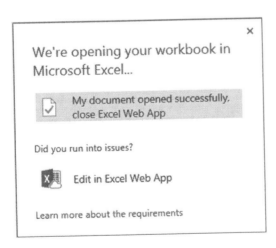

Figure 15-15. *The Edit In Excel confirmation*

5. Assuming that all has gone well and that your worksheet has opened in Excel, you can click My Document Opened Successfully, Close Excel Web App.

6. Switch to Excel.

7. Click Edit Workbook in the warning bar at the top of the spreadsheet (shown in Figure 15-16).

 READ-ONLY   We opened this workbook read-only from the server.   Edit Workbook

Figure 15-16. *The Excel Read-Only warning*

8. Make any modifications using Excel as you normally would.

9. Save the workbook. It may take longer than you are used to because it is being uploaded to SharePoint Online—that is, your Power BI site. The status bar in Excel will look like Figure 15-17 while the workbook is being saved.

UPLOADING TO SHAREPOINT

Figure 15-17. *The status bar in Excel indicating that the file is being saved in Power BI*

10. Close Excel to end your modifications.

Downloading a Copy of an Excel Workbook

There are several valid reasons you may want to download a copy of an Excel BI file from your Power BI site to your local computer. A few possibilities are

- You want to make modifications to the file and need to be sure that you have the latest version.

- You no longer have a copy of the original, or never had a copy, because it was created by someone else.

- You are about to remove the document from the team site and want to keep a local copy, just in case.

Whatever your reasons, one method for doing this is

1. Return to the Home page of the team site. This is shown in Figure 15-18.

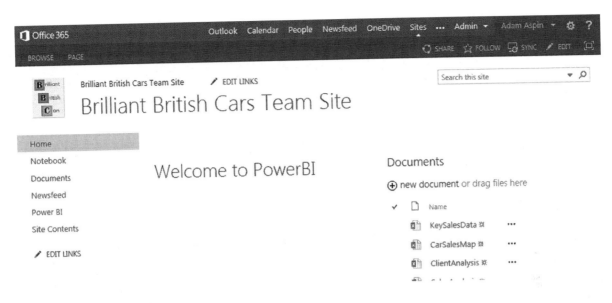

Figure 15-18. *The team site*

2. If you have left the available documents visible on the home page, jump to step 4. If not. . .

3. . . . click on Documents in the navigation list on the left. The Documents page will appear.

4. Click the ellipses (the three dots) to the right of the document name. The document popup window will appear, as shown in Figure 15-19.

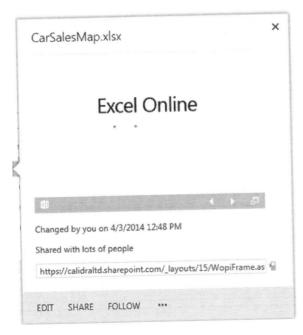

Figure 15-19. *The document popup window*

5.   Click the ellipsis at the bottom of the document popup window. The SharePoint Online document management popup menu will appear, as shown in Figure 15-20.

View Properties

Edit Properties

View in Browser

Edit in Browser

Check Out

Compliance Details

Workflows

Download a Copy

Follow

Shared With

Delete

Figure 15-20. *The SharePoint Online document management popup menu*

6.   Select Download A Copy. The download bar will appear at the bottom of the screen.

7.   Click on the downward-facing triangle at the right of the Save button and select Save As. The Save As dialog will appear.

8.   Navigate to the directory where you want to save the copy, and rename it if necessary.

9.   Click Save.

You will now have a copy of the workbook in the folder where you chose to save it. This will have no effect on the original file on the Power BI site.

___

■ **Note**   For details on the more generic SharePoint functions, such as versioning and checking documents in and out, please consult the SharePoint Online documentation.

___

Removing a Workbook from Power BI

Business Intelligence reports can be transient. The same applies to self-service reports in a Power BI site. Consequently, if you ever want to remove a workbook from your Power BI site

1. Click the ellipses (the three dots) in the bottom right corner of the workbook in either the Documents section or the Featured Reports section and select Delete. The confirmation request shown in Figure 15-21 will appear.

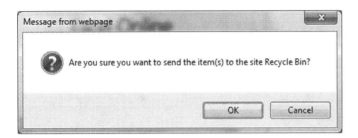

Figure 15-21. Confirm removal of an Excel workbook from Power BI

2. Click OK. The file will be removed from the entire site and will be placed in the SharePoint Online recycle bin. This will effectively remove it from the Power BI site as well as the Documents page of the team site, the team site home page, plus any other pages that you set up to display the worksheet.

You can delete an Excel file just as easily, and using virtually the same techniques, from the team site as well as from the Power BI site. Deleting from a team site will make the file disappear from the Power BI site too.

■ **Note**   If you need to recover a file deleted by accident from the SharePoint recycle bin, please consult the SharePoint Online documentation.

The Power BI App on Tablet Devices

Self-service business intelligence is not limited to PCs or web browsers. If you are using a Windows 8.1 tablet, for instance, you can use the Power BI app to view and interact with Power View reports by filtering, sorting, and highlighting data. Using the Power BI app is not the same as using a browser to access your Power BI team site. First of all, in the app, you will only see the Power View reports for any Excel BI workbooks that you have specifically selected. Second, you can add Excel BI workbooks to the Power BI app from multiple sites.

At the time of writing, the Power BI app is currently only available in a Windows version. Microsoft has recently promised that other versions for other devices will be released soon. So if you are an iPad or Android tablet user, all hope is not lost. Also, it is worth noting that this app is clearly a work in progress that does not, yet ,provide the same full functionality that native Power View in Excel does. I am not going to list any current limitations, because with such a rapidly-evolving product, they may have disappeared by the time this book is published. I advise you to test it out to see just what you can do with this fun tool.

If you are going to try out the examples in this section, you will need to download the Power BI app from the Windows store and connect to your team site as described in Chapter 1.

Running the Power BI App

As you might expect, launching the Power BI app on a tablet is easy:

1. Go to the Windows Start page on your tablet, as shown in Figure 15-22.

Figure 15-22. *The Windows Start screen on a tablet*

2. Tap the Power BI icon. The Power BI page will appear, as shown in Figure 15-23.

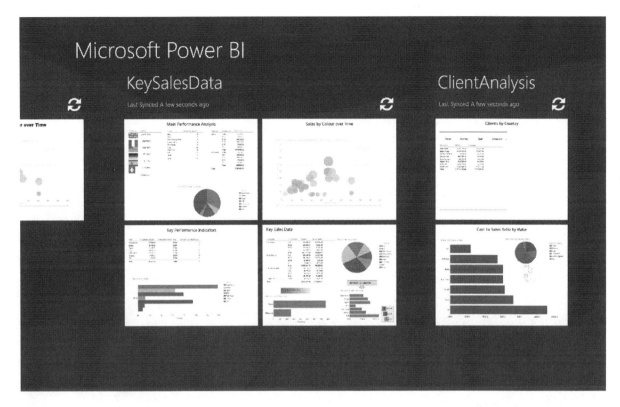

Figure 15-23. *The Power BI screen on a tablet*

Adding Reports to the Power BI App from the Power BI Site

The example I just showed you had a Power BI app where some sample workbooks had already been added. When you start up the Power BI app for the first time, you will probably see a largely blank screen that only shows the message in Figure 15-24:

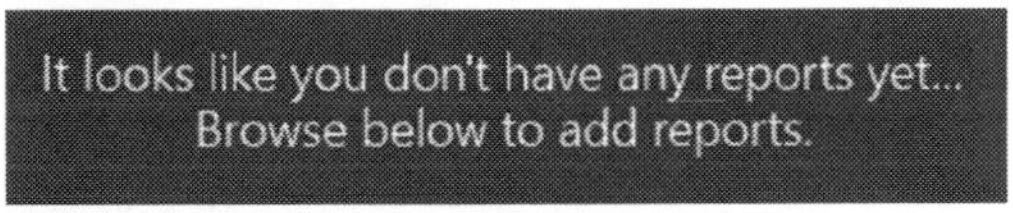

It looks like you don't have any reports yet...
Browse below to add reports.

Figure 15-24. *The Add Reports screen of the Power BI app*

So you need to add some reports from among those already loaded onto your team site. Here's how:

1. In the Power BI app, swipe upward from the bottom of the screen to show the menu (see Figure 15-25).

Figure 15-25. *The Power BI app menu*

2. Tap Browse. The Locations screen will be displayed (see Figure 15-26) showing all the Power BI sites to which you are connected.

Figure 15-26. *The Locations screen in Power BI*

3. Tap on the name of an existing Power BI site. The site screen containing a set of folders will appear, as shown in Figure 15-27.

Figure 15-27. *The site screen of the Power BI app*

4. Tap on Shared Documents. The Shared Documents screen will appear, listing all the available Excel BI workbooks on the site (see Figure 15-28).

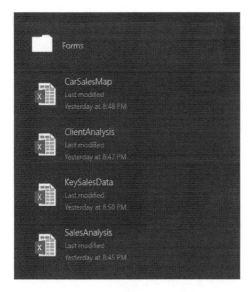

Figure 15-28. *The Shared Documents screen in Power BI*

5. Swipe up on a report that you wish to add. The report will be highlighted and a check mark will appear in the top right corner of the report item. This is shown in Figure 15-29.

Figure 15-29. *Selecting an Excel BI workbook in the Power BI app*

6. Tap Favorite Report in the menu at the bottom of the screen.

7. Click on the back arrow at the top left of the screen three times to return to the main Power BI app screen. All the Power View reports contained in the workbook that you selected will now be visible in the Power BI app.

Removing Reports from the Power BI App

As time goes by and your BI requirements evolve, you will certainly want to remove reports from the Power BI app. This is easy:

1. In the Power BI app, swipe upward from the bottom of the screen to show the menu.

2. Tap Manage Favorites. The Manage Reports screen will appear listing all the available Excel BI workbooks on the site. A part of this screen is displayed in Figure 15-30.

Figure 15-30. *The Manage Reports screen in Power BI*

3. Swipe up on a report that you wish to remove. The report will become highlighted and a check mark will appear in the top right corner of the report item. The menu will appear at the bottom of the screen.

4. Tap Remove. The report will disappear from the Manage Reports screen.

5. Click on the back arrow at the top left of the screen to return to the main Power BI app screen. The report that you removed is no longer visible.

▓ **Note** Removing a report from the Power BI app does not affect the report stored on the Power BI site.

Using Reports in the Power BI App

Now that you have added a few reports to the Power BI app, it is time to see what you can do with them. To put it simply, using a report in the Power BI app is much like interacting with a report in the Excel web app.

Opening a Report in the Power BI App

This is so simple it is almost embarrassing to mention it. Nonetheless, even if you have already guessed, all you have to do is

1. Tap on a report thumbnail to view the Power View report in the Power BI app. An example of this is given in Figure 15-31.

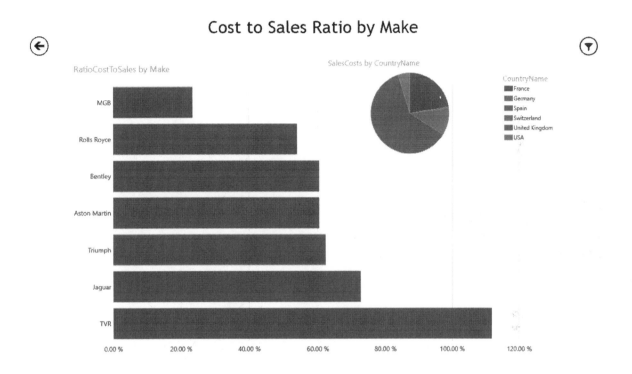

Figure 15-31. *A Power View report in the Power BI app*

To return to the Favorites page of the Power BI app, all you have to do is to tap on the back arrow at the top left of the report.

Filtering a Report in the Power BI App

You can filter reports in the Power BI App much as you did in the Excel web app earlier in this chapter. As an example, I will modify the filters in the ClientAnalysis.xlsx report from the sample files provided with this book.

1. Add the file ClientAnalysis.xlsx to the Power BI app, unless you have already done this.

2. Open the report.

3. Tap on the filter icon at the top right of the report to display the Filters Area.

4. Select View in the Filters Area to modify a report-level filter, or tap on a visualization in the report to modify a visualization-level filter.

5. Modify the filter as described in Chapter 3. An example of interactive filtering using the Power BI app is given in Figure 15-32.

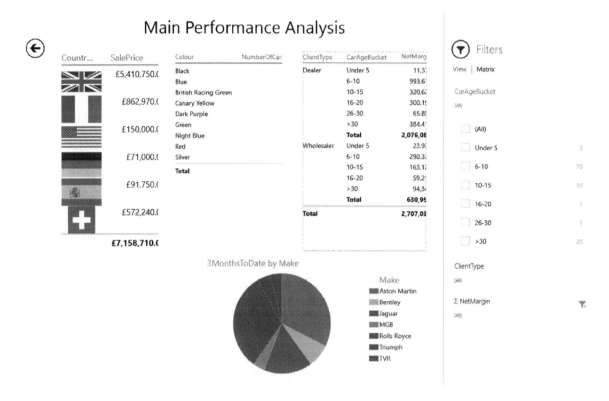

Figure 15-32. *Filtering a report using the Power BI app*

Highlighting or Slicing Data in a Report in the Power BI App

Highlighting data works just as it does in Excel or the Excel web app. To highlight data

1. Tap on a bar, column, or pie slice—or tap on a slicer—and the report will highlight the selection. An example of this is shown in Figure 15-33 where the pie slice Aston Martin is highlighted.

Main Performance Analysis

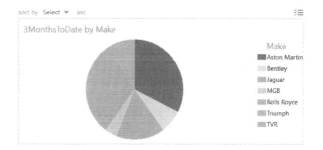

Countr...	SalePrice
🏴	£1,641,000.00
	£445,670.00
🇨🇭	£268,990.00
	£2,355,660.00

Colour	NumberOfCarsSold
Black	2
Blue	4
British Racing Green	1
Canary Yellow	3
Dark Purple	1
Green	4
Night Blue	2
Red	6
Silver	4
Total	**27**

ClientType	CarAgeBucket	NetMargin
Dealer	Under 5	11,370.00
	6-10	369,045.99
	10-15	140,887.00
	16-20	100,623.00
	>30	145,943.00
	Total	**767,868.99**
Wholesaler	6-10	111,160.00
	10-15	86,760.00
	16-20	59,216.00
	Total	**257,136.00**
Total		**1,025,004.99**

sort by Select ▾ asc

3MonthsToDate by Make

Make
- Aston Martin
- Bentley
- Jaguar
- MGB
- Rolls Royce
- Triumph
- TVR

Figure 15-33. *Highlighting data using the Power BI app*

To remove a filter or slicer, just tap it again and the interactive selection will be removed.

Switching Reports in the Power BI App

If all you want to do is switch from one report to another inside the same Excel workbook, you can flip between reports without returning to the Power BI app home screen.

1. Swipe down from the top of the screen. The page thumbnails will appear at the top of the report, as shown in Figure 15-34.

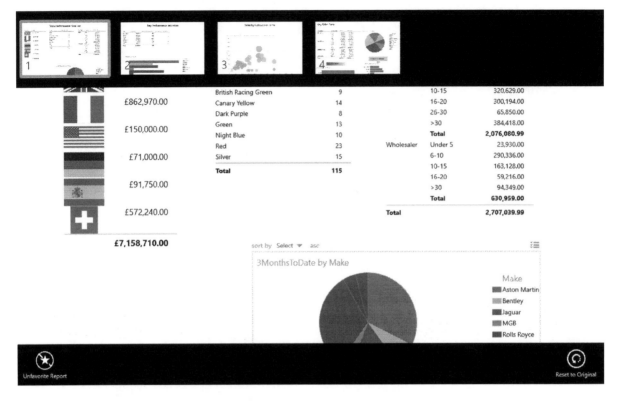

Figure 15-34. Switching pages in a Power BI report

2. Tap on the thumbnail of the page that you want to view.

The page will appear and you can now interact with it.

Synchronizing the Power BI App with the Power BI Site

To ensure that the reports in your Power BI app are completely up to date, you will have to synchronize them from time to time. To do this

1. Tap the Synch icon in the Power BI app Favorites screen, or swipe upward from the bottom of the screen to show the menu and tap the Synch icon.

After a short time the reports in the Power BI app will be updated with the latest versions on the Power BI site. You will know when the operation has finished, because the moving dots across the top of the screen will disappear.

Power BI on Other Mobile Devices

Until the day that the Power BI app is available on other mobile devices, you can always use a web browser (even on a smartphone) to view and interact with Power View reports. This is because the Power View in Power BI not only uses Silverlight, but it can also use HTML 5. This opens up an array of mobile devices on which you can use reports from a Power BI site.

As an example, suppose that you want to view a Power View report on an Android tablet. Here is what to do:

1. Open the tablet's web browser.

2. Connect to your Power BI site.

3. Tap on a report that you want to use. The initial screen will display the message in Figure 15-35.

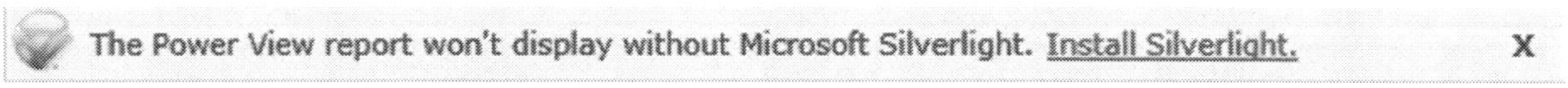

 The Power View report won't display without Microsoft Silverlight. Install Silverlight.   X

Figure 15-35. The Silverlight download message

4. Tap the HTML5 icon at the bottom right of the screen. The Power View report will be displayed and will show a small HTML5 Version icon in the bottom right corner.

You can now filter, slice, and highlight data much as you can when you access Power View reports in a Silverlight-enabled browser.

■ **Note** The Power BI experience using HTML 5 is not yet quite on par with the older and more robust Silverlight version. However, the new version is evolving day by day, and the two could well be on equal footing by the time that this book is published. If this is not yet the case, I can only advise a little patience, as the HTML 5 version will surely match or surpass the Silverlight version one day.

Keeping Power BI Data Up to Date

Once you have loaded a BI workbook into your Power BI site, you have made a great leap forward. You have attained a new pinnacle in the realm of self-service business intelligence by preparing your own data, shaping it, and producing clear, visually attractive output that you can share with your colleagues. However, data is rarely static, and you will most likely want your Power View reports to reflect the latest changes in the source data that underpin your analysis.

Consequently, you *must* ensure that the data in a workbook stored in the cloud can be kept in synch with source data in the corporate network. This way the insights that you have uncovered and shared never need to be out of date. Although it is not complicated, setting up the link between corporate data and SharePoint Online does require some groundwork to be carried out. In essence, you are looking at a two part process:

•   Install a service called the *Data Management Gateway* on a computer on the corporate network that can access SharePoint Online securely and reliably.

•   Set up *scheduled data refresh* (or use manual data refresh if you prefer) using the Data Management Gateway as the channel that connects your Excel BI workbooks on your Power BI site to corporate data.

Once set up, these two elements work together to ensure that your colleagues are always seeing the most up-to-date version of the data that underlies your Power View presentations. Although it can take a few minutes to set up, it is well worth the effort, and it saves you from having to resort to copying new versions of a workbook to a Power BI site to update the data. More critically, once scheduled refreshes are set up, you can trust Power BI to carry out updates for you and avoid the potential embarrassment of forgetting to refresh the data. We will look at these two aspects of automating data synchronization in the next two sections.

Data Management Gateway

The technical definition of the Data Management Gateway is that it is a "client agent that provides access to on-premises data sources in your organization." What this means is that it is a piece of software that you have to install on a networked PC to link the organization to the Data Management Gateway service in SharePoint Online, which handles automated refresh among other things. So what you will have to do is

1. Download a Data Management Gateway to a workstation or server on the corporate network.

2. Install the gateway correctly.

3. Configure the gateway on the on-premises computer.

4. Register the gateway with the Power BI admin center.

Although we say "gateway" as if there were only one, you can, in fact, install up to 200 separate gateways per Power BI tenant. In fact, you could have different gateways to suit varying administrative or organizational requirements.

Let's see this in action and assume that our example enterprise, Brilliant British Cars, only needs a single gateway for the moment. The following sub-sections explain how to set up a Data Management Gateway.

Download a Data Management Gateway to a Workstation or Server on the Corporate Network

Before you can set up a Power BI Data Management Gateway on a corporate PC, you will need to download and install the gateway software. One way to do this is explained in the steps that follow:

1. Go to the Power BI Data Management Gateway download page (currently `http://www.microsoft.com/en-gb/download/details.aspx?id=39717`) and download the appropriate (32-bit or 64-bit version) of the Data Management Gateway local service to a directory on the machine where you want to install the gateway. The .msi file is currently named DataManagementGateway_1.0.5144.2_en-us (64-bit), though you may be choosing the 32-bit version.

2. Double-click the .msi file. The splash page of the Data Management Gateway wizard will appear, as shown in Figure 15-36. Depending on the rights of the user that you are logged in as and your security configuration, you may be asked for confirmation that you want to run this application.

Figure 15-36. *The splash page of the Data Management Gateway wizard*

    3.   Click Next. The End-User License Agreement page of the Data Management Gateway wizard will appear, as shown in Figure 15-37.

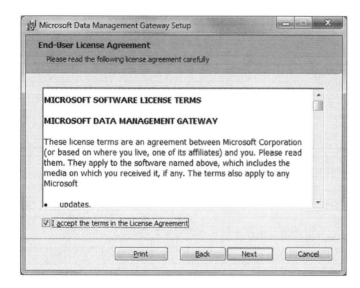

Figure 15-37. *The license page of the Data Management Gateway wizard*

    4.   Check the I Accept The Terms Of The License Agreement box and click Next. The Destination Folder page of the Data Management Gateway wizard will appear, as shown in Figure 15-38.

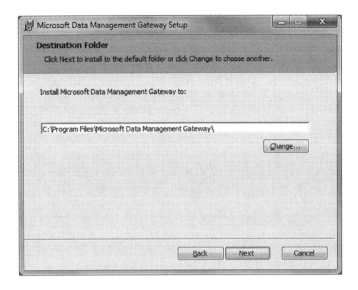

Figure 15-38. *The Destination Folder page of the Data Management Gateway wizard*

5. Accept the default folder unless there are corporate or other reasons to specify a custom folder, and click Next. The Ready To Install page of the Data Management Gateway wizard will appear, as shown in Figure 15-39.

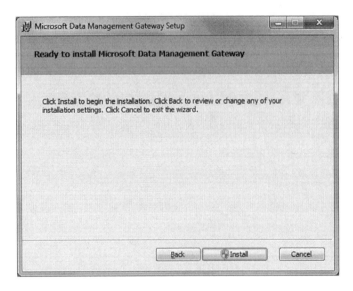

Figure 15-39. *The Ready To Install page of the Data Management Gateway wizard*

6. Click Install. You could be prompted by Windows to allow the installation program to execute; if so, then authorize the program to run. The Completed page of the Data Management Gateway wizard will appear, as shown in Figure 15-40.

Figure 15-40. *The Completed page of the Data Management Gateway wizard*

7. Click Finish. The Wizard will start the Gateway Setup process, and display the Register Gateway dialog.

8. Open your Power BI site in a web browser, as shown in Figure 15-3 at the start of this chapter.

9. Click on the Settings icon (the cog symbol) at the top right of the window.

10. Select Power BI Admin Center. If this is a new session, you may be required to supply credentials. The Power BI Admin Center page will be displayed, as shown in Figure 15-41.

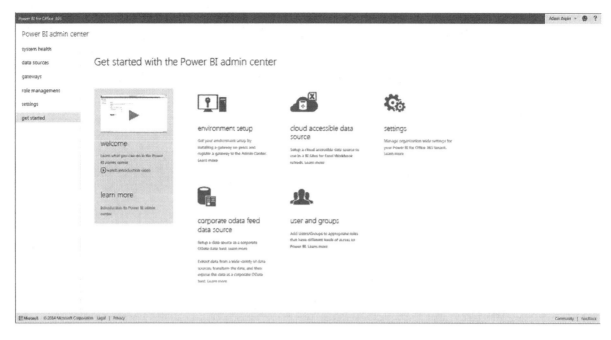

Figure 15-41. The Power BI Admin Center page

11. Click gateways from the menu on the left (unless the Gateways tab is already selected). The Gateways page will be displayed, as shown in Figure 15-42.

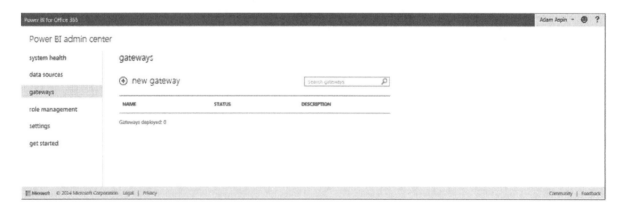

Figure 15-42. The Gateways page of the The Power BI admin center

12. Click New Gateway in the main pane of the Gateways page. The New Gateway page will be displayed.

13. Enter a name for the gateway in the Name box. I will use **SalesGateway** here.

14. Enter a description for the gateway in the Description box. I will add **The main gateway for data updating** here. The New Gateway page will look like Figure 15-43.

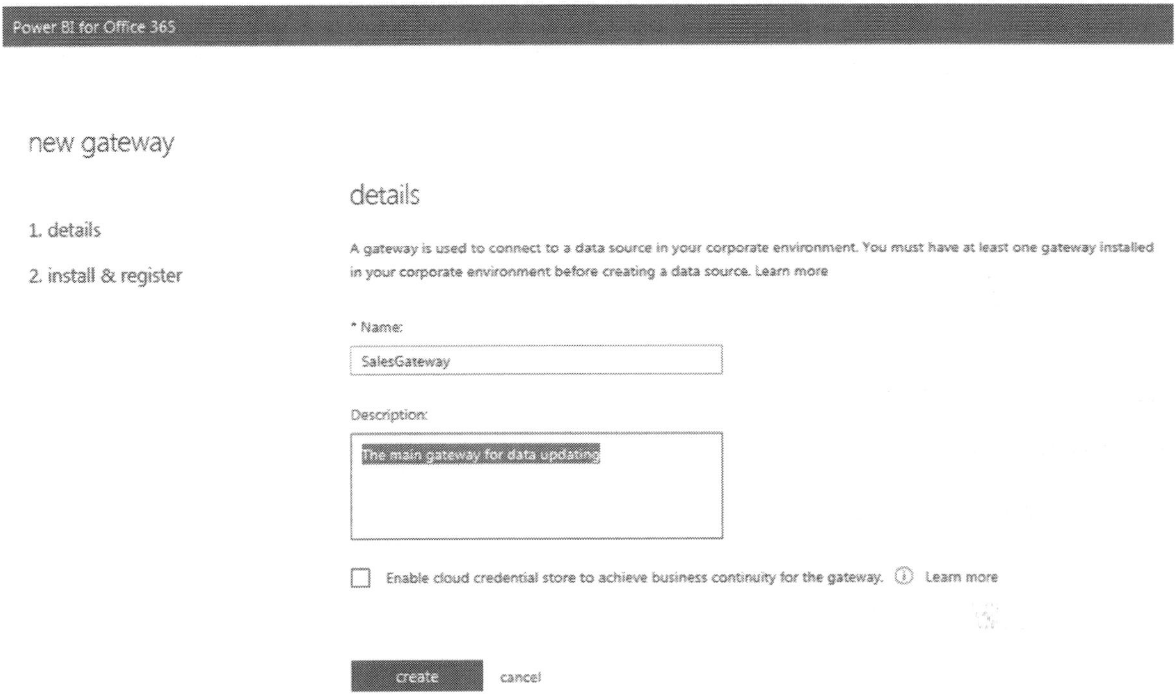

Power BI for Office 365

new gateway

1. details

2. install & register

details

A gateway is used to connect to a data source in your corporate environment. You must have at least one gateway installed in your corporate environment before creating a data source. Learn more

* Name:

SalesGateway

Description:

The main gateway for data updating

☐ Enable cloud credential store to achieve business continuity for the gateway. ⓘ Learn more

create   cancel

Figure 15-43. *The New Gateway page of the Power BI Admin center*

15. Click the Create button. After a few seconds of processing the Install & Register page will appear, as shown in Figure 15-44.

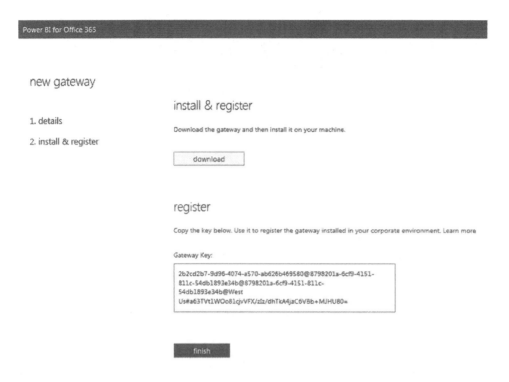

Power BI for Office 365

new gateway

install & register

1. details

Download the gateway and then install it on your machine.

2. install & register

download

register

Copy the key below. Use it to register the gateway installed in your corporate environment. Learn more

Gateway Key:

2b2cd2b7-9d96-4074-a570-ab626b469580@8798201a-6cf9-4151-811c-54db1893e34b@8798201a-6cf9-4151-811c-54db1893e34b@West Us#a63TVt1WOo81cjvVFX/zIz/dhTkA4jaC6VBb+MJHU80=

finish

Figure 15-44. *The Install & Register page for a Power BI Data Management Gateway*

16. Select and copy the gateway key.

17. Switch back to the Gateway Configuration Manager and paste the gateway key into the Gateway Key box. The Gateway Configuration Manager will look like Figure 15-45.

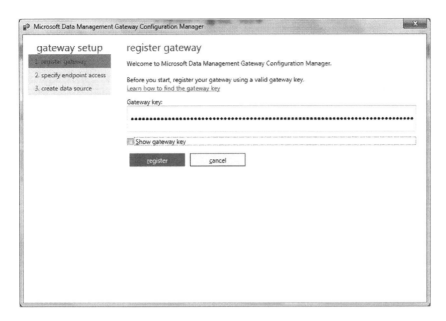

Figure 15-45. *The Register Gateway pane of the Gateway Configuration Manager*

18. Click Register. The Gateway Configuration Manager will display the Specify Endpoint Access pane, as shown in Figure 15-46.

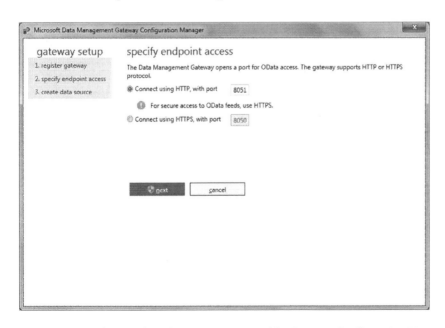

Figure 15-46. *The Specify Endpoint Access pane of the Gateway Configuration Manager*

19. For the moment, accept the default settings by clicking next. The configuration process will probably require you to confirm that you authorize this process to run. The Create Data Source pane of the Gateway Configuration Manager will be displayed, as shown in Figure 15-47.

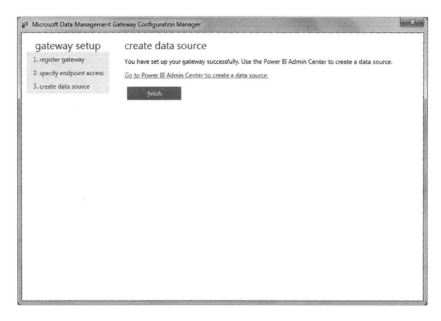

Figure 15-47. *The Create Data Source pane of the Gateway Configuration Manager*

20. Click Finish. The Home page of the Gateway Configuration Manager will be displayed as in Figure 15-48.

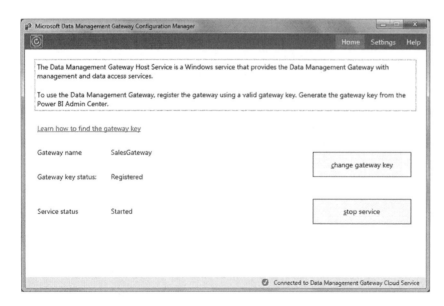

Figure 15-48. *The Home page of the Gateway Configuration Manager*

21. Close the Gateway Configuration Manager (click on the close icon—the X—at the top right of the dialog).

22. Switch back to the Power BI admin center. The Gateways page will display the new gateway, as shown in Figure 15-49.

Figure 15-49. *The new gateway before registration*

This process can take some time to complete—registering the key can take up to 5 minutes in my experience. However, once complete, you have established an essential part of the link between onsite data and self-service BI in the cloud. However, before we proceed to the next step—adding a data source—I have several comments to make concerning data management gateways.

Installing and Configuring a Data Management Gateway from the Power BI Admin Page

First, the process that I just described is not the only way to install a data management gateway. If you prefer, you can start out using the Power BI Admin Center; start at step 8 in the preceding section—and continue until step 16. When you reach step 16, click Finish, and you will see a new gateway, but one that is not registered or started. This is shown in Figure 15-50.

Figure 15-50. *A new gateway that is not yet registered*

From here you can download and register the Data Management service onto the local machine. To do this, click on the ellipses to the right of the gateway name, and select Download Gateway Package Installation Here from the popup, as displayed in Figure 15-51.

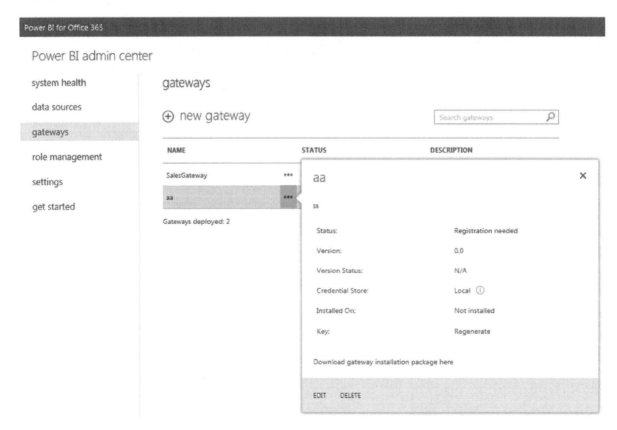

Figure 15-51. *Downloading the gateway application from Power BI*

You will then have to carry out the download and installation process as described in steps 1 to 7 in the last section. The gateway setup process will then run as shown from steps 17 to 21.

The Data Management Gateway Application

The Data Management Gateway Application is installed just like any other piece of software on the local machine. Consequently, you can access it from the Windows Start menu where it should have been pinned during the installation process. If you have unpinned it, then you can find it in All Programs ➤ Microsoft Data Management Gateway ➤ Microsoft Data Management Gateway. Running this application will display the Microsoft Data Management Gateway configuration manager shown earlier in Figure 15-48.

Reregistering a Data Management Gateway Key with the Data Management Gateway Application

There could be times when you need to reregister the gateway on the corporate PC with the Gateway service in your Power BI site. If you ever need to do this,

1. Launch the Data Management Gateway Application. Ensure that the local Gateway service is running.

2. From the Power BI Admin Gateways page (shown earlier in Figure 15-51) click Regenerate.

3. Copy the new key.

4. Switch back to the Data Management Gateway Application. The Microsoft Data Management Gateway Application Configuration Manager will be displayed (you can see this earlier in Figure 15-48).

5. Click Register Gateway. The Register Gateway dialog will appear, as shown in Figure 15-52.

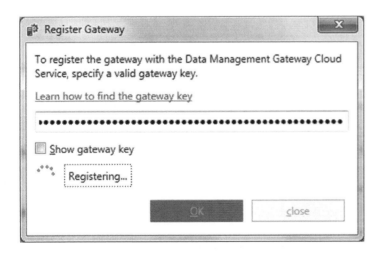

Figure 15-52. *(Re)registering a Data Management Gateway key with the Data Management Gateway application*

6. Paste the key into the gateway key box.

7. Click OK.

8. When prompted to allow administrative access to the Data Management Gateway, click OK.

After a few moments the gateway will be reregistered and operational.

Changing Data Management Gateway Parameters

You can also use the Data Management Gateway application to change any of the initial parameters that you configured when setting up the gateway for the first time. As an example, in the interest of security, you would probably want to switch from the HTTP to HTTPS protocol (if you have not already done this during the initial setup).

1. Launch the Data Management Gateway Application. Click Settings at the top right of the dialog. The Gateway Settings dialog will appear as shown in Figure 15-53.

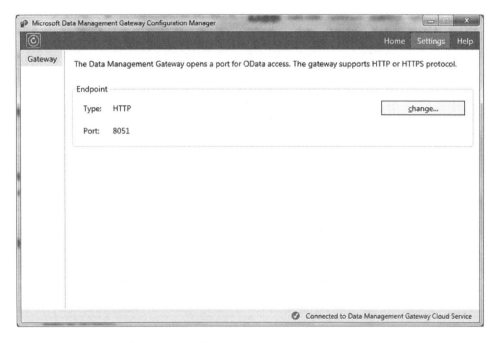

Figure 15-53. *The Gateway Settings dialog*

2. Click Change. The HTTP/HTTPS Endpoint dialog will be displayed as shown in Figure 15-54.

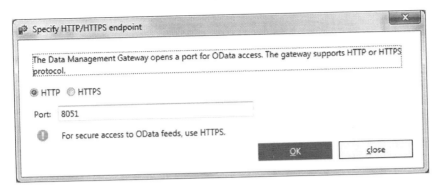

Figure 15-54. *The HTTP/HTTPS Endpoint dialog*

3. Select the HTTPS radio button. The dialog will be modified to accept HTTPS parameters.

4. Enter a valid HTTPS port and select a current SSL certificate. The dialog will look like Figure 15-55.

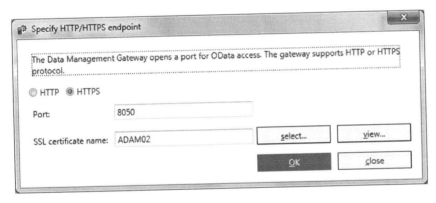

Figure 15-55. *Defining HTTPS parameters for the Gateway*

5. Click OK.

The Gateway is now configured to use HTTPS.

■ **Note** The subject of SSL certificates for security is simply too vast to be described here and has been dealt with exhaustively in many other books and resources. I suggest that you research this subject using your favorite search engine if you need to use SSL certificates.

Stopping and (Re)Starting a Gateway

If you have difficulties when reregistering a Gateway, you may find it helpful to stop and restart the gateway service on the local computer first. To do this

1. Launch the Data Management Gateway Application.

2. Click Stop Service. After a few moments the service status will change to Stopped.

3. Click Start Service. The Gateway service will restart.

Deleting a Gateway

A final aspect of Gateway maintenance is deleting a Gateway. To do this

1. Navigate to the Gateways page of the Power BI Admin Center.

2. Click on the ellipses to the right of the name of the Gateway that you want to delete.

3. Click Delete in the popup (you can see this in Figure 15-51 earlier). The delete confirmation dialog will appear, as shown in Figure 15-56.

are you sure you want to delete this gateway?

This gateway may be used by existing data sources. Deleting the gateway will result in removal of its data sources.

yes   no

Figure 15-56. *The delete gateway confirmation dialog*

4. Click OK.

The gateway will be deleted. This means that you can no longer update workbooks in Power BI that used this gateway to access source data.

Data Sources

With a Data Management Gateway correctly installed and configured, you can now carry out the second part of the preparatory process that will allow Excel BI workbooks in the cloud to be refreshed from on-site data. This phase is called *defining a data source,* and it involves

- Creating a new data source

- Configuring the data source to connect to an on-premises database (only SQL Server or Oracle are currently possible data sources, though this aspect of Power BI is evolving rapidly, and other data sources such as SSAS Tabular warehouses could be available by the time that you read this)

- Supplying security credentials to be used when connecting to the on-premises database

Here is how to carry out this process:

1. Switch to, or open, the Power BI Admin Center.

2. Click on data sources in the menu on the left. The Data Sources page will be displayed as shown in Figure 15-57.

Figure 15-57. *The Data Sources page of the Power BI Admin Center*

3. Click New Data Source. The Data Source Usage page will be displayed. This is shown in Figure 15-58.

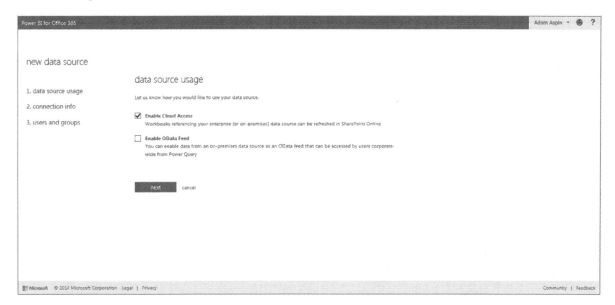

Figure 15-58. *The Data Source Usage page*

4. Leave Enable Cloud Access checked and Enable OData Feed unchecked and click Next.

5. Enter **CarSales** as the Connection Name.

6. Enter **Connection to the CarSalesData database** as the description.

7. Click on the popup menu for the gateway and select the SalesGateway gateway, which you created earlier.

8. Select SQL Server as the data source type from the popup list of available data sources.

9. Select Connection Properties from the Connect Using options.

10. Choose one of the available installed providers. I will choose Microsoft OLEDB Provider for SQL Server in this example. The list of available providers will depend on how the local computer is configured.

11. Enter the name of the SQL Server, including the instance if there is one, in the Server Name box.

12. Enter the database name. If you are using the samples provided with this book, then it will be **CarSalesData**. The data source Connection Info page will look like Figure 15-59.

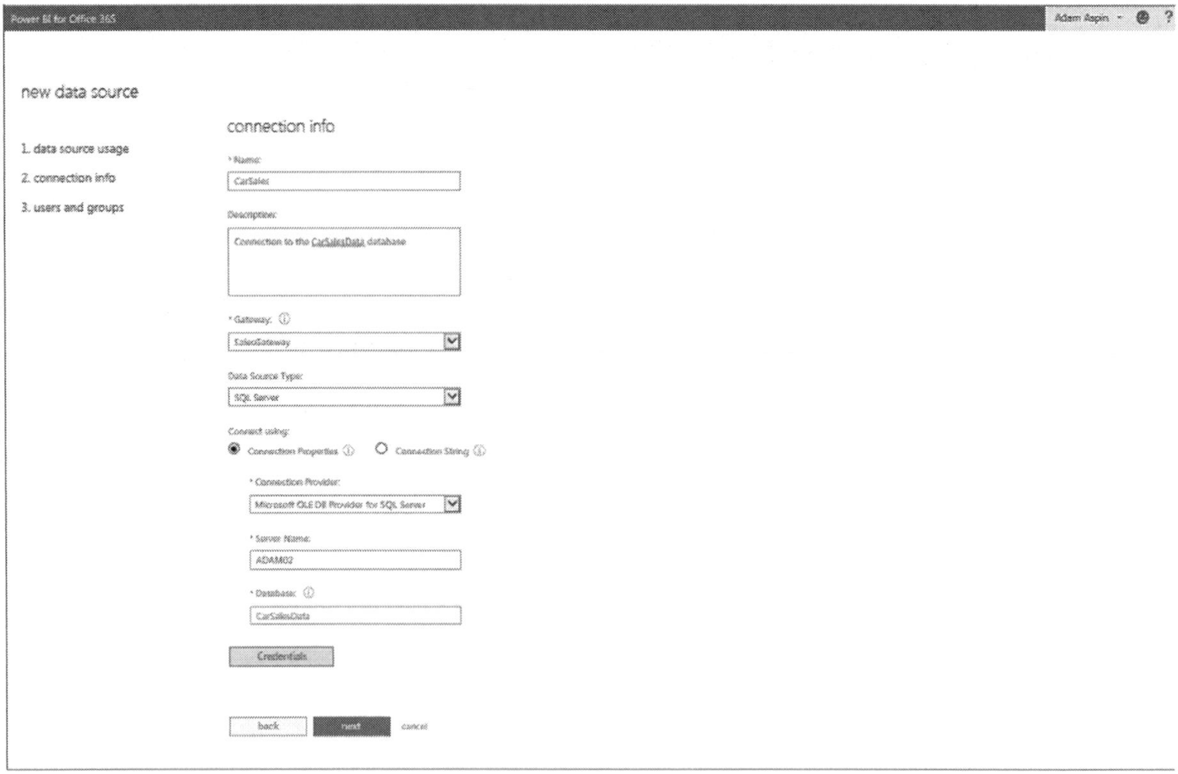

Figure 15-59. *The new data source Connection Info page*

13. Click Credentials. After a few seconds the Data Source Manager Credentials application will ask to be authorized. You can see this in Figure 15-60.

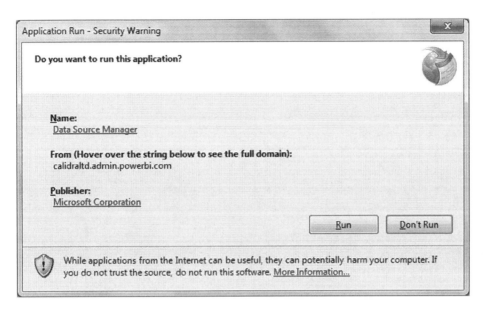

Figure 15-60. *The Data Source Manager credentials application*

14. Click Run. The Data Source Settings application will download and install. You will then see the Data Source Settings dialog.

15. Select Database as the Credentials type.

16. Enter an existing SQL User. I will use **Power BI** in this example (user management is described a little later in this chapter).

17. Enter the database user password. The Data Source Settings dialog will look like Figure 15-61.

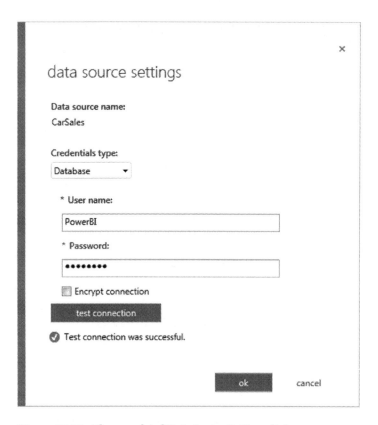

Figure 15-61. *The completed Data Source Settings dialog*

18.   Click Test Connection to ensure that all is well, and (assuming that the connection is
       successful) click OK. The Data Source Settings dialog will close and you will return to the
       Connection Info page for the new data source.

19.   Click Next. The new data source Users And Groups page will be displayed, as shown in
       Figure 15-62.

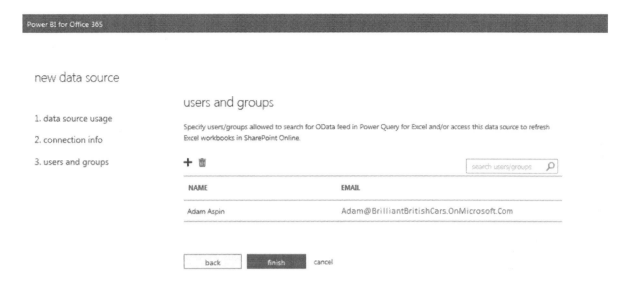

Figure 15-62. *The new data source Users And Groups page*

20. Add any further users by clicking on the plus icon and selecting from the list of existing users.

21. Click Finish. You will see the data source that has been created as in Figure 15-63.

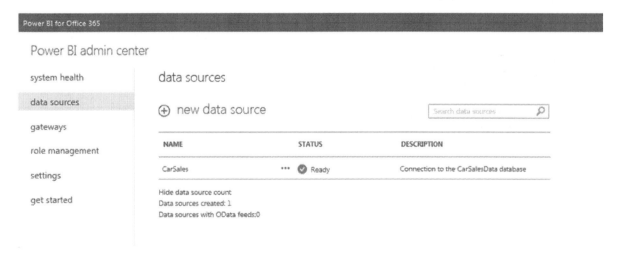

Figure 15-63. *A newly created data source*

▓ **Note**   At step 17 you can choose to encrypt a connection if you wish. This is advisable in practice.

Using a Connection String to Determine Connection Settings

In the previous section you saw how to set up the connection settings for a data source by defining all the separate elements that make up the connection. This can get a little laborious, and so there is another option to configure your data sources if you prefer. It involves copying the connection string from an Excel BI worksheet and using it to set up the data source. Here is how you can do this:

1.   Get a hold of the workbook that has a connection to an SQL Server database.

2.   Open the workbook and switch to PowerPivot (all of this is explained in Chapter 9).

3.   In the Home ribbon click on the Existing Connections button.

4.   Select the requisite connection and click Edit. The Edit Connection dialog will appear.

5.   Click Advanced. The Advanced dialog will appear.

6.   Select the connection string at the bottom of the dialog and copy the connection string.

7.   Cancel out of all the open PowerPivot dialogs.

8.   Switch to, or open, the Power BI Admin Center.

9.   Follow steps 1 to 8 from the previous process in the "Data Sources" section.

10.   Select the Connection String radio button.

11.   Paste the connection string into the Connection String box. The New Data Source page will look like Figure 15-64.

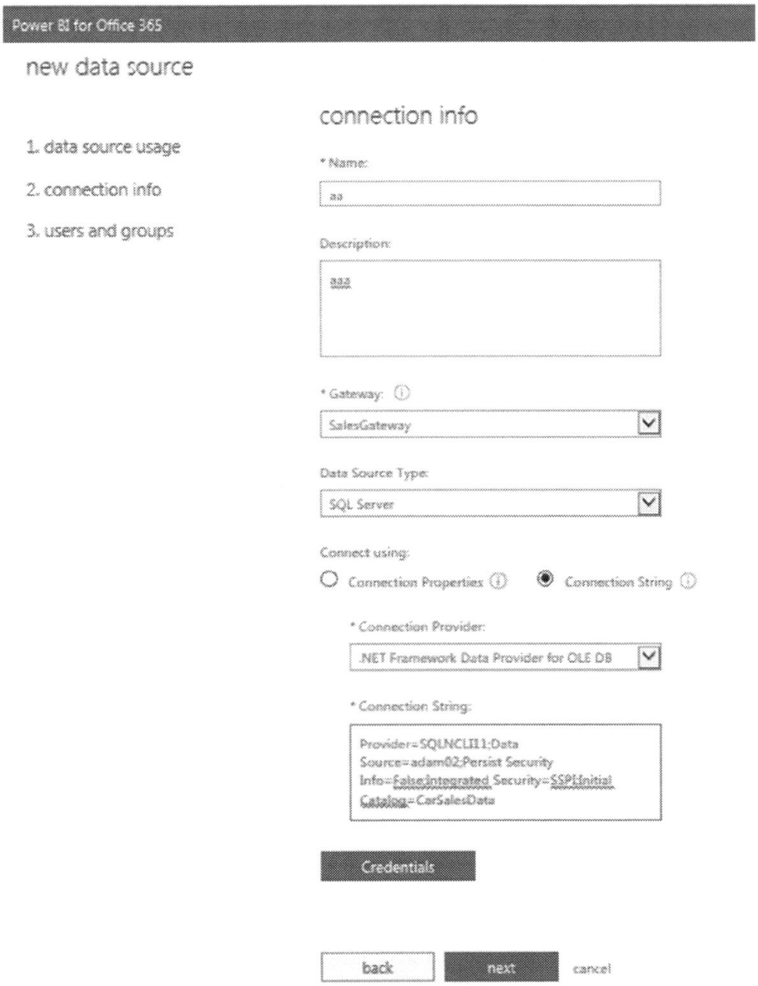

Figure 15-64. *Using a connection string to configure a data source*

12. Continue with steps 13 to 21 from the previous process to complete the data source definition.

■ **Note** You can abandon the creation of a data source at any time by simply clicking the browser back button. Power BI will display a warning dialog to remind you that any unfinished data source will be discarded.

Deleting a Data Source

You may need to manage your data sources once they are set up and running. One core requirement is to delete a data source. Be warned, however, that deleting a data source will prevent workbooks that use this source from being refreshed. To delete a data source, follow these steps:

1. Click on the ellipses to the right of the data source name. The data source popup window will be displayed, as shown in Figure 15-65.

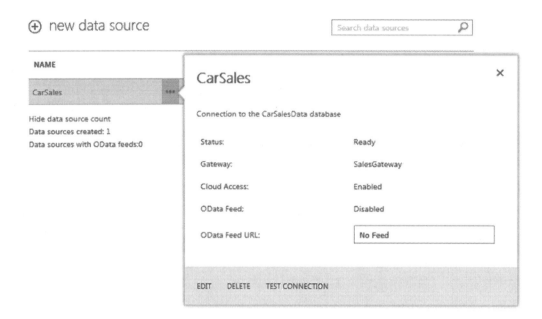

Figure 15-65. *The data source popup window*

2. Click Delete. The confirmation dialog that you can see in Figure 15-66 will appear.

Figure 15-66. *The data source deletion confirmation dialog*

3. Click Yes. The data source will be deleted.

If you have inadvertently deleted a data source that you need, you will have to re-create it.

■ **Note** You are currently limited to 200 data sources for a Power BI tenant. I imagine that this will only be a limitation in the most extreme circumstances.

Data Refresh

So, with the underlying infrastructure in place and working, you can now have Excel BI workbooks in Power BI updated to reflect the latest data changes. There are only two types of data refresh:

- Scheduled data refresh
- Ad-hoc data refresh

■ **Note** As things stand as this book goes to press, you can only refresh data in PowerPivot. So, currently, data loaded into Excel worksheets over a data connection or data accessed using Power Query cannot be refreshed. This, too, could change in the near future.

Scheduled Data Refresh

To begin with, let's see how to schedule a regular automated refresh of the data in a BI workbook that you have uploaded to a Power BI site. Here is how you can do this.

1. Open or switch to your Power BI site.

2. Click on the ellipses at the bottom right corner of the workbook that you want to have refreshed automatically and select Schedule Data Refresh from the popup menu. The Refresh Settings page for this workbook will be displayed.

3. Set the Refresh Schedule to On by sliding the button to the right.

4. Select a data connection from those available.

5. Select a frequency for the data refresh from the Frequency popup. It can be Daily or Weekly.

6. Click inside the Ends By box and select a date when you want the refresh cycle to end from the calendar popup.

7. Set an email to receive refresh failure notifications. The page should look like Figure 15-67.

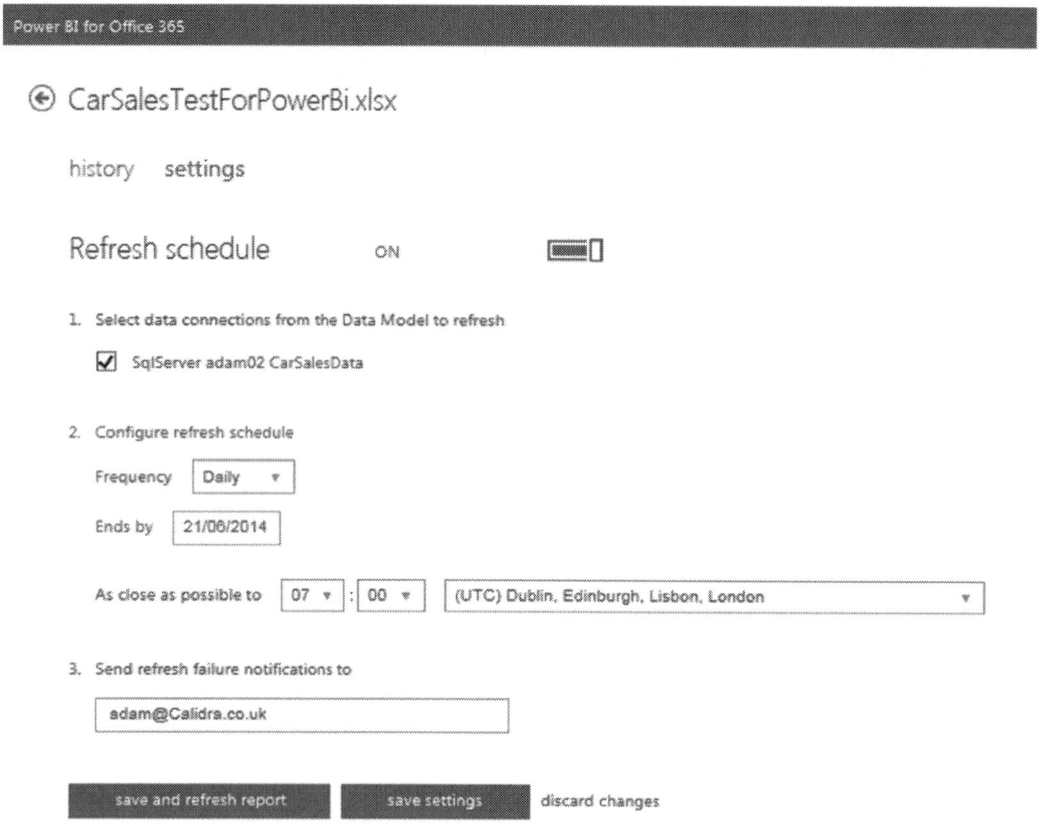

Power BI for Office 365

⊙ CarSalesTestForPowerBi.xlsx

history   settings

Refresh schedule   ON   ▭▭◻

1. Select data connections from the Data Model to refresh

☑ SqlServer adam02 CarSalesData

2. Configure refresh schedule

Frequency | Daily   ▾ |

Ends by | 21/06/2014 |

As close as possible to | 07 ▾ | : | 00 ▾ | | (UTC) Dublin, Edinburgh, Lisbon, London   ▾ |

3. Send refresh failure notifications to

| adam@Calidra.co.uk |

| save and refresh report | | save settings | discard changes

Figure 15-67. *The refresh settings page*

8.   Click Save Settings.

The data will be refreshed according to the schedule that you set.

Ad-Hoc Data Refresh

If you know that the source data has changed and you need to have these changes reflected in the shared workbook as soon as possible, then you can force a refresh of the data. The data refresh will not be immediate, since it can take several minutes, but it will not wait until the next scheduled refresh. Here is how you can force a (nearly) immediate refresh of an existing data source:

1.   Go to the Power BI site that contains the workbook that you want to refresh.

2.   Click the ellipses for the workbook you want to refresh.

3. Select Schedule Data Refresh from the popup menu. The Scheduled Refresh page for the workbook data refresh will be displayed.

4. Click Settings to display the settings tab.

5. Click Refresh Now.

The workbook will be refreshed after a short time.

Using Data Sources

Going to all the trouble of setting up a data source can bring some unexpected advantages. Since you now have a link to corporate data, you can use this to

- Share queries based on a data source to allow colleagues to read specified corporate data that you have shaped, filtered, and transformed.

- Connect to corporate databases over OData and discover and query corporate data.

The following two sections will describe how you can do this.

Shared Queries

Once you have a fully functioning Power BI site, not only can you share the insights that you have developed and expressed using Power View, you can also share any queries that you have created using Power Query. This allows you to avoid having your colleagues duplicate all your hard work sourcing and mashing up data, as well as ensure that a whole team can work from the same data. To share queries, you must first be signed in to Power BI from Power Query.

Sign In to Power Bi from Power Query

To sign in to Power BI

1. In Excel, click the Sign In button on the Power Query ribbon. The Sign In dialog will appear.

2. Enter your Power BI login and password. The Sign In dialog will look something like the one in Figure 15-68.

Figure 15-68. Power BI Sign In dialog

    3.   Click Sign In.

You are now signed in to Power BI. The Sign In button will have changed to Sign Out, and if you hover the cursor over this button, you will see a popup telling you who is currently signed in.

There are several good reasons to sign into Power BI when using Power Query. First, as I mentioned, you can share queries and access queries shared by others. Second, you can use shared data sources when you create your queries, thus ensuring that you have reliable, controlled access to corporate data. This offers users a wider access to the source data than just supplying them with prebuilt queries.

Sharing Queries

To share a query that you have created from inside Excel

    1.   Create a query in Power Query. Use a Power BI data source for the query. This is described in Chapter 12.

    2.   Give the query a suitable name and save it.

    3.   Place the cursor over the query in the Workbook Queries pane (on the right) and click Share from the fly-out. The Share Query dialog will appear.

    4.   Alter the name if necessary and add a description to help your colleagues who are looking at shared queries. The Share Query dialog will look something like Figure 15-69.

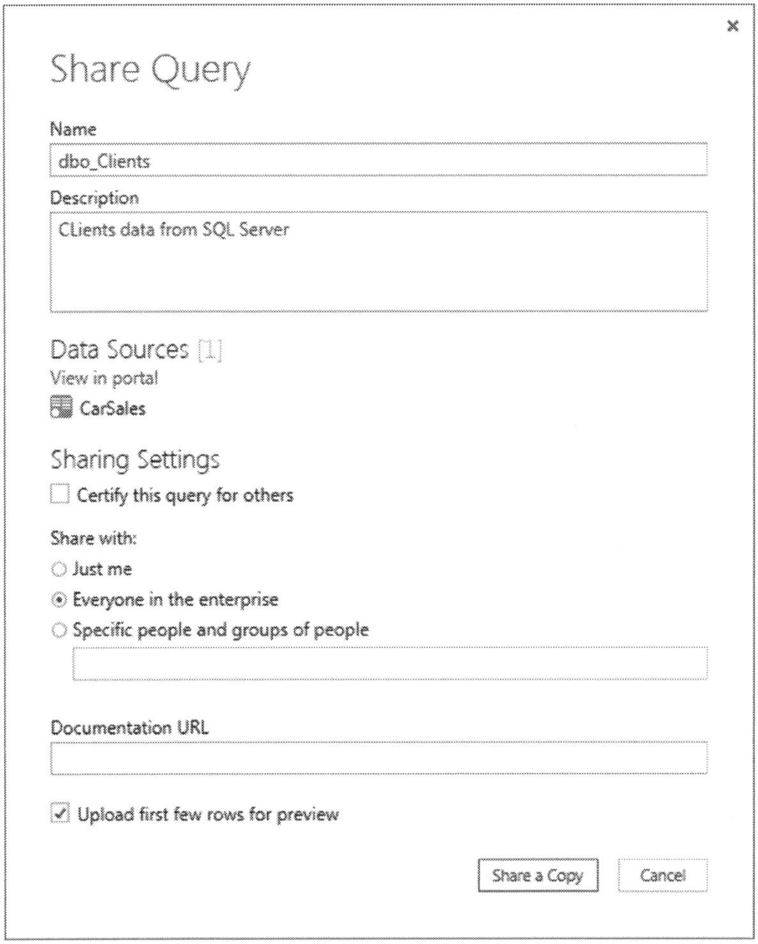

Share Query

Name

dbo_Clients

Description

CLients data from SQL Server

Data Sources [1]

View in portal

▦ CarSales

Sharing Settings

☐ Certify this query for others

Share with:

○ Just me

◉ Everyone in the enterprise

○ Specific people and groups of people

Documentation URL

☑ Upload first few rows for preview

[Share a Copy]   [Cancel]

Figure 15-69. *Shared query on the Power BI site*

    5.   Click Share A Copy.

The query is now shared and available to all your colleagues who are using your Power BI site and that you have authorized to use your queries.

If you are sharing queries, then you will need to make sure that the data a query refers to is available from a Power BI site. In other words, it should be data that has been made available using a data source. If the query references data that is only available on a local disk, for instance, then other users will not be able to use it to return data.

▓ **Note**   You can right-click on a query in the Workbook Queries pane and select Share to display the Share Query dialog if you prefer.

Using a Shared Query

Using a query that has been shared using Power BI is simple:

1. Click Shared in the Power Query ribbon. The Shared Queries pane will be displayed at the right of the Excel worksheet. An example can be seen in Figure 15-70.

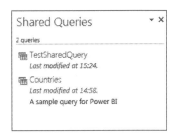

Figure 15-70. *The Shared Queries pane*

2. Double-click the query that interests you (or right-click and select Open or Add to worksheet).

The query will execute and return the data to a new Excel worksheet.

Searching for Shared Queries

If you have access to shared online queries, then you need to know how to look for them. This expands on what we saw briefly in Chapter 13, when looking at Power Query.

1. In Excel, click Online Search in the Power Query ribbon. The Online Search pane will appear.

2. Click Organization in the Power Query ribbon, or select it from the popup at the right of the search box in the Online Search pane.

3. Enter a word or two that you think is part of the query that you are looking for. You can see this in Figure 15-71.

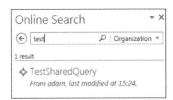

Figure 15-71. *Searching for shared queries*

4. Press Enter or click the magnifying glass icon. Any shared online queries containing the text that you entered will be listed in the Online Search pane.

You can then run the query to return data to an Excel spreadsheet.

Deleting a Shared Query

You can, of course, delete a shared query if you are the query's creator or have sufficient permissions. To do this

1. Place the cursor over the shared query in the Shared Queries pane.

2. Click Delete in the fly-out.

3. Click Delete in reply to the Are You Sure prompt in the fly-out.

Once a query has been deleted you will have to re-create it if you need it again.

Editing Shared Query Settings

The peek window and the popup menu give you a few other options for shared queries apart from those that we have already seen. Principally, you can extend or modify the query properties. To do this:

1. Right-click on a shared query and select Edit Settings (or hover the pointer over the query and select Edit Settings from the fly-out).

The Update Query dialog will appear (which is virtually identical to the Share Query dialog, so I will not reproduce it here). You can modify the query name, description, sharing settings, and documentation URL from here.

OData Feeds

An OData feed allows you to expose on-premises tables and views for colleagues to search using Power Query.

1. Create a data feed where you have checked the Enable Odata Feed box in the Data Source Usage window (you can see this earlier in Figure 15-58).

2. Configure the data access as described previously to establish the connection to an on-site database.

3. When it comes to the Data Settings page of the data feed definition, expand the list of tables and/or views and select the tables and/or views that you want to make available to users. You will see a screen something like Figure 15-72.

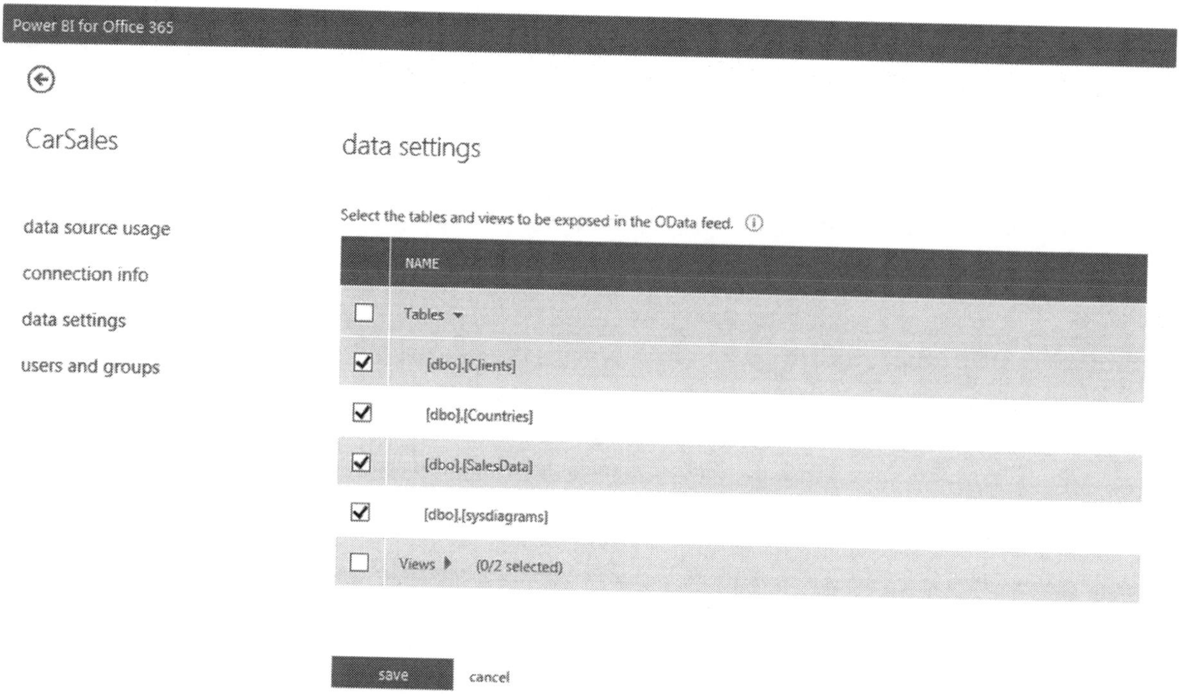

Figure 15-72. *Defining source tables and views for OData*

4. Complete the data source definition as you did previously.

Now you need to find the Odata URL so that you can use it in Power Query. To do this

1. In the Data Sources window in the Power BI admin site, click the ellipses to the right of the data source that you just created. The popup window will appear, as shown earlier in Figure 15-65. This time, however, an Odata URL will appear in the OData Feed URL box.

2. Copy the OData URL.

3. In Power Query, create a query using Odata as the source and the URL that you copied as the reference.

When you use, and share, this query, you will have access to all the selected tables in the data source.

My Power BI

The more you use Power BI, the more Power BI sites you may find yourself using. To help you keep track of key reports from several sites, you can use the My Power BI site. This is simply an overview of all reports you have marked as a favorite (which you saw how to do earlier on in this chapter). So, if you have marked a few reports as favorites, you can see them all together like this:

1. In the Power BI site, click My Power BI at the top right of the page. This is shown in Figure 15-73.

Figure 15-73. *Activating the My Power BI site*

2. Your My Power BI site (visible only to you) will appear in a new browser window with the favorite reports. An example of this is given in Figure 15-74.

Figure 15-74. *A My Power BI site*

Clicking on a report in the My Power BI site will have exactly the same effect as activating it from the Power BI site—it will open the report in the Excel web app. Moreover you can unfavorite a report from the My Power BI site by clicking on the ellipses at the bottom right of the reports and selecting Unfavorite.

Power BI Admin

Self-service does not mean completely self-managing. Although Power BI is designed to function smoothly and with as little management overhead as possible, there are a couple of things that you need to know if you are to manage your Power BI site and ensure that it runs smoothly.

Fortunately you only need to look at a few things:

- Defining the users who can actually manage a Power BI site
- Checking the healthy running of the site

Role Management

Although you (as the Power BI site creator) undoubtedly have the necessary permissions to access the Power BI admin site (and consequently add data gateways and data sources, for example) you may want to add other users so that they can carry out these functions. To add a user with Power BI admin rights:

1. In the Power BI site, click the settings icon (the cog on the top right) and select Power BI Admin Center. This is shown in Figure 15-75. The Power BI Admin Center page will be displayed.

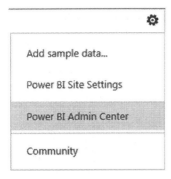

Figure 15-75. Launching the Power BI Admin Center

2.   Click on Role Management in the menu on the left. The Role Management page will be displayed.

3.   Ensure that admin group is the active page (it should be highlighted) and if not, click Admin Group.

4.   Click the add user icon (the plus sign) in the middle of the main page. The Add By Name box will appear as shown in Figure 15-76.

Figure 15-76. Adding a user to the admin site

5.   Enter the first few letters of the user's name and select the appropriate user from the list that appears as you enter the name.

6.   Click the plus icon in the list of users. The user will be added to the list of Power BI administrators.

The Data Steward Group

Another group of users that you can create and manage, but one with less wide-ranging permissions, is the Data Steward Group. This selection of users fulfills a vital role in any enterprise, because they can vouch for the validity of source data. You may remember when sharing queries in a previous section that there was an option to Certify This Query For Others. Data stewards are the only users who are accredited to carry out this task, and consequently, to guarantee that data in a shared query can be trusted. Not even Power BI administrators have this right.

Adding users to the Data Steward Group is virtually identical to what you did previously in the section Role Management when you added users to the Power BI administrators group. The only difference when adding users to the Data Steward group is that at step 3 in this process, you need to click on Data Steward Group before adding the user. Once this is done, users in this group can certify shared queries when creating or editing them. If you look at Figure 15-69 earlier in this chapter, you can see that the Sharing Settings part of the Share Query dialog allows you to certify a query.

___

■ **Note**   The Sharing Settings dialog will only appear in the Share Query dialog if the user is a member of the Data Steward Group.

___

Checking System Health

It never hurts to check that your site is working properly. SharePoint Online logs events that occur over time and lets you view these logs in the Power BI Admin Center. To take a look at the logs

1. In the Power BI admin center select System Health in the menu on the left. The System Health page will be displayed as shown in Figure 15-77.

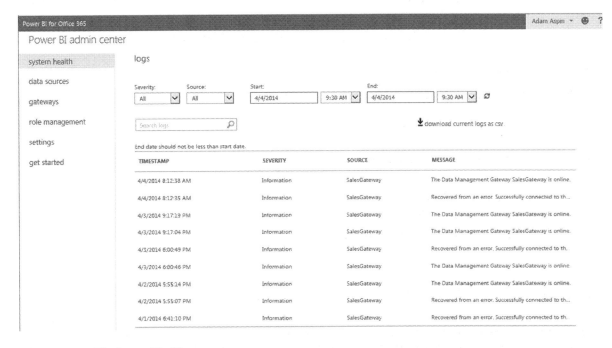

Figure 15-77. The System Health page

As event logs can become voluminous, you can filter the number of records that are displayed and even export the logs to a comma-separated (CSV) file to read in, say, Excel. The available filter options are described in Table 15-1.

Table 15-1. *System Health Options*

Option	Available Choices	Comments
Severity	All, Error, Warning, Information	Lets you choose the type of log record to display
Source	Gateway, Data Source, Job, Role	The sources of system health records you can choose from, and consequently, the area you want to look at
Start Date		Lets you set a start date for log search
Start Time		Lets you set a start time for log search
End Date		Lets you set an end date for log search
End Time		Lets you set an end time for log search
Text Search		Searches the logs for the text that you enter

The main thing to note is that if you change a filter element, such as the source, severity, or a date or time, you will have to click the Refresh icon at the right of the filter elements to update the display.

Exporting System Health Logs

To export log records as a comma-separated file, all you have to do is

1. Click Download Current Logs As CSV. The Save bar will appear at the bottom of the page as shown in Figure 15-78.

Figure 15-78. *The Save bar*

2. Click the popup triangle in the Save button and select Save As. The Save As dialog will appear.

3. Enter a file name, choose a directory, and click Save.

The logs will be saved in a CSV file that you can then open and analyze in, for instance, Excel.

Natural Language Querying

One of the most impressive aspects of Power BI is the ability to query a workbook using ordinary English. This technique, called *natural language querying,* can be used on any workbook that has been loaded into a Power BI site and subsequently enabled for this kind of interactive interrogation. To finish our tour of Power BI, here is how you can apply and use natural language querying with an Excel workbook in Power BI.

1. Navigate to the Power BI site.

2. Click on the ellipses at the bottom right of workbook that you want to prepare for natural language querying. The popup menu will appear as shown in Figure 15-79.

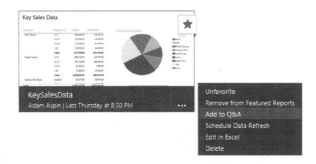

Figure 15-79. *Prepare a workbook for Q&A*

3. Click Add To Q&A. The workbook will briefly display Q&A Enabled.

4. Click Search With Power BI Q&A at the top right of the screen. The Q&A screen will appear.

5. Enter a short amount of text describing the data that you are looking for. In this example, I will use **Show number of cars sold per country**.

6. Press Enter. The query results will appear as shown in Figure 15-80 (assuming that Bing Maps have been enabled).

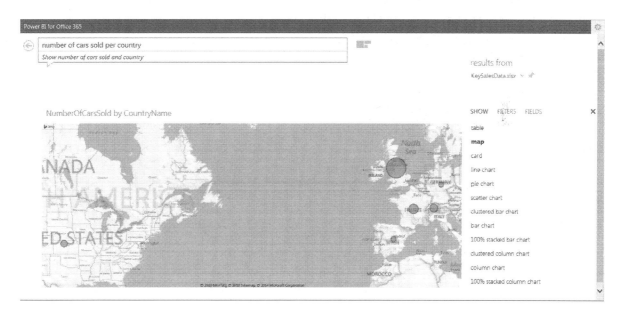

Figure 15-80. *The Q&A page for natural language querying*

As you can see from Figure 15-80, Q&A will select the type of visualization that it thinks answers your question in the most effective manner. If you wish to override this choice, all you have to do is to click on one of the other available options on the right of the window to alter the display type.

Natural language querying will depend to no small extent on the way that you have prepared the data model in PowerPivot. If you remember, back in Chapter 11, I mentioned that it is important to attribute the correct data categories. Well this is also important for Q&A because it allows the natural language query engine to make the correct assumptions. Similarly, giving fields clear and comprehensible names will help the query engine interpret your questions more accurately, and so it will be more likely to return the correct answers. If you add synonyms in PowerPivot to prepare the data for querying, you will likely get even better answers when using Q&A. This, too, is described in Chapter 11.

▓ **Note** Q&A for Power BI is an evolving technology. It is already impressive in its current implementation, but I expect that it will get even better over time. So if it is not perfect for you yet, be prepared to be patient. It will certainly get much better in the future.

Conclusion

Over the course of this book you have seen how to develop the data discovery, modeling, and visualization capabilities of Excel. As the culmination of your journey into self-service BI, this chapter has shown you the new ways you can visualize data, share discoveries, and collaborate from anywhere using the set of technologies that make up Power BI. This has included adding workbooks to a Power BI site, managing the connection to on-premises source data, configuring automated data updates, sharing the queries that you have developed, and allowing controlled access to corporate data using Power Query.

Once you master and implement these techniques and technologies, your Power BI site could really become a true online hub for insight and collaboration, data reuse, and interaction among your colleagues. I sincerely hope that you will have fun using Power BI and develop some really awesome uses for this amazing technology.

APPENDIX A

■ ■ ■

Sample Data

If you wish to follow the examples used in this book—and I hope you will—you will need some sample data to work with. All the files referenced in this book are available for download and can easily be installed on your local PC.

This appendix explains where to obtain the sample files, how to install them, and what they are used for.

Downloading the Sample Data

The sample files used in this book are currently available on the Apress site. You can access them as follows:

1. In your web browser, navigate to the following URL http://www.apress.com/9781430266167.

2. Scroll down the page and click on the tab Source Code/Downloads.

3. Click the link Download Now, and choose a directory where you will save the file HighImpactDataVisualizationWithPowerBI.zip.

You will then need to extract the files and directories from the zip file. How you do this will depend on which software you are using to handle zipped files. If you are not using any third party software, then one way to do this is

1. Create a directory named C:\HighImpactDataVisualizationWithPowerBI.

2. In the Windows Explorer navigation pane, click on the file HighImpactDataVisualizationWithPowerBI.zip.

3. Select all the files and folders that it contains.

4. Copy them to the folder that you created in step 1.

The Sample Data

Once you have installed the sample files you will see the directory/folder structure shown in Figure A-1.

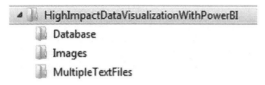

Figure A-1. *The sample data directory structure*

The directories contain the elements outlined in Table A-1.

Table A-1. *The Sample Data Directory Structure*

Folder	Contents
HighImpactDataVisualizationWithPowerBI	Sample Excel files and source data text files.
Database	A backup file of the sample SQL Server database.
Images	The images used in Power View.
Multiple text files	Source files used for Power Query.

Sample Files

There are many sample files included; several are not referenced in the text of the book but are given as examples of what can be done with Power View.

The key sample files referenced in the book are detiled in Table A-2.

Table A-2. *The Sample Data Directory Structure*

File	Description
CarSales.xlsx	The Excel file containing the sample data used in Chapters 2–7 for Power View
PVPresentation.Xlsx	The Excel file containing the sample data used in Chapter 8 for Power View
PowerMapSample.xlsx	The Excel file containing the sample data used in Chapter 14 for Power Map
PowerPivotSample.xlsx	The Excel file that is the basis for building the Power Pivot example in Chapter 9
PowerPivotCodeData.xlsx	The Excel file that is the basis for building the Power Pivot example in Chapter 10
PowerPivotSampleDataset.xlsx	The Excel file that is the basis for building the Power Pivot example in Chapter 11

The various source files used as import examples in Chapters 9 (for PowerPivot) and 12 (for Power Query) are essentially stored in the HighImpactDataVisualizationWithPowerBI directory.

Sample Database

If you intend to follow the examples in Chapter 9 on PowerPivot or Chapter 12 on Power Query, you will need the sample SQL Server data set in the CarSalesData database.

This database is available in the sample data as the file CarSalesData.Bak in the directory C:\HighImpactDataVisualizationWithPowerBI\Database.

Before you can load this database, you will need access to a functioning SQL Server database instance. If you need to, you can download and install the free SQL Server 2014 Express version. It is currently available at the following URL: http://www.microsoft.com/en-in/download/details.aspx?id=42299&WT.mc_id=rss_alldownloads_devresources.

Once installed, you will need to restore the database backup. To do this

1. Open SQL Server Management Studio Express.

2. Open a new query window by clicking New Query in the toolbar.

3. Run the following script.

```
USE [master]
RESTORE DATABASE [CarSalesData] FROM  DISK = N'C:\HighImpactDataVisualizationWithPowerBI\Database\
CarSalesData.bak'
WITH  FILE = 1,  NOUNLOAD,  STATS = 5
,MOVE 'CarSalesData'
TO 'C:\HighImpactDataVisualizationWithPowerBI\Database\CarSalesData_Data.mdf'
,MOVE 'CarSalesData_Log'
TO 'C:\HighImpactDataVisualizationWithPowerBI\DatabaseCarSalesData_Log.ldf'
GO
```

The database will be restored, and can be used in the examples.

Index

509

■ T, U, V, W

■ X, Y, Z

Get the eBook for only $10!

> Now you can take the weightless companion with you anywhere, anytime. Your purchase of this book entitles you to 3 electronic versions for only $10.

This Apress title will prove so indispensible that you'll want to carry it with you everywhere, which is why we are offering the eBook in 3 formats for only $10 if you have already purchased the print book.

Convenient and fully searchable, the PDF version enables you to easily find and copy code—or perform examples by quickly toggling between instructions and applications. The MOBI format is ideal for your Kindle, while the ePUB can be utilized on a variety of mobile devices.

Go to www.apress.com/promo/tendollars to purchase your companion eBook.

Apress®
THE EXPERT'S VOICE™